"During my time at the International Crimin
I led the prosecution of the leaders of the h
victims who shared recollections very much
Nishimwe who tells her story in these pages. Each witness has a sear-ing experience to share, a contribution to our understanding of what occurred and why we must act to prevent such atrocities in the future. *In the Shadows* brings to us accounts of human suffering and survival that might otherwise be lost forever."

Stephen Rapp, *Former U.S. Ambassador-at-Large for Global Criminal Justice, and former international prosecutor at Rwanda and Sierra Leone Tribunals*

"Having walked through the killing fields of Rwanda shortly after the genocide there, I can attest as to the importance of first-hand knowledge of this overwhelming atrocity. *In the Shadow of Genocide* captures such testimonies from those who experienced the genocide and its aftermath and examines critical issues of justice and memory a quarter century later."

Professor David J. Scheffer, *former U.S. Ambassador at Large for War Crimes Issues (1997–2001) and author of All The Missing Souls: A Personal History of the War Crimes Tribunals*

"*In the Shadow of Genocide* is the embodiment of a broader discussion of transitional justice, beyond criminal justice or truth commissions, incorporating the necessary range of concepts of justice and memory that are required for a community to progress after conflict/genocide. An inclusive and diverse range of authors, including Rwandan voices, makes this an important and unique book dealing with the aftermath of genocide and conflict in Rwanda and beyond."

Dr Melanie O'Brien, *Associate Professor of International Law, University of Western Australia; President, International Association of Genocide Scholars*

"This important book provides a holistic look at justice, truth, and memory in post-genocide Rwanda. Its most significant contribution may be in bringing together and preserving diverse and less often heard voices, including those of Rwandan scholars, survivors, artists, and youths."

Jennifer Trahan, *Clinical Professor, NYU Center for Global Affairs and author of Genocide, War Crimes and Crimes Against Humanity: A Digest of the Case Law of the International Criminal Tribunal for Rwanda*

"After a quarter century, one might think that the story of the genocide in Rwanda had been fully told. Then comes *In the Shadows*, providing new accounts and a novel analysis of genocide and recovery, an invaluable contribution to the historical record."

Professor Leila Nadya Sadat, *Director of the Crimes Against Humanity Initiative and Special Adviser on Crimes Against Humanity International Criminal Court Prosecutor*

"*In the Shadow of Genocide* is essential reading on justice and memory in Rwanda since the 1994 Genocide Against the Tutsi. This interdisciplinary book features insightful, original contributions from a diverse array of scholars and practitioners, young and older writers, and Rwandans and non-Rwandans who have conducted significant fieldwork in Rwanda. Highly recommended."

Zachary D. Kaufman, J.D., Ph.D.; *Visiting Associate Professor of Law, Washington University in St. Louis School of Law; Associate Professor of Law and Political Science & Co-Director of the Criminal Justice Institute, University of Houston Law Center Author, United States Law and Policy on Transitional Justice: Principles, Politics, and Pragmatics (Oxford University Press)*

In the Shadow of Genocide

This book brings together scholars and practitioners for a unique interdisciplinary exploration of justice and memory within Rwanda. It explores the various strategies the state, civil society, and individuals have employed to come to terms with their past and shape their future. The main objective and focus is to explore broad and varied approaches to post-atrocity memory and justice through the work of those with direct experience with the genocide and its aftermath. This includes many Rwandan authors as well as scholars who have conducted fieldwork in Rwanda. By exploring the concepts of how justice and memory are understood the editors have compiled a book that combines disciplines, voices, and unique insights that are not generally found elsewhere. Including academics and practitioners of law, photographers, poets, members of Rwandan civil society, and Rwandan youth this book will appeal to scholars and students of political science, legal studies, French and francophone studies, African studies, genocide and post-conflict studies, development and healthcare, social work, education and library services.

Stephanie Wolfe, Ph.D., is an Associate Professor at Weber State University in the Political Science and Philosophy department and a Research Associate in the Department of Ancient and Modern Languages and Cultures, University of Pretoria. Her research focuses on memory and justice following mass atrocities. Publications include The Politics of Reparations and Apologies (2014), and several book chapters on international law, reparations and apologies and memorialization.

Tawia Ansah, Ph.D., J.D., is a Professor of Law, a former Associate Dean for Academic Affairs, and former Acting Dean of Florida International University College of Law. His international experience includes service with the United Nations Field Operation to Rwanda.

Matthew C. Kane, LLM, J.D., is a practicing attorney and offers courses on international criminal law at the University of Oklahoma College of Law. He has been appointed to the list of counsel for the International Criminal Court and publishes extensively on issues relating to the ICC and other war crimes tribunals.

Routledge Studies in Genocide and Crimes against Humanity

The Routledge Series in Genocide and Crimes against Humanity publishes cutting-edge research and reflections on these urgently contemporary topics. While focusing on political-historical approaches to genocide and other mass crimes, the series is open to diverse contributions from the social sciences, humanities, law, and beyond. Proposals for both sole-authored and edited volumes are welcome.

Edited by Adam Jones, University of British Columbia in Kelowna, Canada.

Perpetrators and Perpetration of Mass Violence
Action, Motivations and Dynamics
Edited by Timothy Williams and Susanne Buckley-Zistel

Preventing Mass Atrocities
Policies and Practices
Edited by Barbara Harff and Ted Robert Gurr

Cultural Genocide
Law, Politics, and Global Manifestations
Edited by Jeffrey Bachman

Historical Dialogue and the Prevention of Mass Atrocities
Edited by Elazar Barkan, Constantin Goschler and James E. Waller

A Cultural Interpretation of the Genocide Convention
Kurt Mundorff

From Discrimination to Death
Genocide Process Through a Human Rights Lens
Melanie O'Brien

In the Shadow of Genocide
Justice and Memory within Rwanda
Stephanie Wolfe, Matthew Kane, Tawia B. Ansah

"Mille Collines, Mille Coliques"

Photograph by Sonya de Laat

In the Shadow of Genocide

Justice and Memory within Rwanda

Edited by
Stephanie Wolfe, Matthew C. Kane, and Tawia B. Ansah

First published 2023
by Routledge
4 Park Square, Milton Park, Abingdon, Oxon OX14 4RN

and by Routledge
605 Third Avenue, New York, NY 10158

Routledge is an imprint of the Taylor & Francis Group, an informa business

British Library Cataloguing-in-Publication Data
A catalogue record for this book is available from the British Library

ISBN: 978-1-032-13302-7 (hbk)
ISBN: 978-1-032-13304-1 (pbk)
ISBN: 978-1-003-22859-2 (ebk)

DOI: 10.4324/9781003228592

The Open Access version of this book was funded by Weber State University.

Dedication

—To those whose stories have yet to be told

Contents

List of Figures xiii
Authors Biographies xiv
Contributors Biographies xix
Poet Biographies xxii
Foreword xxiv
Acknowledgments xxx

PART I
Memories of Genocide 1

1 **Memory and Justice: A Personal, Cultural, and Global Experience** 3
MATTHEW C KANE WITH CONTRIBUTIONS BY STEPHANIE WOLFE

2 **Through the Eyes of Children: The 1994 Genocide against the Tutsi in Rwanda** 21
ASHLEE CAWLEY AND STEPHANIE WOLFE WITH CONTRIBUTIONS FROM OMAR NDIZEYE, JACQUELINE MUREKATETE, CONSOLEE NISHIMWE, THÉOBALD KAYIRANGA, JASON NSHIMYE, AND EUGENIE MUKESHIMANA

3 **Experts in the Suffering of Others: Race, Knowledge Production, and the Rwandan Genocide** 44
MJ (MARIE-JOLIE) RWIGEMA

4 **Testimonies of Child Survivors from Gitarama Prefecture: Preserving Memory of the 1994 Rwanda Genocide** 67
MUSA WAKHUNGU OLAKA

PART II
Justice and Society 89

5 **Justice and Transformation within Rwanda** 91
JOSEPH RYARASA NKURUNZIZA

6 **Transitional Justice in the Wake of Genocide: The Contribution of Criminal Trials and Symbolic Reparations to Reconciliation in Rwanda** 110
SAMANTHA J. LAKIN AND CHARITY WIBABARA

7 **"Double Genocide" or Revenge Killings? Did the Liberators of a Genocide Commit Their Own?** 132
JONATHAN R. BELOFF

8 **Moving Forward: Creating a Safe Space for Women Raped during the 1994 Genocide against the Tutsi in Rwanda** 150
ODETH KANTENGWA

PART III
Justice and Memory through Artistic Expression 165

9 **An Open Grave: The Kigali Memorial and the Aesthetics of Memorialization** 167
TAWIA B. ANSAH

10 **Remembering Rwanda through Transnational, Multivocal Narrative** 188
ANNA-MARIE DE BEER

11 **Fictions of Justice in Post-Genocide Films: Conflict Resolution and the Search for Reconciliation** 207
GEORGE S. MACLEOD

12 **Memory and Photographs of Unrepresentable Trauma in Rwandan Transitional Justice** 228
SONYA DE LAAT

13 **Rwandan Youth Speak! Memory and Justice through Poetry** 249
ASHLEE CAWLEY AND STEPHANIE WOLFE POETRY BY JESSICA GATONI, BLISS LIGHT NSHOKEYINKA, CLAUDINE KARANGWA INGABIRE, FRED MFURANZIMA, GUY CADEAU, AND INNOCENT BYIRINGIRO

PART IV
Conclusions 269

14 **Conclusion** 271
TAWIA B. ANSAH

Index 274

Figures

4.1	Gitarama prefecture.	70
4.2	Victims as per IBUKA.	73
12.1	Digitally "stitched" photograph from the *memory → witness* exhibition entitled "I feel at home here" by the author.	240
12.2	Photograph entitled, "I will always tremble whenever I hear voices raised among the leaves of the Banana groves", for the *Memory → Witness* exhibit by the author.	242
12.3	Final photograph in the *Memory → Witness* exhibition entitled, "Redemption," by the author.	243

Authors Biographies

Tawia B. Ansah, Ph.D., J.D., is a Professor of Law, a former Associate Dean for Academic Affairs, and former Acting Dean of Florida International University College of Law. Dr. Ansah's international experience includes service with the United Nations Human Rights Field Operation to Rwanda; with the Department of State and the Organization for Security and Cooperation in Europe (OSCE) in Bosnia-Herzegovina; and with the Council of Europe in the Republic of Kosovo, then a part of the Republic of Serbia. Dr. Ansah has also worked with Canada's Ministry of Justice and with private law firms within the United States.

Jonathan R. Beloff, Ph.D., is an Arts and Humanities Research Council (AHRC) funded Postdoctoral Research Associate at the Department of War Studies in King's College London. His research focuses on the regional politics and security of the African Great Lakes. His first book, titled, *Foreign Policy in Post-Genocide Rwanda: Elite Perceptions of Global Engagement*, published in 2021 by Routledge examines the reasons behind Rwanda's foreign relations. Additionally, he has published academic journal articles, book chapters, book reviews, and editorials on issues facing Central Africa. Since 2008, his travels to the region have led him to work and consult with numerous Rwandan and international government officials. Within these periods of foreign residence, including multiple extended stays in Rwanda, he developed unique skills to engage and consult with a range of different foreign officials as well as Rwandan policymakers in formulating public policy.

Ashlee Cawley, M.A., received her master's degree in international relations with political strategy and communication from the University of Kent's Brussels School of International Studies in 2019. Her essay titled, "Reactionary Withdrawal: Japan's 2018 Decision to Leave the International Whaling Commission," was published in the Brussels Journal of International Studies. Prior to moving to Brussels, Ashlee lived in Gwangju, South Korea, teaching English at two public middle schools. Ashlee attended Never Again Rwanda's Peacebuilding Institute in 2016. She currently resides near Salt Lake City, Utah, where she enjoys writing fiction and working on other creative projects.

Anna-Marie de Beer, Ph.D., is a senior lecturer in French and francophone studies at the University of Pretoria in South Africa. She grew up in Zimbabwe. Her research interests are the relationship between collective trauma and literature as well as francophone autobiography and autofiction. She has published various articles and book chapters on literary representations of the genocide and has traveled to Rwanda to visit genocide sites and interview survivors. Her most recent publication, a monograph titled *Sharing the Burden of Stories from the Tutsi Genocide, Rwanda: écrire par devoir de mémoire*, appeared in May 2020 as part of the Palgrave Series: Studies in Cultural Heritage and Conflict.

Matthew C. Kane, J.D., LLM, is a practicing attorney with a focus on criminal and complex civil law matters. He also teaches courses on international criminal law, comparative criminal law, and comparative responses to terrorism at the University of Oklahoma College of Law. He has been appointed to the list of counsel for the International Criminal Court and previously drafted indictments and arrest warrants for suspected *génocidaires*, among other tasks, at the Office of the Prosecutor for the International Criminal Tribunal for Rwanda. His current research focuses on the development of legal language at the International Criminal Court.

Odeth Kantengwa, PhD Candidate, M.A., is a senior gender expert consultant with Interpeace, Rwanda. Prior, Kantengwa served as a research coordinator with Never Again Rwanda (NAR) and has served as a researcher at the National Commission for the Fight against Genocide (CNLG) in Kigali, where she focused on post-genocide effects and recovery programs. She holds a Master of Arts in genocide studies and prevention obtained from the National University of Rwanda and a post-graduate diploma in research skills from Maastricht School of Management. Kantengwa is a part-time lecturer at the Kigali Independent University where she teaches conflict management as well as policy formulation and implementation courses. Kantengwa has published several articles on motherhood, rape, and the particularities of dealing with effects of rape in post-conflict settings.

Sonya de Laat, Ph.D., is a media historian of humanitarian action, global health, and international development. She is the Global Health graduate academic advisor and a sessional lecturer at McMaster University. She is also an investigator with the Humanitarian Health Ethics research group based at McMaster and McGill universities (humanitarianhealthethics.ca) and an active member of the Canadian Network on Humanitarian History (aidhistory.ca). Recent publications include "Pictures in

Development: The Canadian International Development Agency's Photo Library" (2019) in *The Samaritan State Revisited* and "The camera and the Red Cross: 'Lamentable pictures' and conflict photography bring into focus an international movement, 1855–1865" (2021) in *The International Review of the Red Cross.*

Samantha J. Lakin, Ph.D., is a researcher and practitioner in post-atrocity and post-genocide justice, human security, and African affairs. Her work focuses on issues of memory and justice in states and societies transitioning from mass atrocities and genocide to peace. Dr. Lakin was a Graduate Research Fellow at the Program on Negotiation at Harvard Law School, and a Fulbright scholar in Rwanda and in Switzerland. She holds a Ph.D. in History from the Strassler Center for Holocaust and Genocide Studies at Clark University and a M.A. in International Law and Diplomacy from The Fletcher School at Tufts University. Dr. Lakin's research spans eight years working in Rwanda and surrounding countries in English, French, and Kinyarwanda. Dr. Lakin's first book, *Heroines of Vichy France: Rescuing French Jews during the Holocaust,* co-authored with Paul R. Bartrop, was published with Praeger in 2019.

George S. MacLeod, Ph.D., is an Associate Professor of French at St. Mary's College of Maryland. His research focuses on representations of collective and individual violence in Francophone Africa and the Caribbean. His work on topics ranging from the child soldier novel, Rwandan Tutsi survivor testimony, and the Quebecois zombie film has appeared in peer-reviewed journals such as Research in African Literatures, Contemporary French and Francophone Studies, *The Irish Journal of French Studies*, and *Études littéraires africaines*. His first book – an analysis of Francophone literature, film, and testimony from Africa's post-Cold War period – is forthcoming in Fall 2023 with the University of Nebraska Press.

Linda Melvern is a British investigative journalist, a former member of the award-winning Sunday Times Insight Team. She has written seven books of non-fiction including a fifty-year history of the United Nations, the book becoming the basis for the Channel Four TV series, UN Blues. Three of her books concern the circumstances of the 1994 genocide of the Tutsi. She was a consultant to the prosecution team at the International Criminal Tribunal for Rwanda (ICTR). Her latest book is *Intent to Deceive, Denying the Genocide of the Tutsi* (Verso 2020).

Joseph Ryarasa Nkurunziza is a medical doctor by training. He is the Executive Director and founding member of Never Again Rwanda, a peacebuilding and social justice organization that promotes human rights and peacebuilding among youth and the population at large in

Rwanda and the Great Lakes Region in Africa. He is a core founder and the board chairperson of Healthy Development Initiative, a non-governmental organization that strives to improve both the quality and accessibility of health care for all Rwandans irrespective of their social-economic status. He is currently the chairperson of t Rwanda Civil Society Platform (RCSP) and a board member at the Africa Freedom of Information Centre (AFIC). He has previously served as the chairperson of the Africa Democracy Forum and a 2018 fellow of the Stanford University, Draper Hills program on Democracy, Governance, Development, Civil Society and Rule of Law. He authored and co-authored several publications on the role of civil society and civic participation in Rwanda.

Musa Wakhungu Olaka, Ph.D., received his doctorate in Information Science and Learning Technologies from the University of Missouri - Columbia and is currently the Director of Libraries at Prairie View A&M University. His previous positions include being the Librarian for African Studies, and Global and International Studies at the University of Kansas; Assistant Library Director at Southeast Missouri State University; Librarian for the Holocaust and Genocide Studies Center at the University of South Florida; and a lecturer/librarian in Rwanda where he worked for 6 years.

MJ (Marie-Jolie) Rwigema, Ph.D, MSW, is an assistant professor in the Applied Human Sciences department at Concordia University in Montreal, Canada. She has nearly twenty years of community/social work experience that includes mental health counselling/therapy, arts-based education, community-based research, group facilitation, and documentary filmmaking working primarily with Black, racialized, immigrant, and LGBTQ communities. In 2009, she directed, co-edited, and co-wrote the documentary film "The Rwandan Genocide as told by its Historian-Survivors." In addition to her nearly 20 years of community practice experience, as a researcher and scholar, MJ's work focuses on the interlinkages between political "voice" and "healing" from trauma for politically targeted groups, including research on the perspectives and experiences of Rwandan-Canadian genocide survivors of the 1994 genocide in Rwanda.

Charity Wibabara, Ph.D., completed her doctorate in 2014 from the University of Western Cape in South Africa in collaboration with Humboldt University in Berlin, Germany in Transitional Justice and International Criminal Law. She obtained a Master's degree in international criminal justice in 2010 from the University of Western Cape. She has been a National Prosecutor at the National Public Prosecution Authority since 2015, and currently the coordinator of the International Crimes Department.

Stephanie Wolfe, Ph.D., is an Associate Professor at Weber State University in the Political Science and Philosophy department and a Research Associate in the Department of Ancient and Modern Languages and Cultures, University of Pretoria. She received her doctorate in International Relations at the University of Kent in Brussels, Belgium with a focus on atrocities and the aftermath. Her research led to the 2014 book *The Politics of Reparations and Apologies*, and several other book chapters on international law, reparations and apologies, and justice and memory within the Rwandan context. She is currently leading a research team that has been conducting annual trips to Rwanda to interview genocide survivors and visit memorial sites. This project is entitled *Journey through Rwandan Memorials* (manuscript in progress.)

Fred Mfuranzima is a writer, poet, artist, photographer, and activist, born in 1997 in Rwanda. He is the founder and director at Imfura Arts Center and Imfura Arts for Peace Association, which promotes any form of art that calls for peace, healing, and development of critical thinking in communities within the Great Lakes Region. He has held positions in youth and charity organizations and is an alumnus of the Never Again Rwanda Peacebuilding Institute. Fred has won numerous art awards and international activist certificates. He works hard pursuing his education, overcoming unique challenges with his family of genocide survivors. He believes working together can promote peace and sustainability in Africa.

Nshokeyinka Bliss Light was 7 years old during the genocide against the Tutsi. His grandparents fled to Zaire in 1959, so he grew up there. As his family returned from exile, the perpetrators continued killing the survivors and his grandmother was killed by the defeated regime in the former Gisenyi Prefecture. He is a poet and a teacher of English, Kiswahili, and Literature in secondary education. He has been in touch with different institutions in the war against genocide, such as Never Again Rwanda and other institutions that fight against genocide. Poems are one of the channels he uses to promote peace among citizens.

Foreword

On Denial
Linda Melvern[1]

From the moment the leadership of the Hutu Power movement took control of Rwanda in April 1994, they were determined to distort the reality of events to the outside world. The use of fake news, propaganda, and disinformation was built into their genocidal plans from the beginning. In a masterstroke of public relations, the *génocidaires* placed the United Nations (UN) at the center of their plans, and, as the genocide of the Tutsi spread, the perpetrators used Rwanda's nonpermanent membership on the United Nations Security Council to disguise their intent. The blueprint for their campaign to deny the genocide of the Tutsi then underway can be found in UN documents, in the diplomatic language of cables and letters, and in archives abandoned in Rwandan embassies abroad. In the spring of 1994, the Security Council became a global forum that gave voice to a genocidal regime whose sole policy was the extermination of a part of the population.

In early April, as their extermination program was getting underway, the military and political leaders in Rwanda launched a disinformation operation at the UN headquarters in New York intended to sew confusion and doubt about what was happening. In guarded conversations in the hallways and in letters to the Security Council, the representatives of the Hutu Power, so-called "Interim Government," told fellow diplomats that the large number of civilian deaths was the fault of "the people of Rwanda," for they had spontaneously risen up and attacked "those under suspicion" for the assassination of the President (UN Doc S/1994/531). The *génocidaires* tried to blur the lines between spin and news, between fiction and nonfiction, and to confuse the resumed civil war they were waging against the Rwandan Patriotic Front (RPF), with the mass slaughter of Tutsi families.[2]

In the Security Council, the *génocidaires* promoted the legitimacy of their hastily installed "Interim Government" and argued this government had brought "peace to the people." In a dedicated campaign of falsehood, they denied that a genocide was underway and that the deliberate killing of civilians was steadily progressing country wide. The Foreign Minister of the "Interim Government," Jérôme Bicamumpaka, addressed the Security

Council on May 16, 1994. He officially and publicly denied his government had anything whatsoever to do with civilian massacres:

> The resumption of hostilities by the RPF, along with large-scale massacres of Hutu civilians.... unleashed repressed hatreds and a festering desire for revenge. ... It is said some RPF fighters eat the hearts of men they have killed in order to become invincible.[3]

Among the leadership of the Hutu Power movement were skilled propagandists, including the creators of the hate radio station *Radio Télévision Libre des Mille Collines*. From the outset, these masters of deceit provided a steady stream of fake news to camouflage their *coup d'état* and their elimination of the political opposition on April 7, which they explained as unexpected "political violence." In these first days the *génocidaires* of Rwanda said they had been "powerless" in the face of a series of catastrophic events – events that they themselves had engineered (Melvern, 2020, p. 2).

The *génocidaires* lost the civil war and were chased out of the country by the military forces, the Rwandan Patriotic Army. In response, the *génocidaires* revised their media strategy. A fascinating account describes a week-long policy meeting of the now exiled Army High Command in newly installed offices in Goma, the capital of North Kivu province in Zaire, known today as the Democratic Republic of Congo (DRC).[4] At this meeting, the army officers decided they needed to change the army's disastrous international image in the face of reports about a genocide of the Tutsi.[5] A range of tactics was devised by the army's six-member Commission of Politics and Exterior Relations, which included building contacts with journalists who might be sympathetic to their cause and could report that genocide of the Tutsi was a manufactured story. They decided that the exiled Army had to deploy emissaries to foreign countries to try to shift international opinion. They would need to win the hearts and minds of western journalists. The details of this newly devised public relations program, constructed in makeshift offices in a DRC refugee camp in September 1994, were discovered two years later in a 48-page carefully typed report among a stockpile of documents hurriedly abandoned when the army later fled (Terry, 2002, p. 156).

The same tactics of genocide denial were used in the defense of the *génocidaires* at their trials held at the International Criminal Tribunal for Rwanda (ICTR). Their lawyers argued that the world had been duped by an "effective and educated pro-Tutsi lobby" into believing a genocide had taken place. The claim that the killing of civilians happened "spontaneously" – a feature of the denial presented to the Security Council in 1994 – turned out to be a foundation stone of the defense.[6] In the courtrooms, the *génocidaires'* counsel argued there had been no planning, no conspiracy to murder, and no intent to kill Tutsi. The "intent" to destroy a human group, as required in the 1948 Genocide Convention, was simply lacking. They denied the existence of a *coup d'état* on April 6 and explained that after the assassination of the president, the Rwandan military had been obliged to take charge to avoid a state of anarchy. They argued that the RPF killed the president to deliberately scupper the peace agreement and seize power. To this day, not a shred of evidence has emerged to support such claims (Melvern 2019, 2020).

There was no shortage of scholars, regional experts, and journalists who came forward to testify on behalf of the defendants on trial at the ICTR, or to offer expert reports giving a sympathetic view of the perpetrators. Their stories of denial that they presented to the courts now spread far beyond the courtrooms, and their alternative version of events began to circulate widely on internet sites. The digital age gave the denial of the genocide of the Tutsi a new lease on life and the world's social media was an effective weapon in disseminating denial. The stories promoted by a few former ICTR lawyers, academics, and journalists in France, Belgium, Canada, and the United Kingdom included claims that the death toll was exaggerated, and that the victims brought the catastrophe upon themselves. Today, continued support exists for the defense case of the *génocidaires*.[7] From their prison cells, the convicted *génocidaires* continue to promulgate denialist propaganda and wage a public relations campaign about how they are the victims of a "victors' justice" (Melvern 2019, 2020).

Whether deliberately, or through ignorance or naivety, an increasing number of people collude in efforts to deny the reality of what happened in 1994. They include senior French and Belgian military officers and politicians for whom the reality of events in 1994 is too uncomfortable either for their careers or for other political priorities. These bystanders to genocide, who helped the perpetrators by recognizing as legitimate the "Interim Government," or those who gave their tacit approval to the *génocidaires*, or who tried to cover up their crimes – these people continue to deliberately distort and confuse history.

At first, it was difficult to take denial of the genocide of the Tutsi seriously. Yet over the years numerous collaborators have wittingly (and perhaps unwittingly) helped the *génocidaires* to disguise their criminal enterprise, and whole parts of their story have acquired respectability. There is serious academic work which purports to show that there were no plans to kill Tutsi, and that the killing was just one more episode during a bloody civil war, and the result of political turmoil (Guichaoua, 2015).

For those who care to look, the proof of the planning of the 1994 genocide of the Tutsi is capable of immediate verification. There are available sources of indisputable accuracy. The fact of a planned extermination program is confirmed by investigators appointed by the UN Security Council and is found in the conclusions of the Independent Commission of Experts report describing: "Overwhelming evidence indicates that the extermination of Tutsi by Hutu had been planned months in advance of its actual execution" (S/1994/1125, 1994, p. 12). In December 1994, these experts reported that the 1948 *Convention on the Prevention and Punishment of the Crime of Genocide* had been "massively violated" in Rwanda between April 6 and

July 1, 1994. A conspiracy to destroy the Tutsi population was confirmed as fact by judges at the ICTR. It was confirmed by human rights workers from Amnesty International, Human Right Watch, Oxfam, and the International Committee of the Red Cross whose chief delegate Philippe Gaillard warned a British journalist in January 1994 that planning for genocide was underway. Genocide planning was confirmed by peacekeepers and military observers serving with the UN Assistance Mission for Rwanda, and by its Force Commander, Lt. General Roméo Dallaire. It was confirmed by Belgian intelligence agents. It was confirmed in a milestone report which resulted from a collaborative effort of 18 governments. The prosecutorial knowledge about events in 1994 is publicly available in court transcripts, in the prosecution case at the ICTR, and the decisions of the judges and the appeals available in indictments, testimony, and judgments. A planned and political campaign, the genocide of the Tutsi took place in broad daylight. Between April 6 and July 17, 1994, up to one million people were murdered. The methods of killing had been experimented with in the past and have been documented in human rights reports (Melvern, 2019). Like the Nazi Holocaust, the genocide of the Tutsi was the product of deliberate political design, a plan to exterminate a minority people.

Like denial of other genocides – most notably that of the Armenians and the Nazi Holocaust – the intention of deniers regarding Rwanda is to alter the perception of the crime. Denial is intended to degrade the status of genocide as a unique event. In the case of Rwanda, some people attempt moral equivalence, claiming that not one but two genocides took place, the second a genocide of Hutu. Deniers argue that the entire history of the genocide of the Tutsi needs to be rewritten.

There is nothing "spontaneous" about genocide. Raphael Lemkin, a Polish lawyer, and the father of the 1948 Genocide Convention, believed that the existence of a coordinated plan of action was inherent in the crime itself. A conspiracy against people chosen as victims purely, simply, and exclusively because they were members of the target group. Lemkin explained in *Axis Rule in Occupied Europe* (1944), that genocide was not a sudden and abominable aberration. It was a deliberate and methodical attempt to reconstruct the world (Melvern, 2006, p. 93). Lemkin wrote, "Genocide is a part of history … It follows humanity like a dark shadow from early antiquity to the present time" (quoted in Melvern, 2019, p. 252). Genocide could be both predicted and prevented with international early-warning systems. A key element to genocide is effective propaganda which spreads racist ideology among the populace defining the victim as less than human. This can be seen in Rwanda in the years prior to the genocide.

The denial of genocide is a recognized part of the genocidal process, a part of the crime itself. One of the world's preeminent scholars of genocide, Dr. Gregory H. Stanton (1998), has devised what he calls the *Eight Stages of Genocide*. These stages are classification of the population, symbolization and dehumanization of the target group, organization and polarization of the population, the preparation, and extermination of the group. The final stage in this continuum is denial. Stanton later added two additional stages: discrimination and persecution. In addition, he has determined that denial of genocide accompanies each stage as the crime progresses (Stanton, 2016). Denial ensures the crime never ends.

No tragedy was ever heralded to less effect than the genocide of the Tutsi of Rwanda. Anyone who knew anything about Rwanda knew what was threatened. The world's failure to act before the genocide, or as one million people were slaughtered is one of the greatest scandals of the twentieth century.

The current campaign to deny the genocide of the Tutsi scars Rwandan society. It causes grave offense to survivors. For them, the genocide is not a distant event from 25 years ago but a reality with which they live every day. For them, this is not an academic debate.

The genocide of the Tutsi should be treated with intellectual honesty and rigor. It is one thing to interpret facts differently, and quite another to misrepresent those same facts. For this reason, the memories contained in this book are invaluable. They illustrate for us the terrible reality of genocide and the accounts of the survivors show the difficulties of finding meaningful justice as we seek an understanding of the world's ultimate crime.

Notes

1 For more information on this topic, see Melvern (2020).
2 The Rwandan Patriotic Front was an army created in Uganda to enforce the return home of up to one million Tutsi refugees forced out of the country in purges starting in 1959 and refused return by successive Hutu regimes.
3 UN Security Council. S/PV.3377. Monday, May 16, 1994. A detailed account of the informal meetings of the Security Council which are held in secret appears in Melvern (2019).
4 *'Rapport de la reunion du haut commandement des forces armées Rwandaises et des membres des commissions tenue à Goma du 02 au 08 Septembre 1994'* (Original Copy given to author by Fiona Terry).
5 The *génocidaires* claimed that these were false reports spread by the United Nations and the Western media.
6 In December 2015 after the ICTR closed its doors, there were 93 people indicted and 61 people convicted. "When the ICTR closed its doors in December 2015, 93 people had been indicted and 61 convicted."
7 Among these, but not exclusively, are: French historian Bernard Lugan, Associate Professor of African History at the Jean Moulin University, Lyon, with thirty years of study of the countries of Africa; P. Erlinder, "No conspiracy, no genocide planning ... no genocide?" (Erlinder is lead defense counsel at the ICTR, from the William Mitchell College of Law.) See also www.taylor-report.com and E. S. Herman, "Genocide inflation is the real human rights threat", available at: www.coldtype.net. Also: "No Justice, 'A letter to the UN from some of its political prisoners in Arusha'", (January 2, 2008), available at www.cirqueMinime/Paris (Sites

accessed January 2009). Collins, "Rwanda: obscuring the truth of genocide" (August 13, 2008), available at www.spiked-online.org; Péan, '*Noires fureurs, blancs menteurs*, Rwanda 1990–1994', (November 2005) *Mille et une nuits*.

Bibliography

Collins, B. (2008, August 13). *Rwanda: Obscuring the truth about genocide.* Retrieved from https://archive.globalpolicy.org/security/issues/rwanda/2008/0813rwanda.htm

Erlinder, P. (2008). No conspiracy, No genocide planning ... No genocide? Jurist Legal News and Research.

Guichaoua, A. (2015). *From war to genocide, criminal politics in Rwanda 1990-1994.* (D. E. Webster, Trans.). The University of Wisconsin Press. (Original work published 2010).

Herman, E. S. (2007, October 26). *Genocide inflation is the real human rights threat: Yugoslavia and Rwanda.* Retrieved from http://musictravel.free.fr/political/political75.htm

Lee, J. (2008, December 23). Rwanda: No conspiracy, no genocide planning ... no genocide? *Jurist: Legal News and Community.* Retrieved January, 2019 from https://www.jurist.org/commentary/2008/12/rwanda-no-conspiracy-no-genocide/

Lemkin, R. (1944). *Axis rule in occupied Europe.* Carnegie Endowment for International Peace.

Melvern, L. (2006). Rwanda and Darfur: The media and the Security Council. *International Relations*, *20*(1), 93–104. https://doi.org/10.1177/0047117806060931

Melvern, L. (2019). *A people betrayed: The role of the west in Rwanda's genocide (*2019 ed.). Zed Books. https://read.amazon.com/?asin=B09LQGKZ5Z

Melvern, L. (2020). *Intent to deceive: Denying the genocide of the Tutsi* (2020 ed.). Verso. https://www.amazon.com/gp/product/B07FC2YN2T/ref=kinw_myk_ro_title

No Justice, "A letter to the UN from some of its political prisoners in Arusha'", (2 January 2008), available at www.cirqueMinime/Paris

Péan, P. (2005). *Noires fureurs, blancs menteurs: Rwanda, 1990-1994.* Mille et Une Nuits.

Rapport de la reunion du haut commandement des forces armées Rwandaises et des membres des commissions tenue à Goma du 02 au 08 Septembre 1994

Stanton, G. H. (1998). *The 8 stages of genocide.* Genocide Watch. Retrieved from http://www.genocide-watch.com/images/8StagesBriefingpaper.pdf

Stanton, G. H. (2016). *The ten stages of genocide.* Retrieved from http://genocidewatch.net/genocide-2/8-stages-of-genocide/

Terry, F. (2002). *Condemned to repeat?: The paradox of humanitarian action.* Cornell University Press.

United Nations S/1994/531. (1994, May 3). *Letter dated 94/05/02 from the permanent representative of Rwanda to the United Nations addressed to the President of the Security Council.* Retrieved from https://digitallibrary.un.org/record/197548?ln=ru

United Nations S/1994/1125. (1994, October 4). *Letter dated 94/10/04 from the Secretary-General addressed to the President on the Security Council.* Retrieved from https://www.securitycouncilreport.org/atf/cf/%7B65BFCF9B-6D27-4E9C-8CD3-CF6E4FF96FF9%7D/s_1994_1125.pdf

United Nations S/PV.3377 (1994, May 16). *Security Council, 49th year: 3377th meeting, Monday 94/05/16, New York.* Retrieved from https://digitallibrary.un.org/record/188689?ln=en

Acknowledgments

The editors of this volume would like to thank those who tirelessly helped us with proofreading and editing of numerous drafts, citations, and formatting. Our sincere thanks to Ashlee Cawley, Taylor Covey, Rebecca Fredrick, and Danielle Husberg for getting us across the finish line! In addition, we would like to thank the Hemingway Family and the Hemingway Faculty Development Trust for funding which supported this project throughout its numerous phases.

Part I

Memories of Genocide

1 Memory and Justice

A Personal, Cultural, and Global Experience

Matthew C. Kane

With Contributions by Stephanie Wolfe

Introduction

"The ability to recollect specific past experiences" (Kelly & Lindsay, 1996). It doesn't sound too complicated, but memory is an odd thing. It is, after all, quite limited. We only think of the past – there is no memory of the future. It is selective – we have forgotten far more than we retain. It has a very limited shelf life, as each day we remember less and less of what has gone before. We remember only within the moment, as the past has been consumed by time. What we do recall is limited to what we have observed, a very small slice of our lives, filtered through the predominate narrative, or at least the shared understanding of the event. Such perspective shapes and twists over time, with subsequent events impacted by the memories of the past and the future shaping how we reflect – and understand – what has previously occurred.[1]

Yet memory is who we are, as individuals, families, nations, and peoples. It is never wholly one's own, nor is it ever the exclusive possession of some larger collective.

> All memories, however personal...are linked to ideas we share with many others...A memory occurs to us...because we are surrounded by other memories that link to it...they may be historical, geographical, bibliographic, or political notions of everyday experiences and familiar ways of seeing. These references enable us to determine with increasing precision the contours of a previously isolated past event.
>
> (Apfelbaum, 2010, p. 86; Halbwachs, 1992, p. 173; Lopez, 2015, p. 799 on the topic).

Without memory, we lose our identities. We lose our grief and our hope. As we recognize the importance of memory, we take steps to preserve.[2]

As critical as memories are, we do not exist in the past. We live in the moment, with an eye toward the future. We seek to address what has gone before, to right wrongs and avoid repeated mistakes. Justice is not only the outcome, but the process. Transitional justice, the subset of the term most frequently used in this text, is traditionally defined as "the conception of

DOI: 10.4324/9781003228592-2

justice associated with a period of political change, characterized by legal responses to confront the wrongdoing of repressive predecessor regimes" (Teitel, 2003, p. 69). A field often conceived as highly bureaucratic and legalistic, transitional justice requires more than the legal mechanisms utilized to prosecute perpetrators.[3]

The judicial institutions intended to mete out punishment and compensate victims reflect only one of a number of essential themes. Reconciliation, peace, healing, forgiveness, and truth are all necessary to accomplish a more robust understanding of present conceptions of transitional justice (Clark, 2009; see also Gahima, 2013 presenting a similar list of objectives). As time goes by, an increasing amount of literature is dedicated to the diversity of transitional justice mechanisms. There has been pushback against the dominant narrative within transitional justice, advocating for more exploration of grassroots movements and civil society efforts, as well as how memoirs, film, and photography contribute to survivors' and victims' perceptions of justice. We find that transitional justice should be considered holistically. As such, this volume will bring together legalistic viewpoints, discussions of how memory and space contribute to transitional justice, and artistic responses, including a selection of Rwandan youth poets who reflect upon the history of their country. Ultimately, such perspective reveals not a single unifying feature, but a complex web of varying viewpoints, merging and diverging, intersecting and deviating. At the center, we find personal and collective memories of what has occurred, desires for justice in one form or another, and genuine hope and belief in a brighter future for Rwanda.

***

I have forgotten much about my time at the International Criminal Tribunal for Rwanda (ICTR), at the court in Arusha and on the ground in Rwanda, a prime example of why preservation and documentation are so important. Some memories of that time, however, will remain with me until I remember nothing at all. On a visit to the Murambi Technical School, years before its rebirth as the Murambi Genocide Memorial Centre, I walked the grounds with one of the handful of survivors, who directed my attention to thousands of bodies in room after room. There was no need; despite the liberal use of lye to preserve the corpses, the smell of death was undeniable. Most distinctly, I have etched in my mind the image of a young child whose skull had been split open by a machete. To this day, I feel gut-wrenching nausea contemplating the fear that must have possessed that little one in the moments before her life ended.

While the smell lingered in the air at Murambi, I experienced it the strongest in the courtroom in Arusha. As Emmanuel Bagambiki and Samuel Imanishimwe stood trial at the ICTR, accused of the murders of a number of Tutsis that had sought shelter at a football stadium within yards of the safety of the Congolese border, the prosecution introduced several pieces of fabric taken from exhumed bodies for identification. It only took a moment to understand why the cloth had been stored in an ice chest. The odor was overwhelming. Snippets of dresses and shirts – reminders of those murdered simply because they were identified as Tutsi. What could lead to such depravity? What should be done to address the extraordinary devastation? I was forever affected, but the impact I felt served in large part simply as a reminder that I had not experienced the genocide first-hand. How could someone wake up each morning and function in any meaningful way after having actually experienced genocide?

Dr. Stephanie Wolfe, my co-editor, has had many encounters, both joyous and heartbreaking, with those directly impacted by the mass atrocities committed in Rwanda. She has spent years interviewing Rwandans profoundly affected by the genocide and has visited over 100 memorials scattered throughout the country. Throughout this time, she has visited with survivors, witnesses, memorial workers, and government officials. Sometimes these categories overlap, other times the roles are distinct, and sometimes even adversarial. A recurring theme of these interviews was that of justice. What is justice? How do the survivors experience justice? What does "transitional justice" or even "justice" mean to those that have experienced such brutal crimes? Expectations of justice, like survivors' experiences and lives, have varied greatly. Many spoke of the importance of memory: if no one remembers what happened, then the *génocidaires* won. Dr. Wolfe recalled a discussion with a survivor showing her a new memorial, who broke down in tears when he learned Dr. Wolfe and her team were documenting missing voices. No one had asked his story before. No one was going to remember his family, his experiences. Now someone would.[4]

Transitional justice provides a political reconciliation for those who were once victimizer and victim. It allows a space to, at the very least, coexist. It reasserts the rule of law in a country and stresses that the previous actions were wrong and unacceptable. Yet, all of these conceptions of justice are created to assist those who survived. Drawing on another of Dr. Wolfe's experiences:

> In 2016, we were visiting the mass graves of Kinazi. Our guide walked us to the mass graves, and while there, he explained the history of the region, this site in particular, and the information gathered from witnesses. We couldn't hear from a survivor of this massacre as it was too well organized. Almost everyone had died here, and the one person he knew that had survived moved to Uganda. We heard the horrors and documented the site. Then we left to visit the actual memorial.
>
> Walking through the memorial, the smell of the bodies was overwhelming. We could picture what happened vividly in our minds because of the deep pits turned to graves that we had just visited. Leaving the memorial, I glanced down to see a pair of once bright red shoes. The size – tiny. I broke down crying, the image of a little girl in

> bright red shoes, walking past her headmaster as he decided to kill her was more than I could take. The image, so clear in my mind, continues to haunt me to this day. What is justice for this little girl? What can transitional justice offer her?

Memorials, photography, artistic expression, memories, stories – all are avenues of memory and preservation. To truly engage in transitional justice, we must engage with both the legal system and the memory work.

Before Genocide

The murder of roughly 800,000[5] Tutsis and moderate Hutu did not happen overnight. There was nothing "immediate" about the genocide. The seeds were planted generations before and the roots will last until long after we have all perished. There is a lack of consensus as to precisely when and how the divide between the Tutsi and Hutu arose. Some believe the division was born of ancient migration patterns, with the two groups settling in the region centuries apart. There are general physical characteristics that are often associated with one group or the other that might suggest such genetic diversity. Yet genetic studies have revealed that, at least by the time of the genocide, the groups were extremely similar. Others contend that the labels are economic, with Tutsi historically comprised of pastoralist cattle owners while Hutu agriculturalists farmed the land, giving rise to the possibility that an individual could transition from one group to the other depending on one's financial situation. Regardless, Tutsi and Hutu shared a common language, culture, and history (Khan, 2011; Mamdani, 2002, pp. 41–75).

There is little dispute that colonialism was responsible for stratifying Rwandan society. Following the First World War, Belgium took control of Rwanda from the Germans after a two-decade occupation. In relatively typical fashion, the colonial powers allied themselves with the smaller, controlling faction – the Tutsi king and nobility – thereby ensuring that the leadership of Rwanda would retain its power over the country, while natural resources were stripped from the land and exported to Europe. As a part of this process, the Belgians introduced identity cards, which, notably, included the identification of the bearer as Tutsi, Hutu, or Twa. The line had been drawn (Fussell, 2001; Mamdani, 2002).[6]

In the late 1950s, Hutu disenfranchisement turned to mass violence as more than 20,000 Tutsi were killed in reprisal for an attack by Tutsi governmental actors on a leading Hutu reformist (Eltringham, 2004, pp. 34–50; Mamdani, 2002, pp. 129–131). Hundreds of thousands of Tutsi fled Rwanda, often relocating just across the border in nearby countries. This diaspora would grow and evolve. The Rwandan Tutsi remained refugees, living as temporary residents, their homes just minutes away but beyond their reach (Guichaoua, 2015, pp. 6–13). With limited options available, young men gained military experience as rank and file for various political actors in the region. Many joined with Yoweri Museveni in the Ugandan Bush War and enjoyed his support to create the Rwandan Patriotic Front (RPF) (Reed, 1996; United States Defense Intelligence Agency, 1990).

In 1990, the RPF launched an attack on the Hutu-led Rwandan government, advancing south from Uganda. Backed by various regional and European powers, the Hutu government stopped the advances and celebrated the end of the "October war." The RPF then turned to guerrilla warfare and occupied a northern strip of the country (Kimonyo, 2015, p. 80). The invasion marked a change in the Hutu approach to the Tutsi minority. The Tutsi threat, now realized, provided Hutu extremists with the opportunity to advance their agenda into the mainstream. Concerted efforts were undertaken to identify not only Tutsis in leadership positions within Rwanda, but Hutu that might support more moderate approaches (Melvern, 2000, pp. 61–72). Such potential threats were not limited to government officials, but those with other means of influence – the educated, the artistic, and the affluent. The *Interahamwe*, a civil militia trained by Hutu military officials and equipped by the government, became increasingly militant and anti-Tutsi. Between 6,000 and 7,000 Tutsi and moderate Hutu political opponents were accused of being collaborates of the RPF and imprisoned; in addition, hundreds of other Tutsis were beaten or killed (Kimonyo, 2015; see also Note 4). The situation worsened after the RPF's 1992 attempt to invade Rwanda. Hate propaganda flooded the airwaves and massive shipments of machetes began to arrive in the country (Guichaoua, 2015, pp. 95–142; Melvern, 2009).

Unparalleled Death Comes to Rwanda

On April 6, 1994, an airplane carrying Rwandan President, Juvenal Habyarimana, was shot down as it attempted to land at the Kigali airport, killing all on board. The culprit has not been identified and may never be, although the Hutu government and the RPF immediately pointed fingers at each other (Eltringham, 2004, pp. 111–118). Regardless, the tinder that had been laid over the preceding years was immediately ignited. Targeted murders of Tutsi leaders and Hutu moderates within Kigali began within hours. Within days, targets were expanded to encompass virtually all of Rwanda and all Tutsi – no one was safe. Overnight, one might find a long-time colleague from down the street at their front door with blood on his hands, looking for more.

Many Tutsi turned to local leaders, unable to comprehend that their friends, neighbors, and even relatives might seek to exterminate them, their children, and every Tutsi that could be found. Tutsi would often gather in public places, encouraged by local politicians or clerics, hoping for safety in numbers. Instead, such efforts just made the killings that much more efficient. In the worst of such slaughters, *Interahamwe* would encircle a school or church, throw a few grenades, and begin hacking away. When the effort became tiring, they would return to their nearby camp, to eat and drink until they passed out or were sufficiently refreshed to return to the slaughter.

Over 100 hundred days, 800,000 people – men, women, children, and elderly – were killed. Western states, by and large, found reasons not to intervene. One essential, overly technical debate revolved around a definition: was "genocide" occurring (Scheffer, 2012, pp. 45–68)? The violence only stopped after the RPF had successfully seized control from the Hutu government and the perpetrators were dead or had become refugees themselves.[7] For a detailed accounting of the genocide, see Ashlee Cawley and Stephanie Wolfe's Chapter 2 in this volume.

Legal Mechanisms Addressing the Genocide

Post-genocide Rwanda was in complete disarray. Bodies lined the streets. Infrastructure had been completely disrupted. Individuals vital to basic governmental functions had been wiped from the earth. Such devastation was acutely seen in the judicial system. "Not one court was left operating and of the roughly 800 lawyers and judges in Rwanda before the genocide, only forty were left alive" (Melman, 2011, p. 1277). If those responsible for such atrocities were to be held accountable, alternatives had to be implemented.

The United Nations Security Council (1994a) created the ICTR to prosecute those responsible for genocide and other atrocity crimes while contributing to the process of national reconciliation and restoration of peace and attempting "to strengthen the courts and judicial system of Rwanda" (pp. 1–2). Despite many successes, the ICTR has faced substantial criticism, which will be discussed in Chapters 5 and 6 of this volume. Some have suggested that the tribunal's "foreign genesis, location, and judicial methods have marginalized its relevance to the Rwandan people" (Kamatali, 2006, p. 90; Patterson, 2010, p. 371). In particular, the tribunal's location in Arusha, Tanzania, made it virtually impossible for average Rwandans to participate in or even visit the tribunal,[8] which, additionally, applied a legal framework distinct from their own tradition.[9] According to one author, "a majority of Rwandans feel that the ICTR is 'a useless institution, an expedient mechanism for the international community to absolve itself of its responsibilities for the genocide and its tolerance of the crimes of the [RPF]'" (Scharf & Kang, 2005, p. 917 quoting in part Marks, 2001).[10] Indeed, despite allegations of war crimes committed by RPF soldiers in the immediate aftermath of the genocide, the ICTR has never prosecuted a member of the RPF, or any Tutsi for that matter (Fischer, 2014).[11]

While initial efforts were made to quickly reestablish national courts, it soon became clear that rebuilding would take time (Scheffer, 2012, pp. 69–86, 112). In recent years, the national court system has significantly improved, yet cases of political character often appear suspect.[12] National cases in Rwanda against RPF soldiers seem to protect the defendants rather than provide justice to the victims (Haskell & Waldorf, 2011, pp. 65–66).

Conversely, there is some suggestion that those opposing the government are convicted on limited evidence or coerced confessions (Amnesty International, 2013; European Parliament, 2013).

Nonetheless, the transfer of cases from the ICTR to the Rwandan domestic courts serves as both an endorsement of the local judicial system and an opportunity for observers to gauge the current status of the Rwandan courts.[13] Indeed, three relatively high-profile transferred cases – those of Dr. Leon Mugesera, Jean Uwinkindi, and Bernard Munyagishari – recently resulted in life sentences. As the accused in several other cases transferred to Rwanda from the ICTR remain at large[14] and the Rwandan government continues efforts to obtain extradition of other suspects, the potential for additional national genocide trials is high (Dixon, 2014; Karuhanga, 2014; Musoni, 2013; Rawlinson, 2019).

Despite concerted efforts, the national court system was overwhelmed by the massive numbers of those suspected of genocide and an alternative was necessary to address the extraordinary case load. Some 9,000 suspects were tried by the national courts between 1997 and 2002, while 130,000 sat in prisons awaiting trial (Cruvellier, 2006, p. 169).[15] Inspired by a traditional Rwandan justice system for resolving local disputes, the government set up hundreds of grassroots tribunals known as *gacaca*, where entire communities would witness proceedings, anyone could participate, and local elected leaders would pass judgment on the accused, all with a focus on reconciliation and reintegration (Ngay, 2009, pp. 93–94). After roughly ten years and a million cases, the *gacaca* completed their mandate.[16]

While the subject of much praise, significant criticism of the *gacaca* has emerged, primarily as a result of the relatively informal nature of the proceedings. Among other issues, there were significant concerns with the lack of training and independence of the judges, and the limited rights of the accused, which failed to meet international standards of due process (Amnesty International, 2002, pp. 38–39; Carter, 2007, pp. 41, 48; Doughty, 2016; Sosnov, 2008, pp. 147–149; Westberg, 2011, pp. 355–356). Perhaps most concerning was that the *gacaca* were limited to only try alleged *génocidaires*; thus, RPF members, many of whom committed acts of retaliation and other ethnically motivated violence, have been excluded from prosecution (Haskell & Waldorf, 2011, pp. 53–54).[17] See Chapters 5 and 6 for more information on *gacaca*.

State and Civil Society Contributions to Post-Genocide Reconstruction

While the ICTR, national courts, and *gacaca* all played a critical role,[18] they were, by and large, ill-equipped to address the genocide. It took time to develop the framework for these institutions and to get them up and running. Even then, courts simply could not handle the volume of perpetrators or the national scope of the crimes, although they did evolve to better meet those concerns. To some degree, sharp focus on the legal process came at the expense of other means required for Rwanda to emerge from the genocide (Gahima, 2013, p. xl).

The devastation was so immense and intense that legal proceedings were the least concern of many Rwandans. For many survivors, the very essentials of life were in short supply. Homes had been destroyed, food and transportation limited, and medical care nonexistent. Grief could easily overwhelm – bodies littered many public places, entire families were gone, a woman might be carrying her rapist's child. The needs were much broader reaching than any conceivable judicial mechanism could address. As a result, other entities necessarily stepped into the void, including the government and international and regional organizations (Kimonyo, 2019; Longman, 2017).

Initially, action by international organizations was limited to addressing the refugee crisis in neighboring states, as the violence within Rwanda was too great to allow for in-country assistance. As portions of Rwanda were stabilized, food, water, and other immediate needs were addressed, primarily through United Nations entities. Health professionals from a number of organizations arrived to provide immediate care and addressing key shortfalls, including a safe blood supply and vaccines (Anschütz, 2017; Eriksson, 1996). Significant strides were made to address agricultural shortages, including the provision of seeds and farming equipment (Eriksson, 1996). However, many other areas of concern received little attention.

As the country began to recover from the most obvious and acute concerns, the role of the Rwandan government and civil society became far more impactful, including efforts by the government to mold the collective memory and create its preferred narrative (Kim, 2013, p, 30; Waldorf, 2011). While international aid had done little to address the psychological trauma of the genocide, organizations like Never Again Rwanda (discussed in Chapters 5 and 8) emerged to fill the void. Such local entities have been essential to ensuring that Rwanda and its citizens continue to heal from the genocide and successfully move forward.

A New and Dynamic Contribution to Transitional Justice and Memory of the Genocide in Rwanda

Perhaps the most important contribution of this volume is that it provides a means for a number of Rwandans – scholars, social workers, artists, and survivors – to directly express and preserve their perspectives on the genocide and transitional justice efforts following it. This is by no means a slight to those writing on the topic who are not from Rwanda. Given the vast loss of life, many Rwandans who would have been best suited to make such contributions were themselves victims. Without the efforts of foreign peacekeepers, journalists, academics, and other professionals, many memories of the genocide may have been lost forever. All of the authors in this volume who are not from Rwanda have completed research, field-work, or a variety of other projects within the country itself giving them first-hand experiences that, in many ways, profoundly affected them.[19] In no way attempting to "assume the voice of the victim" (Dauge-Roth, 2010, quoting Lacapra, 2001, p. 98), the non-Rwandan authors have sought, by and large, to assemble the thoughts and perceptions of Rwandans gleaned from personal observation, interviews, first-hand accounts, and other unique sources. The resultant text is rich with new perspectives joining the communal narrative.[20] Roughly a quarter of the authors are from Rwanda and several others are from the Global South. The authors are ethnically and gender diverse, representing a wide range of fields. There is no one story of the genocide, and as such authors hold a variety of viewpoints and use different methodologies, approaches, and philosophies in addressing transitional justice.

The story of Rwanda's genocide has been told and retold many times in the last quarter of a century. As with memory, language changes and evolves. In particular, the preferred terminology of the government and many survivors is "the genocide against the Tutsi." From a legal perspective, this phrase is perhaps most accurate, as the definition of genocide requires that the violence is carried out against a "national, ethnical, racial or religious group" (United Nations Security Council 1994b, Art. 2). However, one specific concern with "genocide against the Tutsi" is that it excludes the thousands of Hutus who were also murdered or were otherwise victimized by those responsible for the mass destruction of life in Rwanda. Thus, a variety of phrases, including the "Rwandan genocide" and the "genocide in Rwanda," have been used by journalists, politicians, academics, and even the authors of this book.

Regardless of the evolving terminology and the growth of literature on Rwanda and its troubled history, the memories of many directly affected by the genocide remain untold. As Linda Melvern highlights, a danger of this "untold story" is the denial and minimization of the genocide, which began during the genocide and has continued to this day.[21] Melvern places great weight on the importance of first-hand accounts to rebut misrepresented facts proffered by those seeking to minimize or deny the genocide. The first section of this volume examines memories of the genocide, through first-hand accounts and critical analysis. In Chapter 2 of this volume, Ashlee Cawley and Stephanie Wolfe assemble interviews from individuals who were children when they experienced the genocide first-hand. These accounts introduce readers to the events of the genocide in a very real and personal way. MJ Rwigema, the author of Chapter 3, presents a critical approach to genocide scholarship, recognizing that the overwhelming majority of academic contributions on the subject are produced by non-Rwandans with highly Westernized perspectives. She concludes that this imbalance warps global views of the genocide and drowns out voices from within Rwanda – an issue that this book makes great efforts bring to the fore. Chapter 4 in this section, written by Musa Wakhungu Olaka, collects and analyzes handwritten accounts of children as they emerged from the genocide.

Chapters 5–8 fall under the umbrella of justice and society following the genocide. In Chapter 5, Dr. Joseph Nkurunziza, executive director of Never Again Rwanda, provides an introduction to institutional transitional justice mechanisms and nongovernmental efforts to recover from the trauma of genocide and build a peaceful and sustainable future. In introducing readers to that civil society organization, Nkurunziza provides a concrete example of just such a mechanism. Chapter 6, authored by Samantha Lakin and Charity Wibabara, addresses the theoretical and sociological aspects of the various legal mechanisms on reconciliation and justice from an internal, Rwandan perspective. Unique options, such as the ICTR and *gacaca* were necessitated by the devastating scope of the genocide; as those options for prosecution ceased, the importance of symbolic measures, such as memorialization and commemoration, increased. All have worked together to advance peace and reconciliation. In Chapter 7, Jonathan Beloff discusses the appropriate classification of thousands of murders of Hutu civilians committed by members of the RPF and the lack of prosecutions for such crimes is examined. Despite the atrocities committed by RPF soldiers, which often go unrecognized, Beloff concludes they simply do not rise to the level of genocide. In Chapter 8, Odeth Kantengwa addresses the long-lasting effects and recovery efforts for women raped and sexually assaulted during the genocide through interviews of those enduring such heinous acts.

The final part of this book addresses artistic efforts to express, memorialize, and consolidate individual and collective memories of the genocide and its aftermath. In Chapter 9, Tawia Ansah examines the Kigali Genocide Memorial Centre, providing insight into the physical construction and effectiveness of the commemorative effort. A walk through the memorial reveals the national narrative at the expense of digressing points of view. Anna-Marie de Beer writes in Chapter 10 of the challenges of collective memory through the literary works of nine African authors who wrote on the genocide, most of them as outside observers, within a few years of its occurrence. These texts provide diverse narratives, much as this book does, prompting thought-provoking questions for the reader. Chapter 11, authored by George S. MacLeod, examines two important pieces of cinematography documenting the genocide. As both reflect the dominant ideology and suffer from the requirement that a good story have a strong ending, they also provide an introduction to a functional transnational justice system. In Chapter 12, Sonya de Laat discusses her personal experience in trying to capture stories and emotions of genocide in still photography. She concludes that such efforts assist in sharing of the trauma, which itself can lead to healing. Finally, Chapter 13 collects the work of several young Rwandan poets, reflecting on the horrors of the past and hope for the future.

Where an Introduction Concludes, a Book Begins

Over a quarter century has passed since the genocide against the Tutsi in Rwanda, yet the memories of these events are still fresh in the minds of those who survived or were otherwise affected by the atrocities. While the country has been rebuilt, the horrors of that summer in 1994 cannot and must not be forgotten. The scope is truly incomprehensible – 800,000 dead, with two million accused of some amount of participation. Humanity itself was dealt a crushing blow. But in such vastness, it is easy to overlook the profound individual effects of the loss of one's loved ones, home, community, and way of life. The accounts collected here are real – actual people with personal stories of devastating loss and remarkable recovery. To borrow from Antjie Krog, we present "the personal story brought, from the innermost of the individual to bind us anew to the collective" (Krog, 2000, p. 86).

This book examines how transitional justice mechanisms have been implemented in the shadow of the 1994 genocide and asks its authors how various strategies have affected individual Rwandans and Rwandan society. It brings together a variety of disciplines from the artistic to the legalistic, with various disciplines explored between. Our desire for this book is simple – that through this effort, memories are preserved that would otherwise be forgotten; that unsung perspectives are examined and ultimately included in the broader effort to remember and learn from such tragedy. The varying perspectives, distinct, unique, and even at times on the fringe or conflicting, coalesce to reveal shared sorrow over what has been, a desire for justice, and hope for tomorrow.

As Father Andre Sibomana wrote a short time after the genocide:

> Our country has just lived through one of the most tragic pages of its history. This ordeal was not necessary. We could have made other choices and human lives could have been spared. Large numbers of people were killed. Justice must search for those who are guilty and try them. Survivors must preserve the memory of this tragedy and learn lessons for the future. The failure to take on the consequences of our past would amount to killing for a second time those whose life has already been stolen
>
> (Sibomana, 1999, p. 153).

Now we proceed, in the shadow of the genocide.

Notes

1 Howe & Knott (2015) discuss: "[W]hat gets encoded into memory is determined by what a person attends to, what they already have stored in memory, their expectations, needs and emotional state. This information is subsequently integrated (consolidated) with other information that has already been stored in a person's long-term, autobiographical memory. What gets

retrieved later from that memory is determined by that same multitude of factors that contributed to encoding as well as what drives the recollection of the event. Specifically, what gets retold about an experience depends on whom one is talking to and what the purpose is of remembering that particular event…Moreover, what gets remembered is reconstructed from the remnants of what was originally stored; that is, what we remember is constructed from whatever remains in memory following any forgetting or interference from new experiences that may have occurred across the interval between storing and retrieving a particular experience. Because the contents of our memories for experiences involve the active manipulation (during encoding), integration with pre-existing information (during consolidation), and reconstruction (during retrieval) of that information, memory is, by definition, fallible at best and unreliable at worst" (pp. 633–634). Thus, as Beil (2011) states, "[m]emory is not so much a record of the past as a rough sketch that can be modified even by the simple act of telling the story…A long list of circumstances…can affect how memories are recorded and replayed, including the emotion at the time of the event, the social pressures that taint its reconstruction, even flourishes unknowingly added after the fact." For an in-depth analysis of how time impacts Rwandan memory of the genocide, see also Brehm & Fox (2016) and Lemarchand (2009) discussing the ambivalence and subjectivity of memory.

2 Dauge-Roth (2010) remarks, "Any memorialization of 'the' past functions always to a certain degree as a powerful legitimizing gesture directed toward the present" (p. 4). In this sense, we must tread carefully; while there is no doubt that Rwanda today has improved since 1994, it is not without its flaws and there is room for significant continued improvement.

3 However, transitional justice has become far more that legal response in a time of significant change. See Hansen (2015) discussing the more encompassing nature of the term in recent years to include a broad group of topics, actors, and occurrences. By way of example, see the broad use of the concept in Roht-Arriaza (2012) and see Lambourne (2015) discussing the importance of transitional justice mechanisms that focus on issues other than legal justice.

4 S. Wolfe, O. Ndizeye, A-M. de Beer, and J. Nkurunziza – Interviews conducted between 2016 and 2019 for the manuscript in preparation: *Journey through Rwandan Memorials*. These interviews were conducted in English, French, and Kinyarwanda, depending on the comfort level and desires of the interviewee. Kinyarwandan translation was conducted by Omar Ndizeye, a genocide survivor and co-author.

5 The number of individuals killed during the genocide remains a debated topic within the international community. Conservative estimates place the number of dead at 500,000 whereas the Rwandan government has stated that 1,071,000 were killed, with 90% being Tutsi. 800,000 was the estimate given by a United Nations expert on population losses and cited by the late Alison Des Forges (1999). See also Vesperini, 2004; and Survivors Fund Statistics. Within this volume, authors are free to utilize whichever statistics they believe to be the most accurate.

6 The Twa, an estimated 1% of the population, were so few that they played no political role in pre-1994 Rwanda and were shunned by both Hutu and Tutsi. During the genocide, some Twa were killed, others became killers; however, their roles were so limited that most studies do not examine them (Des Forges, 1999, pp. 31–33).

7 A number of remarkable accounts exist, reflecting a wide variety of perspectives. See Caplan (2018); Gourevitch (2000); Hatzfeld (2005); Mamdani (2002); Rever (2018); Melvern (2000).

8 As Koosed (2012) remarks: "The rare Rwandan who tries to visit the UN court must take a bus through four countries to get there ... The journey takes two days, and costs around $40 for the bus ticket and $20 for a Kenyan transit visa. This is more than most Rwandans earn in a month" (p. 285).

9 While Rwanda has a civil law tradition, the ICTR bears many traits of the adversarial system "full of 'judicial romanticism' and obscure 'technicalities'...mainly a characteristic of Anglo-Saxon legal culture" (Patterson, 2010, p. 373 quoting in part Moghalu, 2005, p. 176).

10 Also note the "extraordinarily low" knowledge and understanding of the ICTR possessed by the majority of Rwandans (Scharf & Kang, 2005). See also Kamatali (2006, p. 94) and Muna (2004).

11 The only non-Hutu prosecuted by the ICTR was a European who had worked for *Radio Télévision Libre de Mille Collines* and pled guilty to incitement to commit genocide (*Prosecutor v. Ruggiu, Judgement and Sentence,* 2000).

12 The United States Department Of State (2013) recalls that: "the judiciary operated in most cases without government interference; however, there were constraints on judicial independence, and government officials sometimes attempted to influence individual cases..." (pp. 1, 12–14.); see also Rugege (2007, p. 411); and Waldorf (2009, pp. 151–152) discussing domestic prosecution of suspected *génocidaires.*

13 Maunganidze (2012) argues, "until recently most courts - the ICTR and those in Europe - did not believe that the Rwandan courts would be able to provide free and fair trials for genocide suspects. Perceptions are changing, albeit slowly."

14 Eight suspects indicted by the ICTR remain at large. Three are subject to trial by the Residual Mechanism; five by the Rwandan national judiciary. See United Nations International Mechanism for Criminal Tribunals, 2020.

15 See also Scheffer (2012, p. 112) and Chapters 5 and 6 for issues confronted by national courts and the transfer of suspects to the *gacaca* system.

16 The numbers tried by *gacaca* have been reported from 400,000 to 1,958,634. The authors within this volume have been free to utilize the sources they believe to be most accurate. See Brehm et al. (2014, pp. 340–341); Clark (2010, p. 175); Human Rights Watch (2011); Kok (2012); Reyntjens (2013, p. 226); United Nations International Criminal Tribunal for Rwanda (2015). For *gacaca* in general see Clark (2010); Doughty (2015, pp. at 419–437); and Ingelaere (2017).

17 Kamatali (2006, pp. 100–101), cites Roth (2002), that "victims of RPA crimes have virtually no chance of obtaining justice in any Rwandan court, whether military court or Gacaca court." See also Human Rights Watch (2003, 2011).

18 While there are differing opinions and measures of success, "[w]here the ICTR, the national courts, and *gacaca* were, at least in part focused on collectively [establishing an account of how and why the violence occurred] through plural processes, it re-enforced the legitimacy of all three of the court's actions and reduced the potential for popular critique of the courts" (Palmer, 2015, p. 183). The courts have significant effects (both positive and negative) on the development of collective memory of atrocity crimes (Osiel, 1997, 2000).

19 See Dauge-Roth (2010, p. 10) regarding the challenges of the secondary witness.

20 The voices do not, and should not, sound as one. They are as disparate as the individuals who have shared their thoughts and experiences and those who now have the opportunity to discuss and analyze what they find here. See generally, Jessee (2017) on presenting a variety of views and addressing the "danger of a single story." Also see MJ Rwigema's Chapter 3 in this volume for a discussion on Western and non-Western perspective.

21 The phrase "untold story" while utilized here to discuss the voices of those who have not spoken, is increasingly associated with denialism as the BBC documentary *Rwanda's Untold Story* has been widely criticized both inside

and outside of Rwanda. As MJ Rwigema in Chapter 3 states, this untold story narrative includes others those that are "considered 'genocide denial' and 'negationist' discourses." It is to engage with this increasing trend of genocide denialism that we offer up this book as an analysis of fieldwork, research projects, and Rwandan voices of their experiences within Rwanda.

Bibliography

Amnesty International. (2002, December 17). *Rwanda: Gacaca: A question of justice* (Index Number: AFR 47/007/2002). Retrieved from https://www.amnesty.org/en/documents/afr47/007/2002/en/

Amnesty International. (2013, March 25). *Rwanda: Opposition leader's right to a fair trial in jeopardy.* Retrieved from http://www.amnesty.org/en/news/rwanda-opposition-leader-s-right-fair-trial-jeopardy-2013-03-25

Anschutz, K. (2017, January 3). *Cooperation of INGOs in times of humanitarian crises: A case study from Rwanda* [Master's thesis, Linnaeus University]. Retrieved from http://lnu.diva-portal.org/smash/get/diva2:1070967/FULLTEXT01.pdf

Apfelbaum, E. (2010). Halbwachs and the social properties of memory. In S. Radstone, & B. Schwarz (Eds.), *Memory: Histories, theories and debates* (pp. 77–92). Fordham University Press.

Beil, L. (2011, November 28). The certainty of memory has its day in court. *The New York Times.* Retrieved from https://www.nytimes.com/2011/11/29/health/the-certainty-of-memory-has-its-day-in-court.html

Brehm, H. N., & Fox, N. (2016). Narrating genocide: Time, memory, and blame. *Sociological Forum, 32*(1), 116–137. https://doi.org/10.1111/socf.12319

Brehm, H. N., Uggen, C., & Gasanabo, J.-D. (2014). Genocide, justice, and Rwanda's gacaca courts. *Journal of Contemporary Criminal Justice, 30*(3), 333–352. https://doi.org/10.1177/1043986214536660

Caplan, G. (2018). Rethinking the Rwandan narrative for the 25th anniversary. *Genocide Studies International, 12*(2), 152–190. https://doi.org/10.3138/gsi.12.2.03

Carter, L. (2007). Justice and reconciliation on trial: Gacaca proceedings in Rwanda. *New England Journal of International and Comparative Law, 14*, 41–55.

Clark, P. (2009). Establishing a conceptual framework: Six key transitional justice themes. In P. Clark & Z. Kaufman (Eds.), *After genocide: Transitional justice, post-conflict reconstruction and reconciliation in Rwanda and beyond* (pp. 191–206). Columbia University Press.

Clark, P. (2010). *The Gacaca courts, post-genocide justice and reconciliation in Rwanda.* Cambridge University Press. https://doi.org/10.1017/CBO9780511761584

Cruvellier, T. (2006). *Court of remorse: Inside the international criminal tribunal for Rwanda.* The University of Wisconsin Press.

Dauge-Roth, A. (2010). *Writing and filming the genocide of the Tutsis in Rwanda: Disremembering and remembering traumatic history.* Lexington Books.

Des Forges, A. (1999). *Leave none to tell the story: Genocide in Rwanda.* Human Rights Watch.

Dixon, H. (2014, March 4). Kent pastor 'led militia which hacked enemies to death' in Rwanda genocide. *The Telegraph.* Retrieved from http://www.telegraph.co.uk/news/worldnews/africaandindianocean/rwanda/10675970/Kent-pastor-led-militia-which-hacked-enemies-to-death-in-Rwandan-genocide.html

Doughty, K. (2015). Law and the architecture of social repair: Gacaca days in post-genocide Rwanda. *Journal of the Royal Anthropological Institute, 21*(2), 419–437. https://doi.org/10.1111/1467-9655.12213

Doughty, K. C. (2016). *Remediation in Rwanda: Grassroots legal forums*. University of Pennsylvania Press.

Eltringham, N. (2004). *Accounting for horror: Post-genocide debates in Rwanda*. Pluto Publishers.

Eriksson, J. (1996, March 1). *The international response to conflict and genocide: Lessons from the Rwanda experience* [Report]. *The Nordica Africa Institute*. Retrieved from https://www.oecd.org/countries/rwanda/50189495.pdf

European Parliament. (2013, May 23). *European Parliament resolution of 23 May 2013 on Rwanda: Case of Victoire Ingabire*. European Parliament, Council of the European Union. Retrieved from http://www.europarl.europa.eu/document/activities/cont/201306/20130620ATT68096/20130620ATT68096EN.pdf

Fischer, H. (2014, February 25). Rwandan justice under scrutiny at genocide trial. *All Africa*. Retrieved from http://allafrica.com/stories/201402260358.html

Fussell, J. (2001, November 15). *Group classification on national ID cards as a factor in genocide and ethnic cleansing* [Speech transcript]. Prevent Genocide International. Retrieved from http://www.preventgenocide.org/prevent/removing-facilitating-factors/IDcards/

Gahima, G. (2013). *Transitional justice in Rwanda: Accountability for atrocity*. Routledge.

Gourevitch, P. (2000). *We wish to inform you that tomorrow we will be killed with our families: Stories from Rwanda*. Picador.

Guichaoua, A. (2015). *From war to genocide: Criminal politics in Rwanda 1990-1994* (D. E. Webster & D. Webster Trans.). University of Wisconsin Press.

Halbwachs, M. (1992). *On collective memory* (L. A. Coser Trans.). Chicago University Press.

Hansen, T. O. (2015). The vertical and horizontal expansion of transitional justice: Explanations and implications for a contested field. In S. Buckley-Zistel, T. Koloma Beck, C. Braun, & F. Mieth (Eds.), *Transitional justice theories* (pp. 105–124). Routledge.

Haskell, L., & Waldorf, L. (2011). The impunity gap of the international criminal tribunal for Rwanda: Causes and consequences. *Hasting International and Comparative Law Review, 34*(1), 49–85.

Hatzfeld, J. (2005). *Machete season: The killers in Rwanda speak* (L. Coverdale Trans.). Farrar, Straus and Giroux.

Howe, M., & Knott, L. (2015). The fallibility of memory in judicial processes: Lessons from the past and their modern consequences. *Memory, 23*(5), 633–656. https://doi.org/10.1080/09658211.2015.1010709

Human Rights Watch. (2003, August 7). *Security Council: Do not undermine ICTR's independence: Letter to council members on eve of meeting with lead prosecutor*. Retrieved from http://www.hrw.org/news/2003/08/07/security-council-do-not-undermine-ictrs-independence

Human Rights Watch. (2011, May). *Justice compromised: The legacy of Rwanda's community-based Gacaca courts*. Retrieved from http://www.hrw.org/sites/default/files/reports/rwanda0511webwcover_0.pdf

Ingelaere, B. (2017). *Inside Rwanda's Gacaca courts*. University of Wisconsin Press.

Jessee, E. (2017). *Negotiating genocide in Rwanda: The politics of history.* Palgrave MacMillan.

Kamatali, J.-M. (2006). From the ICTR to ICC: Learning from the ICTR experience in bringing justice to Rwandans. *New England Journal of International and Comparative Law, 12*(1), 89–103.

Karuhanga, J. (2014, February 27). Rwanda: Anger as French courts overturns extradition order of genocide suspects. *All Africa.* Retrieved from http://allafrica.com/stories/201402270185.html

Kelly, C. M., & Lindsay, S. (1996). Conscious and unconscious forms of memory. In E. L. Bjork, & R. Bjork (Eds.), *Memory: Handbook of perception and cognition* (pp. 33–67). Academic Press.

Khan, R. (2011, August 30). Tutsi probably differ genetically from the Hutu. *Discovery Magazine.* Retrieved from http://blogs.discovermagazine.com/gnxp/2011/08/tutsi-differ-genetically-from-the-hutu/#.XZ85hFVKhEY

Kim, H. J. (2013). Transitional justice: Politics of memory and reconciliation. In E. Resende, & D. Budryte (Eds.), *Memory and trauma in international relations: Theories, cases and debates* (pp. 30–41). Routledge.

Kimonyo, J.-P. (2015). *Rwanda's popular genocide: A perfect storm.* Lynne Rienner Publishers.

Kimonyo, J.-P. (2019). *Transforming Rwanda: Challenges on the road to reconstruction* (C. Akin Trans.). Lynne Rienner Publishers, Inc.

Kok, N. (2012, February 28). *The closing of the gacaca courts and the implications for access to justice in Rwanda.* Institute for Security Studies. Retrieved from https://issafrica.org/iss-today/the-closing-of-the-gacaca-courts-and-the-implications-for-access-to-justice-in-rwanda#:~:text=The%20closing%20of%20the%20Gacaca%20without%20providing%20any%20way%20for,created%20for%20Rwanda's%20national%20reconciliation

Koosed, D. (2012). The paradox of impartiality: A critical defense of the international criminal tribunal for Rwanda. *University of Miami International and Comparative Law Review, 19*(2), 243–291.

Krog, A. (2000). *Country of my skull: Guilt, sorrow, and the limits of forgiveness in the new South Africa.* Three Rivers Press.

Lacapra, D. (2001). *Writing history, writing trauma.* Johns Hopkins University Press.

Lambourne, W. (2015). Transformative justice, reconciliation, and peacebuilding. In S. Buckley-Zistel, T. Koloma Beck, C. Braun, & F. Mieth (Eds.), *Transitional justice theories* (pp. 19–39). Routledge.

Lemarchand, R. (2009). The politics of memory in post-genocide Rwanda. In P. Clark, & Z. D. Kaufman (Eds.), *After genocide: Transitional justice, post-conflict reconstruction and reconciliation in Rwanda and beyond* (pp. 65–76). Columbia University Press.

Longman, T. (2017). *Memory and justice in post-genocide Rwanda.* Cambridge University Press. https://doi.org/10.1017/9781139086257

Lopez, R. (2015). The (re)Collection of memory after mass atrocity and the dilemma for transitional justice. *New York University Journal of International Law and Politics, 47,* 799–853. https://doi.org/10.2139/ssrn.2406188

Mamdani, M. (2002). *When victims become killers: Colonialism, nativism, and the genocide in Rwanda.* Princeton University Press.

Marks, K. (2001). The Rwanda tribunal: Justice delayed. *Global Policy Forum.* Retrieved from https://archive.globalpolicy.org/intljustice/tribunals/2001/0607icg.htm

Maunganidze, O. A. (2012, February 9). Rwanda's new genocide cases a milestone for domestic prosecutions of international crimes. *Institute for Security Studies*. Retrieved from http://www.issafrica.org/iss-today/rwandas-new-genocide-cases-a-milestone-for-domestic-prosecutions-of- international-crimes

Melman, J. (2011). The possibility of transfer(?): A comprehensive approach to the International Criminal Tribunal for Rwanda's rule 11bis to permit transfer to Rwandan domestic courts. *Fordham Law Review*, *79*(3), 1271–1332.

Melvern, L. (2000). *A people betrayed: The role of the west in Rwanda's genocide*. Palgrave.

Melvern, L. (2009). The past is prologue: Planning the 1994 Rwandan genocide. In P. Clark, & Z. D. Kaufman (Eds.), *After genocide: Transitional justice, post-conflict reconstruction and reconciliation in Rwanda and beyond* (pp. 21–32). Columbia University Press.

Moghalu, K. (2005). *Rwanda's genocide: The politics of global justice*. Palgrave Macmillian.

Muna, B. A. (2004, November). *The early challenges of conducting investigations and prosecutions before international criminal tribunals*. Retrieved from http://www.unictr.org/Portals/0/English%5CNews%5Cevents%5CNov2004%5Cmuna.pdf

Musoni, E. (2013, December 21). Dutch court approves extradition of genocide suspects. *The New Times*. Retrieved from https://www.newtimes.co.rw/section/read/71708

Ngay, R. (2009). Traditional justice and legal pluralism in transitional context: The case of Rwanda's gacaca courts. In J. R. Quinn (Ed.), *Reconciliation(s): Transitional justice in post-conflict societies* (pp. 86–115). McGill-Queen's University Press.

Osiel, M. (1997). *Mass atrocity, collective memory, and the law*. Transaction Publishers.

Osiel, M. (2000). Why prosecute? Critics of punishment for mass atrocity. *Human Rights Quarterly*, *22*(1), 118–147.

Palmer, N. (2015). *Courts in conflict: Interpreting the layers of justice in post-genocide Rwanda*. Oxford University Press. https://doi.org/10.1093/acprof:oso/9780199398195.001.0001

Patterson, P. (2010) Partial justice: Successes and failures of the international criminal tribunal for Rwanda in ending impunity for violations of international criminal law. *Tulane Journal of International and Comparative Law*, *19*(1), 369–395.

Prosecutor v. Ruggiu Case No. ICTR-97-32-I. (2000, June 1). International Criminal Tribunal for Rwanda. Retrieved from https://ucr.irmct.org/scasedocs/case/ICTR-97-32#eng

Rawlinson, K. (2019, April 8). Met police investigate five men over Rwandan genocide claims. *The Guardian*. Retrieved from https://www.theguardian.com/uk-news/2019/apr/09/met-police-investigate-five-men-over-rwandan-genocide-claims

Reed, W. C. (1996). Exile, reform, and the rise of the Rwandan Patriotic Front. *The Journal of Modern African Studies*, *34*(3), 479–501. https://doi.org/10.1017/S0022278X00055567

Rever, J. (2018). *In praise of blood: The crimes of the Rwandan Patriotic Front*. Random House Canada.

Reyntjens, F. (2013). *Political governance in post-genocide Rwanda*. Cambridge University Press. https://doi.org/10.1017/CBO9781107338647

Roht-Arriaza, N. (2012). The new landscape of transitional justice. In N. Roht-Arriaza & J. Mariezcurrena (Eds.), *Transitional justice in the twenty-first century:*

Beyond truth versus justice (pp. 1–16). Cambridge University Press. https://doi.org/10.1017/CBO9780511617911

Roth, K. (2002, August 9). *Letter sent to US Ambassador John Negroponte, President of the UN Security Council.* Human Rights Watch. Retrieved from http://www.hrw.org/news/2002/08/09/letter-sent-us-ambassador-john-negroponte-president-un-security-council

Rugege, S. (2007). Judicial independence in Rwanda. *Pacific McGeorge Global Business and Development Law Journal, 19*(2), 411–425.

Scharf, M. P., & Kang, A. (2005). Errors and missteps: Key lessons the Iraqi special tribunal can learn from the ICTY, ICTR and SCSL. *Cornell International Law Journal, 38*(3), 911–947. http://dx.doi.org/10.2139/ssrn.804607

Scheffer, D. (2012). *All the missing souls: A personal history of the war crimes tribunals.* Princeton University Press.

Sibomana, A. (1999). *Hope for Rwanda: Conversations with Laure Guilber and Hervé Deguine* (C. Tertsakian Trans.). Pluto Press. (Original work published in 1999)

Sosnov, M. (2008). The adjudication of genocide: Gacaca and the road to reconciliation in Rwanda. *Denver Journal of International Law and Policy, 36*(2), 125–153.

Survivors Fund. (n.d.). *Statistics.* Retrieved from https://survivors-fund.org.uk/learn/statistics

Teitel, R. G. (2003). Transitional justice genealogy. *Harvard Human Rights Journal, 16*, 69–94.

United Nations International Residual Mechanism for Criminal Tribunals. (n.d.). *Searching for the fugitives.* Retrieved from https://www.irmct.org/en/cases/searching-fugitives

United Nations International Residual Mechanism For Criminal Tribunals. (n.d.). *United Nations International Criminal Tribunal for Rwanda.* Retrieved from http://www.unictr.org/en/cases

United Nations Security Council. (1994a, November 8). *Statute of the International Criminal Tribunal for Rwanda (as last amended on 13 October 2006)*, retrieved from: https://www.refworld.org/docid/3ae6b3952c.html

United Nations Security Council. (1994b, November 8). *Resolution 955: Establishment of an international tribunal and adoption of the statue of the tribunal.* United Nations. Retrieved from http://unscr.com/en/resolutions/955

United States Defense Intelligence Agency. (1990, November 20). *Rwanda: Unconventional Warfare Prospects*(declassified). https://www.dia.mil/FOIA/FOIA-Electronic-Reading-Room/FOIA-Reading-Room-Rwanda/FileId/204535/

United States Department of State. (2013). *Rwanda country report on human rights practices for 2013.*

Vesperini, H. (2004, April 6). *No consensus on genocide death toll.* IAfrica.com. Retrieved from http://iafrica.com/news/worldnews/314365.htm

Waldorf, L. (2009). A justice "trickle down": Rwanda's first post-genocide president on trial. In E. L. Lutz & C. Reiger (Eds.). *Prosecuting heads of state* (pp. 151–175). Cambridge University Press. https://doi.org/10.1017/CBO9780511575600.011

Waldorf, L. (2011). Instrumentalizing genocide: The RPF's campaign against "Genocide ideology. In S. Strauss, & L. Waldorf (Eds.), *Remaking Rwanda: State building and human rights after mass violence* (pp. 48–66). The University of Wisconsin Press.

Westberg, M. M. (2011). Rwandan's use of transitional justice after genocide: The gacaca courts and the ICTR. *University of Kansas Law Review, 59*(2), 331–367. https://doi.org/10.17161/1808.20180.

2 Through the Eyes of Children

The 1994 Genocide against the Tutsi in Rwanda[1]

Ashlee Cawley and Stephanie Wolfe

With Contributions from Omar Ndizeye,[2] Jacqueline Murekatete, Consolee Nishimwe,[3] Théobald Kayiranga, Jason Nshimye, and Eugenie Mukeshimana

Introduction

I remember vividly the morning of April 7 – it coincided with spring break – so I happened to be with my parents. I was scheduled to go back to my grandmother's house, about two hours away. My father came home; he was very nervous and not himself. He'd been listening with his brother to the radio on the farm, and they had heard that the president had been killed.

It was 1994, and nine-year-old Jacqueline Murekatete, who had been living with her widowed grandmother, was home with her parents and six siblings. She knew that spring break was about to come to an end, and she would soon be going back to her grandmother's village, where she would return to school. What she did not understand was that the assassination of President Juvenal Habyarimana would mark the beginning of the hundred-day genocide in Rwanda. By July, her entire immediate family and most of her extended family would be dead.

The United Nations estimates that approximately 800,000 people were killed that summer (Des Forges, 1999, p. 9). The Rwandan government, however, has estimated the death toll at 1,071,000. In addition, approximately 2 million individuals have been accused of participating in the genocide either through direct killings, informing on those in hiding, or profiting off of the genocide by looting and/or stealing property.[4] This chapter explores the 1994 Genocide of the Tutsi by intertwining experiences of young survivors with historical narrative.[5] While not intended to explain all of the historical or political circumstances of the genocide, this chapter centers the memories of survivors to provide a foundational understanding of the genocide in Rwanda.

DOI: 10.4324/9781003228592-3

Pre-genocide

Memories of childhood are often happy, yet in Rwanda, they were also underwritten by the legacy of historical violence against Tutsi. "I knew I was a Tutsi, and I heard a lot of stories from my parents and grandparents about earlier Tutsi massacres," Jacqueline recalls. "Despite having a sense of that history, for me and many of the children, we always saw it as the past, not that it would ever happen again or that it would ever happen to us in our lifetime." Jacqueline grew up surrounded by loving aunts, uncles, cousins, and friends in Gitarama.[6] Her parents made their living as farmers, but not by choice. Due to the country's strict ethnic-based quota rules, which were designed to limit Tutsis access to higher education (King, 2014), her parents were denied entrance to secondary school, even after achieving exceptional grades and test scores.

Despite being aware of the challenges, Jacqueline's parents encouraged her to study rigorously, in hopes that she would be one of the lucky Tutsis selected to continue her academic pursuits. Two of Jacqueline's uncles had attended university and worked as doctors in Rwanda. Jacqueline recalls that these uncles provided inspiration and drove her to have hope that she too could overcome the ethnic-based obstacles to success.

Théobald Kayiranga, who was eleven years old at the time of the genocide, remembers the challenges of the quota system from his childhood in Cyangugu.[7]

> Every student had a file that said if you were Hutu, Tutsi, or Twa. In order to go to secondary school, you would need to pass an examination and be approved. I remember seeing that all students who succeeded in exams were Hutu, even if there were better Tutsi students. If you were in the top of the primary school, and you got first place, it didn't matter, you couldn't succeed because you were Tutsi. Right before the genocide, when I was in the P-4 level, I was at the top of my class. Even then, I was convinced that I would never go to secondary school.

Théobald recalls how Tutsis were singled out: "My teacher asked all the Tutsi students to stand up in front of our peers so that they would know who the Tutsis were. This happened more than once." Divisionism and ethnic discrimination in the educational system was a common experience throughout both rural and urban areas of Rwanda.

In spite of such discrimination, Théobald has fond memories of his childhood, as he enjoyed close relationships with his aunts, uncles, cousins, siblings, and parents. His father, a successful businessman who owned a thriving farm and bar, was well-respected in the community. "If people had problems, they could come to my father to get advice. Both Hutus and Tutsis would come to my father. He was known as 'someone who would end sorrow.'"

Consolee Nishimwe, who was fourteen at the time of the genocide and grew up in Rubengera,[8] also continues to look back at her childhood with happiness. She recalls, "I was lucky to have such a good family and good parents to help raise me. I have many good memories of my loved ones." Both of her parents worked as teachers at the same school, and instilled in her the value of education, despite the challenges that she faced.

In the years leading up to 1994, Consolee became increasingly aware of the anti-Tutsi sentiment which threatened her family outside the peace of her home. One afternoon when her parents arrived home from work, Consolee noticed that her mother was shaken, and her parents asked her to go into her bedroom. From inside her room, she strained her ears against the door to hear her parents' conversation, "My mom was crying. She said she didn't know what to do about how the Principal was treating him. She told him he should consider getting a different job." Consolee's father was receiving mistreatment at work because of his Tutsi identity, a common occurrence for Tutsis in professional fields.

In spite of the adversity, Consolee's father remained firm in his resolve to continue to help students learn.

> My dad told my mom that he loved his work. He said those who were mistreating him would have to answer to God for what they did. He told Mom he would keep working as a teacher until God was ready for him to stop.

Like her father, Consolee also experienced mistreatment for her Tutsi identity. The conditions only worsened as anti-Tutsi sentiment increased. By junior high school, Consolee had to confront anti-Tutsi jeering from her former friends. She remembers being bullied even while sitting in class:

> My classmate who sat behind me was the mayor's niece. Her name was Annie. She started punching me on the head and called me 'a little Tutsi cockroach.' I was confused. Other classmates had bullied us [Tutsis] before but they hadn't been physical. She started mocking us outside of class. It was alarming how much pleasure she took in picking on Tutsis. People knew what she was doing, but I think no one punished her because they were afraid that they would get in trouble with the mayor.

Consolee recalls how the bullying continued:

> She kept punching me during class. It went on for weeks, but I was too scared to defend myself or even say anything to her. With the way things were going, the Hutu extremists were changing the culture, and they encouraged people to do those kinds of things. I was scared but I didn't tell my parents. Sometimes my teacher came to my house on weekends

> to help with math, so I finally decided to tell him one weekend. I told him that Annie was hitting me and calling me names when he wasn't looking. I thought he'd tell me he'd make her stop. He just said that he'd change her seat. The next Monday, he didn't say anything to Annie or change her seat. I finally realized I'd have to tell my parents. After I told them, they spoke to my teacher, and he changed Annie's seat. I was happy, but she insulted me as soon as she saw me outside of class. After that, I tried harder to keep my distance from her.

Eugenie Mukeshimana, who was a young adult living in the capital, Kigali, at the time of the genocide, heard "You are cockroaches, you are snakes, we could kill you all now and nobody would care!" and other threats while she rode the bus to high school. Due to daily taunts and the hostile environment, she was afraid to walk home even in the middle of the afternoon. When walking down the streets of Kigali, she would hear "We will exterminate you!" and "We will get you someday!" from trucks as government soldiers patrolled the city.

Théobald also recalls threats from militia members in his community.

> I don't remember when the *Interahamwe*[9] came, but they were in my community before the genocide. They were prepared. They would march. They would gather together in this big house and collect materials. The *Interahamwe* would go there to sing songs with lyrics that said, 'We know the Hutu extremist political party is the good political party' and 'We know that the enemy of the Hutus are Tutsis!' I heard them many, many times during the evenings.

"Anytime the Hutus were upset about something, they killed Tutsis," says Jason Nshimye, who was fifteen years old at the time of the genocide. Jason was one of five children, living in a middle-class Tutsi family in the Rwandan countryside. Not long before the genocide began, Jason survived an encounter with another student in which his classmate threatened to kill him, at knifepoint, for being Tutsi. Jason remembers fearing the prospect that because he was a Tutsi, his classmate would not be punished for killing him. He escaped the situation by fleeing when his classmate was distracted. Looking back on the climate leading up to the genocide, Jason comments, "There was no justice for Tutsis, only Hutus." This sense of injustice corresponds to the history of impunity for those who committed crimes against Tutsis which permeated the country in the decades leading up to the genocide.

Genocide

In 1994, the Hutu extremist faction of the government dominated the political climate of Rwanda. The one-party dictatorship arose after the country's independence in 1962 from Belgian colonial rule. President Kayibanda, a

Hutu extremist, led the first republic. He was deposed by Major General Habyarimana, in the 1973 *coup d'etat*. After his assumption of the presidency, Habyarimana increasingly became more authoritarian and oppressive toward the Tutsi minority population. The political party, as the only party, was an authoritarian dictatorship and Habyarimana's inner circle was known to include hard-liner extremists (see Kimonyo, 2016, for more in-depth information on these early years).

Prior to the genocide, Lt. General Roméo Dallaire (2003), Force Commander for the United Nations Assistance Mission for Rwanda, warned the United Nations that he was receiving intelligence that death squads (the *Interahamwe)* were being trained with the goal of rounding up and exterminating the Tutsis (p. 142). Dallaire's warnings were ignored, and his pleas to act were dismissed. On the evening of April 6, the plane carrying Rwandan President Habyarimana and Burundian President Cyprien Ntaryamira was shot down over Kigali by unidentified individuals (Eltringham, 2004).[10] The genocide commenced immediately in Kigali and interviews indicate that by 7 a.m. the next morning, genocidal killings were occurring in distant villages.[11]

Immediately after President Habyarimana's plane was shot down, the *Interahamwe* set up roadblocks in Kigali, forcing all travelers to display their identification cards. These identity cards, originally implemented by Belgian colonial authorities, classified all Rwandans by their paternal ethnicity: Hutu, Tutsi, or Twa.[12] Those whose identity cards stated Tutsi were killed at roadblocks, including men, women, and children.

In *Shake Hands with the Devil,* Dallaire (2003) recalls a meeting where President Habyarimana's death was confirmed. At the meeting, Dallaire repeatedly asserted that the rules of succession dictated that Prime Minister Agathe Uwilingiyimana, a Hutu moderate, was now the head of the government. In violation of the political process, Colonel Bagosora, the head of administration at the Defence Ministry and the primary architect of the genocide, responded that Madame Uwilingiyimana did not have the confidence of the Rwandan people and thus was incapable of governing the nation. The Crisis Committee – Bagosora and other senior military leadership – would instead assume control until a new government was formed. Dallaire continued to insist that Prime Minister Uwilingiyimana had authority as Bagosora and other members of the committee grew increasingly belligerent and insulting toward the constitutionally designated successor (For more information on these events see Dallaire, 2003; Kimonyo, 2016; and *Prosecutor v. Bagosora*).

Prime Minister Uwilingiyimana would remain the head of the government for only fourteen hours. In order to protect the Prime Minister before her planned radio address that would appeal for calm within the country, Dallaire dispatched five Ghanaian peacekeepers and ten Belgian peacekeepers to her residence (Straus, 2006, p. 46). The peacekeepers joined several of her loyal *gendarmes* who were protecting Prime Minister Uwilingiyimana.

In hope of saving her children, the Prime Minister and her husband surrendered to the Presidential Guard and the army. The two were killed immediately, at approximately 10 a.m. The Belgian peacekeepers were taken to a military base where they were tortured and killed in the hours that followed. In addition to these deaths, by noon on April 7, every moderate leader within Rwanda was either dead or in hiding (Dallaire, 2003, pp. 230–245).

The Rwandan Patriotic Front (RPF) was a political refugee organization based in Uganda and comprised primarily of Tutsi refugees who had been forced to flee post-independence Rwanda. In 1990, they launched a military campaign by forcibly entering Rwanda as all previous re-integration measures and permanent resettlement options had failed. The 1990 Civil War concluded in 1993 with the signing of the Arusha Accords. As part of this agreement, a small group of RPF soldiers were quartered in Kigali. When the massacres started throughout the city in April 1994, the RPF[13] began to mobilize troops and informed Dallaire that unless the killings stopped, the RPF would resume military operations. Dallaire passed the message to Bagosora, who dismissed the warnings. In response to the continued massacres, the RPF launched a full offensive on April 8, almost 48 hours after the death of President Habyarimana and the beginning of the genocide (Prunier, 1995, p. 268; Straus, 2006, p. 47). As RPF troops battled for control of the country, the Hutu extremist government consolidated power, and violence against Tutsis and moderate Hutus engulfed the country.

On the morning of April 7, Jacqueline's friends and family were hopeful about their future: "They were a bit worried but somehow thought that their neighbors would never turn on them, that the killings would stop before it reached their village." Jacqueline's father was hesitant to send Jacqueline back to her grandmother's house with such uncertainty in the air. "I didn't fully understand the situation. I wasn't worried at all. I even told my dad to let me go back to my grandmother's. I loved school and looked forward to starting school again." Jacqueline remembers saying a casual goodbye to her parents and siblings, never considering that it could be the last time she would see them.

Jacqueline estimates that the genocide reached her grandmother's village two weeks after she left her parents' home. Seeing crowds of people fleeing through the village, Jacqueline fled with her grandmother and cousin to a nearby commune office. During the nights, Jacqueline would wake to the sounds of screaming; mobs of villagers would come to attack to kill the Tutsis inside.

> They would come with axes, machetes, and hoes to kill us. They [the Tutsi men] could only go outside and try to fight the mobs with sticks and branches. When soldiers would come with grenades, your rock or branch means nothing.

The widespread nature of the genocide was brought about, in part, by hate propaganda produced by Radio Rwanda and *Radio Télévision Libre des Mille Collines* (RTLMC/RTLM) (Temple-Raston, 2005; Thompson, 2007). Consolee recalls hate speech and propaganda being spread when she was a young girl, vividly remembering songs urging people to "exterminate the cockroaches." "It was not only frightening to hear these things over the radio, but even more terrifying to hear similar speech coming from beloved neighbors and friends in everyday life. I couldn't understand why these people turned away from my family." Looking back on the conditions that led up to the genocide, Consolee recognizes the role the radio played in creating an environment of hate: "The extremist-leaning Hutus were easily influenced by the radio. They allowed themselves to hate with intensity." In addition to propaganda, the radio stations directly encouraged murder by broadcasting the names of targets and instructing perpetrators on how to find and kill victims (Temple-Raston, 2005; Thompson, 2007).

Jason's family fled to Mugonero Church with others seeking sanctuary. He recalls:

> After living there for about a week, we heard rumors that our next day would be our last. The following morning the *Interahamwe* arrived with government weapons and started killing everyone. I ran away. Instead of running where they [the killers] could find me, I hid behind a bush.

Like many of the other survivors, Jason fled to the mountains; however, Jason reports that less than 800 of the 4,000 people in the complex escaped. Almost all of Jason's immediate family was killed in the massacre.[14] Elizaphan Ntakirutimana, the pastor of the church, would be the first clergyman convicted by an international tribunal for the crime of genocide for his collaboration with the killers (*The Prosecutor v. Elizaphan Ntakirutimana & Gerard Ntakirutimana*).

The Mugonero Church massacre was not an isolated example. During previous massacres and violent purges in Rwanda, Tutsis had often sought refuge in churches and had been granted safety while within sanctified walls. In 1994, this historical pattern was broken with churches being targeted as massacre sites, and many clergy acting in concert with the killers. Memorial sites have now been established at many churches in recognition of the killings that occurred there. Four churches – Nyamata, Ntarama, Nyarubuye, and Nyange[15]– have been turned into national memorial sites to mark these horrific crimes.

Omar Ndizeye, who was ten at the time of the genocide, is a survivor of the Nyamata Church Massacre in Bugesera.[16] After hearing that the president's plane had been shot down, he fled with his father and six-year-old brother to Kayumba Hill, and then to Nyamata with other Tutsi refugees. Omar recalls:

> The government started transporting killers to the area. When they surrounded us, I saw a big truck of machetes arriving. I couldn't understand

> what was happening because I was only ten years old. Everything was like a film. I saw buses of militias passing by, they were singing 'We will kill you, we will take your properties.' Then, in the afternoon, they started distributing the machetes to the militias, right in front of our eyes.
>
> We watched them take a man out of a house and beat him to death. That's when the feeling started…I can't tell you how I was feeling. It was not a fear or phobia, it was like being paralyzed. Later that afternoon, they made us stand in front of the town office and one of the leaders said, 'I don't want the blood of Tutsis here, go to the church and see the priest. He will see you.' Then the killers started to chase us. They screamed at us that they were going to kill us. I fled with my dad and ran through a school area on our way to the church. Some people were killed running behind us. We were the first people to make it to the church. When we got there, we forced open the door. It was in the evening; you could hear shootings and people screaming all around us. They were killing people nearby.

Over the next few days, the killers moved away and thousands of Tutsi refugees fled to the Nyamata Church complex, with some going into the nearby school, others to the back lot, and others to nearby compounds. Omar was reunited with some members of his extended family, who joined him inside the church. Omar continues:

> Imagine, more than 5,000 people in a cramped church. Parents would put their legs out so that their children could sleep under them or they would hold them. Apart from children screaming and crying, people would talk all night. It was noisy. People were scared. Some people told stories about how Tutsis were killed back in 1959. They said we would die like them. Others would interrupt and say that couldn't happen because we were in a church.
>
> When the militia finally came to kill us in the church, they came with government forces. There was a battle around the church. Suddenly, those who had been fighting to protect us entered inside. That's when I saw the militia through the gates. We could hear them shouting. They started to try and break through. Some of the people in the church had brought rocks with them, so they started throwing stones at the militia to stop them. When they ran out of stones, they threw shoes. Then soldiers came around to the windows and started shooting inside. Whenever someone stood up to throw a stone, they would be shot down. One of my uncles stood up and was shot from the window. Then the militia started throwing grenades inside because the people in the church were resisting. And then it suddenly stopped.
>
> The militia left but they came back with tear gas and more grenades. They threw them through the gate. The smoke took over the whole church. I couldn't breathe. Then people started screaming and crying.

> After some time, the smoke cleared. I could hear my father close to me telling me to wake up. He said, 'Maybe this is the last day' and gave me 100 of Rwandan currency. Then he said, 'Be a man' which in Rwandan also means 'Be strong.' Those were his last words.

The militia then entered the church to kill those who remained alive.

> You could hear the noise of the militia beating people with their knuckles hitting against bone. The next line was for cutting. They'd use their machetes to cut, cut, cut, people. I think they got tired of this, or thought it wasn't working fast enough, because then they started to use grenades again while they kept cutting and beating. I could see the blood and flesh of people exploding from the grenades. I hid myself underneath the benches. By the time the militia got to me, there were so many dead people around me, they passed me and kept beating other people.

The militia would come once more to search the bodies and to ensure everyone had been killed. Omar survived by pretending to be dead; the militia finally left, but not before stealing the money Omar's father had given him. Omar remembers:

> When I finally opened my eyes, the first image I saw was the wife of my uncle. She was sitting in the middle of dead people. One of the grenades had blown off part of her head and shoulder. She spoke with a low voice and said, 'My child you are still alive?' She was very thirsty. She wanted water and asked if I could get her some. I knew I couldn't. I stood up. That's when I saw my father. He was at the top of the bodies. I could see he was cut in the backbone. I went to him because I wanted to know how he was killed. I touched his body and turned over his face. He was beaten up. He had blood coming from his nose and eyes. Then I let him rest on his face again. I couldn't cry when I saw him. I was just paralyzed inside.

Several other children survived the initial massacre; these children helped Omar bring his aunt outside of the church before she died.

Churches were not the only locations where mass killings took place. Many fled to their local administrative commune office believing that the police or local authorities would protect them from the murders occurring, only to find themselves walking to their deaths. Jacqueline initially fled to the commune for safety, but then, one of her uncles, a director of a hospital, paid a Hutu man to fetch them using an ambulance from the hospital as a transport. She recounts: "We said goodbye to the people we were with and left with him." After returning to Rwanda in 2010, Jacqueline learned that over 26,000 people were killed at the commune. Jacqueline and her grandmother were then taken to Nyanza, where they were reunited with her uncle. Being a well-known Tutsi intellectual, her uncle was on many of the kill lists, and knew that if he stayed in Nyanza, he would put their lives at greater risk. He fled, leaving Jacqueline and her grandmother in the care of a Hutu man who he paid to hide them.

Théobald recalls that in Cyangugu, the initial killings were more targeted: "At first, the *Interahamwe* was only killing boys." Théobald fled with his father, older brother, and uncle to hide with Hutu friends in a nearby community. However, because Théobald's father was a well-known member of his community, he knew his presence put his family in danger and separated himself to protect the others. Théobald grew weary of shuffling between families and decided to return to his home to be with his mother.

> Since I was just a small child, I didn't expect anything bad to happen to my mom or dad. When I arrived home, I heard movement, so I started greeting who I thought was my mother, but no one was there. It was only our two dogs. Our house was destroyed, and my mother wasn't there. My neighbor, who was a Hutu woman but had been married to a Tutsi, told me where my mother was.

Théobald joined his mother, members of his extended family, and other Tutsi women and children packed in a small house being guarded by the *Interahamwe*. While there, Tutsi women from Giko, a nearby town, brought news that the same *Interahamwe* had separated mothers from their sons there and burned all male children alive. The next day, the *Interahamwe* told Théobald's group that they wanted to separate the women from the boys. Believing that their sons would be killed, the women gathered together with their children to pray for the last time. Instead of separating them, the *Interahamwe* gathered in a meeting and then left. "They didn't take us away then because they had decided to kill the women and children, too." Théobald remembers:

> The next morning the *Interahamwe* returned. They forced us out of the house and took us to the football ground, where they were going to kill us. However, while they were marching us to the football field, we were stopped by a government policeman. He had a gun, but he didn't kill us. He asked the *Interahamwe*, 'Where are you taking these people?' and they told him they were taking us to a commune office, but that was a lie. He told them, 'At the commune, there is no security, so take them back to the village, where you can have security.'

That night, a Hutu family friend came to the house to tell Théobald's mother that everyone in the house was scheduled to be killed in the morning. Not wanting to leave the rest of their family and loved ones, Théobald's mother remained, but a Hutu friend, who had been hiding Théobald's uncle and brother, took him. While hiding in a banana tree the next day, Théobald discovered another survivor. "She told me that everyone in that small house, including my mom, was killed. The woman survived because she had been using the toilet outside when the *Interahamwe* started killing."

Instances of Tutsi resistance have been reported in many areas in Rwanda; however, few are as well-known as Bisesero, where 40,000 Tutsis died, many having engaged in fierce fighting. Jason was among those at Bisesero, lying in the grass as military-backed insurgents searched for them with dogs. He recalls:

> Every morning, we would wake up and hide. It was important to hide before they came. The grass was tall. If you started to run while they were there, you didn't know where you were going, and you could run into the *Interahamwe*. During the day, they [the *Interahamwe*] were sweeping the land, looking for tracks, and killing people. At night, we could come together. Imagine living the way an animal lives. It hides during the day and lives off the land.

Despite believing no help would come, Jason continued to fight to survive. When thinking about his attackers, he concluded, "I'm tired, but I'm not going to make it easy for you. You will kill me when you're tired, too." Jason almost lost his life when a government official caught him. The man shot the other boys Jason was with; however, when the man aimed to kill Jason, the gun was empty. Jason fled, escaping death again.

As the ordeal went on, Jason remembers experiencing despair and witnessing it in the eyes of those he hid with: "We were tired. Some people decided to throw themselves into the lake. They wanted to kill themselves before the *Interahamwe* could." Jason considered doing the same but refused because suicide violated his religious beliefs. He prayed to God to continue to protect him and sustain him through the horrors of the genocide.

Liberation

It appeared help had finally come when French soldiers arrived in various parts of Rwanda. Operation Turquoise was a French-commanded multinational operation (2,500 troops, all French with the exception of 32 Senegalese) whose purpose according to the United Nations (n.d.) was meant/aiming to "assure the security and protection of displaced persons and civilians at risk." On June 22, the United Nations Security Council passed Resolution 929, which gave the French an intervention mandate under Chapter 7 of the UN Charter with permission to conduct the operation using all necessary means. Operation Turquoise established a "humanitarian protected zone" in the Cyangugu-Kibuye-Gikongoro triangle in southwestern Rwanda (United Nations, n.d.).

The military intervention was not viewed positively by either the RPF or Dallaire, due to France's widespread support of President Habyarimana's regime. As Rwanda was considered to be part of francophone Africa, France maintained support and interest in the country, and upon the commencement of the genocide evacuated many Hutu allies, including the president's widow.

When Operation Turquoise began, the *génocidaires* were convinced that France would support their actions, and thus became even bolder in their killings. When the French arrived, the *Interahamwe* welcomed them, and French flags and colors were displayed (Prunier, 1999, p. 290). According to Dallaire (2003):

> French flags draped every street corner in the capital. "*Vive la France*" was heard more often in Kigali than it was in Paris. RTLM was continuing to tell the population that the French were on the way to join them to fight the RPF. It seemed to me that for every life that Operation Turquoise would save, it would cost at least another because of the resurgence of the genocide.
>
> (p. 437).

Operation Turquoise did support the creation of safe zones for civilians; however, with an insufficient number of troops and a lack of transport capabilities, the French troops were unable to perform large-scale rescue operations. In many cases, the killings continued just kilometers away from French forces (Prunier, 1999, p. 293).

Jason experienced false hope when Operation Turquoise reached his location. Jason and various individuals who were hiding emerged into the open to greet the peacekeepers under the belief that were now saved. The French soldiers stated that it was against their orders to protect them and left the area while Jason and others were still in sight of the killers. Jason recalls that everyone scrambled to hide, but many could not escape and were massacred that day. Jason continued to hide from the *Interahamwe* and credits his faith in God for sustaining him through the genocide: "I saw the hand of God each day. He saved some of us many times and my hope became stronger. Despite the hard circumstances, we lived."

Consolee also relied on her religious beliefs to give her comfort and hope through the hundred-day period. While attempting to escape, Consolee's family was spotted by Hutu extremists. Knowing that he was the primary target, her father ran in a different direction to give his family time to flee for safety. Just minutes after separating from her father, Consolee and her remaining family members hid inside of a loft in a house. They soon heard the men outside laughing and bragging about how they had just killed her father. In this moment of loss, her mother urged Consolee to pray to God. Her mother would again ask Consolee to pray for comfort after her little brothers were murdered. Consolee still remembers the words of her mother: "Just keep praying! God will protect us as he has done before, and if anything happens, he will receive us with the others!" Consolee remembers how prayer gave her strength: "I leaned on prayer. I kept praying constantly. Prayer helped me get through every day." Consolee would also rely on her faith in God as she continued to flee and hide, and after she was sexually assaulted by a relative of a Hutu family hiding her.

After Jacqueline and her grandmother were discovered in the home of the man her uncle had paid to hide them, a mob of killers gathered outside of the house. She recalls:

> I was certain that we were going to die. The killers had the look of death in their eyes, but the Hutu man who was hiding us kept pleading on our behalf. Somehow, they left us alive. Every survivor will tell you that they came face-to-face with people who had the intention to kill them, but for some reason or another, decided not to. We all have those stories.

However, before the mob left, they told the man who had been hiding them that he would have to kick them out or they would return to kill him.

The man told Jacqueline's grandmother that Italian priests who owned a nearby orphanage were taking in children to try to protect them. Jacqueline remembers that, "my grandmother sent me with the man who'd been hiding us to take us to the orphanage. She said she would find another place to hide and come for me in a few days." Jacqueline never found her grandmother's body but does know that after she left the man's residence, she was never heard from again. "Like many other survivors, it's very difficult not to have that closure. Even now, sometimes I think of all sorts of irrational opportunities or scenarios where my loved ones could still be alive."

Omar returned to Kayumba Hill, where he hid with other Tutsi survivors. He had no family to help him, so Omar fetched water for Tutsi families in exchange for food. He remembers:

> We saw two boys coming and running towards our side, telling us that the RPF had come and wanted us to go to them. The older people didn't believe it. They said, 'No, they're just tricking you. They're militia. They just want us to all come down so that they can kill more people together.' But the boys argued, 'No, they saved us. They are *Inkotanyi* [nickname of the RPF soldiers].' So, the group made a decision to have a small group of young men go to check if what they were saying was true. The young men volunteered almost as a kind of sacrifice. They thought if it was the militia, they would try to fight and probably die.
>
> When they came back to tell us it was the *Inkotanyi*… I can't describe such happiness and such joy. There was such an outpour of happiness from all the people. I've never seen such happiness since then. Everyone left singing, eating, having joy. I will never forget what happened when I first saw them. I lost emotions. I was paralyzed. The RPF took us to another area where we were protected at a hospital while the RPF continued the fight against the government.

Eventually Omar was reunited with his mother, Nyinawumwami Nassilah, who had gone to Kigali for medical treatment before the genocide broke out. She had survived, along with Omar's sister, Nyampinga Faridah, by hiding with a Hutu family.

Jason would continue to hide in the hills until the RPF finally arrived at his location and arranged for him to be moved to an orphanage. Believing that his entire family had been killed in the genocide, he could not accept it when his brother came to retrieve him. "I wouldn't talk to him. I thought he was dead. I remember saying, 'Don't talk to me, I don't talk to dead people.'"

As the RPF gained more territory, the orphanage in which Jacqueline found refuge experienced multiple attacks, continuing until the night before the RPF liberated the village. Hutu soldiers came through the orphanage, fleeing the RPF en route to the Congo[17] knowing they had lost. Jacqueline reflects:

> We spent that final night in the basement, packed in with all the other children, believing that the soldiers might bomb the building. They came and packed us in the cafeteria. The priests were begging and bribing them, and there's no logical explanation for why they didn't kill us. Sometimes people would pay or bribe someone not to kill them, and they would still kill them. I tell people it's a miracle. Many of us came face-to-face with death many times, and each time you felt you were going to be killed. Whether it was God, or luck, or chance, we were spared. They knew they had lost the war, so maybe it was the timing, but it could have been anything. It was a miracle.

Jacqueline remembers seeing the RPF soldiers arrive, telling the priests they were going to protect them. Approximately 300 children from the orphanage survived, but Jacqueline could not leave until someone from her family came to retrieve her. Like many children, Jacqueline believed that her family was still alive and she would soon be able to leave the orphanage. Jacqueline's uncle, who had successfully hidden himself before joining the RPF as a doctor, found out she was at the orphanage. He sent a cousin to greet her. Upon his arrival:

> I asked what had happened to my family, and if I could be taken to my parents' village. It was then that he broke down and started crying. He told me that during the genocide, my parents, six siblings, and aunts and uncles were taken by our Hutu neighbors and murdered with machetes in the nearby river.

Consolee found refuge in the French-controlled zone:

> After we heard the good news that the RPF was liberating the country, someone told us that French soldiers were in the area asking for survivors

to come to their camp at a convent for protection. Some of us were skeptical because we had heard conflicting reports about the French. Some said the French had actually come to help Hutus who were fleeing Rwanda because they feared retaliation killings from the RPF. They said the French were even receiving people who were still participating in the genocide. My mom listened to people argue about what to do, and she decided that she was going to take the risk. We traveled there at night, off the main roads to avoid the roadblocks. When we got there, one of the French soldiers guarding the area told us they'd already received too many people and we'd have to turn back, but the person helping us argued with him, saying that if he turned back, we'd be killed. After that, the French soldiers spoke to each other and decided to let us in.

Consolee remained with her mother in French-controlled camps, protected from the genocide that continued around them, until French soldiers informed their group that they would be transferred to an RPF camp.

> The French soldiers dropped us off after the last *Interahamwe* camp, but before we were in RPF territory, they told us they were sorry, and they couldn't take us further. We had to walk the distance by ourselves with no protection. We could see *Interahamwe* killers in the distance and could hear them talking. I prayed to God to make it to the RPF camp before the killers saw us.

Consolee and the other Tutsi refugees were able to safely enter the camp, where they remained under RPF protection until after the conclusion of the genocide.

While Operation Turquoise provided protection to survivors such as Consolee, many survivors believe it also prolonged the genocide by harboring Hutu *génocidaires.* While the RPF liberated Kigali by July 4 and most of Rwanda by July 18, some areas, such as Cyangugu, remained outside the control of the RPF. Ostensibly this area was under international control; however, as previously discussed, many Tutsis did not feel safe under Operation Turquoise. Survivors from these regions report that the genocide continued into the autumn.

After Théobald's mother was killed, he remained in hiding; however, the *Interahamwe* were eventually informed of his location.

> My uncle and brother decided that we were going to have to change the area where we were hiding because everyone knew that Tutsis were in the house. So, during the night, we escaped to our Hutu friend Copain's house to talk with Copain and his brother Jean Paul. They told us that we should go to Munyove because they'd heard that there were still some Tutsis alive there. However, Munyove was four hours away by foot, so we decided that I should stay with Copain.

> Copain had an old toilet outside that used to be for his old house. It was just a hole in the ground, and it had grass and trees covering it. While I was at Copain's, I would spend the night in the house, and spend the day inside the toilet hole. I had to hide there during the day because the neighboring Hutus learned that Copain was hiding Tutsis.

Théobald rotated between Copain and Jean Paul's residences to evade the *Interahamwe.*

Théobald's uncle returned without his brother. The *Interahamwe* had killed his brother on their return from Munyove. In addition, Théobald learned that his father had been killed. Théobald hid as the genocide continued into August: "Everywhere else the genocide stopped by 4 July. In Cyangugu, it was impossible, because the French soldiers were still there. The RPF couldn't liberate our area." With the genocide continuing, Copain and Jean Paul devised a plan to help Théobald and his uncle escape:

> There was only one Hutu man who was willing to take the risk of smuggling Tutsis across Lake Kivu and into the Congo. You had to pay to be taken on a boat. It cost 25,000 Rwandan francs to flee to the Congo. We sold my father's old radio that he'd hidden before the genocide to pay for us, but it was still not enough. Copain's family gave us the rest of the money so we could go.
>
> Arriving there, we gave the money to the man who owned the boat, but once we were sailing, the men who were taking us there stopped and told us; 'You gave the money to our boss. If you don't have additional money to give us, we'll either throw you in the water or take you back to Rwanda so you can be killed.' Before we'd left Copain's house, he'd put money in the back of my shirt—300—to use when we got to the Congo. So, I gave them that 300 and they took us to the Congo.
>
> When we got to the Congo, we found a refugee settlement of Tutsis. Life was hard there. We had nothing to eat. We could only eat mice without rice or beans or anything. I started to carry stones for people that were building houses so I could afford to eat. I had one uncle in the Congo who'd moved there before the genocide began—he lived in a different city. He came and got me, and I moved in with him.

Once the RPF began liberating Cyangugu, the militia and *Interahamwe* started fleeing to the Congo. When *génocidaires* heard Théobald speaking Kinyarwanda, they chased him with the intention of killing him. He fled to his uncle's house, but in light of the new danger to those who had found refuge in the Congo, Théobald and his uncle soon returned to Rwanda to live in a refugee camp. There they were reunited with Théobald's sisters, who had miraculously survived. The RPF would eventually find lodging for the family.

Post-genocide

By July 18, the RPF had secured most of the country. The following day, Pasteur Bizimungu and General Paul Kagame were sworn into office as president and vice-president, respectively, of the new RPF government. The genocide had resulted in the deaths of an estimated 800,000 to 1.071 million, out of an estimated 7.3 million.[18] On July 20, the RPF declared a unilateral ceasefire, but regional upheaval persisted. An estimated 2 million people had fled the country, either in hopes of escaping the genocide itself or in fear of reprisal from victorious RPF forces. This exodus created what is now known as the Great Lakes refugee crisis (Wilkinson, 1997). Other individuals were internally displaced from their homes, and their crops and livestock had been destroyed. The country's infrastructure and social order had been crippled. The new Unity Government was faced with the responsibility of restoring peace and stability to the devastated country.

Life after the genocide was difficult for Omar and his family. With the strain on their living conditions, Omar's academics suffered: "I took on many responsibilities to help. I would fetch water before school, return home to cook lunch, and then go back to school. In the evening I would find firewood." Facing these obstacles, Omar did not believe he would attend secondary school. However, the government established a fund supporting survivors with medical insurance and school fees which allowed Omar to continue his education. Although there was also assistance for survivors to attend university, Omar was determined to receive an academic scholarship. At the time of graduation, he was ranked second in his class and thus recognized his dream, receiving a scholarship to study humanities at Kigali Institute of Education.

Omar recalls, "Even though I had a scholarship, it was still a struggle. Life at the university was not easy at all. That's when I decided to join *Association des Etudiants et Éleves Rescapés du Genocide* (AERG)." Founded on October 20, 1996, at Butare University, AERG functions as an advocacy organization and mutual help association for student survivors. Omar explains:

> The genocide killed families, so we created small families for ourselves. In every group we elected a mom and a dad. We chose them not necessarily on their ages but based on their personalities and leadership abilities. They'd be our parents until they graduated and then, when they'd become 'grandparents,' we'd elect new parents. Families were made up of 12-20 members. At my school, we met every Wednesday to discuss what had happened during the week and what was going on in our lives. We'd talk with those who had exams and those who failed in school, and if someone was having issues, you could send them a small committee for coaching.

Family connections created with fellow genocide survivors continues today. Omar remarks, "When someone is getting married, I go as a brother." Today, the created family maintains contacts through social media.

Omar, as the Executive Secretary of National Coordination at AERG, also initiated the Legal Aid and Counseling Initiative for vulnerable survivors. This was a call center which offered psychotherapy services and legal advice for survivors experiencing property issues. He explains:

> For some, their property was taken by family members because they were young when the genocide happened. For others, they had their property stolen by the people who killed their families. My idea was to introduce a toll-free number where survivors could call to get advice.

This initiative has expanded since its creation and focuses on supporting survivors countrywide.

Omar expresses that after the genocide, locations would trigger his childhood memories:

> Sometimes I avoid coming home to Bugesera. My mom lives very close to where my family's property used to be. You can still see the foundations of my uncle's destroyed home. For other people who come to Bugesera, they see beautiful hills and empty fields. For me, I see the village of Tutsi homes now gone. I see the faces of children I used to know, wearing school uniforms when we walked home from school – khaki for boys and blue for the girls. I see my family members playing football with me as we walked home. I see my old school that was destroyed during the genocide. I see a house and remember that family who used to live there. They were a family of seven children, all of them were killed during the genocide.

Omar worked for Never Again Rwanda, a peacebuilding and social justice organization, and helped lead survivor groups. He has written a memoir of his survival experience, titled *Life and Death in Nyamata: Memoir of a Young Boy in Rwanda's Darkest Church.* He often returns to Nyamata Church and shares his story with others.

In 2004, Théobald went through the *gacaca* justice process. *Gacaca,* which literally translates to "on the grass," is a traditional Rwandan justice mechanism for dispute resolution to address issues related to property (King, 2011). In the aftermath of the genocide, approximately 120,000 genocide suspects were being detained in prisons throughout the country (Clark, 2009). In 2001, as a response to overcrowded prisons and the necessity to instate a justice system to hold perpetrators accountable, the Rwandan government instituted the *gacaca* jurisdictions. Serving as a justice system and a truth commission, *gacaca* comprised around 12,000 community-based courts overseen by locally elected judges, each tasked with judging the cases of genocide suspects. *Gacaca* lasted approximately ten years and processed almost 2 million individuals (Brehm et al., 2014; Clark, 2009; Chapters 5 and 6 this volume).

Théobald recalls:

> When they were doing *gacaca*, I was going to school at the Kigali Institute of Education. It was six hours away from Cyangugu by bus. So, whenever I heard that some of the people who killed my family would be tried, I would take a taxi from Kigali. What *gacaca* did for me personally was give me information. Some perpetrators were convinced to talk about their role in the genocide because if they shared information, their punishment was reduced. So, from that process, I learned things about what had happened. From *gacaca*, I learned that some people, who we thought were innocent, actually participated in the genocide.
>
> *Gacaca* was a very good system, but some perpetrators would say, 'It's not me who did this, it's the people who fled to the Congo!' The murderers of my mother did that. They denied their role and blamed it on the people who are in the Congo. While I was there, I saw the people who had marched us to the football field, so I gave information about that. I also learned about people who had stolen my family's property. When I saw them, I realized how poor they were, so I forgave them.

Today, Théobald maintains close friendships with Jean Paul and Copain:

> I gave them a cow, which is the most precious gift in Rwandan culture. They helped me and they did not participate in the genocide. During the genocide, there were some Hutus who would help some Tutsis, but then also would participate in the killing of others. Those who protected me, they didn't participate in the genocide, and they put their lives in danger. This is why I recognize them as my brothers and as my family.

As the executive secretary of *Groupe des Anciens Etudiants Rescapés du Génocide,*[19] an organization founded by graduate survivors of the genocide, Théobald remarks on the organization's programs:

> We do advocacy work for survivors, and teach them how to create their own jobs, and how they can strive for a better future. We also teach about the genocide and do genocide prevention programs. For me, I'm a Christian, so when I pray, I get peace. But another thing is, I'm social. Helping young survivors is something that has helped me.

In October 1995, Jacqueline immigrated to the United States for adoption by an uncle who had left Rwanda prior to the genocide. She remained silent about her experiences until her sophomore year of high school, when Holocaust survivor David Gewirtzman came to speak at her school:

> Although he had grown up in Poland, I saw a lot of similarities between his story and mine. At one point we were both happy children, Tutsi in

> Rwanda and Jewish in Poland, and how that had all ended: the loss of family, the suffering we had endured, and an environment where everyone had turned against us. I wrote him a letter telling him that I was a survivor of the Rwandan genocide, and he wrote back, and my uncle and I went to visit him. At the time he was going around and sharing his experiences, and I was struggling to come to terms with what had happened. I was sixteen, but I was also at a point in my life where I felt like I had to speak about what had happened. My classmates didn't know about me, just that I was an orphan from Africa. The fact that my family and thousands had died meant nothing to them and I felt a sense of injustice. I felt like I had a responsibility, at least to that classroom, to share my experience.

Today, Jacqueline is an attorney in New York and runs Genocide Survivors Foundation, a nonprofit she founded to raise awareness about genocide and to support survivors. She continues to speak out about her experiences and has done several high-profile interviews and speaking engagements. She believes she has a personal responsibility to speak about the deaths of her loved ones in hopes of preventing another genocide from occurring.

Jason resides with his family in Richmond, Virginia, and is happily married to his wife, another genocide survivor who hid in the Bisesero Hills. He is the proud father of four children. Jason hopes to be a good father and husband and wants to share his experiences to help make the world a better place.

Consolee resides in New York City and, like Jacqueline and Jason, hopes to tell her story to speak against the dangers of hate. In 2012, Consolee published her memoir *Tested to the Limit: A Genocide Survivor's Story of Pain, Resilience and Hope*. Remembering the sorrows and pain of her life and why she has chosen to share her story, Consolee says, "I want my story to help people have hope, no matter how hard and difficult the challenges that face them."

Eugenie immigrated to the United States in 2001 and pursued a degree in social work in Albany, New York. In 2010, she founded the Genocide Survivors Support Network (GSSN), which aims to educate the world about genocide and help survivors heal. For many survivors, GSSN also helps foster a sense of community. "For surviving genocide, there's no real training for therapists on how to help us grieve these things. A lot of the psychologists aren't from Rwanda, so they also are missing the cultural pieces, which are so important for us," says Eugenie. She continues:

> Just being together, sharing memories, doing things together can help us heal. Sometimes, we'll even laugh about it. Someone will say, 'You just screamed the way I did when I was trying to hop over the fence when they were trying to kill me!' and some of us laugh. To people who haven't experienced this, that might sound like a horrible thing to say, but for us,

this is our life, this is what we experienced, and in some ways, we need to be around people who have experienced it to be able to talk about it.

GSSN also seeks to help second-generation and child survivors to connect with their cultural heritage. GSSN provides opportunities for second-generation and child survivors to attend social gatherings to express their feelings about the genocide through group discussions and artwork.

In this chapter, memories of youth survivors have been interwoven with academic commentary to present a summation of the horrific events of 1994 in Rwanda through the eyes of children.. However, these selected memories include mere paragraphs and excerpts drawing from the words of survivors who have lived their own full lives. We are thus given a mere glimpse into that which was experienced by those who survived the 1994 Genocide of the Tutsi. Today, these child survivors, no longer youth, live as adults with memory, meaning, joy, loss, pain, and all the complexities of the human experience.

The effects of the genocide will continue to haunt Rwanda and the world for generations. As the government of Rwanda continues to promote reconciliation and healing, the youth of Rwanda will inherit the country in the shadow of genocide. While this chapter recounts the genocide through the eyes of its children, it also connects to Chapter 13: Rwandan Youth Speak!, which shares the poetry of Rwandan youth who grew up in the genocide's aftermath: those too young to remember the direct events of the genocide, or born in its shadow, who still grapple with the wounds of 1994. Their words, expressed through poetry, continue another segment of this story.

Notes

1 The authors would like to express their gratitude for the Hemingway Faculty Development Trust and family, the Jennings G. Olson family, and the Weber State University Office of Undergraduate Research, whose funding made this research possible. An additional thanks to Julie Ikeda for her assistance and support during the interviewing process in the United States.

2 Omar Ndizeye has published his story of survival in *Life and Death in Nyamata: Memoir of a Young Boy in Rwanda's Darkest Church.*

3 Consolee Nishimwe has published her story of survival in *Tested to the Limit: A Genocide Survivor's Story of Pain, Resilience and Hope.*

4 The *gacaca* courts heard 1,958,634 cases between 2002 and the close of the trials in 2012 (with a 14% acquittal rate). See Brehm et al. (2014, pp. 340–341). Between 1994 and 2006, the national courts heard approximately 10,000 genocide-related cases (Department of Public Information, 2012). The International Criminal Tribunal for Rwanda has indicted 93 people between 1995 and the close of trials in 2012 (International Residual Mechanism for Criminal Tribunals, n.d.).

5 Each contributor was interviewed separately. Their contributions were later combined into this chapter and then sent for their approval.

6 Gitarama has been officially renamed Muhanga and is located in the Southern Province of Rwanda.

7 Cyangugu, formerly known as Shangugu, is in the Rusizi District of the Western Province.
8 Rubengera is a small community within the Karongi district of the Western Province.
9 The *Interahamwe* (meaning "those who work closely together and who are united") was established in 1991 as a youth wing of the *Mouvement Révolutionaire National pour le Développement (MRND).* The Hutu-dominated, extremist party was the only political party allowed in Rwanda prior to the signing of the Arusha Accords in 1993. The youth wing consisted mostly of young, unmarried men, who received military training before the genocide for purposes of "civilian self-defense" to attack the "enemy" in their communities. The *Interahamwe* were trained to kill quickly and witnesses reported not only their brutal methods, but also their targeted killings of Tutsis beginning in 1990. The government provided support for the group via transportation, supplies, and in some cases manpower and weapons (Melvern, 2006, pp. 26–28, 56).
10 As discussed in Chapter 1, we do not know who shot down the plane, however, this has been highly debated. For further review, see Eltringham (2004, pp. 111–118).
11 S. Wolfe, O. Ndizeye, A. De Beer, & J. Nkurunziza, Interviews conducted in July 2016 for the manuscript in preparation: *Journey through Rwandan Memorials.*
12 In 1994, individuals classified as Hutu composed approximately 85% of the county's population, whereas 14% were classified as Tutsi and 1% Twa.
13 For information, see Chapter 7 in this volume.
14 Estimates for the numbers of dead and survivors of massacres vary. For the purpose of this chapter, we defer to estimates provided by the interviewee.
15 The church at Nyange was completely destroyed when the priest, who was a *génocidaire*, ordered the church bulldozed (*The Prosecutor v. Athanase Seromb*). The location of the church was elevated to a national genocide memorial in 2017.
16 Located in the Eastern Province of Rwanda.
17 At the time of the genocide, the Democratic Republic of Congo, referred as the Congo throughout this text, was known as Zaire.
18 The estimated population in 1989 is reported to be between 7.1 million to 7.5 million. See Brehm et al. (2014) as 7.5 million.
19 The organizations AERG and GAERG are discussed further in Chapter 8 of this volume.

Bibliography

Brehm, H. N., Uggen, C., & Gasanabo, J.-D. (2014). Genocide, justice, and Rwanda's gacaca courts. *Journal of Contemporary Criminal Justice*, *30*(3), 333–352. https://doi.org//10.1177/1043986214536660

Clark, P. (2009). *The rules (and politics) of engagement: The Gacca courts and post-genocide justice, healing, and reconciliation in Rwanda.* In P. Clark, & Z. D. Kaufman (Eds.), *After genocide: Transitional justice, post-conflict reconstruction and reconciliation in Rwanda and beyond* (pp. 297–320). Columbia University Press.

Dallaire, R. (2003). *Shake hands with the devil: The failure of humanity in Rwanda.* Arrow Books.

Department of Public Information. (2012). *The Justice and Reconciliation Process in Rwanda.* United Nations. Retrieved January 28, 2022, from https://www.un.org/en/preventgenocide/rwanda/pdf/bgjustice.pdf

Des Forges, A. (1999). *Leave none to tell the story: Genocide in Rwanda*. Human Rights Watch.

Eltringham, N. (2004). *Accounting for horror: Post-genocide debates in Rwanda*. Pluto Press.

International Residual Mechanism for Criminal Tribunals. (n.d.). *The ICTR in brief*. Retrieved December 5, 2021, from http://unictr.unmict.org/en/tribunal.

Kimonyo, J. P. (2016). *Rwanda's popular genocide: A perfect storm*. Lynne Rienner Publisher, Inc.

King, E. (2014). *From classroom to conflict in Rwanda*. Cambridge University Press.

King, R. U. (2011). Healing psychosocial trauma in the midst of truth commissions: The case of gacaca in post-genocide Rwanda. *Genocide Studies and Prevention*, *6*(2), 134–151. https://doi.org/10.1353/gsp.2011.0122

Melvern, L. (2006). *Conspiracy to murder: The Rwandan genocide*. Verso.

Ndizeye, O. (2020). *Life and death in Nyamata: Memoir of a young boy in Rwanda's darkest church*. Amsterdam Publisher.

Nishimwe, C. (2012). *Tested to the limit: A genocide survivor's story of pain* resilience and hope. Balboa Press.

Prunier, G. (1995). *The Rwanda crisis: History of genocide*. Columbia University Press.

Straus, S. (2006). *The order of genocide: Race, power, and war in Rwanda*. Cornell University Press.

Temple-Raston, D. (2005). *Justice on the grass: Three Rwandan journalist, their trial for war crimes and a nation's quest for redemption*. Free Press.

The Prosecutor v. Athanase Seromba, ICTR-01-66. (International Criminal Tribunal for Rwanda, 2006)

The Prosecutor v. Bagosora, ICTR-98-41-T. (International Criminal Tribunal for Rwanda, 2008)

The Prosecutor v. Elizaphan Ntakirutimana & Gerard Ntakirutimana, ICTR-96-10-T & ICTR-96-17-T. (International Criminal Tribunal for Rwanda, 2003).

Thompson, A. (Ed). (2007). *The media and the Rwanda genocide*. Pluto Press.

United Nations. (n.d.). *Rwanda – UNAMIR Background*. United Nations. Retrieved from https://peacekeeping.un.org/en/mission/past/unamirFT.htm on January 28, 2022.

Wilkinson, R. (1997, December 01). *Refugees magazine issue 110 (crisis in the great lates) – Cover story: Heart of darkness*. The United Nations Refugee Agency (UNHCR). https://www.unhcr.org/publications/refugeemag/3b6925384/refugees-magazine-issue-110-crisis-great-lakes-cover-story-heart-darkness.html.

3 Experts in the Suffering of Others

Race, Knowledge Production, and the Rwandan Genocide[1]

MJ (Marie-Jolie) Rwigema

Introduction

In writing about and researching the genocide against Tutsi in Rwanda, I have asked myself a series of questions: How is the Rwandan genocide represented? What kind of knowledge is being produced about the genocide? Does it matter how the genocide is represented? Does it matter by whom it is being represented? If so, why does it matter? How do questions of knowledge production and representation relate to questions of justice, particularly historical justice and symbolic justice? Specifically, as it relates to the Rwandan genocide, I ask: if our understanding is that it was a war between two rival tribes with ancient hatreds, versus a government-sponsored, planned massacre of Tutsi in Rwanda assisted by France and preceded by thirty-five years of systemic racial discrimination (Melvern, 2000), will we reach very different conclusions? Alternatively, the argument that it was a "double genocide" (Verhoeven, 2010) in which Tutsis were killed by Hutu extremists and then Hutus were killed in retaliation by the Rwandan Patriotic Front as a proxy United States imperialist army intent on access to Congo's mineral resources, versus it was an outcome of German and Belgian colonialism (Mamdani, 2001), furthered by postcolonial international financial institutions and international development neocolonialism (Uvin, 1998), we will also lead to very different conclusions.

All of the above are narratives that have been advanced regarding the 1994 genocide in Rwanda. Some have been characterized as the official Rwandan government narrative, while others are considered the academic consensus. Some are the recurring frames used in accounts by mainstream news reports, and others, considered as genocide denial and negationist discourses, described as "the untold story" (Umuvugizi, 2014). The point is that depending on the narrative to which we subscribe, we will have different understandings of who is responsible for genocide, who has been victimized, to whom we may owe reparations, how we should intervene or assist people affected by the violence, and how we ourselves (as Rwandans, or non-Rwandans, policy makers, activists, scholars, or journalists) are implicated in the issue.

DOI: 10.4324/9781003228592-4

I start from the viewpoint that there will always be multiple interpretations of any given event. But for the purpose of this chapter, we should ask: who is speaking and what does their speech imply? Who is served by the speech or narrative? Who is hindered by it? Given how I am positioned as a family member to people who were targeted for death and killed during the genocide solely because of their socially ascribed identity as Tutsi, I will always be inclined to prioritize the views of genocide survivors. Or, as Ntare Sharangabo puts it in response to *génocidaires* who publish work denying the genocide:

> In the case of Rwanda, you will find those who committed it [the genocide] saying in public 'I think…' [and expressing their opinions about the genocide and Rwanda]…[But] there is no 'I think,' there is 'I saw,' and what I saw is that you were there and you had a machete.
>
> (quoted in Rwigema, 2009).

I agree with Sharangabo that critical thought requires us to clearly discern that those who have enacted violence are unlikely to speak honestly or innocently about the violence that they perpetrated. Thus, in the case of mass violence, institutional violence, and systemic violence, we must be able to clearly discern who has been victimized and allow them to speak as the first step in the process of justice. If we cannot discern who has been victimized in genocide with the evidence of hundreds of thousands of dead bodies and the testimonies of thousands of survivors, this likely says more about our positionality in relation to the event than about the reality of what happened.

There is no one viewpoint that is pure and uninfluenced by discourses, needs, and desires. As such, when it comes to crimes like genocide, we must ask: whose perspectives and voice do we prioritize? How do we decide whom to prioritize? What are the implications of speaking, based on differing positionalities? Is it necessary to identify yourself, how you are positioned and implicated, when you speak? And finally: where do speaking, writing, and telling fit into processes of violence like genocide – before, during, and after these events (Taylor et al., 2015)?

In this chapter, I draw from postcolonial thought to reflect on the implications that the discourse on the Rwandan genocide is dominated by non-Rwandan and mostly white, Western knowledge producers. According to Stephanie Wolfe (2014), "Historical justice is focused on the way that societies construct the past in a way that is collectively understood as shared and true" (p. 42). In other words, historical justice is concerned with acknowledging the historical conditions that led to atrocities and the responsibility of various involved parties, and the accurate transmission of that history. Symbolic justice, related to historical justice, is concerned with the actions that are taken to acknowledge past atrocities and injustices: "Its primary focus is not rooted in legalism but in interpretation and memory transmission" (Wolfe, 2014, p. 72), and, "Of the various types of symbolic actions that a state can take it is the apology, the sincere, verbal acknowledgement of responsibility that I consider to be one of the most important aspects of reparation politics" (Wolfe, 2014, p. 73).

I argue that Western discourse about Rwanda, insofar as it maintains a colonial tradition of knowledge production, perpetuates historical and symbolic injustice against Rwandans. Historical and symbolic justice requires an acknowledgment of the colonial and neocolonial role in genocidal violence in Rwanda. Discourses on Rwanda, from the colonial construction of racial/ethnic identities by German and Belgian colonizers, to neocolonial action and inaction by the west pursuant to Rwanda's interests, including United Nations (UN) Security Council discussions during the genocide, media representations at the time of the genocide, and academic discourses, have played a role in creating the conditions for the genocide to happen. These discourses have enabled the obfuscation of third party or outsiders' responsibility for the genocide. Conversations about justice in Rwanda have predominantly focused on holding perpetrators (lower level *génocidaires* and higher-level architects) of the 1994 genocide accountable – either through the International Criminal Tribunal for Rwanda (ICTR) or through the *gacaca* courts. However, conversations about justice rarely implicate non-Rwandan actors.

Aside from the Rwandan government pursuing a case against France for its role in training and supporting military and militia forces responsible for the genocide, the conversation about justice rarely addresses the colonial and neocolonial culpability of the West in creating and supporting the conditions that facilitated the 1994 genocide. The genocidal Rwandan government was largely funded by international aid – up to 70% of the gross domestic product (Uvin, 1998) – and was armed through loans from international financial institutions during the genocide. It was militarily assisted by the French government before, during, and after the genocide (Melvern, 2000). In addition, the German and Belgian colonial powers created the ideological (superior and inferior racial and ethnic identities) and bureaucratic (identity cards) infrastructure for genocide, and then lent their backing to Hutu supremacists. Given this history, we need to interrogate the substance of justice for the colonial/neocolonial forces that were responsible for creating, facilitating, and enabling the conditions that made 1994 possible. And we need to critique the role played by western constructions of its own past and present role, for its culpability for historical, ongoing, and symbolic violence pursuant to the genocide in Rwanda.

Academia, media, and nongovernmental organizations (NGOs) frame narratives about the Third World (Africa and Rwanda in particular) that often view themselves as politically neutral, more objective, or somehow on higher moral ground than that of directly involved parties who are seen as being biased, among other things. This construction of objectivity is inherited from the idea of the European man in Western philosophical traditions as the universal subject – an objective, scientific, knowledge producer – contrasted with the people colonized by European nations, who were constructed as uncivilized and incapable of rational thought (Razack, 2002). It is no longer openly said that Africans cannot, or do not, think. The vast majority of authoritative global level knowledge production about Rwanda – the academic literature, as well as media and pop culture interpretations about the Rwandan genocide – is however produced by non-Rwandans who are mostly white and from the West (Hron, 2011). This, I argue, has the effect of silencing Rwandans and further perpetuating colonial historical and symbolic violence against them. To make this argument, I will turn to three examples of Western discourse about Rwanda: academic, artistic (film), and news media reports.

Academic Discourse on Rwanda

Over the past two decades, I have observed that the vast majority of those recognized in Western academia as experts on the Rwandan genocide are not Rwandan. In analyzing how Western authors write about the genocide (and how they exploit the labor of native informants while erasing their perspectives), Madeline Hron (2011) observed that out of the more than one thousand books written about the Rwandan genocide between 1994 and 2011, only two of those books were written by Rwandans themselves (without collaborators). Similarly, Small (2006) explained that postcolonial publishing patterns have ensured that the West's version of the Rwandan genocide "dominates interpretation and reaction towards the genocide." While there has been an increase since 2011 in texts about the genocide authored by Rwandans, the vast majority of academic writing and cultural production about the genocide remains dominated by white Westerners (Rwigema, 2018). As Zegeye and Vambe (2006) explain, "In contrast to African intellectuals who rush to validate their knowledge by citing European sources… European scholars do not feel compelled to use [or cite] sources of African knowledge when they write about Africa" (p. 11).

As with the books, so it is with academic conferences. For instance, in 2009, I received an invitation to attend an academic conference titled *Remembering Rwanda 15* that was scheduled to coincide with the fifteenth anniversary of the genocide. Of the twenty-two "experts" scheduled to speak, only two listed speakers were Rwandan (one of whom was "TBA" from the Rwandan Association of Toronto). All but three of these speakers were white and from the global North (Taylor et al., 2013, p. 125). In December 2017, a conference at Carleton University focused on exploring the role of the media in the Rwandan genocide included only one Rwandan among its speakers (Journalism and Communication, 2017). Similarly, the 2019 International Association of Genocide Scholars' conference, though hosting numerous panels addressing the Rwandan genocide – twenty-five years later – did not have *any* Rwandan speakers except for myself.

Sherene Razack (2007) describes the theft of Rwandans' pain through the film *Shake Hands with the Devil*: "We become the Rwandans through the understanding that what has happened in Rwanda is a human thing, devoid of historical specificity, devoid, in fact, of Rwandans" (p. 384). Her statement is equally applicable to the theft of knowledge enacted at the academic conferences described above. Apparently, commemorating, educating about, or learning the lessons of the Rwandan genocide does not require Rwandans (Taylor et al., 2013). It seems that non-Kinyarwanda speaking, non-Rwandans are able to analyze Rwandan genocide propaganda in Kinyarwandan. In addition, these same non-Rwandans can author texts, and host conferences asserting their authority on the matter; if we refer to their citations, it seems that no Rwandans were necessary.

After encountering the continual absence of Rwandans and the omnipresence of mainly white Westerners at the Rwanda expert table, I have asked myself and consulted with the literature about why this is the case. Ntare Sharangabo, an independent scholar of Rwandan culture and history, as well as a survivor of the 1994 genocide, explains that the correlation of whiteness with expertise is a colonial continuity. He notes that, "There is a long history of white people claiming the right to speak on behalf of Africans that has its roots from the partition of Africa to recent suggestions at G8 meetings that (western) NGOs should represent Africa" (quoted in Rwigema, 2009). Other authors point to the ways in which the neocolonial development industry, with its unnamed racial hierarchies, reproduces "white expertise" on Africa. Kothari (2006) describes an "authoritative power of whiteness in development" (p. 14) wherein expertise is signified "not always by what is known but by *who* knows" (p. 16). Kothari (2006) points to the reality that this expertise is not based on knowledge and intelligence, but rather on racialized access and privilege. She quotes a development worker: "People don't really believe that I am more intelligent and more knowledgeable because I am white, what they do believe is that I will have greater access to power, to decision-makers and to those who can get things done" (p. 16).

Zegeye and Vambe (2006) also speak to the relationship between knowledge production and racialized power relations. They explain:

> The politics of knowledge production in Africa are defined by power relations. These determine who gets to publish, read, and then distribute knowledge…some people have the political power to authorize certain forms of knowledge and ensure that it has been published and disseminated. Their knowledge is more widely circulated through the technology which they control and monopolize.
>
> (p. 347).

Zegeye and Vambe (2006) name a reality where Europe and North America dominate access to the means of production and distribution of knowledge. Those who have better access to European and North American production agents and markets (such as publishing houses, university presses, and academic journals) are better able to have the knowledge they produced, published, marketed, and distributed. In a context of global white supremacy, it is inevitably the most privileged of Westerners and global elites will have the greatest access to these means of production and distribution. Additionally, Zegeye and Vambe (2006) point to the reality that knowledge production is a process that is tied up with money, status, and power. They explain:

> People are now paid to produce certain types of knowledge and this is a process that inherently excludes the authorization of other forms of knowledge; Knowledge is now a commodity which is bought and sold at the academic market place. It has entrenched itself as power.
>
> (p. 335).

It is not possible in this short space to analyze the literally thousands of academic books and articles written by non-Rwandans on the genocide regarding the ways in which they might perpetuate colonial frameworks. The point I am making is that the *process* of production – the fact of white Western domination in academic knowledge production – is itself problematic and reflects a colonial dynamic that perpetuates injustice. I do believe that more work should be done to explore the ways in which the content of academic scholarship perpetuates colonial continuities in knowledge production about Rwanda. For now, I will turn to two other forms of knowledge production – popular films and newspaper articles on Rwanda – to explore additional examples of colonial continuities in knowledge production.

Popular Culture Discourse on Rwanda

As Nsabimana points out, a primary point of reference about the genocide for many non-Rwandans is the Academy Award-nominated film *Hotel Rwanda*. She states: "Especially after *Hotel Rwanda*, people come and ask 'So what are you, a Tutu or a Tutu?' And then 'Oh it's so sad what happened to the people in your country – oh that's horrible'" (quoted in Rwigema, 2009). It goes without saying that films reach a far larger audience than academic texts. Not only that, but the authors of these films become authorized as a type of expert on the subject matter of the films. As Razack (2007) explains, following a screening of *Shake Hands with the Devil* at the Toronto International Film Festival, audience members came to recognize former head of UNAMIR mission Romeo Dallaire (the subject of the film) and the film's director as de facto Rwanda experts. She states: "If we need to know more about Rwanda, we have only to ask Dallaire or the film's director, as audiences happily did at the Film Festival. That's reality" (p. 386).

While I, and many Rwandans, want people to know as much as possible about the genocide for the purposes of education, commemoration, and justice, the content of these films is also extremely important. They not only reach masses of people, but stand as historical record of the genocide, whether intended to or not. In a context where many of those implicated as perpetrators of the genocide have not been tried for their crimes, many of whom live freely all over the world, and many of whom are actively publishing information denying the genocide – what stands as an accessible historical record is an extremely important matter in the question of historical justice (Rwigema, 2009). I would argue, as others have, that if the purpose of the films is to demonstrate compassion for Rwandans, they have failed miserably on many counts.

Almost all of the popular films have decided that the most important story of the genocide is not that of the targeted Tutsi, but rather the story of either white people who happened to be in Rwanda during the genocide (*Shake Hands with the Devil*, *A Sunday by the Pool in Kigali*, and *Shooting Dogs*) or conflicted Hutu who had to deal with the dilemmas of their relationships to Tutsi (*Hotel Rwanda* and *Sometimes in April*) (Rwigema, 2018). Alexandre Dauge-Roth (2010) shares this view in his examination of Western-produced film representations of the genocide. He argues that many of the films, in addition to "enacting symbolic violence by privileging the accounts of 'so-called experts' over those of survivors" are also rife with historical inaccuracies that "serve the purpose of creating 'white and Hutu redemption' at the expense of truth and telling the stories of Tutsi victims and survivors." Many of the films (*Hotel Rwanda*, *Shooting Dogs*, and *A Sunday by the Pool*) dramatically show the obligatory scene where white expatriates and their pets are evacuated while soon-to-be massacred Rwandans are denied access to these evacuation trucks. Ironically, the films fail to see the connection between those dramatized scenes and their own acts of abandoning Rwandans (again) by centralizing the stories of white people and nonsurvivors in their films (Rwigema, 2018).

In *Stealing the Pain of Others*, Razack (2007) explains that the documentary film *Shake Hands with the Devil*, in centering Romeo Dallaire's story as our entry point into the Rwandan genocide, serves to construct him simultaneously as the primary victim of, hero of, and expert on the genocide. Describing the construction of his victimhood, she states:

> The disembodied observer who is not of the landscape but who hovers over it, Dallaire is the body who suffers and is transformed by it. His is still the principal story of the genocide. When Rwandans speak of their own loss, as they do only very occasionally in this film, the camera pauses briefly, and moves on to the close-ups that inform us who has really been shattered. (p. 383).

Rwafa (2010) agrees with Razack's argument about the centering of Dallaire in his critique of the documentary *A Good Man in Hell*. He states:

> *A Good Man in Hell,* in that it appeals to European morality and conscience while obscuring "African voices" turns "Rwandan cultural and

> political misfortunes into a commodity of affect" in which instead of hearing survivors' voices, we are made to witness European audiences "struggling to create emotional feelings."
>
> (p. 393).

Beyond commodification at the level of affect, Razack (2007) also describes how the theft of pain is turned into a commodification of knowledge and expertise.

Gigliotti (2007), in examining three human rights memoirs written by Westerners who lived in Rwanda during the genocide, shares Razack's perspective that these representations typically re-center white men as simultaneous victims, heroes, and experts. She examines memoirs by Romeo Dallaire, Aidan Hartley (war news correspondent), and Kenneth Cain (lawyer), all of whom were in Rwanda before, during, and after the genocide. After assessing how each of the three authors represents himself, she argues that they do so as world saving moral witnesses, traumatized and transformed by their experiences. She concludes by questioning whether such memoirs can contribute to genocide prevention, or whether they simply re-inscribe the "Western male in a Eurocentric subjectivity, righting and writing the wrongs of racialized western colonialism through scenes of graphic genocide tourism" (p. 95).

In centering the trauma of white Westerners in nonfiction documentaries and memoirs described above, the "based on a true story" films, *Shooting Dogs* and *A Sunday by the Pool in Kigali*, invite us to sympathize with white characters and their moral debates of whether they will stay in Rwanda as the primary story of the genocide (Rwigema, 2018). *Shooting Dogs* was heavily criticized by Rwandans for emphasizing the stories of Westerners, and for constructing white heroes that simply did not exist – in this case, a white Roman Catholic priest who chose to stay with soon-to-be victims (Tumbwebaze, 2013). In a context where the Catholic Church was deeply implicated in enacting the genocide – including priests and nuns killing people – what does it mean to create a story where the white priests and the Church are constructed as heroes, especially when these individuals were anything but heroic according to survivors' accounts?

This narrative choice is contextualized by a long history of white savior narratives in Western filmmaking. As Razack (2007) explains in relation to films on Rwanda: "How do white people, Westerners in general and Canadians in particular, like to see themselves portrayed? The answer is simple: as heroes" (p. 386). Ahmed explains how these representations not only dehumanize Rwandans, but also exonerate white people from responsibility and reconstruct (superior) white subjectivities:

> Not only do such multi-cultural fantasies of becoming involve releasing the western subject from responsibility for the past, but they also

> confirm his agency, his ability to be transformed by the proximity of strangers, *and to render his transformation a gift to those strangers through which he alone can become.*
>
> (Ahmed, quoted in Razack, 2007, p. 386).

Thus, in *Shooting Dogs* and in *Shake Hands with the Devil*, both the Church's and the international community's abandonment and complicity in the massacring of Rwandans have been reinvented as the heroism of white people. Lying about history perpetuates historical and symbolic injustice against Rwandans. Disturbingly, this kind of portrayal has been taken up in Toronto District School Board high school courses on genocide and crimes against humanity (Taylor et al., 2015). Though these courses are intended to cultivate compassion and global citizenship among high school students, activities in which students are invited to imagine themselves as Romeo Dallaire or other peacekeepers maintain the narrative of the white savior (Taylor et al., 2015). Paradoxically, the arguably most heroic UN soldier in Rwanda, Senegalese captain Mbaye Diagne, who personally rescued thousands of people during the genocide, has received negligible recognition for the heroism that ultimately cost him his life.

Like *Shooting Dogs,* the film *Hotel Rwanda* has been criticized by Rwandan survivor/witnesses as inaccurate. Aside from an alarmingly innocent-seeming synopsis on the back of the DVD (innocent until one notices that the genocide is misnamed the 1994 *conflict*), *Hotel Rwanda* has primarily been critiqued for its portrayal of the main character of the film and the choice to highlight his story as an example of heroism in Rwanda (Rwigema, 2018). While this is the first popular film in which a Rwandan is portrayed as a hero during the genocide, and is the first Hollywood film on Rwanda, the amount of backlash it has generated among genocide survivors indicates that the film made problematic representations. For their book *Hotel Rwanda ou Le Genocide Des Tutsis vu par Hollywood*, Ndahiro and Rutazibwa (2008) interviewed 74 people who survived the genocide at *Hotel Mille Collines*, including staff and others who had sought refuge there, to find out their perspectives on the film. All but one of the interviewees agreed that the film is an inaccurate portrayal of both their experiences in the hotel and of Rusesabagina. Most stated that Rusesabagina worsened their experiences after he arrived and began charging individuals to be lodged, fed, and to use communication tools such as faxes and phones. Previously, these services had been provided at no cost, given the context of the genocide.

Additionally, Ndahiro and Rutazibwa (2008) explained that Rusesabagina turned people away who could not pay to enter the hotel. The book was substantiated through interviews and archival documents (that is, notes and communications between *Mille Collines* Belgian parent company Sabena and the staff at the hotel.) The book essentially argued that Rusesabagina was a genocide opportunist, who at best may have helped a handful of personal friends and family, but at worst is responsible for the deaths of people who were turned away, and for compounding the suffering of people who were at his mercy in the hotel. They also questioned the uncritical acceptance of Rusesabagina's version of the story by both Hollywood and by extension, the entire world. This acceptance led to Rusesabagina being awarded a medal of honor from former US President George W. Bush.

It is in these contestations around knowledge – between those with lived experience as victims/survivors of mass violence and those who have the cultural capital to produce and disseminate knowledge about such violence – that illustrate how high the stakes are when it comes to knowledge production (Rwigema, 2018). I argue that, like the 1994 evacuation of non-Rwandans and the deliberate choice of nonintervention by the UN Security Council, recent internationally produced films about the Rwandan genocide send a very clear message. It is a colonially continuous message, that the lives that matter most are white. Since 1994, this message has also been explicitly and implicitly reiterated through mass media coverage about the genocide. I will draw on selected examples of Canadian news coverage of the genocide to make this case.

Canadian Media Coverage of the Genocide

In order to draw a thread between academic, popular culture, and mass media representations of the Rwandan genocide, I will now turn to a number of articles published by the *Toronto Star* in recent years that address the genocide. I have chosen articles that address a number of important issues regarding Canada's relationship to the genocide. These issues include Rwandan genocide perpetrators living in Canada, the Canadian government's knowledge of and action/inaction regarding the genocide, and the efforts of Canadian humanitarians in intervening in Rwandan genocide-related issues.

Media Frameworks and Perspectives

In his article analyzing how the *New York Times* represented the Rwandan genocide in 1994, Chari (2010) argues that, for the most part, the coverage of the genocide fit into four frames: historical baggage, tribalization, western benevolence, and western indifference. He further argues that this type of framing prevented an understanding of socioeconomic, political, and historical factors that contributed to the genocide. It also perpetuated the conflation of the genocide with other crises in Africa, which are constructed as incomprehensible and endemic to the continent. This discourse then justified the nonresponse of governments. Similarly, Cappeliez (2006) argues that the dominant media coverage of the genocide in 1994, including Canadian coverage, reproduced colonial stereotypes of backward, savage African tribes perpetually in conflict that described the violence as essentially incomprehensible. Furthermore, she explains that the coverage positioned the conflict as internal and therefore outside of the interest of Canada, except in relation to Canadian compassion and Canadians' role as international observers.

Cappeliez (2006) goes on to argue that the compounded media images fix certain notions of the genocide in time, ignore other elements of the events, and conflate Rwanda with generalized constructions of Africa and the Third World. These constructions locate the other in a discursive elsewhere, and thus she argues that the representations are ultimately utilized to "reproduce a state-centric international realm that *does not imagine atrocities to be a natural conclusion of the sovereign state*" (p. 19), but rather positions the Canadian and other Western states as good states that intervene with failing states. This discursive construction enabled the Canadian government to engage in a rhetoric of learning lessons to protect humanity facilitated through interconnected public cultural discourses and the media coverage representations of the genocide. All of this ultimately "condition[ed] how the Canadian subject relates to the Rwandan genocide" (Cappeliez, 2006, p. 19).

Similarly, Fair and Parks (2001) argue that colonial frames were central to the coverage of Hutu refugees who fled Rwanda after the genocide. One of their key points is that coverage of the refugee flows that followed the 1994 genocide was much more prevalent than coverage of the genocide itself, because they fit more readily into the frames of what was understood as both a good and easy story for Western media (i.e., a story of the West helping the refugees). These images naturalize refugees as marginalized people to be monitored, taken care of, and pitied by Western humanitarian workers. They also position refugees as objects of knowledge production. This characterization then hindered an understanding that amidst the refugees were *génocidaire*s who weaponized the resources gained from the humanitarian response to further their destructive agenda. This also hindered an understanding that refugees think about and make sense of – *as* knowledge producers – the political circumstances that rule their lives.

Coverage of Canadian Government Response to Rwandan Genocide

In examining disparate articles the *Toronto Star* published in the past decade, I would argue that Cappeliez and Chari's analyses are applicable. Frames justifying indifference persist, such as the construction of the universal moral authority witness-bearing peacekeeper and a false story of Canadian benevolence and compassion. Other frames include the good state intervening with failing states, and colonial stereotypes of backward, savage African tribes that are perpetually in conflict, as well as descriptions of the violence in Africa as incomprehensible. These frames conflate Rwanda with generalized constructions of Africa and the Third World. These narrative constructions which dissociate colonial and neocolonial forces from the violence in Rwanda perpetuate the historical injustice of colonialism.

The first two articles I analyze address the Canadian government's response to the genocide. The next set of articles report on accused genocide perpetrators who were living in Canada. The final two articles discuss the work of Western human rights workers who have intervened in Rwanda and the Great Lakes region as members of helping professions (NGO workers). I am interested in exploring how these newspaper articles, taken together and individually, invite Canadian readers to think about various issues related to the 1994 genocide. What discourses do the articles draw from, explicitly or implicitly, to talk about Rwanda, the genocide, and Canadians' relationships to Rwanda?

An article entitled "Why did Ottawa ignore warnings of Rwandan genocide?" (Black, 2010) shares the details discovered by the *Toronto Star* following the paper trail of 260 pages of documents sent to Ottawa by Canadian diplomats from Rwanda and other East African countries in the months before the 1994 genocide. The use of language such as "never-before-seen documents obtained by the Star" (Black, 2010) positions the newspaper as an investigative, resourceful organization truly in search of answers about why the Canadian government was not responsive to warnings about the genocide. However, the reporter, after tracking the trajectories of telexes sent by Canadian diplomats and interviewing the minister of external affairs at the time, unquestioningly reprints his response that the documents never made it to his or the deputy minister's desk. The author then goes on to quote several other officials, who articulate that the telexes were not acted upon because Rwanda was not considered relevant to Canada's agenda. The Canadian government was well-informed about the likelihood of genocide, and the author concludes that it did not act because of its indifference. With its pages of "never-before-seen" documents, the author fails to answer her own questions of why Canada ignored evidence of the genocide. Instead, a circular answer is offered: Canada was indifferent because it was indifferent. No deeper investigative questions are asked.

If the author was truly interested in exploring questions of Canadian indifference, she would have had to actually discuss the racialized and colonial relations between countries in the Global North and Global South. At the same time, employing the discourse of indifference masks something far more violent than indifference: Canadian complicity. This complicity is seen in the state's actions, both as a donor to the genocidal government and as a UN Security Council member at the time that diplomats chose to withdraw UN troops. The withdrawal and subsequent limiting of the mandate effectively abandoned hundreds of thousands of people to be killed. In simply stating that Canada was indifferent without questioning why, the article itself fits into the frame of Western indifference that Chari outlined. What is most dangerous is that it managed to be indifferent while enacting a written performance of concern and accountability (Rwigema, 2018).

A second *Star* article "Jean Apologize for Canada's role in Rwanda" details the Canadian government's response to the Rwandan genocide. The article describes Governor-General Jean's formal apology to Rwandans in 2010 on behalf of "Canada as part of the international community" (MacCharles, 2010). This positioning of responsibility within an international community is a move that displaces responsibility. Again, we see the idea that the genocide was possible because of the indifference of the international community. The repetition of indifference, without interrogation, normalizes and renders it a plausible explanation in a tautological argument that sounds like this: the genocide happened because we were indifferent, we were indifferent because we were indifferent, we apologize for our indifference, now we realize if we hadn't been indifferent, we could have prevented the genocide (Rwigema, 2018).

None of this mentions the core reason of that indifference that was plainly articulated by former Major Brent Beardsley (2012), Dallaire's Military Assistant in Rwanda. At a week-long genocide studies seminar hosted by the Zoryan Institute that I attended in Toronto in 2012, he stated, clearly and simply: "We left Rwanda because we were racist."

Later in the MacCharles (2010) article, there is a description of Jean being very pleased to see the Rwandan genocide museum's tribute to Dallaire's "unsuccessful efforts." Jean describes Dallaire as a Canadian who tried to protect people in Rwanda. I have heard Rwandans who sought UN protection under Dallaire at *École Polytechnique* directly challenge this construction of Dallaire, which is similar to the other articles about the genocide that project a Canadian angle, usually involving a white hero or helper that is inserted somewhere in the text (Rwigema, 2018).

Interestingly, MacCharles (2010) also included the Rwandan president's response to the apology, after mentioning that President Kagame "shut down two newspapers last week" and that "he faces increasing criticism for stifling dissent." Indeed, I have increasingly observed over the years that Western media discourse about Rwanda includes decontextualized criticisms of the Rwandan government in coverage related to the genocide. While there is obviously a place to critique the Rwandan government, it is the context wherein the critiques are offered that is questionable. The propensity to critique the Rwandan government while obfuscating the role of Western governments, as in these two *Star* articles, illustrates Mutua's (2001) Savages-Victims-Saviors paradigm for understanding how Western media discuss Africa. In this case, the West sees itself as an arbiter of civilized behavior and a regulator of African states' behavior, often characterizing them, explicitly or implicitly, as savage. This characterization is part of a process that disavows the ways in which Western nations continue to colonize African nations and ignores the impact of this colonial relationship on the internal politics of formerly colonized countries.

Coverage of Genocide Trials

Several other *Toronto Star* articles explored the issue of Rwandan genocide perpetrators living in Canada and the ongoing sagas regarding their extradition (or refusal of the Canadian government to extradite them), as well as their trials. One article described the Rwandan government's attempt to have an intellectual architect of the genocide, Leon Mugesera (who was formerly a professor at Laval University in Quebec) deported to Rwanda for trial. The Chiasson (2012) article gave context regarding Mugesera's case, while explaining how the UN Committee Against Torture delayed his extradition to Rwanda. The article managed to represent both the UN and Canada as legitimate arbiters of human rights while engaging in a pretense that UN Security Council member states and Canada do not practice torture. Statements such as "while it (UN) investigates his claims that he'd be tortured in Rwanda" and "if torture is a possibility, he could undergo a genocide-related trial in Canada" (Chiasson, 2012) reinscribe the UN and Canada as civilized entities that have moral authority.

Mutua's critique that nongovernmental human rights reports reproduce "a shameful Third World state that has to be sanctioned and tamed by First World states that define internationally sanctioned civilized behavior" (quoted in McNamee, 2007, p. 311) is applicable to both what the Chiasson article is describing and what the article itself is enacting. In the same moment that the Canadian state is established as moral authority, the Rwandan state is constructed as a savage state, and the UN (whose member states financed and hosted the genocidal government and then abandoned civilians to be murdered during the genocide) is constructed as legitimate arbiter of ethical behavior (Rwigema, 2018).

The article by Chiasson describing Mugesera's case continues the savior-victim-savage framing of previous articles. The author makes a number of statements, such as, "The federal government… has taken necessary steps to ensure Mugesera would be treated fairly in Rwanda", and "The European Human Rights Court and the International Criminal Tribunal for Rwanda…further confirm Rwanda's credibility" (Chiasson, 2012). These comments continue to reproduce colonial relations of power in which Western states and global institutions are positioned as "civilized" and "civilizing" arbiters of justice.

In a similar vein, the *Star* article, "Rwandan pleads not guilty at Canada's second war-crimes trial," describes the beginning of a trial under the Crimes Against Humanity and War Crimes Act of former Rwandan schoolteacher and accused *génocidaire* Jacques Mungwarere (Ditchburn, 2012). The article describes the trial of a Rwandan genocide suspect that took place in Canada, because the Canadian government had refused to extradite him to Rwanda. As with the article on Mugesera, the moral authority of the Western world is uncritically asserted. In contrast to the coverage of Mugesera's court battles, there is no mention of the possibility or question of extradition in Mungwarere's case, and a Canadian courtroom is accepted as a legitimate site to render justice for genocide in Rwanda. Furthermore, as with other articles, the author chooses to insert a line in which the Rwandan government is critiqued, this time through the voice of an expert Canadian academic: "He (Longman) made clear that he has serious difficulties with the current regime in Rwanda which he describes as a dictatorship that has tried to quash dissent and silence critics" (Ditchburn, 2012). The author then goes on to describe the defense cross-examination which focused on "the weaknesses of the genocide-tribunal system in Rwanda that put justice in the hands of citizens at the community level rather than judges and lawyers" with 250,000 elected to local tribunals only receiving a week of training (Ditchburn, 2012). Thus, what should have been reported as the process of putting a Rwandan *génocidaire* on trial ends up putting the current Rwandan government and judicial system on trial.

Coverage of Canadian Humanitarians

The discourse of the superior capacity of Westerners to address Rwandan problems continues in another set of articles that explicitly celebrate the work of Western humanitarians working in Rwanda. The *Toronto Star* article, "Child soldiers: Romeo Dallaire's wrenching return to Africa's 'gang warfare'" is written by Allan Thompson (2012), a Carleton University academic who is regarded as an expert on media and the Rwandan genocide. Over the course of nine pages, it tells us a story, all about Romeo Dallaire. Each word in the article's title has a particular implication.

The use of the word "wrenching" is clearly meant to evoke an emotional response of empathy, though for whom is unclear: Dallaire or the child soldiers? The return and the way it is characterized throughout the narrative – complete with italicized descriptions of Dallaire on the ground in Rwanda with "darkness closing in" (Thompson, 2012) – can be read as a Conrad-esque colonial journey into the heart of darkness, with both "heart of Africa" and "darkness" used to describe parts of his journey. The multiple references throughout the article – encounters with "demons," "devils," in a "Dante's inferno," "dense jungle," "dense bush," and "his Narnia" – are the signifiers that invite us into a journey. A journey with a white hero enacting and claiming his white (colonial) subjectivity through the restoration of good (saving child soldiers) in a mythical, magical, dark "dense bush" where "anarchy reigns" populated by (black) demons and devils (Rwigema, 2018).

The Thompson (2012) article is about Dallaire's transformation from trauma victim, with detailed descriptions of his flashbacks to his first night in Rwanda, to returned glory as military reconnaissance man, to human rights expert and advocate. The focus on Dallaire, which is a story of masculine transcendence over trauma, compares with another article by Black (2009), ostensibly about three Rwandan genocide survivors: Regine King, Leo Kabalisa, and Patrick Sharangabo, living in Toronto. In contrast to the nine-page article on Dallaire's journey, Black's (2009) article dedicates less than a page to all three survivors' experiences combined.

Black (2009) neglects to mention how these survivors have contributed extensively to helping Rwandan survivors both in Rwanda and in Toronto. Regine King, in addition to facilitating the psychosocial Healing of Life Wounds program, wrote a brilliant thesis about this innovative therapeutic program for Rwandan genocide survivors, bystanders, and perpetrators. Leo Kabalisa co-founded Hope for Rwanda's Children, a Toronto-based NGO that has been supporting children orphaned by the genocide to access education, in addition to organizing tours to Rwanda for educators. Black's article is therefore similar to Thompson's article by omission. In the latter, the disproportionate attention given to Dallaire as both a victim and hero of genocide in contrast to actual Rwandan genocide survivors highlights Razack's (2007) argument that the documentation of white peacekeeper trauma during the genocide (especially Dallaire's) has the effect of stealing the pain (and heroism) of Rwandans. This is a perpetuation of symbolic injustice against Rwandans.

Similar to the article which focused on Dallaire, the *Star* discussed the interventions of NGO Save the Children founders Marc and Craig Kielburger post-genocide Rwanda in the article, "How do you teach the unspeakable in Rwanda?" In it, the Kielburgers (2009) ponder the question of how Canadians can teach Rwandans about Rwandan history. In "Stealing the Pain of Others," Razack (2007) argues:

> Our [Canadian] engagement with the world is everywhere depicted as the engagement of the compassionate but uninvolved observer… From our position as witness, we help to mark out the terrain of what is good and what is evil. *Possessed of unique sensibilities*, sensibilities that take us to the depths of grief and trauma, we can diagnose the trouble and act as the advance scout and the go-between.
>
> ([emphasis added], p. 381).

Craig Kielburger and Marc Kielburger (2009), in their description of the work of the foreign NGO Facing History and Ourselves, which develops educational materials for post-conflict countries, enact precisely what Razack describes.

The authors begin by explaining how the Rwandan government has placed a moratorium on the teaching of the genocide for the past fifteen years because of a lack of consensus. However, the NGO Facing History and Ourselves, in partnership with the University of California, Berkeley, and the Rwandan Ministry of Education, is able to start "tackling the history question. … By training teachers to facilitate debate and developing educator resources, the partnership has created a model for teaching" (Kielburger & Kielburger, 2009). The underlying, accepted premise is that Rwandans do not have the capacity to teach their own histories or to independently address the contestations around their history (Rwigema, 2018).

The contestation of history is mentioned in the article as a reason for the genocide, and a reason why it is not being taught. However, in the article, there is a complete erasure of the colonial role in manufacturing the understanding of Rwandan history (for example, the Hamitic hypothesis advanced by European anthropologists) that ideologically fed the genocide (Eltringham, 2006). Thus, the authors could unproblematically suggest that it is appropriate to re-enact a colonial educational relationship with Rwandans (Kielburger & Kielburger, 2009).

In addition to this, Kielburger and Kielburger (2009) link genocide education in Rwanda to issues closer to home. Unfortunately, they framed these issues as "[having] to tackle demons with the civil rights movement in the US and residential schools in Canada." The first point of course is naming the issues closer to home not as genocide and slavery, but as the civil rights movement and residential schools. They then conclude that the take-away lesson in Canadian history is that "Yes, mistakes were committed by everyone," and "It is in teaching those mistakes that the next generation can learn and work towards a better future." Thus, in two lines, they were able to turn Canadian colonialism/genocide (already reduced to residential schools) into a two-sided affair in which "mistakes were committed by everyone" and concluding that genocide education is about teaching about "everyone's mistakes." An organization that does not appear to have accurately grappled with the genocidal history of its own country is ready to help Rwandans, and media coverage celebrates their help.

Media as Injustice

In exploring examples of Canadian media coverage about the Rwandan genocide, my purpose has been to examine how the genocide continues to be represented. I have argued that for the most part, Canadian media coverage, similar to pop culture and academic discourse, continues to dehumanize Rwandans and further a narrative that obfuscates responsibility and accountability for the genocide. Mutua's (2001) savages-victims-saviors paradigm is helpful to understanding how media coverage does this. First, the Canadian government and UN complicity in facilitating the genocide is rewritten as a more innocent indifference, that when followed with apologies, trials, and paper trails reinstates the idea of Canadian benevolence. At the same time, the Rwandan state and its legal system, in contrast to the Canadian state and its legal system, is positioned as inferior and savage ("repressive") in its potential treatment of genocide suspects living in Canada. Finally, as always, white heroes saving Rwandan victims (who are absent in the texts) are profiled as the real story of the genocide. The result: the Canadian reader can feel good about his or her nonimplication in the genocide itself, while identifying with ongoing white heroism and white efforts to save (interchangeable) black victims from (interchangeable) black savages (Rwigema, 2018). This is a perpetuation of both historic and symbolic injustice.

The Implications: Rendering Rwandans Speechless

Trinh T. Minh-ha (1989), in explaining what happens to the other when white anthropologists immerse themselves in discussions about that other, states: "A conversation of 'us' with 'us' about 'them' is a conversation in which 'them' is silenced" (p. 66). Liisa Malkki (1996) echoes this argument when she explains that in the humanitarian field "Representational practices have the effect, as they currently stand of producing anonymous corporeality and speechlessness...testimony about refugees does what [humanitarian crisis] photographs do – silences the refugees...for it tends to be the testimony of 'refugee experts' and 'relief officials'" (pp. 389–390). Malkki (1996), discussing the experiences of Burundian Hutu refugees, is describing a reality where refugees are only called upon to provide their embodied victimhood as opposed to "their own inescapably political and historical assessments of their predicaments and their future" (p. 390).

Nsabimana explains how this process of Rwandan speechlessness (except as embodied victims) is produced:

> So you have things that are set up, there is a person that comes before the survivors testimony, usually western/white, and they talk about the historical and political context of the genocide, and as a support for the intellectual political and sociological analysis – there is a survivors testimony...[and while] there is a place for testimonies, an important place, the problem is the power dynamics, having to almost entertain people in reproducing stereotypes of the helpless victims standing there and for people to come after and patronize you and say "ooh" and then to have the real experts come and explain real things to people
>
> (quoted in Rwigema, 2009, see also Taylor et al., 2013, p. 127).

Nsabimana rightly identifies that implicit in the binary relationship between a white expert who provides intellectual analysis and the black survivor who provides personal testimony is the racist assumption that Rwandans "do not have the intellectual capacity to analyze and explain what happened in their country" (quoted in Rwigema, 2009).

This kind of binary set up, which Minh-ha (1989) describes as: "'Them' is only admitted among us, the discussing subjects, when accompanied or introduced by an 'us'" proliferates beyond lectures and commemorative events where knowledge about the genocide is publicly deployed. It also proliferates among the published academic literature on Rwanda, which is full of (published) white experts who explain and provide analysis based on information from (unpublished and often uncited) Rwandan informants who substantiate and provide evidence (Taylor et al., 2013). For example, Hron (2011) points out that Jean Hatzfield, in several of his books, draws extensively not just from translation but analytical insight about the genocide from a Rwandan research assistant named Innocent Rwililiza, whom he names as an ideal collaborator but whom he never credits as a co-author. This process also occurs with films and mainstream media stories, where white experts, drawing from Rwandan informants, freely utilize their creative license to tell whatever stories they deem important while Rwandan informants end up as the (literal) supporting cast in the stories of their own lives and deaths (Taylor et al., 2013).

This binary set-up is a racialized hierarchy of knowledge production that positions white people as objective experts with legitimate and authoritative knowledge and blacks (Rwandans) as subjective evidence with supportive information (Taylor et al., 2013). It is from this "universal standpoint" (of objectivity) that white moral authority is produced out of the suffering and silencing of blacks (Razack, 2007). It is this sense of moral authority derived from an expertise that is created in myriad ways by white people/Westerners that allows them to play judge and decision-maker. An example of this phenomenon is the expertise of the ICTR. Ntare Sharangabo points out that the moral authority of the ICTR is questionable, given the complicity of the international community in the genocide. He states:

> When the genocide started you had U.N in place who had told us lies about the peace process and evacuations, and when the genocide started, they rolled up and go and you know what's funny, they came back again, set up international courts to judge Rwandan killers, why are you judging them, when they committed it you were there, now you are a good guy?
>
> (quoted in Rwigema, 2009).

His question is made even more pertinent since after two decades, two billion dollars, and only 62 convictions, the ICTR's main accomplishment – the conviction of genocide mastermind Theoneste Bagosora – is problematic. Gerry Caplan (2009), a Canadian academic and political activist, commenting during a commemoration event, argued that the conviction failed to find conclusive evidence of Bagosora implicated in planning the genocide. This lack of a legal pronouncement can be used to support genocide denialist claims that, since if there was no planning by the recognized leader, then there was no genocide to speak of.

Zegeye and Vambe (2006) state:

> There is no culture within which knowledge production does not take place...The politics of knowledge production in Africa are defined by power relations. These determine who gets to publish, read and then distribute knowledge...It is selective knowledge because not all of what has been created as knowledge, or what is authorisable as knowledge, sees the light of day.
>
> (pp. 335–336).

Razack (2007) states:

> How do we give up racial power? By naming it as our own (we who consume the narratives) and by understanding that power has a material base. We can steal the slave's pain, and the pain of Rwandans because they have no personhood that stops us, and because we continue to benefit from their resources. We can mourn with them and avoid any responsibility for the past or implication in the present.
>
> (p. 391).

These scholars are offering us many insights that we can apply as we consider the issue of knowledge production about the Rwandan genocide. They are saying that there is no doubt that Rwandans produce knowledge about the genocide. It is the context of global white supremacy – both in terms of what is recognized as authoritative knowledge, and in terms of differential access to the means of production and distribution – that prevents Rwandan knowledge from being as widely produced, distributed, and accessible as knowledge produced by white people (Taylor et al., 2013).

Peter Uvin (1998), in his work *Aiding Violence,* outlines how structural violence in Rwanda prior to the genocide, as manifested through a top-down and authoritarian Rwandan government and development industry, denied personhood, agency, and voice to ordinary Rwandans. These dynamics, he explains, contributed to the genocide. He argues that ongoing systemic violence by the government and development industry played a key role in creating an environment that facilitated genocide. Similarly, Pauline Ngirumpatse (2009), founder of the organization *Humain Avant Tout,* notes that it is normalized peacetime violence that paves the way for an environment where acute violence such as genocide becomes acceptable. The racism and global white supremacy that created (white) race expertise serves to systemically marginalize and render speechless Rwandan survivors. The genocide of Tutsi in Rwanda was able to happen, as the world watched, for many reasons. As already stated, a primary reason was that the voices of Rwandans did not count (Rwigema, 2018).

Jeanne Umurungi (2009), a Rwandan community activist, noted that when Rwandan-Canadians protested in front of parliament buildings in Ottawa at the beginning of the 1994 genocide, they were ignored by the Canadian government and media because Rwandan voices did not count. Similarly, we have access to news footage from Rwanda in 1994 where people are seen pleading to the person filming them that if they are left they will be killed. We have footage of these voices being ignored and footage of these people being surrounded by killers as cameramen continued to tape. Those voices did not count (Rwigema, 2018).

In the hundred years from when the colonizers arrived in Rwanda to the genocide in 1994, the voices of Rwandans have been ignored by those in positions of colonial power. Racialized power, privilege, and conferred dominance exist. If this reality is denied, either outright or through silence, this denial will continue to reproduce inequity, avoid accountability, and allow those privileged to benefit from the resources of those whose personhood is denied. Historical justice demands that we who benefit from colonial power acknowledge our role in what led to and allowed the genocide to happen. Symbolic justice demands that we sincerely apologize for our past and ongoing role, and take steps to redress and repair, by listening to and centering Rwandan survivors when we discuss the genocide committed against them.

Note

1 This chapter utilizes some research from my Ph.D. Fragments, Webs and Weavings: Rwandan-Canadian Perspectives on the 1994 Genocide against the Tutsi (2018); however, it examines the question of historical and symbolic justice, whereas my previous work is examining social justice, healing, and trauma.

Bibliography

Beardsley, B. (2012). *Presentation.* Zoryan Institute.

Black, D. (2009, April 6). Rwandan survivors recall genocide. *Toronto Star.* Retrieved from http://www.thestar.com/news/world/rwanda/article/614182–rwandan-survivors-recall-genocide

Black, D. (2010, May 22). Why did Ottawa ignore warnings of Rwandan genocide? *Toronto Star.* Retrieved from

Caplan, C. (2009, April 8). [Presentation]. Rwanda's Recovery: Commemorating the 15th Anniversary of the Tutsi Genocide. Toronto, Canada.

Cappeliez, M. (2006). *Memory pools: Representation of the Rwandan genocide in Canadian novel, media, and policy* [Symposium Presentation]. 2nd Annual Graduate Symposium Dalhousie, Dalhousie University.

Chari, T. (2010). Representation or misrepresentation? The New York Time's framing of the 1994 Rwandan genocide. *African Identities, 8*(4), 333–349. https://doi.org/10.1080/14725843.2010.513242

Chiasson, P. (2012, January 11). Leon Mugesera's deportation to Rwanda might be stalled by UN. *Toronto Star.* Retrieved from http://www.thestar.com/news/canada/article/1113903–leon-mugesera-s-deportation-to-rwanda-might-be-stalled-by-un

Dauge-Roth, A. (2010). *Writing and filming the genocide of the Tutsi in Rwanda: Dismembering and remembering traumatic history.* Lexington Books.

Ditchburn, J. (2012, May 28). Rwandan pleads not guilty at Canada's second war-crimes trial. *Toronto Star.* Retrieved from https://www.thestar.com/news/canada/2012/05/28/rwandan_pleads_not_guilty_at_canadas_second_warcrimes_trial.html

Eltringham, N. (2006). 'Invaders who have stolen the country': The Hamitic hypothesis, race, and the Rwandan genocide. *Social Identities, 12*(4), 425–446. https://doi.org/10.1080/13504630600823619

Fair, J. E., & Parks, L. (2001). Africa on camera: Television news coverage and aerial imaging on Rwandan refugees. *Africa Today, 48*(2), 35–57. https://doi.org/10.1353/at.2001.0031

Gigliotti, S. (2007). Genocide yet again: Scenes of Rwanda and ethical witness in the human rights memoir. *Australian Journal of Politics and History*, *53*(1), 84–95. https://doi.org/10.1111/j.1467-8497.2007.00444.x

Hron, M. (2011). Gukora and itsembatsemba: The "Ordinary killers" in Jean Hatzfeld's machete seasons. *Research in African Literature*, *42*(2), 125–146. https://doi.org/10.1353/ral.2011.0048

Journalism and Communication. (2017). *Media and Mass Atrocity: The Rwandan Genocide and Beyond.* Carleton University. https://carleton.ca/sjc/cu-events/media-mass-atrocity-rwanda-genocide-beyond-roundtable/)

Kielburger, C., & Kielburger, M. (2009, April 6). How do you teach the unspeakable in Rwanda? *Toronto Star.* Retrieved from http://www.thestar.com/news/world/rwanda/article/613406–how-do-you-teach-the-unspeakable-in-rwanda

Kothari, U. (2006). An agenda for thinking about 'race' in development. *Progress in Development Studies*, *6*(1), 9–23. https://doi.org/10.1191/1464993406ps124oa

MacCharles, T. (2010, April 21). Jean apologizes for Canada's role in Rwanda. *Toronto Star.* Retrieved from http://www.thestar.com/news/canada/article/798512–jean-apologizes-for-canada-s-role-in-rwanda

Malkki, L. H. (1996). Speechless emissaries: Refugees, humanitarianism and dehistoricization. *Cultural Anthropology*, *11*(3), 377–401. https://doi.org/10.1525/can.1996.11.3.02a00050

Mamdani, M. (2001). *When victims become killers: Colonialism, nativism, and genocide in Rwanda.* Princeton University.

McNamee, E. (2007). Writing the Rwandan genocide: The justice and politics of witnessing after the event. *Law Critique*, *18*(3), 309–330. https://doi.org/10.1007/s10978-007-9015-5

Melvern, L. (2000). *A people betrayed: The role of the West in Rwanda's genocide.* Zed Books.

Minh-Ha, T. T. (1989). *Woman, native, other: Writing post-coloniality and feminism.* Indiana University Press.

Mutua, M. (2001). Savages, victims and saviors: The metaphor of human rights. *Harvard International Law Journal*, *42*(1), 201–245.

Ndahiro, A., & Rutazibwa, N. (2008). *Hotel Rwanda ou le génocide des Tutsis vu par Hollywood.* L'Harmattan.

Ngirumpatse, P. (2009, April 8). *Justice and reconciliation.* [Presentation]. Rwanda's Recovery: Commemorating the 15th Anniversary of the Tutsi Genocide. Toronto, Canada.

Presentation at an event, *Rwanda's Recovery: Commemorating the 15th Anniversary of the Tutsi Genocide* (2009, April 8).

Razack, S. (Ed.). (2002). *Race, space, and the law: Unmapping a white settler society.* Between the Lines.

Razack, S. H. (2007). Stealing the pain of others: Reflections on Canadian humanitarian responses. *Review of Education, Pedagogy, and Cultural Studies*, *29*(4), 375–394. https://doi.org/10.1080/10714410701454198

Rwafa, U. (2010). Film representations of the Rwandan genocide. *African Identities*, *8*(4), 389–408. https://doi.org/10.1080/14725843.2010.513254

Rwigema, M. J. (Director) (2009). The Rwandan genocide as told by its historian-survivors [Film]. Kabazaire Production.

Rwigema, M. J. (2018). *Fragments, webs, and weavings: Rwandan-Canadian perspectives on the 1994 genocide against Tusti* [Doctoral dissertation, University of Toronto]. Retrieved from https://tspace.library.utoronto.ca/bitstream/1807/102940/3/Rwigema_Marie-Jolie_201811_PhD_thesis.pdf

Small, A. (2006). Tierno monenembo: Morality, mockery, and Rwandan genocide. *Forum for Modern Language Studies*, *42*(2), 200–211. https://doi.org/10.1093/fmls/cql008

Taylor, L. K., Rwigema, M.-J., & Umwali, S. (2013). What you see depends where you stand: Critical anticolonial perspectives on genocide education addressing the 1994 Rwandan genocide. In P. P. Trifonas, & B. Wright (Eds.), *Critical peace education: Difficult dialogues* (pp. 115–134). Springer.

Taylor, L. K., Umwali, S., & Rwigema, M.-J. (2015). The ethics of learning from Rwandan survivor communities: Critical reflexivity and the politics of knowledge production in genocide education. In S. High (Ed.), *Beyond testimony and trauma: Oral history in the aftermath of mass violence* (pp. 88–118). UBC Press.

Thompson, A. (2012, April 28). Child soldiers: Romeo Dallaire's wrenching return to Africa's 'gang warfare'. *Toronto Star.* Retrieved from https://www.thestar.com/news/world/2012/04/28/child_soldiers_romo_dallaires_wrenching_return_to_africas_gang_warfare.html

Tumbwebaze, P. (2013, April 5). When Hollywood films got the 1994 genocide wrong. *The New Times.* Retrieved from http://www.newtimes.co.rw/section/read/64614.

Umurungi, J. (2009, April 8). *Canada, genocide and the media: A Conversation.* [Panel Discussion]. Rwanda's Recovery: Commemorating the 15th Anniversary of the Tutsi Genocide, Toronto, Canada

Umuvugizi. (2014, October 13). *Open letter to BBC over genocide denial.* Retrieved from https://umuvugizi.wordpress.com/2014/10/13/1994-bbc-2014/

Uvin, P. (1998). *Aiding violence: The development enterprise in Rwanda.* Kumarian Press.

Verhoeven, H. (2010, September 23). UN report on Rwanda genocide threatens stability in Central Africa. *The Christian Science Monitor.* Retrieved from https://www.csmonitor.com/Commentary/Opinion/2010/0923/UN-report-on-Rwanda-genocide-threatens-stability-in-Central-Africa

Wolfe, S. (2014). *The politics of reparations and apologies.* Springer.

Zegeye, A., & Vambe, M. (2006). Knowledge production and publishing in Africa. *Development Southern Africa*, *23*(3), 333–349. https://doi.org/10.1080/03768350600843010

4 Testimonies of Child Survivors from Gitarama Prefecture

Preserving Memory of the 1994 Rwanda Genocide

Musa Wakhungu Olaka

Introduction

Children's experiences and voices must be included in analyses of genocide. In the case of the Rwandan genocide, these voices and experiences have not been conspicuous and that is why children's testimonies need to be collected, archived, and analyzed in order to get a fuller understanding of the genocide. Throughout Rwanda, children were exposed to horrendous experiences on a daily basis during the 1994 Genocide against the Tutsi. Many were killed and maimed. However, after their rescue, some children who survived would narrate their first-hand experiences. Most of the children who survived were exposed to life-threatening circumstances multiple times, and have endured atrocities repeatedly over several months.

After the genocide, life was never the same. Child survivors endured many hardships, especially when they recalled what they went through. According to a 2003 Human Rights Watch report, close to 400,000 children were orphaned during or slightly after the genocide (Kaplan, 2013). Due to the magnitude of the effects of the genocide, the lived experience of child survivors must be included in analysis of genocide in Rwanda (Dumas, 2019). Unfortunately, the collection and analysis of Rwandan child survivor testimonies have not been as robust and widespread as that of the Holocaust (Cohen, 2007). The most comprehensive collection of genocide testimonies is the USC Shoah Foundation Visual History Archive[1] which now mainly consists of Holocaust testimonies and is viewed as a model to be emulated by those who want to preserve genocide testimonies (Shenker, 2016). This chapter will argue that to understand the full scope and breadth of genocide, it is critically important to collect, analyze, and archive the experiences of the children who suffered its traumas and survived them.

There has been debate regarding ethics and importance of collecting children's testimonies and showing images of the genocide to children. Mukandayisenga (2011) argues that the children get retraumatized, leading to opening of wounds that were already healing. There is a school of thought that views child testimonies as an indictment against perpetrators and therapeutic to the children (King, 2019). Due to these conflicting viewpoints

DOI: 10.4324/9781003228592-5

which were present immediately after the genocide in Rwanda, there are limited numbers of child survivor testimonies. Unfortunately, some of the children bore major physical scars that vividly painted the image of atrocities that were committed.

Most of these child survivors of the 1994 genocide in Rwanda witnessed many atrocities and violent acts being committed (Neugebauer et al., 2018). Tutsis (who were the main target for extermination) suffered the brunt of the genocide and children were not spared. Several children who survived narrated how they witnessed Tutsis being undressed and left to walk naked along the road, one of many acts that perpetrators used to dehumanize and torture their victims (University of South Florida Libraries, 2021).

Additionally, some of the children witnessed firsthand the following atrocities: women and girls raped; people killed by machetes, guns, knives, bows, spears, and arrows; people drowned in rivers including the river Nyabarongo; perpetrators disemboweling pregnant women; toddlers killed by being smashed onto walls; and other small children killed when their necks were twisted between metal bars. Perpetrators further dehumanized Tutsis and moderate Hutus by coercing the ones they arrested to participate in the killing of others. Some of the people who survived were tortured before being released, while others were forced to witness people being killed – often their close associates or family members. Additionally, properties belonging to Tutsis and moderate Hutus were looted and/or burned (University of South Florida Libraries, 2021).

To save their own lives, some of the children who survived the genocide had to hide among dead bodies, while others hid in latrines or in deep pits.[2] It was very common for the killer gangs such as *Interahamwe* and *Simusiga* to extort money from Tutsis and moderate Hutus by promising to spare their lives. In some instances, even after those targeted to be killed offered a bribe, they were later killed by either those they had bribed or by other *génocidaires* (Hatzfeld, 2006).

One major killing field was Gitarama prefecture.[3] Located in the middle of the country, Gitarama prefecture had a long-standing, well-established church system. This prefecture also bordered Kigali, the capital city of Rwanda where mass killings started in April 1994. Five years after the genocide, IBUKA, the umbrella association that comprises various associations for survivors of the 1994 genocide, began a pilot program to collect testimonies of children who survived the genocide. Gitarama prefecture was chosen for the pilot project due to its significance in Rwandan history and also due to its numerous killing fields. Further discussion of its significance is discussed in Section 4. Handwritten testimonies collected from close to 1,000 children from Gitarama document their experiences from the beginning of the genocide until their rescue. At the time of the genocide, these children were between seven and fifteen years old. This chapter highlights how psychological trauma is manifested in the testimonies of these children. This chapter will also comment on the various ways in which those targeted for extermination tried to resist.

Collecting the Testimonies

Prior to 1999 not much effort was expended to systematically collect and preserve testimonies of survivors of the 1994 genocide in Rwanda. However, this situation started to change due to an increasing number of survivor deaths from disease and natural causes. It also became evident that there were many ways in which time affects memory (Viebach, 2019). As time passes and more people die without recording their experiences during the genocide, this much needed information about genocide is lost forever.

In late 1999 and early 2000, IBUKA organized *ingando* (solidarity camps) that brought together close to 1,000 children whose homes were in Gitarama prefecture and who survived the genocide. The purpose was to discuss with these child survivors' issues affecting them and how they could alleviate challenges that they had been experiencing in their lives. By late 1999, these children were between twelve and twenty years old and attending secondary school. Solidarity camps were also put in place as social support mechanisms to help young genocide survivors to bond. IBUKA requested that each child who attended the camps write their testimonies in an exercise book and write what they experienced from the time the genocide began until the time they were liberated.

This was IBUKA's pilot project to collect testimonies from these children, and if successful, IBUKA hoped to scale up the project so that all the children who survived the genocide from all the 12 prefectures in Rwanda (Butare, Byumba, Cyangugu, Gikongoro, Gisenyi, Gitarama, Kibungo, Kibuye, Kigali Ville, Kigali Ngali, Ruhengeri, and Umutara) could record their testimonies, thereby preserving these children's memories. Unfortunately, the nationwide project to collect testimonies from children who survived this genocide was never put in place, partly due to lack of sufficient funds to support collecting the testimonies on a large scale.

Scope and Testimonies Used in This Chapter

Out of the 17 communes in Gitarama prefecture, testimonies from five communes – Masango, Mugina, Bulinga, Mukingi, and Kayenzi – are used in this chapter. These communes were major killing centers and are representative of what happened in the prefecture. Masango represents what happened in the southern part of the prefecture, Mugina represents the east, Bulinga the west, Mukingi the south central, and Kayenzi the north. The chapter will focus on the memory of the children whose homes were in these five communes at the time of the 1994 genocide in Rwanda.

Gitarama Prefecture

Gitarama prefecture was established in 1959 and by 1994, which consisted of 17 communes: Masango, Mugina, Mukingi, Bulinga, Kayenzi, Kigoma,

Nyakabanda, Nyamabuye, Taba, Runda, Murama, Musambira, Tambwe, Rutobwe, Mushubati, Nyabikenke, and Ntongwe. The location of each commune in the prefecture can be viewed in Figure 4.1. Gitarama prefecture was in the middle of the country and bordered Kigali City, the epicenter of the genocide. Due to Gitarama's proximity to the prefectures Kigali City and Kigali Ngali – where the killings started first and a large number of Tutsis got killed – many people fled to Gitarama. This influx of Tutsi's fleeing for their lives ultimately resulting in Gitarama prefecture becoming a major killing site during the genocide.

Gitarama prefecture was also the cradle of evangelism in Rwanda and among the first places in Rwanda where Christian missionaries established

Figure 4.1 Gitarama prefecture.

Source: University of South Florida Libraries (2021).

mission centers. Kabgayi, one of the earliest mission centers established by Catholic missionaries in Rwanda, played a significant role in Rwanda's first republic, headed by Gregoire Kayibanda (Carney, 2011). Some of the priests at Kabgayi were highly influential during President Kayibanda's reign, as he had closely worked with them before ascending to power.

During the genocide, many fleeing violence sought refuge at Kabgayi Catholic Mission. The mission included a cathedral and even a publishing house that published *Kinyamateka*, the oldest newspaper in Rwanda. In addition, there was a seminary, some schools, and a nuns' convent nearby. It was at Kabgayi that many Tutsis were arrested and transported in buses to other locations where they would be killed. A large number of people died at Kabgayi: some contracted cholera and other waterborne illnesses, others died of starvation, and many were murdered when the *Interahamwe* attacked (University of South Florida Libraries, 2021).

In 2006, the administrative structures were changed, and what used to be Gitarama prefecture in 1994 is currently part of the Southern province, one of the five regions/provinces.

Digitizing the Testimonies

The testimonies were digitized by the University of South Florida (USF) Holocaust and Genocide Studies Center (HGSC). Established in 2008, the HGSC was a unit/department in the library and it was meant to bring together faculty members who teach and research about Holocaust and genocide to share their research. The Center was also required to collect rare primary documents, and to help these faculty members to access the documents. At its inception, the HGSC concentrated on growing collections on the Holocaust. As the Center grew, so did the need to provide resources to faculty members conducting comparative research on genocides. Thus, two more collection areas were established: the Armenian Genocide, and genocide and crimes against humanity in the African Great Lakes region.

In late 2011, I was the librarian for HGSC and together with Dr. Mark Greenberg, the Director of HGSC, visited Rwanda and Burundi to start forging partnerships with local institutions working on genocide-related issues. Several potential partners were identified, including IBUKA. The Shoah Foundation had already approached IBUKA about digitizing their materials, but after discussion and careful analysis, IBUKA's leadership decided that the USF should digitize the materials. A memorandum between IBUKA and USF was signed in September 2012 so as to collaborate in the digitization of documents on the Rwandan genocide. Digitization was partly intended to help spur more research on the 1994 genocide in Rwanda, not only at the USF but also in Rwanda and other parts of the world. The other purpose was to preserve rare and unique documents on the 1994 genocide that were in danger of being damaged or destroyed due to the harsh environmental conditions in which they had been stored. The digitization effort would thus secure information in these rare documents for future generations. The digitized content was to be openly accessible in order to encourage teachers across the world who do not have access to primary documents on the Rwandan genocide to have the ability to incorporate some of the documents in their lessons.

Between October 25 and December 2, 2012, I traveled to Rwanda in order to digitize the IBUKA documents. At the end of the five-week digitization process, 12,021 images had been captured and translated to 152.47 gigabytes of storage space. The 12,021 images are equivalent to approximately 16,000 pages, as some double pages were captured in single images. An additional 366 files were retrieved from floppy disks, and are equivalent to about 3,500 pages.

Genocide in Rwanda

The 1994 Genocide in Rwanda claimed close to one million lives. However, Rwandans who characterized themselves as either Hutu, Tutsi, or Twa used to live in harmony before the arrival of colonists who the Rwandan government claims came to sow the seeds of discord (Repubulika Y'U Rwanda Perezidansi ya Repubulika, 1999).

Conflict between the Tutsi, Twa, and Hutu escalated during the Belgian colonial rule. During the initial days of Belgian rule, the colonists favored Tutsis. Belgians appointed Tutsis to positions of power. As a result, Tutsi received formal education that had been established by Christian missionaries. All local chiefs across the country were therefore held by Tutsi in addition to coveted government positions. Belgians employed these discrimination tactics with the hope that it would be much easier to convert the Rwandan masses to Christianity, as all Rwandan kings were Tutsis (Carney, 2011). Hutus were sidelined and tended to be oppressed by the Tutsi chiefs, which greatly angered the Hutu masses. In the late 1950s, conflict between Tutsi and Hutu started to escalate when Hutu masses started to agitate and clamor for political power (Thomson, 2018). Furthermore, major killings of Tutsis by Hutu extremists occurred in 1959, 1964, and 1973 (Mamdani, 2020). The international community paid little attention to the killings, as they saw such killings as common, tribal, barbaric acts characteristic of African countries.

There were many catalysts to the 1994 genocide in Rwanda. Among them include: long-held grudges between the Tutsi and Hutu stemming from colonial days, poor leadership that always wanted to centralize power and exclude others from leadership positions based on ethnicity, and regionalism (Thomson, 2018). In addition, the introduction of multiparty democracy in the early 1990s is viewed to have bred extremist groups, as well as the impact of a declining economy as a result of a slump in coffee prices at the international market. Other economic factors, included the World Bank pushing Rwanda to implement structural adjustment programs, which led to currency devaluation, layoffs, and a reduction in government spending (White, 2009).

Political factors that influenced the genocide included the 1990 Civil War and the use of this conflict by extremist factions. The Rwandan Patriotic Front (RPF), which was mainly composed of Tutsi in exile, attacked Rwanda in 1990 in order to force the government to allow thousands of Tutsi refugees to come back into the country. Hate media flourished in Rwanda in the 1990s, fanning hatred and urging the extermination of Tutsis who were labeled as cockroaches and snakes (Thompson, 2019). This hate and propaganda media included *Kangura* magazine, *Radio Muhabura*, and *Radio RTLM* (Richards et al., 2019). The genocide in Rwanda did not happen by accident. Similar to other genocides, that rarely happen spontaneously, there is planning that tends to take place over a long time (Mugesera, 2014).

The combined political and economic factors, was again, a catalyst for the 1994 genocide. During the hundred days of genocide, it is generally accepted that close to one million Rwandans were killed. However, scholars have provided varied figures, and the methodologies used to arrive at these numbers have been questioned (Tissot, 2020). IBUKA, however, thinks that the one million figure is very conservative.

Figure 4.2 shows IBUKA's breakdown of the 1,389,150 victims per prefecture. IBUKA also counted 118 mass killing sites spread across all the prefectures.

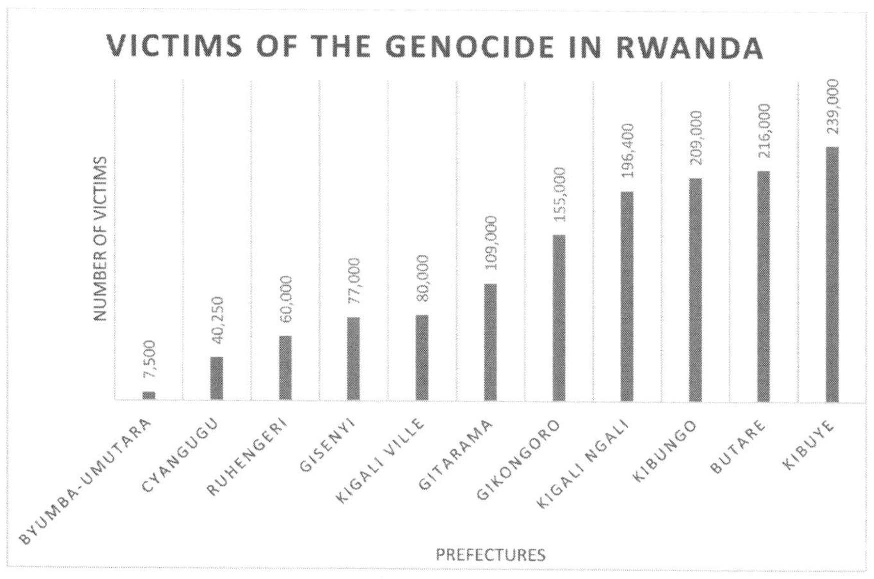

Figure 4.2 Victims as per IBUKA.

Note: This chart was adapted by Musa Olaka and shows number of victims of the 1994 genocide in Rwanda. IBUKA a.s.b.l (n.d.).

Trauma and Genocide

Despite many advances in trauma research, scholars have not come to an agreement as to what constitutes a traumatic experience (Figley, 2012). Historically, trauma used to only refer to physical wounds. However, studies in psychiatry and psychology have contributed to the expansion of the definition to also consider psychological processes (Suarez, 2016). A traumatic experience is now viewed as one that continues to activate an individual's stress long after the actual event, making the individual feel that his or her life, or that of others, is being threatened. Defining trauma based on the magnitude of one's experience to a troubling event, or trauma being a rare occurrence that is also extraordinary in one's life and being able to evoke significant distress in that person's life have all been criticized (Weathers & Keane, 2007). In modern times, it is increasingly being accepted that trauma is "a state of physical and/or emotional shock, which may be a result of real, anticipated, imagined, or forgotten experiences, or encounters that are never static" (Leese et al., 2021).

A traumatic event can affect people differently. This means that the degree and ability for one to cope with a traumatic event also varies (Neugebauer et al., 2018). Duration of exposure to a traumatic event may also affect how the event will impact an individual. In most cases, an individual wants to be set free of the stressors/triggers and to be in control of his/her life, but more often than not ends up feeling helpless (Kaplan, 2013). Magnitude of the stressors may vary depending on how much they are a threat to life and/or their likelihood to cause physical harm (in the perception of the individual). In some cases, trauma causes silence (Leese et al., 2021). One's ability to cope with traumatic experiences is a function of the severity of exposure to the sources causing the trauma, one's culture, and even one's past experiences in life, circumstances in the family, community, or politics (Leese et al., 2021). As a result of the differences in how trauma affects individuals, people should be discouraged from trivializing suffering and traumatic experiences (Suarez, 2016).

The presence or delayed manifestations of trauma for individuals exposed to traumatic experiences as children vary, with survivors experiencing different symptoms as they age and become adults (Hodges et al., 2013). Exposing affected children to therapies at the earliest possible time after the traumatic event may reduce manifestations of traumatic symptoms later in life. Unfortunately, trauma tends to be passed from one generation to another and especially through families (Berckmoes et al., 2017).

This chapter clearly shows that the 1994 genocide in Rwanda was a traumatic event due to the extraordinary number of lives lost and the sustained threat of extermination. This was a human catastrophe that continues to haunt many of the survivors of this genocide. Dr. Nasson Munyandamutsa, a renowned Rwandan psychiatrist, conducted a study on the state of mental health in Rwanda and found that 24–28% of the

Rwandan population suffers from various levels of trauma (Musoni, 2012). However, a more recent meta-analysis indicates that there is a 37% prevalence rate of post-traumatic stress disorder (PTSD) among genocide survivors (Musanabaganwa et al., 2020).

Children and Genocide

Children who are exposed to traumatic experiences during their childhood have a high likelihood of these experiences leading to psychological symptoms later in life. These psychological symptoms may include: anxiety, depression, anger, post-traumatic stress, dissociation, sexual concerns, and "acting out" or externalizing behaviors (Arata et al., 2005). Other symptoms include lack of sleep, having nightmares, constant headaches, wanting to be alone, fear of being alone, being rude, lack of connection to one's family, and lack of confidence in other people (with the exception of other genocide survivors) (Schotsman, 2000).

Children will actively look for ways to cope with their traumatic experiences. They normally try to channel their emotions and thinking, either by being in denial about the trauma or by simply refusing to think about it. This is done in such a way that the children's behavior and social interactions help them avoid or withdraw from what is causing their psychological distress (Punamäki et al., 2004). At the same time, different people tend to handle the same traumatic experience in varying ways, as it depends on the resilience of the individual and also the ability of the individual to get support from his/her family, friends, or community.

Traditional Rwandan Culture and Psychological Trauma

In traditional Rwandan culture, when one started *guhahamuka* (experiencing traumatic seizures), society tended to interpret these attacks to mean that the person had been possessed by evil spirits or simply gone mad/crazy. However, several interventions did exist, and they varied on a case-by-case basis. Normally, the person was given *miti yikinyarwanda* (taken to traditional healers). These traditional healers either tried to exorcise the demons/evil spirits, or gave the traumatized person herbal remedies they could use. There are instances where the person was left alone without any intervention, or the person could be locked inside the house. At times, the victim could be beaten and accused of feigning symptoms. As a whole, the Rwandan culture required people to always exercise patience and self-control when were faced with a major calamity, grief, or sorrowful moments. This was a form of self-control which prevented individuals from exhibiting self-destructive behavior and by extension, affecting the other people around him or her (Bagilishya, 2003; Sinalo et al., 2020). It therefore follows that outward emotional displays of grief or anger tended to be scoffed at.

Experiences of Children in Gitarama Prefecture during the Genocide

Many of the children from Gitarama prefecture who survived the genocide personally experienced horrendous acts and also witnessed some of these acts being committed to other people. As previously discussed, some of their experiences include:

1. Witnessing Tutsis being undressed and left to walk naked on the road;
2. Women and girls being raped;
3. People being killed through the use of machetes, guns, knives, bows, spears, and arrows;
4. People being drowned in rivers;
5. Hiding among dead bodies;
6. Hiding in pit latrines;
7. Children being beaten;
8. Torture intended to dehumanize;
9. Pregnant women being disemboweled;
10. Toddlers being smashed against a wall;
11. Property being burned;
12. Property being looted;
13. Insults and threats;
14. Being hunted down to be killed;
15. Being forced to give up all the money they have;
16. Being forced to kill other people;
17. Going for days without food or shelter.

Psychological Trauma of the Children as Manifested in the Handwritten Testimonies[4]

There are many manifestations that appeared in the testimonies and are clear indicators of psychological trauma. These manifestations include the following.

Avoiding Talking and Wanting to Be Left Alone

R15-00055, a female student from Commune Masango, says, "*...ubwo bambazango kuki ntavuga nkabihorera cyangwa nk'ahaguruka nkigendera nkajya ahobatandeba.*" This student says that while in school, other students would ask her why she never used to talk and, in most cases, she never responded to those students and would go away in seclusion where other students could not see her.

R15-00055, a female student from Commune Masango, says, "*...ubwo nkiga nabi kubera ibibazo by'ukonsigaye njyenyine. Ubwo ngira ikibazo cyokurwarwa mumutwe nkiririwa n'igunze.*" This student narrates how she had challenges in school because she used to spend a lot of time by herself. She goes on to say that she has a mental illness and spends days on end in self-isolation.

Anger

R15-00102, a male student from Commune Mugina, says, "…*Ngako agahinda yansigiye yanteye ntateze kutashima… abo nibo mbashije kuibuka kuko umutima usobetse amaganya ntago usobanura amagambo … igisebe cyirakira aliko inkovu ntabwo ikira ntabwo isabangana.*" This student talks of how he is filled with sorrow and anger and uses a proverb to explain the ever-present sorrow and pain in his heart. This pain and sorrow are so great that he does not even have words to explain what really happened during the genocide.

R15-00061, a female student from Commune Mugina, says, "…iyo *Umuhutu agutera ibisazi kubera ikibazo yewe uwavuga ibyo Umuhutu yakoreye Umututsi usibye ko ntanuwabona icyo abahanisha keretse uwabica bose akabamaraho.*" She explains that whenever a Hutu angers her, she normally wants to remind them about the atrocities Hutus committed against Tutsis. She always feels helpless but wishes she could kill all the Hutus.

Poor Cognitive Function

R15-009, a female student from Commune Masango, has a mentally handicapped brother who had been hacked on his head but survived. She says, "…*Ubu ntabwo mu mutwe hakora neza… ntacyo yishoboreye gukora,*" meaning that the brother is helpless because he cannot mentally function well and has to be assisted at all times.

Sorrow and Depression

R15-00016, a female student from Commune Masango, says, "…*bakabica, abandi bakabatema bakabajugunya mumusarane bakavuga, Imana yabaremye nayo yabanze ugasanga biteye agahinda*" meaning that … they killed and hacked others before throwing them in pit latrines and it was so [painful]/sorrowful when they even said that the God that created them [Tutsis] is the same one that hates Tutsis.

R15-00084, a female student from Commune Mugina, witnessed her father being killed and had to hide in a pit latrine amidst dead bodies. She narrates how she left the pit she was hiding in and went to ask someone to give her a place to sleep (another hideout for the night and was to leave the following morning). The man accepted the student to spend the night at his house, however, the student could not sleep the entire night because she was very fearful and had a lot of sorrow that had been caused by the genocide. This student says, "…*Musabako areka nkaharara bugacya nigendera.*

Umugabo aremera ubwo nalaranye agahinda kenshi numubabaro mwinshi nateragwa nigikomere."

R15-00031, a female student from Commune Masango, narrates how a Hutu man witnessed people being killed, and when he saw the state in which this child was in, he was overcome with sorrow to an extent that he was almost dying "... *uwo musaza yagize agahinda gakomeye nyumayiminota mike gusa ubwo narintegereje ibigiyekumbaho.*" This clearly shows that some bystanders and rescuers were traumatized by seeing atrocities committed against Tutsis.

R15-00019, a female student from Commune Masango, narrates how she was overcome with grief and sorrow to an extent that she could not even manage to eat, "*...Ibyo kurya nabashije kubihabwa ntabyambujije no kunanirwa kubirya. ...abona fite agahinda kenshi...*" This student was later arrested (by a killer gang). She was waiting for her turn to come before she could be killed and she had no doubt that death was imminent. She narrates that, "*...ahasigaye mu mutima wange ngira ubwoba bwinshi, uratangira uratera cyane. Nibwo naratangiye gutabaza uwiteka cyane mu mutima wanjye.*" This means that her heart started pounding so much due to extreme fear and she had no alternative other than to start praying and praising God in silence with the hope that God could save her from her captors.

R15-00011, a female student from Commune Masango, discusses how a man called Mudahunga was brutally killed by being slashed with machetes and thrown into a pile of dead bodies. His wife was so traumatized that she collapsed and died. "*...Mugabo witwa Mudahunga akaba yarapfuye nabi cyane. Bamutemaguye bamuta mu ntumbi ...mugore we yahise nawe apfa kubera agahinda.*"

Hysteria/Epileptic Fits and Fainting

R15-00019, a female student from Commune Masango, managed to flee into Zaire (current day Democratic Republic of Congo) with a Hutu family that was sheltering her. When she was told of the death of her maternal aunt who was a nun, she narrated that she was overcome by trauma and experienced deep sorrow before starting to act like a crazy person. She screamed and shouted out what she had seen during the genocide. "*...Nahise ngira umubabaro ukabije cyane, mpita numva mbaye décourage muri njyewe. Naratuye numva kubaho kwanje ntako noneho numva ndiyanze nibwo nahise mera nkumusazi mpita mba toromatise... navugaga ibyo nabonye byose muntambara ariko bigenda binyishsushyanya mbere, nsubira kubibona, nkarushana kuvuza induru.*"

R15-00016, a female student from Commune Masango, says, "... *twabonye byinshi namaso yacu... twabonye benshi bahahamuka.*" This means that survivors saw so many atrocities and witnessed many people traumatized, became hysterical, and even fainted.

R15-0030, a female student from Commune Masango says, "...*mwakwita ku bibabaro byacu kuko nibyinshi numudadufasha bizatwiramo ibisazi*." This student is requesting that children who survived the genocide be attended to since many of them have deep-seated internal sorrow and challenges. She stated that if these challenges are not addressed, then some of the children will end up being mad/mentally unstable.

Crying Whenever One Thinks About or Starts to Narrate What Happened during the Genocide

R15-00016, a female student from Commune Masango, says, "...*Twavuga Byinshi ariko byatugirira ingaruka, ntabwo twabirangiza*," meaning that the student would like to narrate more, but fears the mental repercussions on herself because it would retraumatize her. She therefore narrates only a small part of her experience during the genocide.

R15-0009, a female student from Commune Masango says, that, "...*ariko iyo mbyibutse ndarira*," meaning that whenever I recalled what happened, I start crying.

R15-00046, a male student from Commune Masango narrates, "...*sinabivuga ngo mbirangize kuko ari bibi ntabasha kubivuga bidatuma nikomeretse n'umutima*." He explains how he risks having a heartache and mental breakdown. He states what he experienced was very horrendous and he cannot even complete narrating what happened during the genocide.

Being Ready to Die

R15-00031, a female student from Commune Masango, saw so many people being killed that she was ready to die. She did not even try to hide from the attackers. She openly walked along the road so that she could also be killed. "...*Njeze kumunota wa nyuma wo gupfa, Imana ntiyabyemeye ubwo nafashe inzira ndagenda ariko mubyukuri sinarinzi aho najyaga niyemeje kunyura kumuhanda gusa ntakwihisha kuko numvaga ahasigaye wagirango bwanje nabushyize mumaboko y'imana mvuga ati ahasigaye mwami wanjye unjeze uko ushaka*."

R15-00019, a female student from Commune Masango, was starved for so long that she felt she was ready to die and accepted that death was imminent "...*Nari nkitinya gupfa cyane ... numva inzara... ntarupfu rurenze urwo*." In other words, the extreme hunger that this student experienced made her feel that she was not any better than a dead person.

Inability to Function and Look after Oneself

R15-00025, a female student from Commune Masango, writes how the genocide reduced some children to being helpless and unable to properly function or even look after themselves. "... *Dore bana bamwe na bamwe basigaye ntacyo bazimarira kubera kuibuka abobajyenye agahinda kandi barenga. Bajyanye agahinda, Imana yonyine izabibukira.*"

Wishing to Be Dead

R15-00020, a female student from Commune Masango, remembers what happened and wishes that she would have been better off had she died during the genocide. "*…hari igihe mbangayika nkavuga ngo niyo nza kuba narapfuye.*" This is due to the many challenges the student experienced after the genocide. Simply because the genocide has come to an end does not mean that survivors are safe and are going to live a happy life.

Resistance during the Genocide

Despite being outnumbered by genocide perpetrators, who were also better equipped with weapons, Tutsis and moderate Hutus tried to fight back against their attackers. There were moments when those targeted to be killed managed to achieve some success. Below is a list of forms of resistance as manifested in handwritten testimonies of children from Gitarama prefecture.

Resistance by Churches and Religious People

There were many Hutu church members who were against killing Tutsis. They organized some of their congregation and hid as many Tutsis as they could, or made every effort to help the Tutsis flee. One of the students who survived the genocide clearly shows the role these Christians played. Student R1512X wrote in Kinyarwanda which translates as follows, "…the following morning, some of the men who used to pray at the parish my father headed held a meeting and agreed to give us refuge yet they were Hutus. That is when my sister and I went and hid at Habineza Wellers' home that was in Nyagihamba in Commune Musambira."[5]

Resistance by Hutu and Tutsi Who Were Persecuted

In some of the communes, Hutus and Tutsis organized themselves and fought *Interahamwe*. It is evident that in some localities, the push to kill Tutsis was being done by people who were not from those localities. Had there not been these external forces, there is a likelihood that some areas would have witnessed less killing. R15-00046, a female student from Commune Mugina, shows how gangs came and attacked her village and how Hutus and Tutsis in her neighborhood fought the attackers. She says,

> …all those people had sought refuge in the church near our home. About two days after fleeing to take refuge at the church, getting to the

church, the killer group called *Interahamwe* attacked the church to kill us. Whenever the gang came to attack, we would organize ourselves and fight the gangs. Men on our side used spears, clubs, and machetes while us children fought the gang using stones. We were at times lucky to repulse the gangs. Whenever we repulsed the killer gang, it would go and rearm itself and attack us with grenades and they managed to kill some of our people. Later, a killer gang called *Simusiga* that was mainly comprised of Burundian refugees and hardcore *Interahamwe* came and attacked us.

Resistance and Dissent by School Administrators

Despite the fact that the genocide started when schools were on vacation, a few teachers played a role in protecting students who were in their custody. R15-0043 was a male student from Commune Masango who narrates how his school's principal, who was a Hutu, managed to save more than 35 Tutsis. He narrates:

> The army sergeant kept on telling the school's director that, "Director, really? You had hidden all these thirty-five Tutsis yet Tutsis are the ones who killed Habyarimana. Are you not the one who admitted them to study in this school? Now you have hidden all these Tutsi snakes." The Director asked for forgiveness but the soldiers refused to forgive him. We also asked the soldiers for forgiveness but all in vain. When they heard that the major in the army was coming, they told us to go away but promised to come back and deal with us. By then it was already noon and some of the Hutu students said, "let us go have lunch and leave those snakes [referring to Tutsi students] alone." After finishing eating they said, "What had taken place had nothing to do with us [Hutu]." By then we were so scared because we knew that the soldiers were going to come back and take us to be killed. After the soldiers left, our school Director returned and told us that those soldiers were the army major's bodyguards and they had tried to coerce the Director to bribe them with money. Afterwards, the Director told us to go and have our lunch but we refused to go.

Resistance and Dissent by Community

R15-00080, a male student from Commune Mugina, says, "A day after Habyarimana died is when villagers from Cyeru came and attacked Kiyonza and they were carrying guns and other weapons. When the attackers started killing people, all the people (Hutus, Tutsi, and Twa) in Kiyonza worked as one team and fought back the attackers. Later, when Hutus from Kiyonza became aware of the attackers' main motive, they stopped fighting the attackers and said that they were not going to die with Tutsis because of something that was an issue affecting Tutsis only. Some of the people (Hutu) from Kiyonza who had helped fight the attackers, later on became the people who started killing our people (Tutsi)."

Resistance and Dissent by Being Hidden by Neighbors and Good Samaritans

R15-89x, a male student from Commune Masango, talks of how he survived:

> ...at the time that I was hiding at the traditional medicine man's home whose name was Siriro, I informed them that two of my sisters were hiding at our neighbor's home in Buhanda while another sister was hiding in the home of an old lady called Nyamurundi. I was not at Siriro's home for long before a man called Viyatori came to visit. Viyatori's home was in a place called Saruheshyi in Commune Mukingi and what brought this man to visit this medicine man was because his wife was pregnant. It was not Viyatori's first time to visit Siriro's home and the two knew each other and were friends. Siriro then told Viyatori, "my dear, do me a favor and go and hide that child for me because the father is in Kigali and it is possible that he may even have been killed."

Resistance and Dissent by Friends and Relatives

R15-87XX, a female student from Commune Mugina, narrates,

> When we arrived at the home that they [some refugees] were hiding in, the owners of that home told us that we were too many and they could not give us refuge. It is then that the owners of the home requested another home to hide me where I spent one night before leaving in the morning to go to my older sister's home. She was married to a Hutu man and I only slept in her home for one night because killer gangs kept coming to that home so that they could take her away to be killed.

Bribing to Survive

Some students survived because they either bribed those attacking or the people whose homes they were hiding in managed to bribe the attackers. In some instances, people paid as much as 45,000FRW ($315), and in other instances, they gave attackers property they had. Student R15-80XZ says the following:

> ...they hid me and after a couple of days, the killer gang came and rounded us up and took us to the pit where they were killing people and dumping the bodies. When we reached the pit, the person at whose home I was hiding came and gave the killers some money so that they could release me. I returned to that person's home and within no time

the gang came and picked me up and loaded me in a vehicle together with people whom they were going to drown in river Nyabarongo. People in the home that I was hiding in came again and paid my captors some money so that they could release me. On being freed, the people from the home that had given me refuge took me and went and hid me somewhere in Kavumu near Nyanza ...

Intervention/Support Provided to Children from Gitarama Prefecture Who Survived the Genocide

Many institutions put in place programs to child survivors. One method of support included paying school fees for these children to enable them to continue with their education. The government put in place programs such as *Fonds d'Assistance aux Rescapés du Génocide* (FARG) to support these children by paying their tuition.

In some of the testimonies, the children acknowledge that had it not been for this fund, they could not have attended school. This would have had a myriad of negative effects in life. Female student R15-0009 said "*...ntaza kubona ikigega nari kwichwa na gahinda kenshi*," which means, "...Had I not been supported by a fund that is paying for my schooling, I could have been devastated with sorrow." This student also says that she does not want to be alone; she wants to be with other children she can talk to. Research has shown that it is important for schools to meet the behavioral and emotional needs of students, and that meeting these needs is critical in the student's healing process (Little & Akin-Little, 2011). In the case of children from communes Masango, Mugina, Bulinga, and Kayenzi, none of the students talk of having received any intervention from the schools that they attended. It seems that the schools that these students attended most likely did not have any psychological trauma intervention mechanisms in place.

A female student, R15-00055, believes that time heals. "*Ubwo ariko ibibazo byagiye bigabanuka ndakokemeza ndiga mbona ndatsinze*," which means, "... and that is how the challenges and problems that I was facing kept on reducing, and I continued with my schooling and eventually performed well."

Most of the children from Gitarama prefecture who survived the genocide received little to no psychological support from their school to assist with the recovery process. Since issues dealing with the 1994 genocide were rarely discussed in schools, it is reasonable to argue that teachers may have been afraid of talking about the genocide. It is only in acute traumatic cases that teachers intervened. Unfortunately, immediately after the 1994 Rwanda genocide, most of the teachers in schools were not trained and had no education on managing students who were traumatized (Obura, 2003). In 2006, IBUKA employed a few high-school graduates who received one year of training in counseling from *Association Rwandaise* (Denborough & Mukamana, 2020). By 2012, IBUKA had laid off all its professional mental health counselors due to financial constraints. The one who remained could not handle all the survivors needing psychological help and the situation was worse in the communes. There had been disagreements between the *Commission Nationale Lutte Contre le Genocide* (CNLG), which is the National Commission for the Fight Against Genocide, and the department of Psychosocial Consultation Center in Rwanda's Ministry of Health over how traumatized genocide survivors should be cared for, with each organization accusing the other of failing to support traumatized survivors, particularly during the genocide commemoration period in the month of April (Musoni, 2012). Unfortunately, a National Mental Policy had only been in place since 2010 (Republic of Rwanda Ministry of Health, 2010). Decades later, Rwanda still did not have sufficient qualified professional mental health counselors although positive strides have been made to increase the number of mental health professionals. As of 2020, Rwanda had 13 psychiatrists (Devex, 2021). In 2019, it was reported that there were also 381 psychiatric nurses and 599 trained clinical psychologists (Kalisa et al., 2019).

Social support is critical in reducing the severity of trauma (Wang et al., 2021). The communal culture in Rwanda and close-knit family structures have been pillars in reducing impact of trauma among genocide survivors (King, 2019). Narrative therapy is now being trailed with some genocide survivors to try to validate their pain and to encourage healing (Uwihoreye, 2021). Other current approaches that are being employed in Rwanda in order to understand serious issues arising from living through conflict or genocide include the art-based approaches (Denov & Shevell, 2021). Effort to mitigate trauma among Rwandan genocide survivors is very noble. However, immediately after the genocide, survivors were required to live with perpetrators in the same neighborhood to encourage reconciliation, which was a long-term government policy. Reconciliation is a process and does not simply happen because people have been forced to live together by the state (Prieto-Ursúa et al., 2019). Despite reconciliation efforts, trauma still lingered among survivors.

Conclusion

Testimonies of child survivors from Gitarama prefecture are sufficient evidence that the voices of children also need to be heard and be taken seriously. Children can contribute detailed accounts of what transpired during the genocide including resistance and traumatic events. As a whole, these testimonies provide a very unique perspective to the genocide because they tend to speak about what transpired at very specific locations within the communes in Gitarama. Voices of child survivors were notably absent during the *gacaca* court proceedings. These testimonies ought to have been used as evidence during *gacaca* court hearing across Gitarama prefecture because children also need justice yet their testimonies were never used.

The history of genocide in Rwanda through lived experiences of child survivors from Gitarama prefecture and across the nation therefore needs more in-depth analysis. Unfortunately, scholarship on genocide in Rwanda has paid little attention to voices of child survivors, atrocities that were committed against children, in addition to how ordinary Tutsis in Gitarama prefecture resisted and fought back against attackers during the genocide. Other aspects including the role of school administrators in resisting perpetrators and protecting Tutsi students need more research.[6]

Many child survivors of Gitarama prefecture were traumatized. In human beings, trauma can have lingering effects and therefore must be taken seriously in order to improve people's lives and the need to continue rebuilding the country after a genocide. However, only a handful of students indicate in their written testimonies that there were interventions that had been put in place to help them overcome the trauma during and after the genocide. There were many other students who did not write about being traumatized in their testimonies, though this should not be construed to mean they were not showing symptoms. Rather, this may be attributed to the fact that Rwanda is a very oral society, and these students may not have felt comfortable expressing themselves with the written word. Additionally, the children were not directed to specifically talk about traumatic experiences.

The provision of psychosocial support for children in postconflict situations must be given utmost priority to reduce the impact that trauma has on child survivors and their offspring. The children who wrote these testimonies are now adults with families of their own. A longitudinal study needs to be done to find out how trauma evidenced in their testimonies continues to manifest in their adulthood. The types of mechanisms that these children have used to cope with trauma through the years also need to be investigated. The challenges that students faced during the genocide were immense, and it is unfortunate that many survivors ended up facing a host of other problems long after the genocidal killing came to an end. In this chapter, I have argued that children's experiences and voices must be included in analyses of genocide. Collecting and digitizing these testimonies play a role in amplifying these voices, thereby preserving the experiences of children who survived the genocide in Rwanda so that people have a better understanding of what happened to the children, during and immediately after the genocide. The clear evidence of trauma and unique accounts of resistance support the claim that children's stories are significant and must be taken into account – both to understand the genocide and to mitigate the dangerous effects trauma could have on the future of individuals and the country.

Notes

1 This archive was established by the Shoah Foundation and has more than 55,000 oral histories mainly of Holocaust survivors. Recently, oral histories from other genocides have started being incorporated in this digital archive.

2 These stories were recorded in the testimonies we collected, but are also mentioned in Chapter 2 of this volume which recounts survivor experiences during the genocide.
3 In 1994, Rwanda was divided into eleven regional administrative units called prefectures, and this number increased to twelve in 1996. In 2002, prefectures were renamed provinces, and in 2006, the provinces were reorganized into major five administrative regions/provinces.
4 Codes have been used to represent actual names of children who wrote the testimonies discussed in this chapter due to the sensitive nature of the testimonies.
5 All testimonies used in this chapter were originally written in Kinyarwanda. Quotations in English that have been used in this chapter were translated from Kinyarwanda to English by Musa Wakhungu Olaka. Quotes in English without accompanying Kinyarwanda text were used to reduce bulkiness of the chapter.
6 Avenging the genocide seemed absent in these children's testimonies. Maybe the children could not document the need for revenge because by the time the testimonies were being written, the Rwanda government was strongly advocating for reconciliation, and most Rwandans rarely go against government policy.

Bibliography

Arata, C. M., Langhinrichsen-Rohling, J., Bowers, D., & O'Farrill-Swails, L. (2005). Single versus multi-type maltreatment: An examination of the long-term effects of child abuse. *Journal of Aggression, Maltreatment & Trauma*, *11*(4), 29–52. https://doi.org/10.1300/J146v11n04_02

Bagilishya, D. (2003). Mourning and recovery from trauma: In Rwanda, tears flow within. *Transcultural Psychiatry*, *37*(3), 337–353.

Berckmoes, L. H., Eichelsheim, V., Rutayisire, T., Richters, A., & Hola, B. (2017). How legacies of genocide are transmitted in the family environment: A qualitative study of two generations in Rwanda. *Societies*, *7*(3, 24). 10.3390/soc7030024

Carney, J. J. (2011). *From Democratization to Ethnic Revolution: Catholic Politics in Rwanda, 1950–1962*. [Unpublished doctoral dissertation]: The Catholic University of America.

Cohen, B. (2007). The children's voice: Postwar collection of testimonies from child survivors of the Holocaust. *Holocaust and Genocide Studies*, *21*(1), 73–95.

Denborough, D., & Mukamana, A. (2020). Survivors supporting survivors: Recalling the history of the Ibuka counselling team. *International Journal of Narrative Therapy & Community Work*, (2), 1–7.

Denov, M., & Shevell, M. C. (2021). An arts-based approach with youth born of genocidal rape in Rwanda: The river of life as an autobiographical mapping tool. *Global Studies of Childhood*, *11*(1), 21–39. 10.1177/2043610621995830

Devex. (2021, December 25). *How Rwanda is spearheading efforts to tackle mental health*. Retrieved from https://devex.shorthandstories.com/how-rwanda-is-spearheading-efforts-to-tackle-mental-health/index.html

Dumas, H. (2019). When children remember: A history of the Tutsi genocide through the eyes of children (1994–2006). *International Review of the Red Cross*, *101*(1), 37–57. 10.1017/S1816383119000171

Figley, C. R. (2012). Childhood and adolescent trauma: An overview. In *Encyclopedia of trauma: An interdisciplinary guide*. Sage.

Hatzfeld, J. (2006). *Machete season: The killers in Rwanda speak*. Farrar, Straus and Giroux.

Hodges, M., Godbout, N., Briere, J., Lanktree, C., Gilbert, A., & Kletzka, N. T. (2013). Cumulative trauma and symptom complexity in children: A path analysis. *Child Abuse & Neglect*, *37*(11), 891–898. http://dx.doi.org/10.1016/j.chiabu.2013.04.001

IBUKA a.s.b.l (n.d). *Itsembabwoko ryo mu w'1994; Imurika ku itsembabwoko*. IBUKA.

Kalisa, J., Schäfer, I., Püschel, K., Mutesa, L., & Sezibera, V. (2019). Fostering the training of professionals to treat trauma and PTSD in Rwanda: A call for structured training curriculum. *Rwanda Public Health Bulletin*, *1*(2).

Kaplan, S. (2013). Child survivors of the 1994 Rwandan genocide and trauma-related affect. *Journal of Social Issues*, *69*(1), 92–110. https://doi.org/10.1111/josi.12005

King, R. U. (2019). The true healing is healing together: Healing and rebuilding social relations in postgenocide Rwanda. *Peace and Conflict: Journal of Peace Psychology*, *25*(1), 49–60. http://dx.doi.org.pvamu.idm.oclc.org/10.1037/pac0000357

Leese, P., Crouthamel, J., & Köhne, J. B. (2021). *Languages of trauma: History, memory, and media*. University of Toronto Press.

Little, S. G., & Akin-Little, A. (2011). Responses to childhood trauma: An international perspective. *School Psychology International*, *32*(5), 441–447. https://doi.org/10.1177/0143034311402915

Mamdani, M. (2020). *When victims become killers: Colonialism, nativism, and the genocide in Rwanda*. Princeton University Press.

Mugesera, A. (2014). *The persecution of Rwandan Tutsi before the 1990-1994 genocide*. Dialogue Editions.

Mukandayisenga, M. R. (2011, April 13). *Igihe*. Retrieved December 27, 2021, from Ese abantu babona bate ihagarikwa ryo kwerekana filimi za jenoside mu ruhame?: http://www.igihe.wikirwanda.org/cache/news-15-53-11940-1html

Musanabaganwa, C., Jansen, S., Fatumo, S., Rutembesa, E., Mutabaruka, J., Gishoma, D., Uwineza, A., Kayiteshonga, Y., Alachkar, A., Wildman, D., Uddin, M., Mutesa, M. (2020). Burden of post-traumatic stress disorder in postgenocide Rwandan population following exposure to 1994 genocide against the Tutsi: A meta-analysis. *Journal of Affective Disorders*, *275*(1), 7–13. 10.1016/j.jad.2020.06.017

Musoni, E. (2012, February 4). CNLG, MoH Differ Over Handling of Trauma Cases. *New Times Rwanda*. Retrieved June 30, 2021, from https://www.newtimes.co.rw/section/read/49039

Neugebauer, R., Forde, A., Fodor, K. E., Fisher, P. W., Turner, J. B., Stehling-Ariza, T., & Yamabe, S. (2018). Are children or adolescents more at risk for post-traumatic stress reactions? *The Journal of Nervous and Mental Disease*, *26*(1), 11–18.

Obura, A. (2003). *Never again: Education reconstruction in Rwanda*. UNESCO Institute for Educational Planning.

Prieto-Ursúa, M., Ordóñez, Á, & Dushimimana, F. (2019). How can it be possible? Psychological processes of reconciliation after the genocide in Rwanda. *Papeles Del Psicólogo/Psychologist Papers*, *40*(1), 57–63.

Punamäki, R.-L., Muhammed, A. H., & Abdulrahman, H. A. (2004). Impact of traumatic events on coping strategies and their effectiveness among Kurdish children. *International Journal of Behavioral Development*, *28*(1), 59–70. https://doi.org/10.1080/01650250344000271

Republic of Rwanda Ministry of Health (2010). *National mental health policy in Rwanda*. Ministry of Health.

Repubulika Y'U Rwanda Perezidansi ya Repubulika. (1999). *Ubumwe bw'abanyarwanda: Mbere y'abazungu n'igihe cy'ubukoloni; Mu gihe cya repubulika ya mbere*. Kigali: [Unpublished report].

Richards, H. K., Baele, S. J., & Coan, T. G. (2019). Studying "radio machete": Towards a robust research programme. *Journal of Genocide Research*, *21*(4), 525–539. 10.1080/14623528.2019.1652017

Schotsman, M. (2000). *A l'ecoute des rescapes: Recherche sur la perception par les rescapés de leur situation actuelle*. GTZ.

Shenker, N. (2016). The Holocaust as a paradigm for documenting genocide testimonies. *History & Memory*, *28*(1), 141–175.

Sinalo, C. W., Irakoze, P. C., & Veale, A. (2020, October 15). Disclosure of genocide experiences in Rwandan families: Private and public sources of information and child outcomes. *Peace and Conflict: Journal of Peace Psychology*. 10.1037/pac0000521

Suarez, E. B. (2016). Trauma in global contexts: Integrating local practices and socio-cultural meanings into new explanatory frameworks of trauma. *International Social Work*, *59*(1), 141–153. 10.1177/0020872813503859

Thompson, A. (2019). *Media and mass atrocity: The Rwanda genocide and beyond*. CIGI.

Thomson, S. (2018). *Rwanda: From genocide to precarious peace*. Yale University Press.

Tissot, R. (2020). Beyond the "numbers game": Reassessing human losses in Rwanda during the 1990s. *Journal of Genocide Research*, *22*(1), 116–124. 10.1080/14623528.2019.1703250

University of South Florida Libraries. (2021). *Rwanda Youth and Children's Testimonies*. Retrieved 07 01, 2021, from http://genocide.lib.usf.edu/rwandanchildrenstestimonies

Uwihoreye, C. (2021). I will keep your secret: Ijoro ribara uwariraye Kandi ntamvura idahita - from psychological suffering to recovery in Rwanda. *International Journal of Narrative Therapy & Community Work*, *1*, 10–59.

van der Hart, O., & Steele, K. (1999). Relieving or reliving childhood trauma? A commentary on Miltenburg and Singer (1997). *Theory & Psychology*, *9*(4), 533–540. https://doi.org/10.1177/0959354399094005

Viebach, J. (2019). Of other times: Temporality, memory and trauma in post-genocide Rwanda. *International Review of Victimology*, *25*(3). https://doi.org/10.1177/0269758019833281

Wang, Y., Cheung, M., Wang, N., Yu, X., & Kenardy, J. (2021). Social support and posttraumatic stress disorder: A meta-analysis of longitudinal studies. *Clinical Psychology Review*, *85*. 10.1016/j.cpr.2021.101998

Weathers, F. W., & Keane, T. M. (2007). The criterion a problem revisited: Controversies and challenges in defining and measuring psychological trauma. *Journal of Traumatic Stress*, *20*(2), 107–121. 10.1002/jts.20210.

White, K. R. (2009). Scourge of racism genocide in Rwanda. *Journal of Black Studies*, *39*(3), 471–481. doi: 10.1177/0021934706297877.

Part II

Justice and Society

5 Justice and Transformation within Rwanda

Joseph Ryarasa Nkurunziza

Introduction

After the tragedy of the 1994 Genocide against the Tutsi in Rwanda devastated the country, the government of Rwanda immediately recognized the need for massive reconstruction efforts. The government focused on rebuilding the country's economy, infrastructure, education and healthcare systems, and establishing provisions to meet the basic needs of all Rwandans. Also pertinent to the reconstruction efforts of the government was the question of how Rwandans would confront the tragedy and move forward to repair the social fabric and promote socio-economic development (Kimonyo, 2019).

The achievement of stability and peace depends on how well a society deals with its past (Sarkin, 2001). In post-conflict societies, one critical question governments face is how to handle those accused of human rights violations. Within Rwanda, a variety of methods are employed to bring perpetrators to justice and to promote unity, reconciliation, and preservation of memory. A new state had to be founded on a commitment to respect human rights and a dedication to the rule of law, but also had to take into account the trauma experienced by the country and inherent challenges in bringing about reconciliation and unity between parties when the memories of the genocide were still very fresh. However, sometimes the aims of achieving national reconciliation, building unity, and reconstructing necessary institutions are in conflict with conventional understandings of justice (Sarkin, 2001).

Pursuant to the latter, criminal prosecutions involve trials for those considered most responsible for mass human rights abuses, such as people in positions of power who instigated, planned, and led human rights abuses among the greater population (Wolfe, 2014). Truth commissions are designed to document and analyze the abuses that occurred, with the aim of learning from them and making recommendations to prevent future violations of human rights (Hayner, 2011). Reparations initiatives are geared toward repairing the damage caused by human rights abuses (de Greiff, 2006). For instance, rebuilding a victim's house that was destroyed and

DOI: 10.4324/9781003228592-7

offering a genuine and official apology for the trauma incurred by victims address both the monetary and emotional damage caused by abuse. Such initiatives are overseen and led by governments to ensure that the wrongs of the past are addressed so that citizens can move forward (Posner & Vermeule, 2003). Security system reforms involve re-establishing institutions – such as police and military forces, which may have formerly been responsible for systematic murders and other abuses – designed to protect citizens in an atmosphere of genuine trust (Teitel, 2000). Finally, memorialization efforts are initiatives put into place to ensure societal memory of the abuses that occurred during the period of conflict with the goal of preventing such acts from happening in the future. Memorialization efforts are seen as "mechanisms to restore the dignity of victims and survivors, including exhumations, tombstones, memorials and monuments and the renaming of streets and public facilities" (Naidu, 2004, p. 2). Although all those forms of reparations are relevant, this chapter focuses on a particular form of transitional justice applied in Rwanda after the 1994 Genocide against the Tutsi, namely, the *gacaca* courts.

Transitional justice is an adapted form of justice that focuses on the promotion of conditions for peace, reconciliation, and democracy in societies recovering from genocide, ethnic cleansing, and other human rights abuses (ICTJ, n.d.). Teitel (2003) defines it as "the conception of justice associated with periods of political change, characterized by legal responses to confront wrongdoing of repressive predecessor regimes" (p. 69). Transitional justice involves a series of complementary procedures that address the various or widespread complexities of restoring peace, stability, and healing in post-conflict societies. Transitional justice procedures often include criminal prosecutions, truth commissions, reparations initiatives, security system reforms, and memorialization efforts (Teitel, 2003; for a comprehensive understanding of the concept of transitional justice in general see Girelli, 2017; Lawther, et al., 2019; O'Donnell & Schmitter, 1986; Teitel, 2000).

In this chapter, I argue that peace and justice are inextricably interlinked. While justice often refers to a punishment for the offending party for a given crime, peace is defined as a "long-term condition that must be facilitated for the future" (Clark, 2009, p. 191). For survivors of genocide, threats of continued violence and societal instability undermine the justice process, as well as the healing and reconciliation processes. Therefore, in order to achieve transitional justice and reconciliation in post-genocide Rwanda, it is necessary to not only employ successful justice mechanisms but also mechanisms which will aid in the establishment of peace. In this regard, it is necessary to not only analyze the effectiveness of the instruments of justice within Rwanda, but also examine efforts to safeguard peace in society.

This chapter begins by exploring the ways Rwanda sought to bring those guilty of genocide to justice by looking at the strengths and weaknesses of international and domestic methods of transitional justice, including the International Criminal Tribunal for Rwanda, national courts, and a traditional system called *gacaca*. It then discusses the important role of civil society organizations (CSOs) in the nation's recovery by highlighting the peacebuilding, human rights, and reconciliation work of one CSO, Never Again Rwanda (NAR).

Justice and Reconciliation in Rwanda: A Nation on Trial

Because the 1994 Genocide against the Tutsi resulted in such an astonishingly large number of lost lives – not to mention mutilations, theft, and destruction – Rwanda was left with hundreds of thousands of accused (Clark, 2009). The post-conflict government faced massive challenges in deciding how to deal with such a large number of accused persons, how to deliver justice to an even greater number of traumatized victims, and how to promote reconciliation between perpetrators and victims. Three main mechanisms of justice were utilized: the International Criminal Tribunal for Rwanda, the national courts system, and *gacaca* courts.

The International Criminal Tribunal for Rwanda

The objective of the International Criminal Tribunal for Rwanda (commonly known as the ICTR) is summarized in its full title assigned by United Nations (UN) Security Council Resolution 955 (1994): *International Criminal Tribunal for the Prosecution of Persons Responsible for Genocide and Other Serious Violations of International Humanitarian Law Committed in the Territory of Rwanda and Rwandan citizens responsible for genocide and other such violations committed in the territory of neighboring States, between 1 January 1994 and 31 December 1994*. Many question whether the court has achieved this elaborate goal. This section will examine the effectiveness of the ICTR within the context of the goals of the aforementioned transitional justice model.

The UN established the ICTR in Arusha, Tanzania, in 1995, with the mandate to prosecute those responsible for genocide as well as grave and serious violations of international humanitarian law committed in Rwanda (Corey & Joireman, 2004). The first trial – of Jean Paul Akayesu, the former mayor of Taba in Rwanda's Southern Province – began on January 9, 1997.

Over the lifetime of the tribunal, some positive outcomes were achieved, notably, the ICTR's contribution to the development of international law. For the first time in history, a conviction for genocide was arbitrated by an international tribunal, with Jean Paul Akayesu being the first person to be found guilty of the crime. The ICTR was also the first international tribunal to hold members of the media responsible for inciting acts of genocide through broadcasting. In addition, the ICTR was the first forum to recognize rape as a means of perpetrating genocide. The ICTR boasts indicting 93 "high-ranking military and government officials, politicians, businessmen, as well as religious, militia, and media leaders" and sentencing 63 of them throughout the tribunal's twelve years of activity (International Criminal Tribunal for Rwanda, n.d.). This, however, is only a fraction of the full number of people involved in the extermination of nearly 1 million people.

Although the tribunal was a landmark for international law, it has received extensive criticism. Peter Uvin and Charles Mironko (2003) argue that the court served only to appease the international community's morality by trying to make amends for its failure to intervene in the 1994 genocide. In *Western and Local Approaches to Justice in Rwanda* they write:

> The ICTR is not a form of deterrence … nor does it impact on dynamics of reconciliation or lighten the burden on the Rwandan justice system. Rather, it is about symbolic politics; we, the international community, *do* care about Rwanda, *are* outraged by it, and solemnly pledge to show our disapproval. This move was necessary in the light of the total inaction of that same community during the genocide, which was widely perceived as shameful
>
> (p. 220).

Jean-Marie Kamatali (2006) argued, rightly, that "the ICTR has invested very little in bringing justice and reconciliation to Rwandans" (p. 102) and that, in order to deter future crimes, international tribunals should be held in the country where humanitarian crimes occurred. Indeed, the court's initial weakness came with the decision to establish a tribunal in Arusha, Tanzania, outside of Rwanda and far from victims of the genocide. The UN Secretary General, Boutros Boutros-Ghali, supported this choice and stressed the importance of ensuring that "not only the reality but also the appearance of complete impartiality and objectivity in the prosecution of persons responsible for crimes committed by both sides" (United Nations Security Council, 1995, p. 10). While the decision was based on a principle that assumed that "some degree of distance from the events in question strengthened the perception of impartiality of the work of the international tribunal" (Moghalu, 2002, footnote 16), it failed to recognize that this strategy would also distance the tribunal from the very people who had been victimized by the events in 1994, and would deny them access to the trials and the closure the trials could potentially bring. This distance created a barrier in the healing process for those whose rights were so outrageously violated. "Denying victims such rights by the ICTR is not only a justice delayed, but also a justice denied," writes Kamatali (2006, p. 96).

The victims and the Rwandan community as a whole were overlooked, or worse, considered but ultimately ignored, in this process. The activities of the ICTR were foreign to Rwandans, not only with regard to the location where the tribunals were held, but also in practice. Bernard Muna (2004) stated that "the ICTR remained foreign to Rwanda and the Rwandan people, the very society it was designed to help."

Thus, disconnected from the Rwandan people, it was very difficult for the ICTR to respond to the expectations of Rwandans and to initiate reconciliation within society. Reconciliation refers to a "pragmatic way to deal with profound changes involving past injustices in order to achieve some other desired purposes such as building peace, nurturing democracy, promoting human rights and delivering justice, among others" (Sinh Nguyen Vo, 2008, para. 4). Without a sense among the Rwandan population that some level of justice had been delivered, how could they possibly move on in their recovery as a nation?

National Courts and Other Mechanisms

The Rwandan national courts also played a role in prosecuting those accused of the crime of genocide. Rwanda's national judicial system had been completely destroyed due to the genocide and had to be rebuilt from the ground up. Compounding this challenge, the national courts were also attempting to deal with thousands of genocide charges and other genocide-related cases. The government of Rwanda, with the assistance of international donors, went to extensive and novel lengths to restructure and rebuild an independent judiciary to fight impunity and to train judges, lawyers, investigators, and police. By 1996, it was estimated that 841 judges and 210 prosecutors had been trained (Brehm et al., 2014).

By 1998, after two years of trials carried out in the national court, Rwanda still faced massive justice challenges. With an estimated 120,000 people imprisoned and awaiting trial, the courts had only been able to handle 1,292 cases – just under 650 cases per year (National Service of Gacaca Courts, 2012). This is not because of slow rate of conviction, but rather because the national courts were simply not equipped to deliver justice on such a large scale. At the rate the courts were going in 1998, it would have taken nearly two hundred years to try all 120,000 accused (Corey & Joireman, 2004). Even as the courts doubled their productivity – completing an average of a little more than 1,000 cases per year by 2002 (National Service of Gacaca Courts, 2012) – justice would have taken over hundred years to be delivered through the conventional system. This would simply be infeasible, not to mention unjust. Furthermore, the estimated number of accused did not include the many perpetrators who were still roaming free, which would later be discovered through the *gacaca* proceedings.

In 1999, the government of Rwanda established a National Unity and Reconciliation Commission. Pursuant to Article 178 of the Constitution of the Republic of Rwanda, and law No 35/2008 of 08 August, the Commission had eight objectives which included: "to educate, sensitize and mobilize the population in areas of national unity and reconciliation;" and "to denounce and fight actions, publications, and utterances that promote any kind of division and discrimination, intolerance, and xenophobia" Through this commission, the government of Rwanda sought to educate the entire population on the importance of peace, unity, and reconciliation.[1]

By 2002, it was clear that the conventional justice mechanisms could only do so much. Having tried 7,181 cases by that time, and with around 120,000 accused still detained (Human Rights Watch, 2008, 2014), something needed to be done, not only to speed up the process, but to help heal Rwandan society, which was still profoundly wounded by the atrocities of 1994.

Gacaca Courts

After the ICTR and the efforts of the national courts, there were still hundreds of thousands of prisoners waiting for their cases to be heard. The rate at which the ICTR and the conventional courts were processing cases was far too slow to deal with the extremely large number of accused in a reasonable amount of time. To respond to that challenge, the government of Rwanda began planning for the transition of judicial responsibilities from the national courts to the traditionally based *gacaca* model. While a pilot phase of the trials commenced in June 2002, the government officially established the *gacaca* courts in March 2005 (Brehm et al., 2014, p. 336). More than 12,000 community courts were created across the country to begin to deal with the aftermath of 1994 swiftly, efficiently, and fairly, all the while respecting Rwanda's culture and traditions (Ingelaere, 2008).

The *gacaca* courts are an adaptation of a traditional and local mechanism for conflict resolution in Rwanda that predated the colonial period in the country. *Gacaca* translates to "an open, grassy area" in Kinyarwanda. Before the 1994 genocide, *gacaca* were typically outdoor spaces where community members would gather before elected judges, who were usually elders, respected and recognized in their communities as having high moral standards. The entire community would participate in the process of resolving minor judicial cases. Traditionally, *gacaca* was designed to encourage reconciliation and forgiveness between the person who committed an offence and the victim who was hurt by the crime. The best outcome of traditional *gacaca* proceedings would involve a confession by the perpetrator of the crime, who would give a description of the wrongs they committed, convince the community that they were truly sorry for their actions, and ask for forgiveness for their crime. The guilty party would compensate the victim to make amends for the crime (such as replacing a stolen item, offering a service to make up for the harm caused) and provide the community members at the *gacaca* with food and drink as a symbol of reconciliation and renewed peace (Vandeginst, 1999).

The *gacaca* system, which was used to handle an enormous number of cases in Rwanda, is unique compared to conventional justice mechanisms in the way that it involves entire communities or, in this case, the entire society. The courts not only had the aim of delivering the appropriate punishment to criminals, they also obligated everyone affected by the offence to participate in the process of restoring peace. In this way, the *gacaca* courts took an inclusive approach to transitional justice: since Rwanda's entire population was affected by the genocide, the entire population was included in the judicial process that followed. In 2001, some 250,000 lay judges, the majority of Hutu (Clark, 2012) were elected by the people in their respective communities and trained to carry out the judicial proceedings in accordance with Rwandan law.

During the preparations for the *gacaca* trials, some deliberate decisions were made, most notably that no lawyers would be routinely involved in the trials. This was done for two reasons. The first was simply to deal with a logistical issue. After the genocide, the judicial system had been decimated and there were simply not enough professional judges and lawyers in the country to handle the hundreds of thousands accused who were waiting to be tried (Clark, 2012). Second, there was "a widespread fear that lawyers would distort the process by dominating hearings and intimidating participants" (Clark, 2012, p. 4). Indeed, the process provided an open forum where survivors were surrounded by community members in a location that was familiar and therefore comfortable to them, giving them a safe space where they could express their pain, be heard and have their feelings validated – not only by perpetrators, but also by their community at large – and could begin the long transition from trauma to healing.

The *gacaca* courts were seen as legitimate by Rwandan citizens because of their democratic nature (through the election of judges), and their familiarity as a method of justice linked to Rwandan tradition. After a perpetrator confessed to a crime, witnesses in the community would come forward to either corroborate or contest the version of events. In this way, the *gacaca* courts, by their nature, put a strong and deliberate emphasis on revealing the truth about exactly what happened during the genocide, incorporating one of the aforementioned components of transitional justice. The process "promoted reconciliation by allowing victims to learn the truth about the death of their relatives, and by giving the opportunity for the guilty to confess their crimes, to declare their remorse and to ask for forgiveness from the community" (National Service of Gacaca Courts, 2012).

The *gacaca* courts were a path chosen by the government of Rwanda to ensure not only that justice and peace could be realized but, more importantly, that the nation was engaged in its own rehabilitation and healing. Through the *gacaca* proceedings, it was not just a matter of accused *génocidaires* appearing before the courts to be judged and punished in the event of a guilty verdict. It was about delivering truth to the survivors of the genocide in a public forum. It was about bringing a sense of closure to those whose relatives disappeared during the genocide, by revealing the location of their loved ones' remains. It was also about rebuilding relationships that seemed broken beyond repair, by offering opportunities for perpetrators to admit to their crimes, to apologize for the pain they had caused, and to set up conditions for forgiveness to take place. The *gacaca* system was a necessary, homegrown solution applied to an extremely daunting task. It was designed by Rwandans, for Rwandans, to provide a foundation upon which the entire nation could start to heal.

Although hearing the truth could often be highly traumatizing to genocide survivors, after some time, many found relief and a sense of peace in knowing what had happened to their friends and relatives and being able to locate them and honor them with a proper funeral and burial – something they otherwise would have been denied. Although the perpetrators could never make up for their crimes, at least there was some solace that came from admissions of wrongdoing, expressions of remorse, acts of disclosing the truth, and efforts to make reparations. Through the process of truth-hearing and truth-telling, Rwandans had to come together as one to discuss the event that ruptured the Rwandan society (Saugman, 2012).

Criticism and Support of the Gacaca Courts

The *gacaca* courts officially completed their term on May 4, 2012. Despite its strengths, the process received extensive criticism from the international community. For instance, Human Rights Watch (2008) criticized the proceedings for the lack of legal representation afforded to defendants who were put on trial in its publication, *Law and Reality: Progress in Judicial Reform in Rwanda*: "The accused had no access to counsel in *gacaca* jurisdictions…although that right is guaranteed by the Rwandan constitution and by the International Convention on Civil and Political Rights to which Rwanda is party" (p. 18).

However, this criticism was uninformed. According to the National Service of Gacaca Courts (2012), the *gacaca* trials did not prevent defendants from seeking a lawyer to represent them and, although it was rare, some did use this option. Rather, lawyers were not given a central role in the proceedings because *gacaca* courts, by nature, function through public participation in accordance with the Rwandan history and culture.

In his book, *Inside Rwanda's Gacaca Courts: Seeking Justice After Genocide*, Bert Ingelaere (2016) points out that the *gacaca* courts failed to fulfill their five goals, and that often the goals were taken as outcomes, preventing scholars from an unbiased view of the courts' accomplishments and failures. Elsewhere, Ingelaere (2008, 2009) argued that the *gacaca* courts, in straying from the traditional practice and moving into a more prosecutorial practice, limited its own effectiveness in reconciling Rwandans and thus became an "invented tradition."

In 2009, IRIN (*Integrated Regional Information Networks*, now *The New Humanitarian*) assessed the strengths and weaknesses of the trials and noted that the *gacaca* courts may have failed to meet the judicial needs of women raped during the genocide. It also noted that because the nature of *gacaca* courts was a public forum of justice, they did not allow for videotaped, private testimony of rape cases – an element that may have deterred rape survivors from coming forward. However, in 2008, the government legislated Organic Law No. 13/2008, which allowed the courts to hold private, confidential hearings to protect the survivors of these acts (IRIN, 2009).

Other scholars (such as Clark, 2010) have argued that while the *gacaca* courts had some drawbacks, they nevertheless achieved remarkable results in terms of peace and justice and should be lauded for their accomplishments in the face of remarkable challenges. Nicola Palmer (2015) argues that given the differing views of the *gacaca* courts, some scholars believed that some testimony offered during the trials were coerced or mandated. However, according to Palmer, this is neither a necessary nor fair interpretation, and to say that different people hold different views is merely to understand the complexities of the *gacaca* process. In addition, the *gacaca* courts allowed each community to determine the truth of their experiences of the genocide and to open a dialogue where before there had been silence.

Although the trials did have some other challenges, such as bribery and corruption – something acknowledged by Rwanda's National Service of Gacaca Courts (Musoni, 2006) – the problem with the criticisms was that many did not take into account the very difficult task of bringing justice to Rwanda faced and the impossibility of resolving these additional issues without significantly delaying the proceedings. The Rwandan government had to balance two competing, but equally important components of justice: providing justice in a reasonable amount of time and providing justice that was fair to survivors and perpetrators. Due to certain inevitable practical challenges, sometimes there had to be tradeoffs.

In the end, over one million suspects were tried on charges related to their involvement in the genocide, due to new accusations that arose during the *gacaca* proceedings. To deal with such a large number of accused, the reconciliatory nature of the *gacaca* provided opportunities for many perpetrators to confess and show genuine remorse to those impacted by the crime. In return, their sentences by the courts would be reduced depending on the severity of their crimes (Musoni, 2006).

Considering the challenges Rwanda faced after the Genocide against the Tutsi, the *gacaca* courts were the only judicial solution that had the ability to process more than one million cases of genocide-related crimes that emerged from the chaos of 1994. In a country that had been ignored in its time of most dire need, Rwanda picked up the pieces and came up with a solution that fit its unique needs in light of a genocide with an unbelievable amount of public participation. While the trials had some imperfections, it should be admitted that the process achieved far more than the ICTR and the national courts in terms of creating cohesion, promoting peacefulness, and aligning with the principles of much-needed transitional justice. The *gacaca* courts were crucial in setting the foundation for reconciliation in Rwanda.

Rwanda's Long Walk to Recovery

In addition to the prosecution of hundreds of thousands of people, Rwanda faced another challenge in terms of the restoration of unity and reconciliation. In the years since the genocide, the government of Rwanda has established a system of stable governance and restored relationships with neighboring and foreign countries as well as the international community. In order to achieve these tasks, the government required, and continues to require, the involvement and support of many stakeholders, including citizens and CSOs. CSOs in Rwanda fulfill a variety of functions, from helping citizens deal with and heal from their memories of atrocities to assisting them with livelihood activities. Their work has been instrumental in helping Rwandans reconcile with each other. This section focuses on how one CSO, NAR, has focused on peacebuilding, governance, and healing in its work in Rwanda and internationally. As a co-founder of NAR, I have been involved in every aspect of its work since its founding in 2002.

Transformation within Rwanda

Today, the positive model of economic development represented by Rwanda is impressive and recognized around the world as an unlikely, but highly welcomed, success story. By 2013, Rwanda was the tenth fastest-growing world economy, and had made great progress toward achieving its Millennium Development Goals (International Monetary Fund, 2013). Rwanda's two five-year Economic Development and Poverty Reduction Strategies implemented from 2008 to 2018 resulted in an average annual growth of 7.2% for its economy and 5% for its gross domestic product (GDP). Rwanda aspires to become a Middle-Income Country by the year 2035; however, has entered its first recession since 1994 due to COVID lockdown and social distancing measures (World Bank, 2021). To achieve its progress toward becoming a Middle-Income Country, Rwanda has adopted various policies leading to economic stability, including an investment in infrastructure, access to health care, and access to education.

However, there are still many areas with room for improvement. While great progress has been made by the government, no government can effectively implement all desired policies without support. The cooperation of partners within the society is required to effectively and efficiently implement policy. This helps ensure that the government's initiatives are realized to their full potential and that they benefit Rwandan society to the greatest extent possible.

Role of Civil Society Organizations in the Reconstruction Process

CSOs in the developing world exist for a number of reasons, including supporting the government, acting as a check and monitor on government activities, and helping to bring about sustainable development (Cross, 2001). CSOs, especially local ones, are well-equipped for this task because they have the required expertise, special insight into the needs of their peers, commitment, and knowledge in various contexts through specialization in their given field of expertise. In addition to being comprised of members of the community, local CSOs have the necessary proximity to the population to ensure sustainability of governmental or nongovernmental projects. As Florea (2005) rightly states, CSOs have become "searchlights, illuminating and drawing attention to particular causes and conflicts and influencing both the participants and the outside world community" (p. 45).

As previously mentioned, the 1994 Genocide against the Tutsi decimated the human capital of Rwanda and the credibility of its institutions. Nongovernmental and civil society organizations now play a key role in the healing process that has led to sustainable peace in Rwanda. Such organizations have made great progress in building governance capacities of relevant institutions in Rwanda and in implementing healing initiatives, such as dialogue clubs in the communities.

Local CSOs in Rwanda have been engaged in the promotion and protection of human rights by strengthening national capacities. Through their promotion of decentralization – a priority of the Rwandan government that is working to give more power to local leaders – CSOs have ensured not only that participatory decision-making processes are available to all Rwandans, but that Rwandans understand how to use these mechanisms (Joint Government Assessment Report). As a result, citizens are better connected with their government and involved in the process of policy-making, and the policies created are designed to most effectively benefit the Rwandan population.

Many local CSOs such as NAR, the Youth Association for Human Rights Promotion and Development, and the *Ligue Rwandaise pour la promotion et le defense des droits de l'Homme* have been concentrating their efforts on human rights, peacebuilding, and reconciliation to ensure sustainable peace, raise citizens' awareness of societal issues, and increase citizens' participation in the decision-making processes.

NAR is a peacebuilding and human rights organization that arose in response to the 1994 Genocide against the Tutsi. "Guided by a vision of a nation where citizens are agents of positive change and work together towards sustainable peace and development," the organization "aims to empower Rwandans with opportunities to become active citizens through peacebuilding and development."[2] NAR places a particular emphasis on youth as the future of a peaceful society. With almost two decades of experience, the organization is one of the leading national peacebuilding organizations in Rwanda. NAR runs four programs, including peacebuilding, governance and human rights, youth engagement, and research and advocacy. Through its peacebuilding program, NAR organizes many activities, including a biannual Peacebuilding Institute. The Institute brings together young Rwandans, international students, and professionals, who are presented with valuable opportunities to reflect on the following question: "What can Rwanda teach the world?" They examine this question while studying the themes of genocide history and prevention; transitional justice, unity, and reconciliation; women, peace, and security; and good governance and peacebuilding.

NAR's governance and human rights program "[engages] youth in decision-making processes within their communities to foster a just and democratic society and to teach young people how to become active citizens. NAR also promotes human rights and empowers youth to act as advocates of their own rights." NAR's research programs underpin the entire organization to ensure that the work NAR does will address real challenges and will make a real difference in the lives and futures of Rwandan citizens.

Never Again Rwanda in Peacebuilding

The NAR peacebuilding program is based on the understanding that the horrors of the genocide in 1994 need to be studied, discussed, and analyzed for sustainable peace and development and to ensure that it never occurs again. Stories of what, how, when, and why the genocide happened, along with examinations of the serious consequences it created, need to be studied and understood by young people and the general citizenry alike.

Youth were specifically targeted and manipulated to kill their fellow Rwandans during the 1994 Genocide against the Tutsi (Barrett, 2019; Hintjens, 1999). They are, likewise, a prime group that should be targeted when it comes to rolling out peacebuilding initiatives. These initiatives include education and skills to resist manipulation by those in positions of power, and to promote peace amongst their peers. Twenty-eight years have passed since the genocide. The majority of the youth today were not yet born when the genocide occurred and therefore did not personally experience the atrocities; hence, the need for education on the effects of hatred and the importance of building peace.

In order to ensure a lasting peace, the youth must be understood and partnered with to help them realize their potential to become key drivers of social change. In order to tap into the potential of youth in promoting a peaceful society, NAR established a Peacebuilding Institute. The Institute strives to empower young people with skills to prevent and overcome violence and ethnic divides as they explore the question, "What can Rwanda teach the world?" The Peacebuilding Institute is a venue for international, regional, and Rwandan youth, usually university students, to discuss the 1994 Genocide against the Tutsi as well as to draw lessons learned from that terrible experience.

Participants explore the topic of genocide history and prevention through visits to historical sites, lectures, and group discussions about the 1994 Genocide against the Tutsi. They learn from Rwanda's experience, the causes of genocide, the warning signs, and how political leaders manipulated the youth into participating in the genocide by convincing them to kill their fellow citizens. Participants are encouraged to read about the genocide, to discuss different perspectives and theories on what factors triggered and caused the genocide, and to reflect on the extremely painful implications of the genocide on the lives of most Rwandan citizens.

After discussing the genocide, participants also explore the topic of transitional justice. They debate on the role of the ICTR, the national courts, and the *gacaca* courts. They do this through meetings with legal experts and Rwandan government officials to hear about how Rwanda handled the aftermath of the genocide. They learn about memorialization efforts, the role of the National Unity and Reconciliation Commission, and the National Commission for the Fight against Genocide from the people who work in these institutions. The students are encouraged to analyze the various elements of transitional justice that were adopted in Rwanda and to share their ideas about the strengths, weaknesses, opportunities, and threats moving forward for Rwandan society. After analyzing Rwanda's experience, they brainstorm and discuss how they might make use of Rwanda's transitional justice mechanisms in other post-conflict societies. In this way, participants actively learn from Rwanda's tragedy and are equipped with the tools that they need to help them deal with violence that may have occurred in other communities, including their own, in order to prevent future abuses and to pave a path for peace.

The Peacebuilding Institute later added a theme on women, peace, and security in order to explore the ways in which women are instrumental in preventing, keeping, and building peace. Through this theme, the students also learn about the formal mechanisms for including women in the peacebuilding process, as well as ways to build gender sensitive programs in peacebuilding in order to create a gender inclusive environment and draw on the strengths of all people in helping to build peace.

The final topic covered in the Peacebuilding Institute is good governance and peacebuilding. The students learn about Rwanda's governance structure and how genocide prevention is built into the legislative structure of the country. They study Rwanda's decentralization efforts and learn about how the country seeks to engage the population so that they can take ownership in the country's reconstruction. They learn about campaigns that seek to re-establish positive ethnic identities (for example, "We are all Rwandan"), rather than perpetuate divisive ideologies. The students are also afforded the valuable opportunity to interact with Rwanda's politicians and to ask them questions about the challenges in governing a country recovering from genocide and to seek their advice on how to build peace in other societies. As with the other themes, the participants engage in debate to analyze the strengths of and challenges to Rwanda's system, and they collectively discuss how reconstruction efforts that have worked in Rwanda might be applied to other societies to promote lasting peace.

The main aim of each Peacebuilding Institute is to help participants become part of a network of smart, young leaders who can effectively reflect together on how to build sustainable peace through a collaborative learning experience. It also aims to equip the students with the skills they require to become peacebuilders in their own communities and to share their understanding of the genocide history, its consequences, and the way that Rwanda has rebuilt with their families, neighbors, colleagues, and fellow students when they return home, so that they too have opportunities to learn from the 1994 genocide and its aftermath.

Ultimately, the Peacebuilding Institute plays the role of a public forum for genuine dialogue on how to deepen engagements that are in support of the total elimination of genocide not only in Rwanda, but throughout the entire world.

Never Again Rwanda in Promoting Human Rights

While the government and Rwandan civil society have made, and continue to make, extensive efforts to raise awareness of human rights and encourage public participation in governance, many citizens still believe that platforms upon which they can freely express their opinions and voice their concerns about issues that affect their lives are not accessible to them. Access to certain services designed to benefit citizens is still restricted in certain circumstances – for instance, some disabled people are still prevented from applying for jobs due to stereotypes about their capabilities, despite it being their right to have chances for employment equal to any other Rwandan citizen.[3] This is likely due to the lack of human rights education. Many Rwandans are simply not aware of the current structures in place that are designed to help each citizen access their fundamental human rights or to solve any problems that still exist.

In practice, human rights abuses, lack of political opposition, and fear and suspicion point to an underlying fragility and unpredictable future for a country. While Rwanda continues to be deservedly heralded for its achievements by an international community still nursing a collective guilt for its failure to prevent and respond to the 1994 genocide, there is still a fragility that exists beneath the surface which poses a risk to the country's long-term stability. It is therefore important to renew emphasis on human rights in order to continue to consolidate the post-genocide gains made and to ensure their sustainability.

With a deep understanding of this unique context, NAR provides free and safe dialogue spaces to encourage civic participation and to broaden human rights discussions. Since young people have incredible potential for sparking social change, NAR's projects have already prepared thousands of youth to promote human rights throughout the country, which will slowly but surely erode old ideas that have divided Rwanda's citizens in the past in favor of a more inclusive society for all. These human rights activities will have far-reaching implications irrespective of diversity and difference.

Never Again Rwanda in Societal Healing and Reconciliation

NAR acknowledges the importance of societal healing and reconciliation as prerequisite for the sustainability of all other programs, whether governmental or nongovernmental. Through its reconciliation initiatives,

NAR "aims to contribute to the consolidation of a peaceful and inclusive Rwandan society enabled to overcome the wounds of the past and to peacefully manage conflicts and diversity." These initiatives also encourage empowerment among the citizens to influence government programs and policies that are responsive to their needs.

Societal healing and reconciliation is achieved through dialogues where citizens, including the youth, participate. After gradually building trust and helping people to feel comfortable in these environments, the dialog forums enable community members to openly discuss sensitive topics and to initiate a collective healing process. With the guidance of trained facilitators, the forums allow communities to identify and reach consensus on priorities and proposed solutions. The initiative also helps populations effectively engage decision makers with the assistance of the media, and it helps citizens fully participate in Rwandan governance by making use of "new and existing mechanisms for citizen participation, and to jointly implement activities in support of their shared vision of the future" (NAR).

Through the healing process, NAR places a particular emphasis on engaging the youth, tapping into their potential for becoming leaders of peace in their communities by encouraging a spirit of dialogue as a conflict resolution mechanism, teaching critical thinking when it comes to analyzing complex situations, promoting collaborative reflection, and enabling them to experience and make use of arts, sports, media, and public outreach as avenues for expression. To complement the Government of Rwanda's work, NAR empowers groups of citizens to use new and existing mechanisms to interact with decision makers at local, district, and national levels around the priorities of citizens and their communities. This will ultimately increase citizens' participation in governance matters and ensure that policies reflect and respond to their needs.

Conclusion

The role of peace and security in ensuring the continued development and well-being of a country simply cannot be stressed enough. These two elements are prerequisites for all reconstruction and development processes, particularly in post-genocidal societies where stability is dependent upon each and every citizen. Emerging from the tragic events of 1994, Rwanda has made impressive efforts and has had a remarkable rebound with numerous successes.

But a government, however strong, cannot achieve the full potential of its desired development when acting alone. All stakeholders need to be involved at all levels. The role of civil society in the reconstruction process of Rwanda is crucial in assisting the government to achieve its aims and in ensuring a stable, prosperous future for the country. NAR serves as an example of how CSOs can complement the government's efforts and support it in achieving its desired objectives. The organization uses a variety of approaches to assist Rwandans in coming to terms with their past while continuing to encourage reconciliation and unity to promote a strong, peaceful future. In this way, NAR ensures that its efforts align with the government's objectives in order to build a better Rwanda.

Just twenty-eight years after the genocide, remarkable progress has been made, and by making use of the strengths of CSOs and partnering with them, improvements can continue to be made in the ongoing journey of rebuilding the country. Transitional justice mechanisms put into place in Rwanda in an attempt to come to terms with the genocidal legacy and achieve reconciliation are reasonably successful, but many challenges remain. The ICTR, national courts, *gacaca* system, and other justice mechanisms have played a significant role in Rwanda's post-genocide transformation process to varying success. Domestic organizations such as NAR fulfill a vital purpose, addressing needs that the government and external organizations are unable to meet. By utilizing education, peacebuilding, and other reconciliation tactics, NAR helps Rwandans obtain justice through the guarantee of nonrecurrence and truth promotion – two pillars of transitional justice identified by the United Nations Special Rapporteur, Mr. Pablo de Greiff.[4] Ultimately, NAR serves as a concrete example of a functioning transitional justice mechanism, revealing what Rwanda can teach the world about justice, unity, reconciliation and good governance.

Notes

1 For more information about the law, see Law No. 35/2008 of 2008 Determining the Organization and Functioning of the National Unity and Reconciliation Commission. Further information can also be found on http://www.nurc.gov.rw/index.php?id=83 (Accessed November 11, 2014).

2 For more information about Never Again Rwanda, visit its website at http://neveragainrwanda.org/ (accessed January 24, 2022).

3 The rights of persons with disabilities (along with the rights of all other Rwandan citizens) are protected principally by the Constitution. The rights of persons with disabilities are additionally protected by the National Laws N° 01/2007 on the Protection of Persons with Disabilities in general and N° 02/2007 on the Protection of Former War Combatants with Disabilities. Additionally, Rwanda ratified the Convention on the Rights of Persons with Disabilities and its Optional Protocol on 15 December 2008 without qualification. For more information, see 'Initial Report of Rwanda on The Implementation Of The Convention on The Rights of Persons With Disabilities' (March 2015), available at: http://www.minijust.gov.rw/fileadmin/Documents/International_Reports/Inintial_report_UNCRPD_-_Final_Version_08th_April_2015.pdf

4 Full Statement by Pablo de Greiff, UN Special Rapporteur on the promotion of truth, justice, reparation and guarantees of nonrecurrence, at the conclusion of his official visit to Sri Lanka, available at: https://lk.one.un.org/news/full-statement-by-pablo-de-greiff-un-special-rapporteur-on-the-promotion-of-truth-justice-reparation-and-guarantees-of-non-recurrence-at-the-conclusion-of-his-official-visit/ (accessed September 10, 2019).

Bibliography

Barrett, J. (2019). *Child perpetrators on trial: Insights from post-genocide Rwanda.* Cambridge University Press.

Brehm, H. N., Uggen, C., & Gasanabo, J.-D. (2014). Genocide, justice, and Rwanda's gacaca courts. *Journal of Contemporary Criminal Justice, 30*(3), 333–352. https://doi.org/10.1177/1043986214536660

Clark, P. (2009). The rules (and politics) of engagement: The gacaca courts and post-genocide justice, healing and reconciliation in Rwanda. In P. Clark, & Z. D. Kaufman (Eds.), *After genocide: Transitional justice, post-conflict reconstruction and reconciliation in Rwanda and beyond* (pp. 297–320). Columbia University Press.

Clark, P. (2010). *The gacaca courts, post-genocide justice and reconciliation in Rwanda.* Cambridge University Press.

Clark, P. (2012). How Rwanda judged its genocide. *Counterpoints.* African Research Institute. Retrieved from https://africaresearchinstitute.org/newsite/wp-content/uploads/2013/03/How-Rwanda-judged-its-genocide-E6QODPW0KV.pdf.

Corey, A., & Joireman, S. F. (2004). Retributive justice: The gacaca courts in Rwanda. *African Affairs, 103*(410), 73–89. https://doi.org/10.1093/afraf/adh007

Cross, T. (2001). *Comfortable with chaos: Working with UNHCR and the NGO's; Reflections from the 1999 Kosovo refugee crisis.* United Nations High Commissioner for Refugees. Retrieved October 10, 2019, from https://www.unhcr.org/3b03e2774.html.

de Greiff, P. (Ed.). (2006). *The handbook of reparations.* Oxford University Press.

de Greiff, P. (2014). *Report of the Special Rapporteur on the promotion of truth, justice, reparation and guarantees of non-recurrence.* United Nations Human Rights Council. Retrieved September 10, 2019, from https://digitallibrary.un.org/record/780680.

Florea, S. (2005) *The role of NGO's in post-conflicts reconstruction: A partnership with the United Nations* [Unpublished doctoral dissertation]. The University of Webster.

Girelli, G. (2017). *Understanding transitional justice: A struggle for peace, reconciliation, and rebuilding.* Palgrave Macmillan.

Hayner, P. B. (2011). *Unspeakable truths: transitional justice and the challenge of truth commisions* (2nd ed.)Routledge

Hintjens, H. M. (1999). Explaining the 1994 genocide in Rwanda. *The Journal of Modern African Studies, 37*(2), 241–286.https://doi.org/10.1017/s0022278x99003018

Human Rights Watch. (2008, July 25). Law and reality: Progress and judicial reform in Rwanda. Retrieved from https://www.hrw.org/report/2008/07/25/law-and-reality/progress-judicial-reform-rwanda.

Human Rights Watch. (2014, March 28). Rwanda: Justice after genocide-20 years on. Retrieved from https://www.hrw.org/news/2014/03/28/rwanda-justice-after-genocide-20-years.

Ingelaere, B. (2008). The gacaca courts in Rwanda. In L. Huyse, & M. Salter (Eds.), *Traditional justice and reconciliation after violent conflict learning from African experiences* (pp. 25–60). IDEA.

Ingelaere, B. (2009). Does the truth pass across the fire without burning? Locating the short circuit in Rwanda's gacaca courts. *The Journal of Modern African Studies*, 47(4), 507–528.

Ingelaere, B. (2016). *Inside Rwanda's gacaca courts: Seeking justice after genocide.* The University of Wisconsin Press.

International Center for Transitional Justice [ICTJ]. (n.d.). What is transitional justice?: ICTJ. Retrieved January 20, 2015, from https://www.ictj.org/about/transitional-justice.

International Criminal Tribunal for Rwanda. (n.d.). The ICTR in Brief. Retrieved August 26, 2019, from https://unictr.irmct.org/en/tribunal.

International Monetary Fund. African Department (2013). *Rwanda: Poverty reduction strategy paper.* International Monetary Fund. Retrieved from https://www.imf.org/en/Publications/CR/Issues/2016/12/31/Rwanda-Poverty-Reduction-Strategy-Paper-41127.

IRIN. (2009, June 23). Jury still out on effectiveness of `Gacaca' courts. *The New Humanitarian.* Retrieved February 5, 2015, from http://www.irinnews.org/report/84954/rwanda-jury-still-out-on-effectiveness-of-gacaca-courts.

Joint Government Assessment Report-Common Country Assessment – Rwanda 'Governance, Justice, human rights and national reconciliation' *paper 6* (2009).

Kamatali, J. M. (2003). The challenge of linking international criminal justice and national reconciliation: The case of the ICTR. *Leiden Journal of International Law, 16*(1), 115–133. https://doi.org/10.1017/s0922156503001067

Kamatali, J.-M. (2006). From ICTR to ICC: Learning from the ICTR experience in bringing justice to Rwandans. *New England Journal of International Law and Comparative Law, 12*(1), 89–103. Retrieved from: https://ssrn.com/abstract=2652831

Kimonyo, J. P. (2019). *Transforming Rwanda: Challenges on the road to reconstruction.* Lynne Rienner Publishers.

Lawther, C., Moffett, L., & Jacobs, D. (Eds.). (2019). *Research handbook on transitional justice.* Edward Elgar Publishing.

Moghalu, K. C. (2002). Image and reality of war crimes justice: External perceptions of the International Criminal Tribunal for Rwanda. *The Fletcher Forum of World Affairs, 26*(2), 21–46.

Muna, B. (2004, November 25). *The early challenges of conducting investigations and prosecutions before international criminal tribunals* [Speech]. Given at the Observations at the Colloquium of Prosecutors of International Criminal Tribunals.

Musoni, E. (2006, September 27). Rwanda: Graft threatens gacaca courts. *All Africa.* Retrieved September 8, 2015, from https://allafrica.com/stories/200609280010.html.

Naidu, E. (2004). Symbolic reparations: A fractured opportunity. Centre for the study of violence and reconciliation.

National Service of Gacaca Courts. (2012, June). *Gacaca Courts in Rwanda.* Retrieved February 05, 2015, from the Republic of Rwanda Ministry of Justice. http://www.minijust.gov.rw/uploads/media/GACACA_COURTS_IN_RWANDA.pdf.

O'Donnell, G. A., & Schmitter, P. C. (1986). *Transitions from authoritarian rule: Tentative conclusions about uncertain democracies.* Johns Hopkins University Press.

Palmer, N. (2015). *Courts in conflict: Interpreting the layers of justice in post-genocide Rwanda.* Oxford University Press.

Posner, E. A., & Vermeule, A. (2003). Reparations for slavery and other historical injustices. *Columbia Law Review, 103*(3), 689–748. https://doi.org/10.2307/1123721

Rwanda: Law No. 35/2008 of 2008 Determining the Organization and Functioning of the National Unity and Reconciliation Commission [Rwanda], 8 August 2008, available at: https://www.refworld.org/docid/4a3f87922.html [accessed January 24, 2022]

Sarkin, J. (2001). The tension between justice and reconciliation in Rwanda: Politics, human rights, due process and the role of the gacaca courts in dealing with the genocide. *Journal of African Law*, 45(2), 143–172.

Saugman, F. (2012). *Gacaca Courts: Lessons Learned in Transitional Justice*. Retrieved November 14, 2014, from http://www.consultancyafrica.com/index.php?option=com_content&view=article&id=1088:gacaca-courts-lessons-learned-in-transitional-justice-&catid=60:conflict-terrorism-discussion-papers&Itemid=265

Sinh Nguyen Vo, D. (2008) *Reconciliation and conflict transformation* [essay, University of Notre Dame]. Retrieved on November 11, 2014, from https://www.beyondintractability.org/casestudy/vo-reconciliation

Teitel, R. G. (2000). *Transitional justice*. Oxford University Press.

Teitel, R. G. (2003). Transitional justice genealogy. *Harvard Human Rights Journal, 16*. Retrieved from: https://digitalcommons.nyls.edu/cgi/viewcontent.cgi?article=1339&context=fac_articles_chapters

United Nations International Criminal Tribunal for Rwanda. (n.d.). *The ICTR in brief*. Retrieved August 26, 2019, from https://unictr.irmct.org/en/tribunal

United Nations Mechanism for International Criminal Tribunals. (1994). *UN Security Council Resolution 955*. Retrieved January 20, 2015, from http://www.unmict.org/ictr-remembers/docs/res955-1994_en.pdf

United Nations Security Council Resolution 955 S-RES-955 (1994) of 8 November 1994. UN Security Council resolution 955 on the establishment of an International Tribunal and adoption of the Statute of the Tribunal, November 8, 1994 available at http://www.un.org/Docs/scres/1994/scres94.htm

United Nations Security Council. (1995, February 13). *Report of the Secretary-General pursuant to paragraph 5 of the Security Council Resolution 955*. Retrieved from https://digitallibrary.un.org/record/198227?ln=en

Uvin, P., & Mironko, C. (2003). Western and local approaches to justice in Rwanda. *Global Governances*, *9*(2), 219–231. Retrieved from: https://www.jstor.org/stable/27800476

Vandeginst, S. (1999, November 8–12). *Justice, genocide, and reparation after genocide and crimes against humanity: The proposed establishment of population gacaca tribunals in Rwanda*. [Conference presentation]. All-Africa Conference on African Principles of Conflict Resolution and Reconciliation, United Nations Conference Center, Addis Ababa, Ethiopia.

Wolfe, S. (2014). *The politics of reparations and apologies*. Springer.

World Bank (2021). *Overview: Rwanda*. Retrieved January 22, 2022, from https://www.worldbank.org/en/country/rwanda/overview

6 Transitional Justice in the Wake of Genocide

The Contribution of Criminal Trials and Symbolic Reparations to Reconciliation in Rwanda

Samantha J. Lakin and Charity Wibabara[1]

Introduction

Immediately following the genocide against the Tutsi, Rwanda's legal system was left dismantled and destroyed. To prosecute the large number of genocide suspects, it became clear that employing various court systems would be necessary. As a result, the administration of justice in post-genocide Rwanda was implemented by different entities. In addition to legal processes that focused on prosecuting genocide suspects and perpetrators, Rwanda further applied symbolic efforts to achieve justice and reconciliation. Symbolic processes – genocide memory, commemorative ceremonies, psychosocial support for victims, and educational assistance, among other initiatives – became paramount as Rwanda continues to attempt to bring their society together after the devastation of the genocide.

At the international level, the International Criminal Tribunal for Rwanda (ICTR) was established by United Nations resolution 955 (1994) to prosecute the organizers and masterminds of the genocide, while Rwandan national courts handled cases of the remaining suspects (Organic Law N° 08/96, 1996). However, the national courts lacked the capacity to deal with the vast majority of alleged perpetrators in a fair and timely manner. To increase their impact and respond to the growing culture of impunity, Rwanda chose to implement alternative justice mechanisms. In 2001, Rwanda introduced a modern version of the traditional *gacaca* courts[2] to focus on the significant number of cases of suspects charged with "low-level" crimes, with the goal of reintegrating these suspects into their communities. Additionally, nonjuridical mechanisms were implemented by the Rwandan government, survivors' organizations, national civil society, and international organizations. These processes focused on symbolic reparations and symbolic meaning, in the form of apologies, truth-telling, and engaging in acts of genocide remembrance.

Despite the issue of unequal justice arising from the use of international, national, and *gacaca* courts in the Rwandan case, prosecuting those accused of serious international crimes such as genocide nevertheless

DOI: 10.4324/9781003228592-8

constitutes a milepost toward the achievement of national and global transitional justice. The adjudication of those accused of genocide is predicated on central goals of justice, accountability, deterrence, reconciliation, and ending impunity (Behrendt, 2001, p. 97; Harmon & Gaynor, 2004, p. 403; Schabas, 2006, p. 69).

This chapter focuses on the following key issues and debates as Rwanda engaged in court-based and symbolic forms of justice after the genocide. First, the authors examine the role and impact of different courts, tribunals, and the *gacaca* system as means to address the post-genocide problems of intergroup reconciliation. The authors further identify key impacts of the individualization of guilt and the acknowledgement of responsibility that resulted from courts, trials, and *gacaca,* including the role that legal prosecution played in uncovering truth about past instances of violence. The authors examine these questions in the context of established historical indicators of reconciliation in other post-conflict societies (de Greiff, 2010, pp. 20–25; Ramsbotham, 2005; Wallensteen, 2002, p. 15).

Legal prosecutions and legal precedent provide one way to memorialize the events of the genocide, but it is not the only means. The second focus of this chapter considers non-legal efforts toward reconciliation and justice through the institutions and mechanisms of genocide memorialization. The authors conclude that whereas much of the literature on post-genocide Rwanda focuses on the legal mechanisms, the Rwandan context provides a rich example of the potential synergies between legal, societal, and symbolic means of achieving these goals. This chapter reflects on the Rwandan case which heavily employed both legal and symbolic forms of transitional justice, highlighting how a society grapples with its traumatic past.

Transitional Justice: The Rwandan Context

Legal frameworks on transitional justice have long played a prominent role in responding to grave atrocity crimes, including crimes of genocide. The International Center for Transitional Justice (n.d) provides a useful definition of transitional justice as, "the ways countries emerging from periods of conflict and repression address large-scale or systematic human rights violations so numerous or serious that the normal justice system is incapable of providing an adequate response" (https://www.ictj.org). Legal scholar Miriam Aukerman (2002) further highlights complications for transitional justice when the scale of the atrocities is defined as "radical evil" (p. 43). Transitional justice and peace studies scholar Brandon Hamber (2006) concludes that transitional justice can only be a "good enough" attempt at providing justice and redress to victims, as nothing can bring back the lives lost, and the potential of those lives. Acknowledging these challenges, the Rwandan government, civil society, survivors' organizations, and other citizen groups still decided to attempt creating senses of justice after the genocide and work toward reconciliation among Rwandans. Among the numerous attempts at justice, this chapter focuses on three examples that represent varied approaches toward justice-seeking in the aftermath of the genocide: the establishment of the ICTR, *gacaca* courts, and genocide memorialization efforts.

Initial assumptions in the years immediately following the genocide focused on retributive legal efforts as the best way to serve the needs of the population. However, assuming the primacy of court-based systems as the most appropriate way to create senses of justice rendered and to foster reconciliation in Rwandan society was both flawed and incomplete. According to international legal scholar Mark Drumbl (2007), although legal forms of justice have been the favored approach to helping states and societies recover from conflict, symbolic components are also recommended for states seeking to successfully provide justice. Original research conducted for this chapter validates Drumbl's findings, showing that both legal and symbolic responses to the genocide in Rwanda have positively influenced the road toward reconciliation.

The ICTR's Contributions to Reconciliation

The United Nations Security Council (UNSC) established the ICTR in the immediate aftermath of the genocide, in November 1994, to prosecute those most responsible for planning and implementing the genocide.[3] The prosecutions were intended, *inter alia,* to contribute to delivering justice for thousands of survivors who were experiencing pervasive and lasting effects of the genocide on a daily basis. At the outset, survivors had mixed perceptions, hopes, and doubts about the ICTR. Faith in the UN's institutional capacity and willingness to affect change in Rwanda was low. The UN Security Council that established the ICTR in 1995 was the same Security Council that had turned a blind eye to atrocities in Rwanda less than a year earlier, when Rwandans were being butchered en masse during a "machete" genocide,[4] which many experts referred to as "preventable" (African Union, 2000).

The technical ability of tribunal judges was also problematic. As the ICTR was a blend of common and civil law systems, trial chamber judges came from both legal traditions. Some judges were former academics or government officials who had no experience managing a courtroom (Des Forges & Longman, 2004). The use of both civil and common-law procedures in the application and interpretation of the ICTR's Rules of Procedure and Evidence also became a daunting task. For example, Rule 89 stipulates that the Chambers are not bound by national rules of evidence.[5] The Chambers of the ICTR repeatedly underscored that neither of the two legal systems prevailed at the Tribunal. The decisions rendered by the Chambers confirm that styles and solutions inspired by both systems were applied. This arrangement caused specific challenges for the operational functions of the ICTR.[6]

Although there have been positives and difficulties in the cooperation between the Tribunal, genocide survivors, the Rwandan government, and other UN member states, the consensus within Rwanda seems to be that for all its challenges, the tribunal left a strong legacy in Rwanda. For instance, some Rwandans expressed that the ICTR was successful in its mandate to hold accountable the highest level of perpetrators (Des Forges & Longman, 2004). The Tribunal indicted ninety-three genocide suspects, tried seventy-five cases, and convicted sixty-one *génocidaires*. The trials completed by the Tribunal challenged the historical impunity that existed for decades in Rwanda. However, the ICTR is criticized by many survivors for failing to punish those who planned the genocide prior to its occurrence. To hold the planners and organizers of genocide accountable, prosecutors would have to have demonstrated an intent to destroy members of a protected group, the specific intent requirement under the Genocide Convention.

In addition to holding the so-called "big fish" genocide perpetrators accountable, the Tribunal made substantial contributions to international criminal jurisprudence. The Tribunal became the first international court to interpret the definition of the crime of genocide enshrined in the 1948 Geneva Convention. The ICTR's judicial notice in the case of Karemera, the genocide against the Tutsi in Rwanda, is a matter of law (United Nations International Residual Mechanism for Criminal Tribunal, 2006). Additionally, under the legal provisions of command and superior responsibility, the ICTR held accountable military, government, and media leaders for human rights violations committed by their subordinates during genocide. The landmark case of Jean Paul Akayesu, former *bourgmestre* of Taba commune, set legal precedent by defining and recognizing rape as a means of perpetrating genocide (Wibabara, 2014). These legal advances under international law have functioned separately from the question of restorative justice outside a legal framework, such as victim reparations and compensatory actions for emotional pain, torture, and loss of life suffered by the victims.[7] This does not discount the enormous symbolic value of the legal response to genocide, as noted in the following discussion. To cite Antonio Cassese (1994), "The role of the Tribunals cannot be overemphasized. Far from being vehicles for revenge, they are tools for promoting reconciliation and restoring peace" (p. 16, see also Barria & Roper, 2006; Burnet, 2008; Clark, 2011).

Trials by both national and international courts have facilitated the official, public acknowledgement of genocide (including acknowledgement of the intent to destroy members of the Tutsi people) in Rwanda and explored the causes of such violations (Graybill & Lanegran, 2004). In doing so, they have restored the dignity of those who have been victims of grave crimes (Nsanzuwera, 2005, p. 948; Rettig, 2011, p. 194). Acknowledgement affirms that a victim's suffering is a result of injustice and is worthy of attention through convicting offenders to avoid historical revisionism (Werle, 2009, p. 101; Zorbas, 2009, p. 127). Acknowledgement of genocide acts in trials sets a moral standard, which provides a basis for restoration of relations between victims and perpetrators (Shnabel et al., 2008).

Gacaca

While there are differing opinions and measures of success regarding courts focusing on genocide perpetrators, according to Nicola Palmer (2015), "[w]here the ICTR, the national courts and *gacaca* were, at least in part focused on collectively [establishing an account of how and why the violence occurred] through plural processes, it re-enforced the legitimacy of all three of the court's actions and reduced the potential for popular critique of the courts" (p. 183).

In 2001, the Rwandan government enacted *Organic Law N° 40/200 of 26/01/2001, Setting Up "Gacaca Jurisdictions" and Organizing Prosecutions for Offences Constituting the Crime of Genocide or Crimes Against Humanity Committed Between October 1, 1990 and December 31, 1994*. The 2001 law identified four crime categories, originally distinguishing between attacks committed with intent and those committed without intent (art. 51). In 2004, the law changed to reflect three categories, without consideration of criminal intention (Organic Law N° 16/2004, art. 2).

Category One crimes included leading, planning, and inciting the genocide, and committing acts of rape as a weapon of genocide. Category Two crimes included killings and serious assaults, and Category Three covered stealing, destroying, looting, or damaging property. Until June 2008, Category One suspects continued to be tried by the conventional courts, including the ICTR and national courts in Rwanda, while *gacaca* courts handled Category Two and Category Three cases. However, in May 2008, in response to slow and lengthy cases in the Rwandan national courts and citizen advocacy around the importance of gendered violence including rape, the Rwandan parliament transferred many cases from Category One to *gacaca*, including cases of sexual violence (Human Rights Watch, 2014). The *Gacaca* Law also established the administrative structure of *gacaca,* forming more than 9,000 courts throughout the country, each with nine *inyangamugayo* (community "judges") elected based on their respected position and reliability among community members (Organic Law N° 16/2004, art. 13).[8] *Gacaca* was coordinated by the National Service of Gacaca Jurisdiction under the Ministry of Justice.

During *gacaca* trials, suspects were given the opportunity to admit their responsibility and to contribute to the shaping of a new Rwandan society (*Umuryango Nyarwanda*). This took the form of public gatherings where the perpetrators personally apologized to the victims in front of the community, acknowledging their role in killing Tutsi (Bornkamm, 2012, p. 69). *Gacaca* also helped many families find the bodies of their loved ones and provide a burial ceremony for them. Perpetrator confessions helped obtain truth, which furthered attempts for Rwandan communities to address past crimes and begin restoring human dignity (Gready, 2010). Establishing truth has contributed to meaning and justice by providing clarity regarding past violations, which paves the way for prosecution of past human rights abuses and for creating a historical record of past events (Bornkamm, 2012, pp. 26–27, 91; South Africa, 1999, p. 112). Additionally, documentary material, transcripts of the hearings, videos, and individual statements all contribute to establishing factual records and archives. Court archives can be especially useful to promoting justice if they are made available to the public for education and historical preservation.

Like all aspects of transitional justice in Rwanda, views on *gacaca* are polarized between those who see them as tools of social control to those who exalt their justice- and reconciliation-bearing qualities. In his nuanced book, *Inside Rwanda's Gacaca Courts: Seeking Justice After Genocide*, Bert Ingelaere (2016) determines that *gacaca*'s impact on truth, justice, and reconciliation was mediated by the fact that victims and perpetrators live together in modern Rwandan communities, which complicates the pragmatic realities of daily life. Some Rwandan individuals used *gacaca* to seek advantage, whether to settle scores which may have had nothing to do with the events of 1994, or to reduce their sentence or reparation payments. Although there were cases of real reconciliation, Ingelaere (2016) argues that *gacaca,* rather than resulting in widespread reconciliation, was part of an uneasy "living together" that has been marked by a range of reactions, from revenge killings to silence and mistrust. Although driven by the desire to find judicial truth, *gacaca* was influenced by strategic testimony and "pragmatic truth." This argument shows that the results of *gacaca* on reconciliation are difficult to measure, and depend on what variables and factors are considered.

The ICTR, Gacaca, and "Local" Justice

A common understanding of transitional justice involves the important role of courts like the ICTR and *gacaca* for victims and for the effort to realize reconciliation between them and the legacy of violence is the discovery of the truth of what happened. According to the South African Truth and Reconciliation Commission (South Africa, 1999, p. 110), there are various kinds of truth that would arguably help in reconciliation, such as factual or forensic truth, personal or narrative truth, social or dialogue truth as well as healing and restorative truth (see also Brounéus, 2008; Haws, 2009; Hazan, 2010, p. 157; South Africa, 1999, p. 110). For instance, formal courts are better geared to establish forensic truth than narrative or healing truth, with the latter most likely to emerge from restorative mechanisms (Burnet, 2008; Fierens, 2005, p. 918).

Gacaca courts were able to try large numbers of perpetrators in a short period of time. Yet they sometimes created further cleavages in society, especially when released perpetrators returned to their homes privately harboring grievances and different experiences during the period of the genocide, which they shared with their children and family members while living alongside survivors (Clark, 2010, p. 175).

Concerning trials by Rwandan national courts, the pursuit of "forensic" truth also contributed to the goal of reconciliation. The purpose of these trials was to uncover the past, contributing to accountability and retribution. By exposing the negative side of the past, those responsible for violations of human rights were held accountable for their actions, which in turn combatted the culture of impunity and established deterrence (Rwanda. National Unity and Reconciliation Commission, 2020). National court trials helped in the reconciliation process, especially when the courts held itinerant hearings in Rwandan communities where the crimes were committed. Such processes afforded hearings to persons held on criminal charges in remote places.

As designed by the Rwandan government, *gacaca* aimed to provide an additional mechanism for holding perpetrators accountable. Sometimes, at *gacaca* meetings, perpetrators disclosed the locations of the remains of murdered victims. As Taylor and Lederach (2014) note, knowing "essential truths" about where loved ones are buried is a central factor that impacts victims' abilities to make sense of past suffering. These confessions assisted in creating satisfaction around "essential truths" and many victims reported that burying their loved ones provided closure.

Scholarship by Lars Waldorf, Bert Ingelaere, and Anu Chakravarty discuss *gacaca*'s significance in understanding how local Rwandans engage with a state-led justice process. Waldorf (2006) states that "critics of international criminal justice often…assume that criminal accountability for genocide, crimes against humanity, and war crimes is better handled at the national level. While this assumption may well hold true for established liberal democracies, it is far more problematic for post-conflict successor regimes" (p. 5).

As such, *gacaca* proceedings had limitations, especially from a Western legal perspective. *Gacaca* could not provide accused perpetrators with due process under the law. Different authors criticize *gacaca* decisions, concluding that some decisions were subject to local and national interference. Additionally, judges were not trained in legal impartiality, and could make decisions that would favor their personal situations (Bornkamm, 2012; Chakravarty, 2016; Waldorf, 2006).[9] However, regarding reconciliation, "some of the participants in the *gacaca* displayed transformative agency in shared expressions of integrity, sorrow, and regret" (Chakravarty, 2016, p. 324). This modeling can have a positive impact on shaping expectations and behavior, through which Rwandans prioritize justice and peace over violence.

Overall, trials conducted by the ICTR, national, and *gacaca* courts established a historical record of events with legally binding consequences. As such, trials contribute to reconciliation by documenting the truth, even if incomplete (Freedman et al., 2011, p. 297; Moghalu, 2009, p. 88; Sisk, 2011, p. 73).

Conclusory Comments on the Legal Framework

The above section looked at the extent to which the ICTR and *gacaca* trials aided reconciliation of the population in Rwanda. Ultimately, although the processes in these legal mechanisms for finding the truth were different, they each had in common the attempt to address past crimes to ensure restoration of human dignity (Gready, 2010). Establishing truth contributes significantly to the process of reconciliation by providing clarity regarding past violations (Bornkamm, 2012, p. 91; South Africa, 1999, p. 112).

There remained, of course, tensions and disagreement regarding how the trials might facilitate a process as complex as reconciliation (Barria & Roper, 2006, p. 364; Cassese, 1998; Fierens, 2005, p. 915; Fletcher & Weinstein, 2002, p. 585; Swart, 2008, p. 100). Since there is no perfect justice mechanism for such grave abuses like crimes of genocide, criminal trials cannot accomplish everything regarding retribution and restoration. The limitations of legal frameworks as a response to genocide pointed toward a more creative and multidimensional approach to transitional justice (Mukherjee, 2011; Richters et al., 2005, p. 207). Inevitably, in Rwanda as elsewhere, sociocultural symbolic processes such as truth commissions and memorialization were used alongside penal prosecutions to address past human rights violations (Clark, 2009, p. 463; Tomuschat, 2006, p. 160).

This research does not conclude that criminal trials can never facilitate reconciliation (Richters et al., 2005, p. 207; Mukherjee, 2011). However, when retributive justice mechanisms are favored, their application may result in justice that is viewed as incomplete or inappropriate for the specific post-genocidal context. To deal effectively and comprehensively with a legacy of grave crimes, it was necessary for Rwanda to look beyond criminal justice and consider the concept of restorative justice (Arenhövel, 2008, pp. 577–580; Fierens, 2005, p. 918; Rettig, 2011, p. 206). Ultimately, a coordinated relationship between the various established measures formed an important basis for reconciliation.

Nonjuridical Justice and Symbolic Reparations

While legal cases and punishment of perpetrators have played a significant role in providing justice and holding perpetrators accountable in Rwanda, several symbolic elements were also incorporated to build public trust and integrate victims and former perpetrators into post-genocide Rwandan society (Hamber, 2006). Ordinary justice systems inevitably fall short of redressing the harms done to individuals, except in the aggregate. As such, this justice gap has begun to be filled by the introduction of nonjudicial processes and institutions. One significant nonjudicial, symbolic form of justice are reparations.

Reparations programs take two basic forms: material and nonmaterial. The latter might be termed "symbolic" as it is not based on material compensation.

That is, reparations may include important symbolic displays and demonstrations even when they do not include a material component, such as monetary compensation. Examples of non-material reparations include public apologies from state authorities, public rites and ceremonies, and the establishment of memorials and commemoration ceremonies to remember lives lost. The public dimension in such symbolic actions can help recognize what happened during the conflict and who was victimized. Public acknowledgment, both by the state authorities and by the rest of society, plays an important role in overcoming the exclusion victims have suffered and therefore assist in the efforts toward post-genocide reconstruction (Magarell, 2007).

De Greiff (2008) makes the distinction in effect between symbolic (nonmaterial) and material reparations on the basis of their different limiting factors. For the latter, de Greiff includes financial capacity, questions regarding whether and how much money can recompense an individual whose entire family was murdered, and the sense that that accepting monetary payments for mass death is like accepting blood money.

Symbolic and material reparations are situated within the sub-fields of two broader areas: transitional justice and memory studies after trauma. The main rationale for providing reparations to victims of past mass crimes is to repair the harms suffered and to acknowledge that what happened to them was wrong (Laplante, 2013). Roht-Arriaza (2004), advocating for both material and nonmaterial reparations, asserts that reparations programs must address abstract needs such as justice and accountability, while at the same time providing the practical means for victims to rebuild their lives. According to Hamber and Wilson (2002):

> Psychologically speaking, the so-called symbolic acts of reparation such as reburials, and material acts of reparation such as payments… [can] play an important role in processes of opening space for bereavement, addressing trauma and ritualizing symbolic closure. They acknowledge and recognize the individual's suffering and place it within a new officially sanctioned history of trauma
>
> (p. 38).

Hamber and Wilson (2002) further state:

> Symbolic representations of the trauma, particularly if the symbols are personalized, can concretize a traumatic event, and help reattribute responsibility. The latter stage is important because labeling responsibility can appropriately redirect blame towards perpetrators and relieve the moral ambiguity and guilt survivors often feel
>
> (p. 38).

Similarly, Rachel Ibreck (2012) discusses the potential of symbols such as genocide memory practices. She relates to Olick and Robbins (1998), who state, "What we learn of the past through present discourses, symbols and practices bears on how we each remember it and on our relations with others" (p. 99). Building on the relational aspects of engaging in memorialization, Booth (2006) extends this argument further, stating that "Memory cements social bonds, and shared memories are a foundation for the possibility of creating ethical and just communities" (p. 70). Ibreck (2012) discusses meaning-making based on Olick and Robbins and Booth's assertions. She says:

> As such, the ritual of genocide commemoration, envisaged as a means to express shared grief and solidarity with the victims and to join in a moral condemnation of violence, also has a significant part in constructing the meaning of past atrocities and in creating moral and political communities
>
> (p. 99).

In constructing moral and political communities, meaning-making begins to take place via the presence and recognition of symbolic mechanisms, which allow for the potential of new identities to be created, informed by past experiences of violence, yet optimistic about a future where such victimization will be acknowledged and prevented.

Hearty (2019) and Olsen et al. (2010, p. 980) place symbolic reparations within the broader field of transitional justice. As with juridical responses to genocide and the quest for reconciliation, both symbolic and material reparations have their limits and challenges. For instance, Hearty (2019) claims that symbolic reparations often have greater moral importance "because they are better placed to address the causes and consequences of, rather than resultant material needs arising from, past harms" (p. 6). Symbolic reparations can provide opportunities to reflect back upon the violence and crimes that took place. The ability to understand what systems, processes, discrimination, ideology, and abuses of power created the situation for such mass violence in the first place is important in helping people see themselves represented and acknowledged in the historical narrative, or alternate ones.

Similar to the court systems and fact-finding initiatives, massive legal reparations programs often cannot calculate or quantify with any degree of certainty the harm done to each individual victim. Even the most generous program will fall short if the expectation is to repair all harm. Furthermore, calculating individual harm and providing a monetary value for losses as a result of genocide could be perceived as an offensive process by victims and survivors, further dehumanizing lives lost. As such, individual monetary reparations might not be the most appropriate way to provide redress for harms caused by the genocide.

Additionally, for many victims, symbolic reparations are simply not enough to contend with the depth of psychological pain suffered by a survivor, and the assumption that they might be able to provide such closure is flawed (Hamber, 2006). Social psychologists, political scientists, and legal scholars who research victimhood agree that any symbolic justice processes can create situations of competition and hierarchies of victimhood (Berry, 2017; Bouka, 2013; Butler, 2009; Fujii, 2009; Krystalli, 2021). Our research shows that when symbolic reparations processes are based on legal and social definitions of victimhood that are not agreed upon, different groups can use claims of victimhood to disrupt justice and reconciliation efforts. Synergy and agreement between state entities, social groups, and victim communities about who is a victim, of what crimes, and why their victimhood is legitimate, is essential to promote transformational and lasting justice and reconciliation, and to minimize cases of victim hierarchies (Berry, 2017; McEvoy & McConnachie, 2012).

Communal Symbolic Reparation Efforts

In the case of Rwanda, symbolic reparations have taken the form of communal efforts to redress past crimes. The most salient aspect of communal, symbolic reparations is the capacity for symbolic justice initiatives to impact a person's ability to make meaning out of past harms, to restore their faith in the future, providing a positive basis under which to engage in the post-genocidal society (Hamber, 2006, p. 562). Hamber notes that the impact of symbols in this regard is often greater than more targeted, individualistic reparative gestures. Although symbols cannot bring back the dead, and they cannot undo the harm suffered by victims, nevertheless they may show an attempt by the state to redress the human rights abuses that have occurred and help survivors re-enter society as valued and equal citizens.

The most prominent forms of symbolic reparations are the memorials, both physical and ephemeral. Hamber and Palmary (2009) identify the following:

Constructing commemorative monuments to all victims of human rights abuses, or creating a national memorial or process of memorialization;

- Erecting plaques and tombstones, or building new cemeteries;
- Creating national days of remembrance, thanksgiving, or reconciliation;
- Organizing campaigns and cultural celebrations that promote reconciliation;
- Reburials, exhumations, commemorative services, and marking and honoring mass graves (p. 328).

Reparations programs, particularly memorialization, are an inherently political project. They can help constitute a new political community (de Greiff, 2008, p. 462). According to de Greiff, reparations relate to a broader political agenda by broadening the concept beyond the juridical concern with individual claims. That is, the political aim of memorials and forms of memorialization such as truth commissions include recognition, civic trust, social solidarity, psychosocial healing, and re-entry for survivors into the civic and political life.

Genocide Memorials as Symbolic Reparations

Monuments, museums, and memorial sites aim to serve as a vehicle for the intergenerational transmission of historical memory, as do narratives and annual rituals of remembrance (Hamber, 2006, p. 567). Ideally, memorialization is a process that satisfies the desire to honor those who suffered or died during conflict and a means by which to examine the past and address contemporary issues. Processes of memorialization aim to promote social recovery after violent conflict; however, when improperly implemented they can reinforce sentiments of victimization, discrimination, and desire for revenge. These processes manifest differently depending on who initiates them, the stage of the conflict, and the kind of society that emerges after the violence ends (Barsalou & Baxter, 2007).

Transitional justice scholars who focus on post-genocide Rwanda, including Mwambari (2020), Major (2015), Jessee (2017), Viebach (2014), Fox (2019), Wolfe (2020), and Lakin (2016), each discuss how memorialization in Rwanda is part of the state's efforts to promote shared identity, unity, and reconciliation. Additionally, through memorials and public genocide commemorations, the post-genocide government seeks to generate legitimacy based on a shared understanding of Rwanda's history and genocidal violence. According to the former National Commission for the Fight Against Genocide, there are approximately 250 memorial sites in Rwanda, almost all of which mark locations of massacres during the genocide. Their authenticity is linked to the violence that occurred at the site itself (Wolfe, 2020). Memorial sites in Rwanda can be found in churches, local government offices, and even school compounds where people were murdered during the genocide.

Kwibuka ("to remember") commemoration ceremonies take place annually from April 7 to July 4. These ceremonies are highly ritualized, performative, and symbolic. Survivor testimonies, burials, and prayer are central. Ceremonial symbolism, public participation, and legally mandating the week of April 7 to 13 as a national period of mourning reinforce the significance of the genocide as an event that impacted the lives of all Rwandans. Furthermore, per Hamber et al., (2010), the deep investment in sites of memory from every level of society, and the contested nature of those sites, can be a powerful catalyst for productive new dialogue and public engagement with regard to creating a sense of communal justice.

Public Memory, State, and Individual Narratives

In his article, "Can There Be a Political Science of the Holocaust?", political scientist Charles King (2012) addresses the formation of narratives through individual survivors' memories and their role in interrogating public memorial sites, spaces, and processes. The intersection of private remembrance ceremonies and public memory expressed at different memorial sites and spaces creates a template for what becomes a nation's "public memory." The latter, however, can be influenced by the state, as in the case of Holocaust memory in the current state of Israel, or the case of memory of the 1994 genocide against the Tutsi in present-day Rwanda. According to King (2012), the:

> sheer scale of Holocaust victimhood, its direct link to the long history of European antisemitism, and the memorialization of both in museums, monuments, and popular culture, have given rise to a lattice-work of 'public memory' that can present a challenge to scholars seeking to analyze events in a new light
>
> (p. 324).

Our research identifies a set of central questions when considering the roles public memory plays in different aspects of a post-genocidal society, like Rwanda. When do Rwandans feel compelled to take part in commemoration activities or visit memorials? When Rwandans attend public genocide commemorations, they listen to the same speeches, testimonies, songs, and prayers delivered during the ceremony. At the same time, however, each individual Rwandan has personal reflections when they attend a public commemoration, and they are diverse in how they relate to the public and collective memory presented. Does visiting memorial sites and attending genocide commemorations yield solidarity among Rwandans collectively (King, 2012; Lakin, 2020)?

Christopher Browning's (1992) research discusses the dangers of showing history as monolithic and based around a single story. His research asks scholars to consider how to portray the social, political, economic, cultural, and ideological complexities within and across various groups (leaders, perpetrators, survivors, moderates, resisters, rescuers, children, etc.) in order to represent the diversity of conflict and to minimize the black-and-white portrayal of victim and perpetrator that often characterizes the description of mass violence to the public. Hamber (2006) notes that memorials are more successful in achieving the goals above if survivors are part of the design and creation process, and if the symbolism personally relates to their suffering and has meaning for them. In short, for reparations to function as effectively as vehicles of reconciliation, they must provide the space for survivors to express their sadness, rage, and ambiguity as they struggle to come to terms with the psychological and emotional impact of their loss (p. 567). Memorials can create the physical and emotional space for survivors to reconstruct their identity as survivors of conflict in a new society, and to start the process of restoring their political and social ties.

The Potential of Memorial Spaces in Rwanda

Memorials can provide a space to allow survivors to grieve and to place their histories into a socio-political context. In Rwanda, however, the politics of memory is ever-present (Edkins, 2003). Just as genocide memory can be politicized, it can also be depoliticized. Depoliticizing genocide remembrance and recognizing the shared humanity of all Rwandans can positively impact the utility of *inzibutso* (genocide memorial sites) and *Kwibuka* (genocide commemoration ceremonies) as places of dialogue and reconciliation.

Memorials have the ability to shape the discourse surrounding issues of rebuilding and reconciliation in post-conflict societies by bringing the issue of survivors' memory to the table. Memorials can help identify what role memory, personal narratives, and history play in public conversations (Wolfe, 2020, pp. 82–83). At the same time, memorials are part of a worldwide cultural memory of mass human rights violations. Leaders can manipulate memorialization processes to conform to a specific retelling of history, one that fits with the narrative of those who want to manipulate the history. To limit the misuse of genocide narratives, national and social memorialization efforts must connect, based on a shared understanding of the past.

According to the current Rwandan government, the primary purpose of memorials is to show the undeniable history of the genocide that took place. Memorial sites in Rwanda take various forms in order to preserve the history. Some memorial sites, like the Kigali Genocide Memorial (Gisozi), provide an historical background to Rwanda's history of genocide, coupled with video testimonies, artistic sculptures, and paintings representing victims' suffering, photographs, and artifacts.[10] Other memorial sites, like Murambi or Nyarubuye, display bones, clothing, and last possessions of victims.[11] Both approaches are intended to combat genocide denial and to preserve the historical accuracy of accounts of the genocidal violence that took place in 1994. In addition, both western-style museum exhibits and raw memorials of bones in churches provide respectful burial spaces for the dead. These become sacred spaces for survivors: victims come to the physical place where people were massacre, separating from their daily lives and from the larger commemorations to the genocide.[12]

Both types of memorial sites, Western and "raw," contribute to these goals, yet there is still debate around which sites, if any, are most meaningful for survivors, and for Rwandans writ large. In addition, there is the question of whether survivors feel compelled to visit memorials outside of the hundred days of commemoration, and what they experience when they visit the memorial sites.

In Rwanda, as in many post-genocide societies, transitional justice mechanisms such as memorialization can be viewed along a spectrum. On one end, transitional justice in Rwanda can promote positive psychosocial healing, can validate survivors' experiences, and can help rebuild trust in the new society and faith that the new state will protect them from future violations. On the other end of the spectrum, transitional justice in Rwanda legitimizes state-building efforts. Elements of both positions exist in a dynamic relationship, overlapping in time and space, at times posing challenges toward reconciliation, and at other times resting comfortably together.

However, after an unprecedented genocide that involved mass participation and significant human casualties, Rwanda engaged in an equally unprecedented journey to provide justice and reconciliation. Rwanda faces the continued challenge of meeting the needs of various stakeholders with different needs after the genocide. As Rwanda is a relatively young post-genocide nation, and as every individual living in Rwanda at the time was affected by the genocide in some way, the potential for reconciliation remains positive based on the attention paid to justice-seeking mechanisms, and the diverse approach to restorative and retributive justice that the country has adopted.

Conclusions

After the genocide, Rwanda's legal and governmental systems were destroyed and left with no institutional capacity. The challenge of rebuilding the country, including legal and public institutions, seemed daunting and nearly impossible. One of the most urgent requirements for rebuilding was to implement legal efforts to prosecute the large number of genocide suspects and perpetrators, which resulted in a multi-leveled system of courts to try offenders under both national and international law. In addition, memorials were built as early as 1994 and 1995, and continue to be built and visited three decades after the events.

As Rwanda looks to its future, its memory of the past events has been shaped by both the trials and the various forms of genocide memory, both formal and informal. Within the legal domain, the closing of the *gacaca* courts in 2012 and of the ICTR in 2014 has left the remaining work of adjudicating the genocide to the national courts. In addition, the ICTR closing provided an opportunity to refocus reconciliation efforts around symbolic measures, including memorialization, commemoration, and reparations. In short, Rwanda's response to the genocide over the past decades has shifted from its legal response, in the main, to memory work that is more specifically cultural, societal, and communal. To promote and reinforce the legal efforts toward reconciliation, the social and cultural work have had to be both meaningful and inclusive.

As discussed in this chapter, reconciliation and justice can be measured by a number of indicators, and they are by no means standardized. The success of justice-seeking programs in post-genocide Rwanda depends upon the definitions used to identify how the society has recovered.

We have suggested that for all the limitations inherent to both legal and nonlegal vehicles toward justice and reconciliation, nonetheless there is evidence that they are being achieved in Rwanda through the various forms of reparations, both material and symbolic, even if it does not look like the ideal view of reconciliation promoted by a segment of transitional justice theorists discussing other post-conflict states. For instance, although there have been revenge killings immediately after the genocide in Rwanda, they have been limited, and while animosity may exist on an individual level, for the most part it is not acted upon in daily Rwandan society.

In addition, in a radical break from the past, the children of genocide survivors and the younger generation in Rwanda are being educated in a system that encourages critical thinking and stresses the importance of individual choice in the face of propaganda or external pressure, all approached from a standpoint of pride in being Rwandan. While it may be unrealistic to ask genocide survivors to forgive perpetrators for their actions, coexistence as a form of reconciliation occurs on a communal level, even if individual Rwandans do not feel reconciled. Economic cooperation, renewed friendships, and family relationships have developed as the social fabric of Rwanda has been rebuilt over the past three decades, and the robust justice agenda in Rwanda has promoted the recovery of relationships in Rwanda. It is in these highly contextual ways that Rwanda is on its path toward reconciliation.

The shift from legal to symbolic measures has an additional significance for reconciliation efforts: this is because memorials and commemorations do not have fixed meaning. Rather, they have a "built-in polyvalence, a degree of slipperiness, which allows nuanced meanings to co-exist" (Brown, 2013, p. 282). The fact that memorialization and commemoration represent dynamic and ever-changing meaning of the relevant symbols (the memorial, the commemoration) may provide more space and opportunities for past injustices to be named and explained, and for current injustices to be debated and called out in a way that changes in its social and political acceptability as time distances the society from the past violence. According to transitional justice and peace scholar Kris Brown (2013):

> Students and practitioners of symbolic reparation will need to examine how their commemoration will find its place within a multiplicity of discourses. Counter narratives to the state or international non-governmental organization (INGO) branded 'meta-narrative' of transition and peace will certainly exist
>
> (pp. 282–283).

Memory is labile, and the post-legal memorialization of an event such as genocide, with its complexity and scope, must contend with that complexity and scope. Within that dialogic space between Rwandans and outsiders, between the accused and the victims, even between the survivors and the dead, the work of justice, reconciliation and peace, continues at a different register through the filaments of these symbolic and communal gestures.

Finally, timing is important. There is no standard timeframe for how a state and a society comes to terms with its past, genocidal or otherwise. Additionally, theories of transitional justice are constantly changing as scholars and practitioners conduct research and look at different post-conflict states and societies. No system exists yet that is equipped to deal with extraordinary human rights abuses. Attempting to find a perfect system may be overpromising what transitional justice can realistically do, setting such efforts up for failure. The words of Mahmood Mamdani (2015), a preeminent scholar on identity and social justice in Africa, highlight these findings. Mamdani concludes that societies must move from pursuing legal justice to creating social justice in the aftermath of atrocity crimes and genocide. Social justice has the potential to lead to future reconciliation as a combined and sustained effort between legal and symbolic transitional justice mechanisms.

Notes

1 The views presented in this chapter are expressed by the authors in their capacities as independent academics and scholars of transitional justice. The chapter does not represent the views of the authors' professional positions or affiliations.
2 In 2001, Organic Law N° 40/2000 of 26/01/2001 governing the creation of *gacaca, Gacaca* Courts and Organizing the Prosecution of Genocide Crimes and other Crimes against Humanity committed in Rwanda entered into force and was replaced by the 2004 Organic Law.
3 UN Security Council resolution 955 on the establishment of an International Tribunal and adoption of the Statute of the Tribunal, November 8, 1994 available at http://www.un.org/Docs/scres/1994/scres94.htm
4 Hutu militias predominantly used machetes to kill Tutsi civilian during the genocide.
5 See International Criminal Tribunal for Rwanda, Rules of Procedure and Evidence entered into force June 29, 1995.
6 International and national courts and tribunals have significant effects (both positive and negative) on the development of collective memory of atrocity crimes, justice, and reconciliation. For more information, see Osiel, 1997.
7 Redress and Survivors Fund et al. (2012), "The right to reparation for survivors: Recommendations for reparation for survivors of the 1994 genocide against the Tutsi," October 2012 p. 13. Retrieved from http://survivors-fund.org.uk/wp-content/uploads/2012/11/Right-to-reparation-Final.pdf on January 9, 2022
8 Article 5 of the 2007 law decreased the number of judges required to a panel of 5–7.
9 For more information on critiques of *gacaca* courts, see: Brehm et al., 2014; Clark, 2010; Kaitesi, 2014.
10 Fieldnotes, Lakin, August 2014.
11 Fieldnotes, Lakin, July 2018.
12 Executive Secretary, IBUKA. Interview by S. Lakin. Field Notes. June 6, 2013.

Bibliography

African Union (2000). *Rwanda: The preventable genocide.* Retrieved on December 20, 2019, from https://www.refworld.org/docid/4d1da8752.html

Arenhövel, M. (2008). Democratization and transitional justice. *Democratization*, *15*(3), 570–587. https://doi.org/10.1080/13510340801991114

Aukerman, M. J. (2002). Extraordinary evil, ordinary crime: A framework for understanding transitional justice. *Harvard Human Rights Journal*, *15*(39), 39–98.

Barria, L. A., & Roper, S. D. (2006). How effective are international criminal tribunals? An analysis of the ICTY and ICTR. *The International Journal of Human Rights*, *9*(3), 349–368.https://doi.org/10.1080/13642980500170782

Barsalou, J., & Baxter, V. (2007, January 1). The urge to remember: The role of memorials in social reconstruction and transitional justice. *United States Institute of Peace*. Retrieved September 10, 2020, from https://www.usip.org/publications/2007/01/urge-remember-role-memorials-social-reconstruction-and-transitional-justice

Behrendt, U. P. (2001). *Dealing with the 1994 genocide: A comparative analysis of usefulness of the ICTR and Rwanda's national prosecutions* [Master's thesis, University of Western Cape].

Berry, M. E. (2017). Barriers to women's progress after atrocity: Evidence from Rwanda and Bosnia-Herzegovina. *Gender & Society*, *31*(6), 830–853. https://doi.org/10.1177/0891243217737060

Booth, W. J. (2006). *Communities of memory: On witness, identity, and justice*. Cornell University Press.

Bornkamm, P. C. (2012). *Rwanda's gacaca courts: Between retribution and reparation*. Oxford University Press.

Bouka, Y. (2013). (Oral) History of violence: Conflicting narrative in post-genocide Rwanda. *Oral History Forum d'Histoire Orale*, *33*, 1–26. http://www.oralhistoryforum.ca/index.php/ohf/article/view/538

Brounéus, K. (2008). Truth-telling as talking cure? Insecurity and retraumatization in the Rwandan gacaca courts. *Security Dialogue*, *39*(1), 55–76. https://doi.org/10.1177/0967010607086823

Brown, K. (2013). Commemoration as symbolic reparation: New narratives or spaces of conflict? *Human Rights Review*, *14*, 282.

Browning, C. R. (1992). *Ordinary men: Reserve police battalion 101 and the final solution in Poland*. Harper Collins.

Burnet, J. E. (2008). The injustice of local justice: Truth, reconciliation, and revenge in Rwanda. (2008), 3 *Genocide Studies and Prevention*, *3*(2), 173–193. https://doi.org/10.3138/gsp.3.2.173

Butler, J. (2009). *Frames of war: when is life grievable?* Verso.

Cassese, A. (1994). ICTY First Annual Report, UN Doc. A/49/342, S/1994/1007. available Retrieved from: https://www.icty.org/x/file/About/Reports%20and%20Publications/AnnualReports/annual_report_1994_en.pdf

Cassese, A. (1998). Reflections on international criminal justice. *The Modern Law Review*, *61*(1), 1–10. https://doi.org/10.1111/1468-2230

Chakravarty, A. (2016). *Investing in authoritarian rule: Punishment and patronage in Rwanda's gacaca courts for genocide crimes*. Cambridge University Press.

Clark, J. N. (2009). The limits of retributive justice: Findings of an empirical study in Bosnia and Hercegovina. *Journal of International Criminal Justice*, *7*(3), 463–487. https://doi.org/10.1093/jicj/mqp041

Clark, P. (2010). *The gacaca courts, post-genocide justice and reconciliation in Rwanda: Justice without lawyers*. Cambridge University Press. https://doi.org/10.1017/CBO9780511761584

Clark, J. N. (2011). The impact question: The ICTY and the restoration and maintenance of peace. In B. Swart, A. Zahar, And G. Sluiter (Eds.), *The legacy of the International Criminal Tribunal for the former Yugoslavia* (pp. 55–80). ICTY Outreach Programme. https://doi.org/10.1093/acprof:oso/9780199573417.003.0003

de Greiff, P. (2008). Justice and reparations. In P. de Greiff (Ed.), *The handbook of reparations* (pp. 153–175). Oxford University Press. https://doi.org/10.1093/0199291926.003.0013

de Greiff, P. (2010). A normative conception of transitional justice. *Politorbis*, *50*(3), 17–30.
Des Forges, A., & Longman, T. (2004). Legal responses to genocide in Rwanda. In E. Stover & H. M. Weinstein (Eds.), *My neighbor, my enemy: Justice and community in the aftermath of mass atrocity* (pp. 49–68). Cambridge University Press. https://doi.org/10.1017/CBO9780511720352.005
Drumbl, M. A. (2007). *Atrocity, punishment, and international law*. Cambridge University Press. https://doi.org/10.1017/CBO9780511611100
Edkins, J. (2003). *Trauma and the memory of politics*. Cambridge University Press.
Fierens, J. (2005). Gacaca courts: Between fantasy and reality. *Journal of International Criminal Justice*, *3*(4), 896–919. https://doi.org/10.1093/jicj/mqi069
Fletcher, L. E., & Weinstein, H. M. (2002). Violence and social repair: Rethinking the contribution of justice to reconciliation. *Human Rights Quarterly*, *24*(3), 573–639.
Fox, N. (2019). Memory in interaction: Gender-based violence, genocide, and commemoration. *Signs: Journal of Women in Culture and Society*, *45*(1), 123–148. https://doi.org/10.1086/703498
Freedman, S. W., Weinstein, H. M., Murphy, K. L., & Longman, T. (2011). Teaching history in post-genocide Rwanda. In S. Straus, & L. Waldorf (Eds.), *Remaking Rwanda: State building and human rights after violence* (pp. 297–315). The University of Wisconsin Press.
Fujii, L. A. (2009). *Killing neighbors: Webs of violence in Rwanda*. Cornell University Press.
Graybill, L., & Lanegran, K. (2004). Truth, justice, and reconciliation in Africa: Issues and cases. *African Studies Quarterly*, *8*(1), 1–18.
Gready, P. (2010). "You're either with us or against us": Civil society and policy making in post-genocide Rwanda. *African Affairs*, *109*(437), 637–657. https://doi.org/10.1093/afraf/adq038
Hamber, B. (2006). Narrowing the micro and macro: A psychological perspective on reparations in societies in transition. In P. de Greiff (Ed.), *The handbook of reparations* (pp. 560–582). Oxford University Press. https://doi.org/10.1093/0199291926.003.0017
Hamber, B., & Palmary, I. (2009). Gender, memorialization, and symbolic reparations. In R. Rubio-Marin (Ed.), *The gender of reparations: Unsettling sexual hierarchies while redressing human rights violations* (pp. 324–380). Cambridge University Press. https://doi.org/10.1017/CBO9780511596711.010
Hamber, B., Sevcenko, L., & Naidu, E. (2010). Utopian dreams or practical possibilities? The challenges of evaluating the impact of memorialization in societies in transition. *International Journal of Transitional Justice*, *4*(3), 397–420. https://doi.org/10.1093/ijtj/ijq018
Hamber, B., & Wilson, R. A. (2002). Symbolic closure through memory, reparation and revenge in post conflict societies. *Journal of Human Rights*, *1*(1), 35–53. https://doi.org/10.1080/14754830110111553
Harmon, M. B., & Gaynor, F. (2004). Prosecuting massive crimes with primitive tools: Three difficulties encountered by prosecutors in international criminal proceedings. *Journal of International Criminal Justice*, *2*(2), 403–426. https://doi.org/10.1093/jicj/2.2.403
Haws, C. (2009). Suffering, hope and forgiveness: The Ubuntu theology of Desmond Tutu. *Scottish Journal of Theology*, *64*(4), 477–489. https://doi.org/10.1017/S0036930609990123

Hazan, P. (2010). *Judging war, judging history: Behind truth and reconciliation* (S. Meyer de Stadelhofen, Trans.). Stanford University Press.

Hearty, K. (2019). Problematising symbolic reparation: 'Complex political victims', 'dead body politics' and the right to remember. *Social and Legal Studies*, *29*(3), 343–354. https://doi.org/10.1177%2F0964663919869050

Human Rights Watch. (2014, March 28). *Rwanda: Justice after Genocide – 20 years on.* https://www.hrw.org/news/2014/03/28/rwanda-justice-after-genocide-20-years/.

Ibreck, R. (2012). A time of mourning: The politics of commemorating the Tutsi genocide in Rwanda. In P. Lee, & P. N. Thomas (Eds.), *Public memory, public media and the politics of justice* (pp. 98–120). Palgrave Macmillan.

IBUKA, The Survivors Fund, & REDRESS. (2012). Right to reparation for survivors: Recommendations for reparation for survivors of the 1994 genocide against the Tutsi. Retrieved from http://survivors-fund.org.uk/wp-content/uploads/2012/11/Right-to-reparation-Final.pdf

Ingelaere, B. (2016). *Inside Rwanda's gacaca courts: Seeking justice after genocide.* The University of Wisconsin Press.

International Center for Transitional Justice. (n.d.). *What is transitional justice?* Retrieved: September 19, 2019, from https://www.ictj.org/about/transitional-justice

Jessee, E. (2017). *Negotiating genocide in Rwanda: The politics of history.* Palgrave Macmillan.

Kaitesi, U. (2014). *Genocidal gender and sexual violence: The legacy of the ICTR, Rwanda's ordinary courts and the gacaca courts.* Intersentia Press.

King, C. (2012). Can there be a political science of the Holocaust? *Perspective on Politics*, *10*(2), 323–341. https://doi.org/10.1017/S1537592712000692

Krystalli, R. C. (2021). Narrating victimhood: Dilemmas and (in)dignities. *International Feminist Journal of Politics*, *23*(1), 125–146. https://doi.org/10.1080/14616742.2020.1861961

Lakin, S. (2016). Symbolic justice in Rwanda: An analysis of local perspectives. *Identity, Culture & Politics: An Afro-Asian Dialogue*, *17*(1), 38–59.

Lakin, S. (2020, June 12). Redefining justice: How local perspectives of genocide memory inform and practice in Rwanda. *Georgetown Journal of International Affairs.* Retrieved from https://gjia.georgetown.edu/2020/06/12/redefining-justice-how-local-perspectives-of-genocide-memory-inform-policy-and-practice-in-rwanda/

Laplante, L. J., (2013). The plural justice aims of reparations. In S. Buckley-Zistel, T. Koloma Beck, C. Braun, & F. Mieth (Eds.), *Transitional justice theories* (pp. 66–84). Routledge Publishers. Retrieved from https://papers.ssrn.com/sol3/papers.cfm?abstract_id=3038951

Magarell, L. (2007). *Reparations in theory and practice.* International Center for Transitional Justice. Retrieved from https://www.ictj.org/publication/reparations-theory-and-practice

Major, L. (2015). Unearthing, untangling and re-articulating genocide corpses in Rwanda: Déterrer, démêler et réarticuler les corps du génocide au Rwanda. *Critical African Studies*, *7*(2), 164–181. doi: https://doi.org/10.1080/21681392.2015.1028206.

Mamdani, M. (2015). Beyond Nuremberg: The historical significance of the post-apartheid transition in South Africa. *Politics & Society*, *43*(1), 61–88. https://doi.org/10.1177/0032329214554387

McEvoy, K., & McConnachie, K. (2012). Victimology in transitional justice: Victimhood, innocence and hierarchy. *European Journal of Criminology*, *9*(5), 527–538. https://doi.org/10.1177/1477370812454204

Moghalu, K. C. (2009). Prosecute or pardon? Between truth commissions and war crimes trials. In C. L. Sriram, & S. Pillay (Eds.), *Peace versus justice? The dilemma of transitional justice in Africa* (pp. 69–95). Oxford University Press.

Mukherjee, G. (2011). Achieving reconciliation through prosecution in the courts: Lessons from Rwanda. *Conflict Resolution Quarterly*, *28*(3), 331–348. https://doi.org/10.1002/crq.20026

Mwambari, D. (2020). Music and the politics of the past: Kizito Mihigo and music in the commemoration of the genocide against the Tutsi in Rwanda. *Memory Studies*, *13*(6), 1321–1336. https://doi.org/10.1177/1750698018823233

Nsanzuwera, F.-X. (2005). The ICTR contribution to national reconciliation. *Journal of International Criminal Justice*, *3*(4), 944–949. https://doi.org/10.1093/jicj/mqi066

Nyseth Brehm, H., Uggen, C., & Gasanabo, J.-D. (2014). Genocide, justice, and Rwanda's gacaca courts. *Journal of Contemporary Criminal Justice*, *33*(3), 333–352. https://doi.org/10.1177/1043986214536660

Olick, J. K., & Robbins, J. (1998). Social memory studies: From "collective memory" to the historical sociology of mnemonic practices. *Annual Review of Sociology*, *24*(1), 105–140. https://doi.org/10.1146/annurev.soc.24.1.105

Olsen, T. D., Payne, L. A., & Reiter, A. G. (2010). The justice balance: When transitional justice improves human rights and democracy. *Human Rights Quarterly*, *32*(4), 980–1007. https://doi.org/10.1353/hrq.2010.0021

Organic Law N° 08/1996 of 1996 (1996). On the organization of prosecutions for offences constituting the crime of genocide or crimes against humanity committed since 1 October 1990.

Organic Law N° 16/2004 of 19/6/2004 (2004). Establishing the organisation, competence and functioning of Gacaca courts charged with prosecuting and trying the perpetrators of the crime of genocide and other crimes against humanity, committed between October 1, 1990 and December 31, 1994.

Organic Law N° 40/2000 of 26/01/2001 (2001). Setting up "Gacaca Jurisdictions" and organizing prosecutions for offences constituting the crime of genocide or crimes against humanity committed between October 1, 1990 and December 31, 1994.

Osiel, M. J. (1997). *Mass atrocity, collective memory, and the law*. Transaction Publishers.

Palmer, N. (2015). *Courts in conflict: Interpreting the layers of justice in post-genocide Rwanda*. Oxford University Press. https://doi.org/10.1093/acprof:oso/9780199398195.001.0001

Ramsbotham, O. (2005). The analysis of protracted social conflict: A tribute to Edward Azar. *Review of International Studies*, *31*(1), 109–126.

Rettig, M. (2011). The Sovu trials: The impact of genocide justice on one community. In S. Straus And L. Waldorf, (Eds.), *Remaking Rwanda: State building and human rights after mass violence* (pp. 194–209). The University of Wisconsin Press

Richters, A., Dekker, C., & De Jonge, K. (2005). Reconciliation in the aftermath of violent conflict in Rwanda. *Intervention*, *3*(3), 203–221.

Roht-Arriaza, N. (2004). Reparations in the aftermath of repression and mass violence. In E. Stover & H. M. Weinstein (Eds.), *My neighbor, my enemy: Justice and community in the aftermath of mass atrocity* (pp. 121–139). Cambridge University Press. https://doi.org/10.1017/CBO9780511720352.009

Rwanda. National Unity and Reconciliation Commission (2020). *Rwanda Reconciliation Barometer 2020*. Retrieved from: https://www.rwandainthenetherlands.gov.rw/fileadmin/user_upload/Netherlands_user_upload/Documents/Updates/RWANDA_RECONCILIATION_BAROMETER_2020__N.pdf

Schabas, W. A. (2006). *The UN international criminal tribunals: The former Yugoslavia, Rwanda and Sierra Leone*. Cambridge University Press.

Shnabel, N., Nadler, A., Canetti, Nisim, D., & Ullrich, J. (2008). The role of acceptance and empowerment in promoting reconciliation from the perspective of the needs-based model. *Social Issues and Policy Review*, *2*(1), 159–186. https://doi.org/10.1111/j.1751-2409.2008.00014.x

Sisk, B. (2011). The role of the UN archives in the long-term legacy of the ICTY. In R. Steinberg (Ed.). *Assessing the legacy of the ICTY* (p. 73–74). Martinas Nijhoff Publishers. https://doi.org/10.1163/ej.9789004186248.i-318

South Africa. (1999). *Truth and reconciliation commission of South Africa report*. Vol. 1. The Commission.

Swart, B. (2008). Damaska and the faces of international criminal justice. *Journal of International Criminal Justice*, *6*(1), 87–114. https://doi.org/10.1093/jicj/mqm082

Taylor, L. K., & Lederach, J. P. (2014). Practicing peace: Psychological roots of transforming conflicts. *Global Journal of Peace Research and Praxis*, *1*(1), 12–31.

Tomuschat, C. (2006). National prosecutions, truth commissions and international criminal justice. In G. Werle (Ed.), *Justice in transition - prosecution and amnesty in Germany and South Africa* (pp. 157–168). Berliner Wissenschafts-Verlag.

United Nations International Residual Mechanism for Criminal Tribunal. (2006, June 20). ICTR appeals chamber takes judicial notice of genocide in Rwanda. Retrieved from https://unictr.irmct.org/en/news/ictr-appeals-chamber-takes-judicial-notice-genocide-rwanda

United Nations Security Council. (1994, November 8). *Resolution 955: Establishment of an international tribunal and adoption of the statute of the tribunal*. United Nations. Retrieved from http://unscr.com/en/resolutions/955

Viebach, J. (2014). Aletheia and the making of the world: Inner and outer dimensions of memorials in Rwanda. In S. Buckley-Zistel, & S. Schafer (Eds.), *Memorials in times of transition* (pp. 69–94). Intersentia.

Waldorf, L. (2006). Mass justice for mass atrocity: Rethinking mass justice as transitional justice. *Temple Law Review*, *79*(1), 1–87.

Wallensteen, P. (2002). *Understanding conflict resolution: War, peace, and the global system*. Sage.

Werle, G. (2009). *Principles of international criminal law* (2nd ed.). T.M.C. Asser Press.

Wibabara, C. (2014). *Gacaca courts versus the international criminal tribunal for Rwanda and national courts lessons to learn from the Rwandan justice approaches to genocide*. Nomos Verlagsges Mbh & Co KG.

Wolfe, S. (2020). Memorialization in Rwanda: The legal, social, and digital constructions of the memorial narrative. In E. M. Zucker., & D. Simon (Eds.), *Mass violence and memory in the digital age* (pp. 19–44). Palgrave Macmillan. https://doi.org/10.1007/978-3-030-39395-3_2

Zorbas, E. (2009). What does reconciliation after genocide mean? Public transcripts and hidden transcripts in post-genocide Rwanda. *Journal of Genocide Research*, *11*(1), 127–147. https://doi.org/10.1080/14623520802703707

7 "Double Genocide" or Revenge Killings? Did the Liberators of a Genocide Commit Their Own?

Jonathan R. Beloff

Introduction

On the night of April 6, 1994, the aircraft carrying the Presidents of Rwanda and Burundi was mysteriously shot down on its approach to Kigali International Airport. The flight originated from Arusha, Tanzania, where regional leaders had been pressuring Rwandan President Juvenal Habyarimana to implement a peace agreement between his government and the Tutsi-dominated rebel group, the Rwandan Patriotic Front (RPF). The killing of Habyarimana resulted in Hutu ideological extremists organizing and perpetrating the deaths of over 800,000 Tutsis and moderate Hutus within a hundred-day time span. The massacres ended on July 19 when the RPF's military wing, the Rwandan Patriotic Army (RPA), was able to drive the interim genocidal government out of Rwanda and into eastern Zaire, now known as the Democratic Republic of Congo (DRC).

Allies of the previous administration questioned why the heroes of the genocide killed an estimated 25,000–45,000 innocent Hutu civilians (Des Forges, 1999, p. 728). Twenty-eight years after the genocide, the narrative of Hutu deaths as part of an organized "double genocide" by the RPF is yet again being told by new media avenues as seen in the BBC documentary, *Rwanda's Untold Story* (Reyntjens, 2015), and through new books (Wrong, 2021, pp. 365–380).

Within Rwanda, little public or media attention is paid to Rwandan Hutu deaths caused by the RPA. They are typically hidden from public discourse or ignored by official discourse. This has hindered public discussion on how to remember those who died during the Civil War of 1990 who were not directly involved in the military campaigns or victims of the subsequent 1994 Genocide against the Tutsi. National memorials and commemorations often only focus on how Hutu genocide perpetrators butchered the local Tutsi population (Longman, 2017, pp. 260–267). Comparisons between the deaths of Tutsis and Hutus during the genocide as well as any discussion of a post-genocide reconciliation between the two victim groups of the genocide and of the RPA killings are extremely

DOI: 10.4324/9781003228592-9

limited. This is a result of post-genocide Rwandan elites' fear that discussion that memorializes Hutus killed, or attempts at reconciliation between former RPA fighters and Hutu victims, might overshadow the horrors of the genocide. This concern raises the question of whether these deaths should properly be characterized as "revenge killings," or as a "double genocide" of or against the Rwandan Hutu population, in whole or in part, in order to establish a Tutsi-dominated state.

In this chapter, I attempt to answer this important question. The subject has become controversial over the years. I will focus on the RPA killing of Hutus during that same time period as the genocide of the Tutsis. I will not address the post-genocide killings of Hutus, such as the 1995 Kibeho massacre (Prunier, 2009, pp. 38–41), which occurred after the RPF had taken over the state. I argue in this chapter that of the two opposing views, the scholarship that characterizes the killings by the RPA during the genocide of Tutsis and moderate Hutus in the months leading up to July 1994 as "revenge killings" is more persuasive than the argument that these killings constituted a "double genocide" of the Hutus. In short, despite the horror of some of those massacres by the RPA soldiers, those killings do not rise to the level of, or indicate, an intent to commit genocide. Indeed, a strong rebuttal argument to the "double genocide" theory is proposed by the current RPF-dominated Rwandan government: the idea that the theory is tendentious. The "double genocide" believers are simply deniers of the original, or the only real, genocide of the Tutsis in 1994.

The chapter is organized into five main sections. The first section details my methodology in collecting the information. The research stems from the existing scholarly literature and my own field research interviews. The second section examines the core beliefs and training of RPA troops before the genocide. Examining the RPF's ideology of ethnic unity is important for understanding the psychological rationale for its participation in the killing of Hutu civilians even as the soldiers swept toward Kigali in an attempt to end the genocide. The third section focuses on the killings themselves, with particular emphasis on the early documented cases immediately following the initiation of the genocide; that is, the killings that occurred at the Rwandan-Tanzanian border, and those liquidations involving members of the Catholic Church. In the fourth section, I explain why these murders took place.

The cases of mass killings of Hutu civilians cited in this chapter are not compendious but illustrative, an attempt to explicate their rationale. The fifth and final section is focused on how, since 1994, the killings are remembered within both official and informal discourses. Their occurrence during the genocide of the Tutsis complicates the memorialization of that larger event, a fact that is often used to deny the genocide as such. How, therefore, the killings are characterized and memorialized has implications for the memorialization of the genocide itself and, thereby, the nation's attempts toward reconstruction and reconciliation.

Methodology

The sensitive nature of this subject made conducting field research rather complicated. Some scholars have suggested that the subject highlights the dangers of performing research in Rwanda (Clark, 2013). However, the aim of this research was to better understand the history of the Rwandan Civil War and how the RPA killings factor into the nation's understanding of Rwanda's past. Various qualitative methods were used for this research. It began with grounded theory to prevent any prior biases from the author's experiences in Rwanda. Grounded theory is the mechanism of using qualitative information extracted from field research data to create a theory to explain a social phenomenon (Creswell, 2009). After the primary research period, this research utilizes triangulation methodology (Davies, 2001) to examine the validity of informant's responses in light of the existing literature. This methodological model provided me with the best mechanisms to extract information from the semi-structured interviews I conducted among numerous Rwandans living in Rwanda during multiple visits to Rwanda and abroad.[1] The interviewees provided support, information, and guidance. Many informants within the Rwandan government and military (Rwanda Defence Force[2] or RDF) were willing to discuss this subject, despite what some scholars describe as an oppressive research environment which could hinder openness to discuss this subject (Beloff, 2017, pp. 50–53). Many RPF informants held some association with the RPA killings. Association ranged from soldiers having been accused of participating, or being a commanding officer of soldiers who conducted the killings, or even, one informant, being responsible for prosecuting in military courts soldiers who engaged in the killings.

Conducting research within Rwanda was difficult at times as Rwandans, whether government or military elites, or citizens, would avoid publicly discussing the subject. However, established relations with elites provided me the opportunity to explain the purpose of the research. Informants were opened to discuss the sensitive subject once I established that I had not drawn any prior conclusions regarding the killings and with regards to how I engage with Rwandans.

The chapter leaves out the interviewees' names to protect their identities. In addition, it substantially utilizes previously published scholarly literature to prevent any accusations of bias, by supporters and detractors alike, toward the double genocide theory. On the contrary, as I hope to show, these two main sources, my own fieldwork interviews, and the extant literature, support my overall theory that the RPF did not plan or conduct a double genocide based on the known case studies of killings by its troops.

While conducting this research, I did not face any significant limitations or hindrance from any military or political elite actors. My experience differed from those of Rever (2018) and Sundaram (2016), who performed research on similar highly sensitive subjects in Rwanda. Rather, many informants admitted the sensitivity of the subject and supported my research. One of my informants commented on their hope that one day, my research could be used to make society more aware of the Civil War's history in a context that did not detract from the significance of the genocide.[3]

Ethnicity and the Rwandan Patriotic Front

The RPF originated from the first wave (1959–1962) of exiled Tutsi refugees, which stemmed from the departure of the Belgian colonial power and the rise of the first Hutu President Grégoire Kayibanda (Melvern, 2000, pp. 17–21; Prunier, 1997, pp. 54–60). From 1962 until the beginning of the Rwandan Civil War in 1990, tens of thousands of Tutsis were forced to flee their Rwandan homes and move into poorly maintained refugee camps in the surrounding nations of Burundi, Tanzania, Uganda, and Zaire. The dire conditions of the refugee camps and the lack of economic activity heavily influenced the refugees' belief in the need for equality and self-determination for what they considered the ideal civic society. Many wanted a return to the pre-colonial socio-economic structure, others the creation of a post-colonial system that mimicked the socialist systems being erected in other parts of Africa (Waugh, 2004, pp. 7–27).

In 1973, Major General Juvenal Habyarimana conducted a military *coup-d'état* against President Kayibanda and assumed political power in Rwanda. Many Tutsis within and outside Rwanda believed the new Habyarimana administration could bring a decline in anti-Tutsi pressures and public policies. However, new anti-Tutsi government policies were enacted, and more Tutsis fled the country, to such an extent that new pressures mounted from the exiled community for a right of return policy. In addition to the new influx of refugees, frustration with the dire situation within the exiled Tutsi population grew. Refugees experienced anti-Rwandan racism and corruption by their host governments. This was especially the case in Uganda under the political rule of Idi Amin and of Milton Obote (Kimonyo, 2019, pp. 18–47).

With conditions in regional nations growing worse, the refugees felt it increasingly necessary to pressure the Habyarimana administration to allow them to return to their homeland. Tutsi, as well as ideologically moderate (or even anti-extremist) Hutus, who sought refuge in Uganda lived together with little to no ethnic tension. Most saw themselves as victims of Hutu extremists, and thus saw each other as Rwandans and as fellow victims, whether based on politics or ethnicity (Rucyahana, 2007, p. 38).

The desire to leave the refugee camps and return to Rwanda transformed into action in 1987. The refugee-led Rwandese Alliance for National Unity Congress, which would later be renamed as the Rwandan Patriotic Front (RPF), crafted the Eight-Point Programme, which would be the ideology of the refugee movement (Beloff, 2021, p. 40; Crisafulli & Redmond, 2012, pp. 52–62; Rusagara et al., 2009, p. 187). The Eight-Point Programme specified the belief in "one Rwanda," a country that accepted all Rwandans no matter their ethnic identity. This transethnic belief held significant importance to the core of the rebel group that became the RPF.

In order to spread this ideology among the growing number of refugees fleeing the country before the Civil War, a military movement (the Rwandan Patriotic Army[4] or RPA) was created. Political teachings, known as *Ingando,* became as significant as the military training. During these political lessons, troops were instructed in the newly-formed RPF's vision of Rwanda's history. This stressed how the German and Belgium colonial powers had created and enforced ethnic differences and beliefs to retain political and economic control over the territory.

The *Ingando* policies advanced by the RPF promoted the idea of a unified people ("one Rwanda"). *Ingando* countered the long history of ethnic divisionism which, even after independence, had been exploited by the series of Hutu governments in power. Divisionism enabled those governments to maintain power and caused a disenfranchised Tutsi population to become targets of violence, and to flee the country in waves during the 1960s, 1970s, and 1980s.

One of the macabre ironies of Rwandan history is that the "ethnic-free Rwanda" that the RPF was proposing through *Ingando* was matched, rhetorically, by the "ethnic-free Rwanda" promoted by the extremists associated with Habyarimana's government, except that their objectives were radically opposed. *Ingando* represented ethnic transcendence, an end to divisionism through unity, whereas the extremists envisioned an ethnic-free Rwanda through the mass extermination of the Tutsis.

In the guerilla bases and refugee camps before the Civil War, the rebel soldiers received an education in reconciliation and equality between Hutu and Tutsi. Some RPF leaders were concerned that if they did not address and emphasize the subject of reconciliation, there was a strong possibility that they might lose control over their soldiers, resulting in killings to avenge the loss of their loved ones once they entered Rwanda (Kimonyo, 2019, pp. 180–181). Many RPA troops and international aid workers would later credit the *Ingando* classes for the limited number of RPA killings and, indeed, limited any temptation to formulate and foment of an intent to eradicate Hutus, during the 1994 liberation of Rwanda (Gourevitch, 1998, p. 219).

After a failed attempt to invade the country in October 1990, the RPF implemented more civics classes for its soldiers while they were stationed in the forest on the Virunga volcanoes (Kinzer, 2008, p. 84). The "political commissars" of the RPF focused on informing the soldiers about the current political landscape in Rwanda, how to interact peacefully with the local population, regardless of ethnicity to gain the community's support and trust, and how to establish an internal military structure to prevent abuses (Crisafulli & Redmond, 2012, pp. 31–41; Kinzer, 2008, pp. 53–54; Waugh, 2004, pp. 53–54). In addition, punishments for criminal acts committed by RPA soldiers, such as robbery and murder, were meted out in the hope of gaining the trust of the Rwandan public.

Throughout the RPA's first (1990) and second (1992) attempts to invade Rwanda, its troops focused on positively interacting with the local population to demonstrate that its actions were based not on ethnicity, but on a commitment to establish an inclusive government for all citizens. During raids on Rwandan Government military outposts, all possible attempts were made by the RPA to prevent civilian casualties and to make the public aware of its intentions (Kinzer, 2008, pp. 33–34, 88–89).

Although predominantly a Tutsi rebel force, there were many disaffected Hutus within the ranks of the guerilla army. For instance, during the January 22, 1991, rebel attack on the northwestern city of Ruhengeri, RPA soldiers released many political prisoners in the hope that they would join their rebel movement (Melvern, 2020, p. 88; Rucyahana, 2007, pp. 49–51). Although the RPF recruitment of Hutu foot soldiers remained low, many Hutus did join the movement to support a democratic transition of political power (Rusagara et al., 2009, p. 178). This military structure was vastly different from that of the armed forces of Rwanda at the time, the *Forces Armées Rwandaises* (FAR), which actively prohibited any Tutsi from serving (Melvern, 2000, p. 101; Prunier, 1997, pp. 168–169).

RPA Killings

While the Hutu extremist-led Rwandan government perpetrated the genocide during the hundred-day period in 1994, the RPA was busy liberating large sections of the country. It is worth noting that for some it was considered controversial to describe the military campaign during the genocide as a "liberation" rather than an "invasion." Some Rwandans feared that the approaching RPA would seek vengeance for the murder of the local Tutsi population (Rusesabagina & Zoellner, 2006, p. 168; Wrong, 2021, p. 240). However, other Rwandans, both Hutu and Tutsi, saw the approaching RPA as a source of peace and physical security (Kayihura & Zukus, 2014, pp. 116–126). For the majority of Rwandans, the invading force brought an end to the killings and a return to some form of normalcy (Doughty, 2016, pp. 61–62).

Nevertheless, some RPF-held territory continued to experience bloodshed despite the removal of genocide forces (Gribbin, 2005, p. 161). Unlike before, violence was directed at Hutu individuals who RPA soldiers believed had either organized or participated in the murders of the local Tutsi population.[5] That is, the motivation to kill these Hutus was more from vengeance or suspicion than from any intent to destroy the Hutu population as such.

Alison Des Forges estimated that the RPA killed 25,000–30,000 civilians (Doughty, 2016, p. 62; Lemarchand, 2009, pp. 88–91; Prunier, 1997, pp. 266–268, 342, 359–362; Straus & Waldorf, 2011, p. 17). The massacre of Hutu civilians occurred sporadically, especially within the rural areas (Waldorf, 2011, pp. 49–50). The Kabgayi massacre is the largest and most well-known of all the killings.

On April 11–12, 1994, the RPA prevailed in its first major battle against the FAR in northeastern Rwanda. Given the ease with which the RPA defeated the FAR, the RPA and RPF leadership determined that the new war was winnable and decided to focus all of its attention on achieving victory (Des Forges, 1999, p. 538).[6] As more of the country was liberated by the RPA, and the genocide became more widely known and witnessed by the RPA soldiers themselves, the RPA's central command focused on finishing the war as early as possible in order to stop the atrocities. According to my informants, this unfortunately led to a reduced concern among RPF political leadership about those killings of Hutu civilians carried out by its troops.[7]

The RPF considered the *Interahamwe,* a Hutu extremist genocide militia group that carried out the genocide and, indeed, members of any pro-Hutu militias, to be enemy combatants. This, in effect, allowed its soldiers to kill civilians whom they believed had participated in the genocide (Prunier, 2009, pp. 306–307; Waugh, 2004, pp. 167–168, 175).[8] The first major massacre resulting from this conception of the terms of conflict was on April 15 at the community of Sake, in the former Kibungo prefecture near the Rwandan-Tanzanian border. Genocide perpetrators fled with civilians to the Tanzanian border, fearing retaliation. The RPA attacked the group at Kanazi Hill and killed hundreds. This event is confirmed through the United Nations High Commission for Refugees (UNHCR), which reported the killing of refugees who were fleeing to Tanzania (Des Forges, 1999, pp. 541–552). Further massacres by RPA troops during the hundred days of the genocide took place in the Nteko sector in the Gitarama prefecture; Mututu in the Butari prefecture; the Nzangwa mosque in Bugesera, as well as several others (Des Forges, 1999, pp. 542–544).

As the war raged on and the RPA's soldiers became more aware of the genocide, random acts of murder against civilians suspected of participating in or supporting the genocide grew. Des Forges documented most of the attacks that took place from the end of May through to early July (Straus & Waldorf, 2011, p. 17). In response to the allegations of such massacres, the RPA stated that the soldiers responsible for these crimes would either face disciplinary action by their commanders or military trials for their crimes (Des Forges, 1999, pp. 557–558; Gribbin, 2005, p. 124). The record of any punishments these troops received for having killed Hutu civilians, however, remains unavailable (Kinzer, 2008, pp. 260, 329–330).

The Catholic Church had been one of the most powerful institutions used by the previous Rwandan Presidents, Kayibanda and Habyarimana, to secure political power and preach ethnic hatred against the Tutsi populations (Beloff, 2015, pp. 106–112; Carney, 2013, p. 193; Mbanda, 1997, pp. 60–61). Many within the RPF held an opinion of the Church that differed radically from those held by the past Hutu-led Rwandan governments. The former saw the Catholic and Anglican Churches as a primary cause of underdevelopment and corruption both in Rwanda and on the African continent as a whole.

Some within the RPF viewed the church as a too-dominant player in public affairs that needed to be restrained in order to prevent religious corruption of government officials. Others, however, believed that the Church could be a significant ally, as it had been for prior regimes, once the RPF gained political power. However, the Churches' involvement in the genocide made them a target for many RPA soldiers.

As noted, the most widely known massacre of Hutu civilians, allegedly based on revenge, occurred at the Kabgayi Catholic Church Center outside of Gitarama on the June 3. Pope John Paul II had formally requested protection of the church from Lt. General Romeo Dallaire along with the United Nations Assistance Mission for Rwanda (UNAMIR) troops, but these forces proved to be ineffective. Most of the residents at the religious site decided to stay and wait for the incoming RPA soldiers. The religious leaders were risking their lives as they had participated in earlier genocide-related crimes, whether as instructing congregates to participate in the massacres or spreading ethnic violence through religious sermons. On June 3, a number of the RPA soldiers, having invaded and secured the region, went into the monastery with the aim of killing its religious leaders. RPA troops entered the church facility and murdered the archbishop along with three of his bishops (Vincent Nsengiyumva, Thaddee Nsengiyumva, and Joseph Ruzindana), ten priests and around 1,500 other Hutu victims (Gribbin, 2005, p. 141; Prunier, 1997, pp. 270–271; Melvern, 2000, p. 206).

A former RPA commander, who was responsible for the capture of the church, noted how he had ordered his troops to capture and hold all those inside. He was not at Kabgayi during its capture; however, and discovered within a day or two that some of his soldiers had ignored his orders. He would later testify at a closed-door military trial against those soldiers for disobeying his orders, but admitted that he understood why some soldiers saw the need to commit revenge and kill defenseless civilians after having witnessed the horrors of the genocide for nearly two months.[9] UNAMIR was able to coordinate with the RPA and the FAR to have the bodies transferred to the interim government for a proper burial (Beloff, 2015, p. 214).

When Dallaire pressed the RPF about the Kabgayi murders, the RPF acknowledged the event and blamed a breakdown in military command stemming from RPA soldiers losing their sanity after witnessing atrocities. In Dallaire's words: "Quite simply, they killed the princes of the church out of vengeance, their discipline frayed to the breaking point by the atrocities they'd witnessed" (Dallaire, 2004, pp. 414–418). Other reports state that the RPF forces blamed the deaths on the lack of training received by the accused officers, who had only recently been recruited. Skeptics of the RPF's explanation believe that the motive for the massacre at this specific church, and of Vincent Nsengiyumva in particular, stemmed from his relationship with the Habyarimana regime (Lewis, 1994). During Habyarimana's presidency, Nsengiyumva was one of his influential allies within the church, promoting government policy pursuant to an ideology of hatred against the Tutsi (Prunier, 1997, pp. 270–272; Wallis, 2019, pp. 265–267, 270–274). Whatever the true reason for the murders, it provided the fleeing genocidal government with the propaganda opportunity to coax many Hutus to flee into Zaire.

In 1995, in response to the alleged killings in Kabjayi and elsewhere, the UNHCR created the Gersony Mission, a four-member team tasked with uncovering evidence of widespread human rights violations committed by the RPA. United Nations (UN) consultant Robert Gersony and his team estimated that up to 45,000 Hutus died or "disappeared" as a result of targeted killings by RPA troops (Des Forges, 1999, pp. 553–556; Kimonyo, 2019, p. 113; Lemarchand, 2009, p. 104; Wrong, 2021, pp. 265–267, 270–274). The report was designed to determine the motive and intent for the killings, but was suppressed by leading members of the UN after the RPA (which succeeded to the RPF) questioned the report's methodology.

The RPA demanded that the sources of the derogatory evidence be presented so it could cross-analyze the testimonies (Gribbin, 2005, pp. 141, 160–161; Kimonyo, 2019, pp. 113–115). No follow-up studies were performed until Alison Des Forges wrote *Leave None to Tell the Tale*. Both the UN report and Des Forges' publication questioned the predominant belief that the RPF were the "clean good guys" in the conflict, compared with the "bad guys"[10] of the Hutu extremist groups. The UN report's suppression has convinced some Great Lakes region scholars (e.g., Reyntjens, Prunier, Pottier, and Lemarchand) that the RPF is determined to prevent any mention of the killings in order to keep playing the "genocide guilt card" that is seen as pivotal to its foreign policy (Cowell, 2012, p. 45; Lemarchand, 2009, pp. 73, 95–106; Pottier, 2002, pp. 79–81; Reyntjens, 2016; Rieff, 2002, pp. 179–180).

Understanding the Killings

Most of the research conducted on the Rwandan genocide has attempted to understand the local social dynamic that saw neighbors killing their neighbors (Fujii, 2009; Straus, 2006). This chapter seeks to ascertain the rationale for the killings undertaken by the RPA by understanding why they happened: whether they were committed to avenge the massacre of Tutsis, or whether they evinced an intent to eradicate Hutus. Unlike the 1994 genocide, or other genocides such as the Holocaust, there is an absence of confirmed data to prove a link between the individual actions of soldiers who committed the murders and any planning and execution of a genocidal strategy crafted and enacted by the military establishment of the RPA. On the contrary, my research suggests that the reasons why the assassinations occurred has to do with the dynamics of the Rwandan Civil War, the RPF establishment (Ugandan-origin rather than newer troops), the military and civics training, and – the least understood psychological issue – the effects of the massacres of Tutsis on the soldiers.

When the Arusha Accords peace treaty[11] was brokered, the RPA consisted of around 15,000 troops, although some estimates have the number as high as 20,000 (Prunier, 1997, pp. 193, 270). The FAR, on the other hand, had around 40,000 troops (Gourevitch, 1998, p. 157). These numbers do not include foreign-based troops, including the UNAMIR troops that ranged from around 270 to 2,500 troops throughout the conflict, or hired mercenaries (Dallaire, 2004, p. 88; Kinzer, 2008, pp. 153–157). By the end of the genocide in July 1994, the RPA numbered around 40,000 troops (Gourevitch, 1998, p. 222). This dramatic increase in the number of troops was a result of how quickly territory was conquered.[12]

During the first weeks of the genocide, the FAR chain of command had very little concern for whether or not its troops participated in the genocidal killings. Its main concern was to try to protect the nation for what it saw as a Tutsi-led invading army. However, by the third week of the hundred-day genocide, the FAR began to focus its attention on assisting the *Interahamwe* with their daily massacres (Kimonyo, 2016, p. 366). With this shift in military operations, the RPA found it easier to invade and hold the newly liberated territories. The biggest problem that the RPF/RPA leaders encountered was the limited supply of soldiers available to continue the invasion into western Rwanda, as well as hold on to the recently conquered territories. To solve the problem of troop shortages, the RPA accepted nearly anyone willing to fight against the genocidal government (Kinzer, 2008, pp. 189–191).

While most veteran RPA troops originated from Uganda, many of the newly recruited troops were from Burundi or Zaire, where Tutsi populations faced harsh persecution at the hands of local Hutu supremacists. These new, young, predominantly Tutsi RPA soldiers saw a chance to seek revenge for the horrors inflicted on them. Additionally, many fighters seemingly disregarded the Eight-Point Programme goal of a united Rwandan identity, instead perceiving the RPA as a pro-Tutsi rebel group seeking to gain political and/or financial power for the Tutsis in a new, post-conflict Rwandan society.

The new RPA soldiers were a mixed blessing. They provided the rebel force with the numerical strength it needed to continue its operations, namely, to end the genocide through the liberation of the country. However, these soldiers were trained very differently from the original troops who participated in the 1990, 1991, and 1992 campaigns.[13] As stated before, those earlier soldiers received *Ingando* instruction on how to interact with civilians.[14] One of the key political teachings of *Ingando* was the RPF's responsibility to stop the cycle of ethnic violence that had afflicted Rwanda since the beginning of colonization. These lessons were either never given to the new recruits, or significantly shortened. Newly enlisted personnel received, on average, a week of military and political training (Prunier, 1997, p. 270). Thus, they were not as disciplined and knowledgeable about the core beliefs of the RPA's as earlier recruits had been.

The original troops also witnessed the genocidal horrors performed against their distant Tutsi relatives. Some related these experiences to previous abuses perpetrated to a lesser extent against their own families throughout the region. Anger from witnessing the results of these inhuman, genocidal acts, combined with fear that they might occur again, coupled with a lack of proper military training, steered some of the original RPA soldiers to take revenge against Hutu civilians. As such, their actions were not so different from the second group, the newer recruits, who joined the RPA during the liberation, and who were survivors of the genocide. In short, both groups would have been motivated by revenge.

In the midst of the genocide, Tutsi civilian survivors felt compelled to join the RPF and RPA for various reasons. Some joined because they felt unable to continue their lives; they had lost their families, friends, crops, and cattle and were left with the sense that they had very little reason to live. Some joined to try to stop the genocide in other parts of the country. Others joined because they wanted to fight against the forces of the genocide government as an act of revenge for their lost families.[15]

Equally susceptible to vengeance were the older RPA troops from Uganda whose mental state quickly deteriorated after discovering the horrors that had occurred in their ancestral villages. The core of the RPA were Rwandan Tutsi refugees who resided in Uganda (Rusagara et al., 2009, pp. 173–177). For two or three generations in exile, they had heard stories about their ancestral homelands. Rwandan history is based on oral tradition, which resonates deeply with children (Kinzer, 2008, pp. 16–18). Only a few of these Rwandan exiles were able to visit their homeland before 1994. Unfortunately, the *Interahamwe* specifically targeted any family members of RPF/RPA members/collaborators who did not flee the country prior to 1994.

Some RPA troops were able to liberate their ancestral villages or visit them after liberation. They encountered the destruction of the Tutsi population, which often included their relatives. The emotions that ran through these soldiers' minds are unimaginable. The troops from the refugee camps in Uganda had spent most of their childhood hearing stories of the beauty of their homeland and of the family members who had not emigrated or fled during past pogroms. For soldiers who had joined the RPA in the hope of reconnecting with family members who still resided in those lands, seeing them dead created mental insanity (Kinzer, 2008, pp. 116–119). As such, most RPA soldiers viewed the remaining Hutu villagers with suspicion and distrust (Prunier, 1997, p. 266), questioning whether they had participated in the murders or whether they had attempted to save any of the victims. With their families dead, some troops saw no possible future and thus did not consider the consequences of committing acts of murder. The RPA troops who killed unarmed Hutu villagers, on the evidence presented to me, were mentally insane. They were enraged and sought to avenge the deaths of their loved ones and the desecration of their ancestral homesteads. There was no evidence that they harbored a specific desire to commit massacres against the Hutu population based solely on their ethnicity or following explicit military orders to do so.[16]

The killing of Hutus seemed to be individual acts rather than a grand conspiracy by the RPF to butcher the Rwandan Hutu population (Dallaire, 2004, p. 479; Reed, 1996, p. 499). Behind most of the noted cases of killings by RPA soldiers are stories that depict the mental breakdown of individual soldiers, many of whom, afraid of prosecution by the RPA's military court, subsequently committed suicide.[17] The number of cases prosecuted by the RPF's successor, the RPA's military court, remains unknown (Gribbin, 2005, p. 164; Gourevitch, 1998, pp. 223, 246, 346; Kinzer, 2008, pp. 191–193; Peskin, 2011, p. 180).

The conclusion, based on the interviews and the literature, that the RPA killings were motivated by revenge and not with any genocidal intent, is not meant to justify the murders of innocent civilians. It does make a difference; however, how the killings are characterized. I argue that the most appropriate locus for definitively determining how to characterize those killings is the legal forum. In the following section, I argue how the Rwandan justice system and the International Criminal Tribunal for Rwanda are the most appropriate sites to discover and promote the truth behind these tragic events.

Remembering Those Who Died

During the 2010 Rwandan Presidential Election, opposition candidate Victoire Ingabire visited the Kigali Genocide Memorial to pay her respects to the 250,000 genocide victims buried there. It has become customary for Rwandan and international political, business, and civil society leaders to pay their respects at the memorial (Guichaoua, 2021). However, Ingabire's visit became mired in controversy after she publicly stated the need to memorialize Hutus who had been killed by the RPA during the Civil War (Jones, 2016, p. 350). The comments themselves were controversial, but equally problematic was where she said them: at the Kigali Genocide Memorial. A memorial guide who witnessed the speech told me of his disbelief, not so much of her comment but because of the location.[18] For him, and multiple others at the memorial, the comments were controversial because the memorial's focus is on remembering those who were killed during the genocide rather than during the Civil War.

Ingabire's speech closely tracks what Melvern (2020) and others have described as the minimization of the genocide of the Tutsis and the attempt to foster a moral equivalence between the deaths of Hutus killed by the RPA and those killed by genocide forces (pp. 121–122, 143, 177–196). However, Reyntjens (2013, pp. 48–49, 247), Thomson (2018, pp. 182–184, 225–228), and Longman (2017, p. 165) categorize Ingabire's comments and her later arrest by the Rwandan government as the latter's attempt to silence her and others regarding the RPA killings, and as a way for society to forget that part of the history of the Rwandan Civil War and the genocide. There are no memorials for Hutus killed during the Rwandan Civil War. Longman (2017) notes that some victims of the RPA were buried alongside genocide survivors at the nation's many genocide memorials (p. 142).

Longman (2017) writes that the RPA killing of Hutus during that period is often purposely ignored by the government during genocide commemorations or conversations about the genocide (p. 142). The historical narrative of the RPF as the "good guys" combating the "bad guys" of the genocidal former government and its genocidal actors leaves little room for discussion of RPA killings of Hutu civilians. During conversations with Rwandans in Kigali and Gisenyi, a former center of power during the Habyarimana regime, all commented on how civilian casualties during the Civil War and particularly the genocide are known (within society) to have happened. However, many have accepted the government narrative of the necessity for the history of the killings to be minimized in public spaces in order for Rwandan society to remain stable. When asked when society will engage in open conversations about the killings, one Hutu genocide survivor commented, "Maybe one day for our grandchildren. We [Rwandan society] are still too fragile for it. Like with politics [political openness], we need to have a few generations of stability before we are ready to discuss it."[19]

The argument for stability is also given as a reason why the scope of the *gacacas'* (a community-based court system that promotes dialogue and reconciliation between victims and *Interahamwe*) was limited to genocide crimes (Longman, 2017, pp. 112–115). The *gacaca* courts focused on promoting justice and reconciliation between genocide perpetrator and victims (Clark, 2010, pp. 1–28). None of these trials prosecuted any members of the RPA for their crimes during the genocide. This has caused controversy, with some scholars such as Peskin (2011, pp. 173–182) and Reyntjens (2013, pp. 78, 99–105, 132–138) asking whether the post-genocide RPF-led government has exerted political pressure to obstruct court investigations into RPA crimes during the genocide. Despite some calls for action, public discussion on promoting historical justice for these victims has largely been absent within Rwanda (Jessee, 2017, p. 78).

While Thomson (2012), Rever (2018), and Longman (2017) would characterize the government's policy of silence as an attempt to whitewash history and to secure RPF power, many of my informants perceived the policy, as noted, as a strategy to promote stability, even if it meant that the victims of RPA killings were not memorialized.[20] Once the nation had reached long-term security and development, these informants said, then society will be able to discuss the RPA crimes without the fear of a return to violence. This belief also held among the former RDF members. During a 2019 conversation, a former RPF commander said, "They [RPF killings] will be discussed by a generation who doesn't know if they are Hutu, Tutsi or Twa. They won't want to kill each other at that point."[21] While the nation awaits this post-ethnic period, victims of the RPF killings are typically publicly ignored, despite most of the society being fully aware of the RPA soldiers who committed them.

Conclusion

When RPA soldiers had returned to the homes they had once fled, they found friends and family members massacred in the most brutal acts imaginable. One would be hard pressed to imagine a soldier, faced with this scenario, not wishing to retaliate. There is no doubt that these individual soldiers did use their weapons and killed members of the Hutu population. However, the fact of these killings, even *en masse*, does not prove that there was an overall goal by the RPA to carry out a double genocide. The RPA killings totaled approximately 25,000 or 1–2% of the total 1.5 million deaths during the 1990–1994 Civil War and the genocide (Prunier, 2009, pp. 342–359). The low number of killings can be attributed to the RPF's express policy of trying to end the cycle of ethnic hatred and massacres, and to gain the trust and support of the local population toward the establishment of a new and inclusive future government. The low number of Hutu deaths relative to the genocide of the Tutsis also resulted from the RPA's attempt to help the many new Hutu refugees, who had fled during the end of the genocide, feel that they could safely return to Rwanda under the RPF's philosophy that all Rwandans have the right to live in Rwanda (Reed, 1995, p. 52).

There is evidence that some of the soldiers who participated in the killings either committed suicide or were convicted in military courts for their crimes (Prunier, 2009, pp. 342–363). This is further proof that the killings were based on vengeance, for it would be unlikely that the soldiers would face a penalty for their participation in the killings if these acts were condoned by the RPA. However, the total number of RPA (formerly RPF) troops prosecuted, convicted, and sentenced by the military tribunals is unknown and, by all reports, unlikely ever to be revealed. This lack of transparency about the Hutu massacres will always make this subject controversial.

It is understandable that the RPF-led Rwandan government would not want to deviate from the dominant historical narrative as part of its ongoing effort to prevent a future genocide. Justice for the victims of the killing of innocents, however, is not the only element missing from that official narrative. The government's silence, and the silence of society at large, regarding these events means that a part of Rwandan history is largely absent from the public discussion of the memorialization of the events of 1994.

I have argued that the preponderance of evidence suggests that the RPA killing of Hutus during the genocide of the Tutsis was likely motivated not by the intent to destroy the Hutu population, but from revenge. Given the silence on the issue within official Rwandan discourse, the idea of a double genocide, not definitively disproved by this lack of transparency, will remain a sensitive issue, because it represents a society not fully reconciled with its past.

I suggest that it is difficult for Rwanda, as with any post-conflict society, to sever itself from the shackles of its bloody history while parts of that history are silenced or suppressed. Rwandans, whether members of the ruling elite, the military, or civil society, are well aware how the country has not settled this part of its history. As a result, Thomson (2018), Reyntjens (2018), Mann and Berry (2016), and Longman (2017) question the RPF's continued role in the progression and success of post-genocide Rwandan society, specifically whether the government has fostered a stable environment for economic development. On the one hand, Rwandan history within the country is taught through the RPF's own perception and construction of history, with the genocide centering that perception and functioning as the primary focal point. Nevertheless, on the other hand, that construction of the recent past includes the suppression of the RPA killings which are largely left out of the nation's memory. Mention of them remains culturally and politically sensitive as seen, for instance, in the arrest of Ingabire during an election based on transnationalism in Rwanda (Jones, 2016).

Ultimately, therefore, the current public policy of being overly cautious when discussing the genocide creates a strong breeding ground for genocide denial to take root. It also can be problematic for long-term social stability as reconciliation between Rwandans will be incomplete.

Notes

1 The research periods are as follows: June to July 2012; January to June 2013; July to December 2014; August 2016; and August to October 2019.
2 In 2002, the Rwandan Patriotic Front changed its name to the Rwanda Defence Force.
3 Interview with an unnamed Rwandan government official in September 2014.
4 The Rwandan Patriotic Front (RPF) was the political rebel actor with its military being the Rwanda Patriotic Army (RPA).
5 Interview with an unnamed RDF commander in May 2013.
6 Interview with an RDF officer in September 2014.
7 Interview with an unnamed RDF commander in May 2013.
8 Interview with a former RDF commander in May 2013.
9 Interview with a RDF commander in December 2014.
10 These terms are often used by writers such as Johan Pottier, Gerard Prunier, and Filip Reyntjens to describe how the RPF illustrated the conflict for Western audiences (Pottier, 2002, pp. 33–34, 339–340).
11 This agreement created a permanent ceasefire for the Rwandan Civil War (1990–1994 accords were in 1993) between the warring RPF and the Habyarimana regime. It orchestrated a democratic transition from the previous one-party state of the Habyarimana regime, with Habyarimana retaining his Presidency but allow for different political parties to participate in the Parliament.
12 Interview with an unnamed RDF commander in May 2013.
13 Interview with an unnamed former RDF commander in September 2014.
14 These courses still exist to promote Rwandan unity for returning refugees (Purdekova, 2018, pp. 174–202).
15 Interview with RDF officials in May 2013.
16 Interview with ten RDF officials from May to June 2013.
17 Interview with ten RDF officials from May to June 2013.
18 Interview with a Kigali Genocide Memorial tour guide in August 2016.
19 Interview with Rwandan Hutu survivor of the genocide in December 2014.

20 Interviews with Rwandans between: August 2016, August to October 2020.
21 Interview with a former RDF commander in August 2019.

Bibliography

Beloff, J. R. (2015). The historical relationship between religion and government in Rwanda. In M. Rectenwald, R. Almeida, & G. Levine (Eds.), *Global secularism in a post-secular age* (pp. 205–222). De Gruyter. https://doi.org/10.1515/9781614516750-014

Beloff, J. R. (2017). The limitations of research space for the study of Rwanda. *The SOAS Journal of Postgraduate Research*, *10*(2016–2017), 48–60.

Beloff, J. R. (2021). *Foreign policy in post-genocide Rwanda: Elite perceptions of global engagement*. Routledge.

Carney, J. J. (2013) *Rwanda before the genocide: Catholic politics and ethnic discourse in the late colonial era*. Oxford University Press. https://doi.org/10.1093/acprof:oso/9780199982271.001.0001

Clark, P. (2010). *The gacaca courts, post-genocide justice and reconciliation in Rwanda: Justice without lawyers*. Cambridge University Press. https://doi.org/10.1017/CBO9780511761584

Clark, P. (2013, November 28). Must academics researching authoritarian regimes self-censor? *Times of Higher Researcher*. http://www.timeshighereducation.co.uk/features/must-academics-researching-authoritarian-regimes-self-censor/2009275.fullarticle

Cowell, F. (2012). Participatory rights in Rwanda: genocide ideology laws and the future of political space. In M. Campioni & P. Noack (Eds.), *Rwanda fast forward: Social, economic, military, and reconciliation prospects* (pp. 45–59). Palgrave MacMillan. https://doi.org/10.1057/9781137265159_4

Creswell, J. W. (2009). *Research design: Qualitative, quantitative, and mixed methods approaches*. Sage Publications, Inc.

Crisafulli, P., & Redmond, A. (2012). *Rwanda, Inc.: How a devastated nation became an economic model for the developing world*. Palgrave Macmillan.

Dallaire, R. (2004). *Shake hands with the devil: The failure of humanity in Rwanda*. Da Capo Press.

Davies, P. H. J. (2001). Spies as informants: Triangulation and the interpretation of elite interview data in the study of the intelligence and security services. *Politics*, *21*(1), 73–80. https://doi.org/10.1111/1467-9256.00138

Des Forges, A. L. (1999). *Leave none to tell the story: Genocide in Rwanda*. Human Rights Watch.

Doughty, K. C. (2016). *Remediation in Rwanda: Grassroots legal forums*. University of Pennsylvania Press.

Fujii, L. A. (2009). *Killing neighbors: Webs of violence in Rwanda*. Cornell University Press.

Gourevitch, P. (1998). *We wish to inform you that tomorrow we will be killed with our families: Stories from Rwanda*. Picador.

Gribbin, R. E. (2005). *In the aftermath of genocide: The US role in Rwanda*. iUniverse.

Guichaoua, A. (2021, May 5). In Rwanda, genocide commemorations are infused with political and diplomatic agendas. *The Conversation Africa*. https://theconversation.com/in-rwanda-genocide-commemorations-are-infused-with-political-and-diplomatic-agendas-160283

Jessee, E. (2017). *Negotiating genocide in Rwanda: The politics of history*. Palgrave Macmillan.

Jones, W. (2016). Victoria in Kigali, or: why Rwandan elections are not won transnationally. *Journal of Eastern African Studies*, *10*(2), 343–365. https://doi.org/10.1080/17531055.2016.1187816

Kayihura, E., & Zukus, K. (2014). *Inside the hotel Rwanda: The surprising true story… and why it matters today*. BenBella Books.

Kimonyo, J.-P. (2016). *Rwanda's popular genocide: A perfect storm*. Lynne Rienner Publishers.

Kimonyo, J.-P. (2019). *Transforming Rwanda: Challenges on the road to reconstruction*. Lynne Rienner Publishers.

Kinzer, S. (2008). *A thousand hills: Rwanda's rebirth and the man who dreamed it*. John Wiley & Sons.

Lemarchand, R. (2009). *The dynamics of violence in central Africa*. University of Pennsylvania Press.

Lewis, P. (1994, June 12). June 5-10: New atrocities in Africa; Three bishops and 10 priests are slaughtered in Rwanda as tribal killings go on, *New York Times*, *https://www.nytimes.com/1994/06/12/weekinreview/june-5-10-new-atrocities-africa-three-bishops-10-priests-are-slaughtered-rwanda.html*

Longman, T. (2017). *Memory and justice in post-genocide Rwanda*. Cambridge University Press.

Mann, L., & Berry, M. (2016). Understanding the political motivations that shape Rwanda's emergent developmental state. *New Political Economy*, *21*(1), 119–144. https://doi.org/10.1080/13563467.2015.1041484

Mbanda, L. (1997). *Committed to conflict: The destruction of the church in Rwanda*. Society for Promoting Christian Knowledge.

Melvern, L. (2000). *A people betrayed, the role for the West in Rwanda's genocide*. Zed Books.

Melvern, L. (2020). *Intent to deceive denying the genocide of the Tutsi*. Verso.

Peskin, V. (2011). Victor's justice revisited: Rwandan Patriotic Front crimes and the prosecutorial endgame. In S. Straus, & L. Waldorf (Eds.), *Remaking Rwanda: State building and human rights after mass violence* (pp. 173–183). The University of Wisconsin Press.

Pottier, J. (2002). *Re-imaining Rwanda: Conflict, survival and disinformation in the late twentieth century*. Cambridge University Press. https://doi.org/10.1017/CBO9780511491092

Prunier, G. (1997). *The Rwanda crisis: History of a genocide*. Columbia University Press.

Prunier, G. (2009). *Africa's world war: Congo, the Rwandan genocide, and the making of a continental catastrophe*. Oxford University Press.

Purdekova, A. (2018). *Making Ubumwe: Power, state and camps in Rwanda's unity-building project*. Berghahn Books.

Reed, W. C. (1995). The Rwandan patriotic front: Politics and development in Rwanda. *Issue: A Journal of Opinion*, *23*(2), 48–53. https://doi.org/10.2307/1166507

Reed, W. C. (1996). Exile, reform, and the rise of the Rwandan patriotic front. *Journal of Modern African Studies*, *34*(3), 479–501. https://doi.org/10.1017/S0022278X00055567

Rever, J. (2018). *In praise of blood: The crimes of the Rwandan patriotic front*. Random House Canada.

Reyntjens, F. (2013). *Political governance in post-genocide Rwanda*. Cambridge University Press. https://doi.org/10.1017/CBO9781107338647

Reyntjens, F. (2015). The struggle over truth – Rwanda and the BBC. *African Affairs*, *114*(457), 637–648. https://doi.org/10.1093/afraf/adv042

Reyntjens, F. (2016). (Re-) imagining a reluctant post-genocide society: The Rwandan patriotic Front's ideology and practice. *Journal of Genocide Research*, *18*(1), 61–81. https://doi.org/10.1080/14623528.2016.1120464

Reyntjens, F. (2018). Understanding Rwandan politics through the longue durée: From the precolonial to the post-genocide era. *Journal of Eastern African Studies*, *12*(3), 514–532. https://doi.org/10.1080/17531055.2018.1462985

Rieff, D. (2002). *A bed for the night: Humanitarianism in crisis*. Simon & Schuster.

Rucyahana, J. (2007). *The bishop of Rwanda: Finding forgiveness amidst a pile of bones*. Thomas Nelson, Inc.

Rusagara, F., Mwaura, G., & Nyirimanzi, G. (2009). *Resilience of a nation: A history of the military in Rwanda*. Fountain Publishers Rwanda.

Rusesabagina, P., & Zoellner, T. (2006). *An ordinary man: An autobiography*. Penguin Books.

Straus, S. (2006). *The order of genocide: Race, power, and war in Rwanda*. Cornell University Press.

Straus, S., & Waldorf, L. (2011). Introduction: Seeing like a post-conflict state. In S. Straus, & L. Waldorf (Eds.), *Remaking Rwanda: State building and human rights after mass violence* (pp. 3–24). The University of Wisconsin Press.

Sundaram, A. (2016). *Bad news: Last journalists in a dictatorship*. Doubleday.

Thomson, S. (2012). Peasant perspectives on national unity and reconciliation: Building peace or promoting division? In M. Campioni, & P. Noack (Eds.), *Rwanda Fast forward: Social, economic, military and reconciliation prospects* (pp. 96–110). Palgrave Macmillan.

Thomson, S. (2018). *Rwanda: From genocide to precarious peace*. Yale University Press.

Waldorf, L. (2011). Instrumentalizing genocide: The RPF's campaign against 'Genocide Ideology'. In S. Straus, & L. Waldorf (Eds.), *Remaking Rwanda: State building and human rights after mass violence* (pp. 48–66). The University of Wisconsin Press.

Wallis, A. (2019). *Stepp'D in blood: Akazu and the architects of the Rwandan genocide against the Tutsi*. Zero Books.

Waugh, C. M. (2004). *Paul Kagame and Rwanda: Power, genocide, and the Rwandan patriotic front*. McFarland & Company, Inc.

Wrong, M. (2021). *Do not disturb: The story of a political murder and an African regime gone bad*. Public Affairs.

8 Moving Forward

Creating a Safe Space for Women Raped during the 1994 Genocide against the Tutsi in Rwanda

Odeth Kantengwa

Introduction

In the spring of 1994, Rwandans endured a cataclysmic genocide against the Tutsi. In one hundred days, more than one million people perished (Republic of Rwanda, 2002). The widespread killings, torture, and rape left the country's social fabric in shambles. During the genocide, rape, gang rape, sexual torture, sexual slavery, and forced marriage were used systematically as weapons against 250,000–500,000 women and girls (Amnesty International, 2004, p. 4). The genocide resulted in human and material losses, psychological trauma, and social disruption.

In this chapter, the term genocidal rape refers to forced sexual penetration that is "committed with intent to destroy, in whole or in part, a national, ethnical, racial or religious group" (UN General Assembly) by inflicting bodily and mental harm, causing death, group destruction, or preventing future births (Reid-Cunningham, 2008). Female survivors of genocidal rape face unique challenges as individuals. Not only are they traumatized by the experience of living through genocide, but they also endure the psychological trauma that accompanies rape. While rape was itself stigmatizing, the sexual torture of these women often resulted in unwanted pregnancies or HIV. Perpetrators of sexual violence were recruited for their HIV-positive status. Many rapes were thus explicit attempts to pass on what was, at the time, an inevitably fatal disease to victims, their children, and future sexual partners (Kantengwa, 2014). The birth of children which were the products of such atrocities posed additional burdens and increased the likelihood of exclusion of the mothers from society (Denov & Piolanti, 2019; Woolner et al., 2019).

Specific instances of mass violence committed during the 1994 genocide against the Tutsi cannot be understood without a close consideration of their causes and consequences (McGarty, 2014). This chapter documents genocidal rape as one of mass violence that has complex and long-term consequences for female survivors. It also documents inspiring stories of their healing processes, made possible through the contribution of the project titled *Appui aux victimes de violence sexuelles* supported by the *Hôpitaux Universitaires de Genève* (HUG).

DOI: 10.4324/9781003228592-10

Since these women faced distinctive challenges after the genocide, support groups for women who experienced genocidal rape during the 1994 Genocide Against the Tutsi were facilitated through *Médecins du Monde*. In these groups, women began to discuss their experiences with the facilitation of a psychotherapist. Recent research has recognized the therapeutic benefits of group therapy for participants, particularly in the context of acute or chronic psychological trauma (Gishoma et al., 2014). With this in mind, *Médecins du Monde* helped to facilitate support groups for female survivors of genocidal rape by providing transport services, psychological (medical) assistance, as well as economic services. After the conclusion of the *Médecins du Monde* program, female survivors maintained a social space, sharing personal stories to support each other, but lacked material support and assistance. This was particularly the case for survivors who were infected with HIV or raising children born of rape. Thus, victims may have shared their stories with others, but could not escape the social stigma associated with poverty and the lack of psychological assistance resulting from genocide.

In response to this need, Never Again Rwanda (NAR), a Rwandan nongovernmental organization (NGO), with funding from *Hôpitaux Universitaires de Genève* (HUG), expanded a support project for female survivors of genocidal rape (*Appui aux victimes de violence sexuelles*), allowing for these women to transform their social space into a safe space. Understanding the differences between a social space and a safe space is key to understanding the needs of survivors of the genocide. A social space is merely a gathering place for people to come together and discuss their shared experiences. While the power of sharing emotions should not be minimized (Pennebaker et al., 2001), it was a combination of sharing personal stories with facilitation from psychotherapists and material support that created a safe space.

Within these safe spaces, true healing for these female survivors could begin. This chapter shows that through the *Appui aux victimes de violence sexuelles* project, women survivors would meet and share their experiences as well as propose solutions for their daily problems. In such safe spaces, these women are removed from areas with social stigma and isolation. They can participate in income-generating activities as well as engage with psychological professionals to share their stories and provide solutions to their daily problems. Given the above, this chapter endeavors to answer the following two research questions:

1 How do female survivors of genocidal rape describe effects resulting from genocidal rape?
2 What role does the sharing of personal stories in a group facilitated by psychotherapists play in the post-genocide healing process?

While most scholars focus on the attempt to explain genocide, there is very little work examining the effects of rape that resulted from the 1994

Genocide against the Tutsi in Rwanda. The contribution of the role of sharing personal stories in a safe space to the post-genocide healing process has received little to no attention in the published literature on the aftermath of political violence, conflict, genocide, and rape. Toward a larger understanding of the genocide and its effects, it is critical, however, to examine the ways sharing of personal stories in safe spaces advances our understanding of how group sharing influences the life chances of female survivors in the healing context of post-genocide Rwanda.

Beyond the Expectations of *Appui Aux Victimes De Violence Sexuelles* Project: The Creation of a Safe Space

The late Professor Dr. Naason Munyandamutsa, a psychotherapist, family therapist, and then country director of NAR, met with a HUG staff member assisting in the mental health department in Rwanda and shared his concerns regarding women raped during genocide. The HUG staff member decided to pay a visit with Professor Munyandamutsa to one of the support groups for these women. During their visit, women expressed their problems and what they thought would be helpful to them at the moment. From their expressed needs and priorities, Professor Munyandamutsa drafted a project proposal. From there, the two (Dr. Munyandamutsa and the HUG staff member) traveled to Switzerland to raise awareness of issues concerning female survivors of genocidal rape in Rwanda with the Swiss government.

As a response, the government of Switzerland, through the *Département de la solidarité internationale*, collaborated with HUG to initiate the project in Rwanda in 2012, as an attempt to offer family-based care and comprehensive services – including material and psychosocial support – to 144 females and their family members, particularly 16 children born of genocidal rape. The purpose of this project was specifically to satisfy the needs of women by getting them into psychotherapy groups and having them engage in economic activities that equally served as therapeutic.

The project provides resources to initiate income-generating activities, basic medical care through paying medical insurance, agriculture education programs, and training for women survivors of genocidal rape. Most program activities are led by female survivors with additional facilitation by trained psychotherapists, which helps women to become "agents of change" in their communities.

Women engaged in the project have had a quicker healing time than other female genocidal rape survivors who did not participate in the initiative.[1] Belonging to a group and accessing services in a safe environment restores individual dignity, which in return reduces social stigma and allows these women to re-enter society, ultimately helping to rebuild social relationships that were destroyed during the genocide and restore the social fabric of Rwanda.

Methods

Through the use of qualitative methodology, this chapter aims to understand how female survivors of genocidal rape perceived the sharing of personal stories in groups, how the HUG project facilitated the creation of a safe space, and how the project contributes to healing in post-genocide Rwanda.[2] Qualitative methods help researchers to respond to a social problem by producing a set of broad research questions, rather than a narrow hypothesis. As the researcher investigates the problem, the research questions become narrower and lead to the creation of a conceptual framework (Blumer, 1969). Purposive sampling was used and data were collected through in-depth interviews and group discussion with women who had been raped during the genocide. In order to best understand the experiences of the female respondents of this study, the researcher encouraged these women to guide the conversation and share their stories in a way in which they felt comfortable. The researcher listened with sensitivity and encouraged responses to questions when necessary.

Selection Criteria

Although genocidal rape affected all the regions of Rwanda harshly, this research focused on female survivors of genocidal rape from the Southern Province of Rwanda. Respondents were identified through NAR. Selection criteria required that respondents be female survivors of genocidal rape and members of the *Appui aux victimes de violence sexuelles* project supported by HUG. Respondents were excluded from the sample if they had a severely limited ability to communicate with the researcher due to cognitive or emotional impairments. Of 38 women who were identified, two women who had agreed to be interviewed found it difficult to proceed with narrating their experience about raising children born of rape and chose to discontinue participation.

Data Collection Methods

The study's research approach was qualitative, and the data were gathered through 14 in-depth interviews and two focus group discussions involving six to 13 participants. The in-depth interviews lasted between 120 and 210 minutes in spaces selected by the respondents (usually at the offices of the HUG project, or at the fieldwork site where female survivors carry on their income-generating activities). Interviews and group discussions began with open-ended questions such as, "Please tell me your life story, and share with me whatever you think is relevant." The researcher lets the respondents talk about whatever they wanted, in whatever order they chose, touching on topics that they chose. Over the course of the interviews and discussion, the following questions were asked in each case: "How would you describe yourself during the genocide?" and "What role does sharing of personal stories in a group play in your post-genocide healing process?"

Interviews and the focus group sessions were conducted in Kinyarwanda, recorded (with permission of the interviewees), and later transcribed and translated into English. In conducting in-depth interviews as well as group discussions, the researcher immersed herself in the data and ongoing assessments for forty-five days before the final analysis.

Qualitative Data Analysis

As Ellsberg and Heise (2005) explain, there are many ways to analyze qualitative data. Generally, however, analysis involves organizing the data according to specific criteria, reducing it to a more manageable form, displaying it in a form that aids analysis, and interpreting it.

Most of the data analysis was done after data collection and transcription of field notes and interviews was complete. The researcher read and reread the data to form a consistent interpretation. From the life stories of the female members of the HUG project, the researcher identified three elements that form the respondents' narratives:

1 Psychosocial and economic effects resulting from genocidal rape;
2 The need for a safe space in post genocide society;
3 The importance to respondents of sharing personal stories in a group.

Results

This section does not exhaust every effect resulting from the genocide. However, narratives from female survivors reflect the majority of the horrors experienced during the 1994 genocidal rape in Rwanda. Many of the discourses presented in this section reflect the women's experiences before the establishment of the *Appui aux victimes de violence* sexuelles project.

Psychological Consequences

Female survivors of genocidal rape often experience psychological trauma long after the sexual torture occurs. For the respondents, genocide left psychological scars that often prevented them from engaging in normal social activities. A thirty-nine-year-old woman whose father was forced to witness her rape reported:

> After all this time I am still troubled by his death and the way they forced him to witness the way I was raped...Whenever these experiences come in my mind, I look for a quiet place and isolate myself for some hours...When I think back to the genocide of 1994, a feeling of coldness comes over me and I start to shiver...[3]

Survivors' friends and neighbors unwittingly, by their mere presence, extended the physical and emotional intrusion of genocidal rape in the lives of these women. As the respondent described, lingering fears can lead to social isolation when survivors feel a loss of safety and control over themselves and their environment.

The respondents articulated the view that the systematic attacks by genocide perpetrators resulted in not only a loss of control, but also a lack of self-awareness and human dignity. One respondent described being gang raped by members of the militia and the *Interahamwe*, saying "Everyone in that group came and tasted me like an object of pleasure." She struggled to narrate the impact of genocide, crying, "I find myself as a person who has lost my value, my dignity as a mother and a woman. I feel ashamed and see myself as an outcast in the society." Far worse, she found that she could not escape from people that triggered a traumatic reminder of her rape: "It is one thing to be raped and it is another to be raped in public by gangs with whom you are to live together after they are released."

Post-traumatic stress disorder, panic disorders, and social phobias can prevent these women from participating in normal activities. A forty-five-year-old woman with a gynecological injury due to rape described a common doctor's visit:

> A male doctor told me to lie down on the gynecological table for examination. I lay down, but then after like one minute, I saw a group of three young men coming into the room [following the doctor]. I fell down and ran away. This group of young men reminded me of how *Interahamwe* raped me as a group...After coming back to my senses, I was told that these young men were doing their internship in that hospital.

The above testimonies indicate that genocidal rape continues to traumatize survivors. In Rwanda, women were raped as part of a systematic, genocidal campaign, and as such were treated like objects. Women lost their sense of humanity and worth and often experienced constant retraumatization because they lived near and interacted with former perpetrators and their families. Beyond the impact of rape on individual women in Rwanda, respondents also reported that they worried they could potentially pass on their fears and insecurities to their children born out of rape.

Social and Economic Consequences

In Rwanda, like other nations around the world, rape can carry a severe social stigma. Rwandan women who were raped did not want to reveal their experience to others, fearing that the community would reject them. The social stigma was particularly acute for those infected with HIV. These women, who already isolated themselves because they felt unsafe and "lacking emotional warmth," found that they had to hide their most painful experiences from Rwandan society for fear of social stigma. This stigma forced one respondent to move from her village to "another province where no one knew about [her] experience." A sixty-five-year-old describes this acute fear of rejection:

> We (referring to herself and her friends) decided to keep silent about the horrors we had endured instead of being considered as prostitutes. We thought that if our sexual torture became known, the community would stigmatize and marginalize us. We decided to keep quiet because some people in the community, when they found out that our friends had been raped and that they had sexually transmitted diseases, particularly HIV, said that if they had survived then they must have collaborated with perpetrators of the genocide [worked as prostitutes]. This means that if we reveal our experience, we are likely to face the same stigma.

Respondents reported that because of the persistent stigma attached to rape and HIV/AIDS, many of them were discouraged from ever coming forward to seek help or meet with friends to share their experiences. Some respondents even said that their friends suffered unnecessarily and died in silence because they lacked hope and were unable to access well-designed programs that would have met their needs.

The challenges resulting from raising children born of rape were not limited to social stigma. Respondents also reported economic difficulties related to raising children. One mother of a child born of rape said, "I was always troubled by how I will pay the school fees for my daughter. I failed to concentrate on what I could do while surrounded by that problem. It made me feel sorrowful and bitter." To address this issue, most female interviewees got married immediately after the genocide. From what they reported, these early marriages did not last. Some of the women mentioned that getting married that quickly, and often that young, would not have been a priority, but for the inability to deal with the economic challenges.

The Importance of a Safe Space

A psychological counselor from NAR noted the importance of group sharing for survivors of genocidal rape:

> When a person has experienced the levels and multiplicity of physical and emotional traumas that survivors had to deal with, it is never easy for them to heal and get to the normal way of life, especially if she does not open up to someone in a safe space and more especially to someone she trusts and confides in. These females felt like their world had come crashing down on them and that they were unable to pick up their pieces.

Without a safe space in which to share, it can be extremely difficult for traumatized women to heal. Surrounded by constant reminders of the horrors they have faced and unable to vocalize their emotions, women can feel even more isolated and depressed. A forty-six-year-old woman spoke about her life before joining the *Appui aux victimes de violence sexuelles* project as "a nightmare." Without family or friends, she was completely alone and could not face completing even simple daily tasks. She said:

> Though I felt like I should share my experience because I felt like bursting, the people around me did not care and would not see directly through my heart, though they were able to observe that I was withdrawn and not making any progress, as I failed to concentrate on activities I attempted to do...

A participant in the *Appui aux victimes de violence sexuelles* project recognized this survivor's symptoms and invited her to open up to other female survivors in a safe space. The woman at first was hesitant:

> What exactly confused me at the time was that I could not find the right words to narrate what I went through and I hesitated if that was the right time to say and more so if these were the right people to share with. And sometimes I asked myself if what she suggested was going to help me despite the fact that my heart kept convincing me that I should get someone to share with my psychological burden.

Thus, it became clear that the safe space provided a much-needed outlet. The exceptional psychological and social effects of genocidal rape on female survivors in post-genocide Rwanda created the need for programming, in addition to providing an outlet, that also included material and social services as well as a safe space for women to meet. *Appui aux victimes de violence sexuelles* exemplified this type of project: it provided material support and helped women form collectives, but it also gave women a place they felt truly accepted and heard as individuals. According to a psychological counselor from NAR, providing a safe space "has been helpful to them in a way we did not even expect as we started this process." In fact,

> Once [the women] shared their experience we realized that negative emotions started vanishing. This as well helped them quite generally later to develop emotional expression in collective situations, such as commemorations, grouped in associations, religious ceremonies, and other social rituals which seemed too difficult immediately after genocide ended in Rwanda.

Group sharing as well as professional counseling allowed survivors to overcome struggles that could have broken them in the past. For example, psychosocial counselors worked with women before and after they testified at *gacaca*. Together, the survivor and her counselor would prepare for confronting a potential perpetrator and the difficulty of sharing testimony. This professional training, as well as the support of other survivors in the association, allowed female members to participate more actively in *gacaca*, a process which can help to heal themselves as well as Rwandan society at large.

Beyond emotional growth, the country director of NAR said that promotion of group sharing "restores social bonds, increased social cohesion, and group survival."[4] By connecting survivors together to share their stories, the program enables individual women to rebuild their sense of self and form communal bonds that contribute to the creation of a new social fabric in Rwanda. For respondents, these meetings were more than just a chance to express themselves. According to one respondent, "Belonging to our group can be equated with belonging to a class. We learnt how to live a meaningful life." Sharing personal stories allows respondents to learn new skills from one another, build new networks, accept their pasts, move forward with their lives, and just plain feel better.

Because survivors are at different stages in the healing process, they can collaborate and generate solutions to individual struggles. Respondents indicated that they learned "social skills" from their fellow survivors, which allowed them to communicate better with their home communities. Furthermore, sharing of personal stories inspires women to work through the social trauma associated with their children born from rape. One survivor with a child born of rape commented, "I learned from our friends that there is no way we can run from commitments as mothers, especially when we see the challenges ahead." Another woman commented that she learned from her collective:

> We now have to be conscious not only for our own interests but for our children as well. We are now determined to give our contribution to remove pain in the world by acting with compassion and by service as a role model.

Working through problems as a multi-leveled group, with women at different stages of the healing process, prompted women to learn skills from each other that were essential to overcoming social phobia and re-entering society. In addition, the respondents were able to overcome the social stigma associated with having a child born from rape and reassume their roles as mothers. This network of women and their families created a community within Rwanda that can promote healthy reconciliation.

Respondents also highlighted how sharing of personal stories during the *Appui aux victimes de violence sexuelles* project encouraged them to accept their realities, find the strength to continue with daily activities, and envision a brighter future. Before sharing their stories, many women had refused to acknowledge the very real problems they struggled with, including HIV, because they could not process them. The safe space provided assisted women in confronting their realities, and also provided a safety net comprised of friends and medical services to help them through their struggles. One woman explained:

> We had to look for a way to deal with our psychological traumas. We chose to face them because we have a reason to live for. Of course, at first we were inactive and we would sometimes get intimidated but at last we accepted the challenge of living with such effects and we finally courageously embraced the opportunity that comes with lessons of going through traumatic situations like genocide and rape.

The process was not easy. Another respondent asked herself how it could be possible to be happy again after a traumatic event like genocide. The *Appui aux victimes de violence sexuelles* group participants worked through the issue:

> When I joined my friends, who I felt can easily help me only because we share the same experience, the only thing they started with was to tell me that maybe acceptance of the past is a better concept. For us to start our journey to healing we need to first accept what befell us and thereafter we look for the ways to go about them. The things I used to fear even to think about, it was now high time to face and accept what happened.

These survivors recognized their past and were determined to find strength in it, to find meaning in life even if confronted with hopelessness. Listening to one another's stories and supporting each other through grief and anger helped to move these women into their futures. They learned essential coping mechanisms that allowed them to accept the troubles they had experienced in the past as well as any problems they might encounter in the future.

These women are more than just members of the same project; they became friends who understood each other's struggles. One respondent said:

> We do not dwell only on problems; we also have to get and say positive words and enjoy good moments because we have them. As we shared our social emotions even in difficult or problematic situations, our bodies relaxed.

When asked about economic support they received, female survivors in this study spoke about their appreciation for the material support they received. One of them narrated:

> Before *Appui aux victimes de violence sexuelles* project, I was always deeply impoverished and struggled with the responsibilities of taking

> care of my siblings. Due to this lack of financial support, my life was disturbed by stress, fear, and suffering. I am so grateful for HUG project because I know it could have been even possible to die, but *Appui aux victimes de violence sexuelles* project provides us with economic support. We [referring to herself and her group members] are engaged in income-generating activities and we can meet many of our basic needs and we are no longer isolated.

This is not to suggest that all women were completely healed by the program. Healing is an ongoing process, and not all women would be at the same level. Some of them would not yet have accepted what befell them, such as those who had been both sexually abused and infected with HIV. However, the overwhelming success of sharing of personal stories in a safe space funded by HUG's *Appui aux victimes de violence sexuelles* project was illustrated in the change in tone the respondents used when speaking of their future. Instead of using words like "hopeless" and "weak," respondents described themselves as "strong" and "determined." They looked forward to the future and were ready to encounter life again.

Conclusion

Female survivors of genocidal rape experience a litany of psychological symptoms and material problems that can follow them for years after their actual traumatic incident. Seemingly harmless situations can trigger a memory for rape survivors, who may relive the event as though it were occurring in the present. Consequently, survivors of rape can feel like they have no protection and are always vulnerable to attack (Hassan, 2003). Furthermore, after being treated so horrifically, women can feel as if they have lost their value as humans, and often exhibit symptoms of guilt, self-blame, and depression (Jewkes et al., 2002). Many respondents reported that because of the persistent stigma attached to rape and HIV/AIDS experienced during the genocide, they felt discouraged from seeking help or meeting with friends to share their personal stories. Female survivors often isolate themselves from society and feel as if no one in their communities can understand their pain.

The narratives show that the most traumatizing and challenging process for mothers before the *Appui aux victimes de violence sexuelles* project was the lack of a safe space comprised of both material and psychological support. The life stories of female respondents of this study, especially before the establishment of the project, were marked by traumatic memories related to both physical and psychological torture from genocidal rape. This continued and was reported to cause severe stress. The traumatic emotions resulting from genocidal rape also damaged women's perceptions of themselves. Some reported that in the period immediately after genocide, they could not see themselves as protective mothers. One of them commented, "I was aware that my harsh reaction to my child, including not breastfeeding my baby girl, from genocidal rape was bad for her, but I did not have the strength to act otherwise." This is in line with other research which highlights how some mothers felt that it was better not to tell their children what they went through during genocide. This research indicates that though such women chose not to share such experiences, their children still confronted them, seeking information about their identities (Dunlap et al., 2004).

After the 1994 Genocide against the Tutsi, survivors of rape formed informal social spaces where they shared their traumatic emotions and experiences with one another. As this study indicates, sharing of personal stories in a group and the creation of a safe space for women raped during the genocide were vital to their healing journey and their ability to re-enter society. Herman (1995) suggests that, regarding healing trauma resulting from mass violence, it is generally agreed that letting out what was previously kept in is better than attempting to repress and forget painful memories. The formation of associations that provided material support and group sharing allowed survivors to escape the stigma of their communities and permitted them to self-actualize. Hassan (2003) confirms that solidarity among victims of atrocities such as rape provides the strongest protection against terror, despair, shame, and stigma.

The analysis of participants' life stories shows that groups serve as families where female survivors work together to solve problems. Through sharing in these safe spaces, survivors feel loved, recognized, and cared for. In my research on women with children born from genocidal rape in Rwanda, I discuss the narratives of females' experiences and their reports on the importance of sharing traumatic emotions with people who went through similar tragedies. My research highlights the fact that group sharing is a powerful tool that helps women survivors of rape deal with their daily problems. It helps to break down feelings of isolation, secrecy, and shame (Kantengwa, 2014).

These women's life stories reflect the need to provide them with environmental, material, and social resources to assist them in navigating their healing journey. The major resources that women and their children lack are material resources, social support, connection, and care. Social isolation, especially for those in the rural areas, is a challenge to their healing process. Sharing their personal stories in a group was reported by program participants as providing mutual support that helped them learn psychological and economic strategies for dealing with painful emotional events.

Hazelwood and Burgess (1995) also show that the formation of social bonds is vital to the survivors' healing journey, as the length of time required for healing is connected to the quality of an individual's intimate relationships. Indeed, Zraly et al. (2013) postulate that understanding how patterns of courageous emotional expression among collective sexual violence survivors are supported or constrained by the social and structural forces operative within the post-conflict and post-genocide context. Therefore, the safe spaces created through the *Appui aux victimes de violence sexuelles* project rehumanize the female survivors and allow them to rejoin their communities. Social spaces act like mini networks, encouraging reconciliation and adding to the diversity of Rwanda's new social dynamic.

Indeed, the lessons learned from this study are not only applicable to female survivors of genocidal rape in Rwanda, but also to other victim groups within the country. The genocide traumatized the entire country, tearing apart Rwanda's social fabric and isolating individuals in their pain and suffering. To move forward as a nation, different groups need to form associations to talk about their experiences during genocide and receive material support. These networks of smaller groups allow individual Rwandans to heal after the genocide and promote the creation of a healthier, more hopeful Rwandan society. Safe spaces have been formed for students, widows, orphans, and other facets of society, and many of them have experienced the same success as the survivors of genocidal rape discussed in this chapter.

For example, the Association of Genocide Survivor Students (AERG) and the Group of Former Genocide Survivor Students (GAERG) were created when students in higher learning institutions who lost their families after the genocide needed a support network. AERG and GAERG created artificial families composed of students acting as a "mother," "father," and "children" who set up rules to live together as nonbiological families. Sharing stories among families is one of AERG's most important dynamics. This informal emotion-sharing allows students to support each other morally, while the material support offered by the program helps student survivors work through academic and socioeconomic problems.[5] *Benishyaka* ("Those with Courage") was created to defend the interests of widows and orphans of the liberation war led by the Rwandan Patriotic Front. The association gathers widows and orphaned children of deceased soldiers together to exchange their emotions. The program also pays for school fees for orphaned children. *Benishyaka* creates a safe space where orphans can receive material help and work through traumas unique to student survivors. These children are Rwanda's future, so ensuring their ability to heal is an extremely worthwhile goal.[6]

This chapter reflects the life stories of the specific subset of women survivors of genocidal rape who are members of the *Appui aux victimes de violence sexuelles* project. There are, however, avenues for further research within the field. For example, stories from female survivors of sexual torture experienced during the genocide indicate the significant impact of these experiences on the children born from the concomitant rape. In my own research, I found that the legacy of silence around genocidal rape as well as sexual torture has become a critical issue for the children. As they come of age and plan for marriage, starting families, and launching their own professional lives, these children increasingly express the need to understand how much their identities have been shaped by the circumstances of their birth within the cauldron of violence (Kantengwa, 2014). Research should be performed on this new generation of Rwandans born of genocidal rape: how they identify themselves, how society treats them, and how they view the future.

Rwanda experienced a terrible tragedy in the spring of 1994. Yet, by sharing their experiences with people who can understand their pain, individuals and groups have begun to move forward from their trauma, reconcile, and re-engage with society in newer, healthier ways. Rwanda's story of emotion-sharing can serve as an example for other post-conflict states. After trauma, victim groups should be encouraged to come together in safe spaces to tell their stories. Post-conflict governments should be urged to promote the creation of such spaces that provide material support and emotional sharing. The state would thereby enable the individual, the group, the community, and the nation as a whole to move forward into a brighter future.

Notes

1 This observation is informed by an interview I conducted with a Rwandan psychotherapist who compared the outcomes of the beneficiaries of the project with other female genocidal rape survivors in the surrounding region (some of whom were recipients of other projects but did not include the package of benefits as provided through HUG/NAR).
2 This article pulls from a research study (strategy, criteria, data collection, and analysis) that was also utilized in Kantengwa (2014). The questions and conclusions, however, depart from my previous works.
3 Focus Group Discussion in Huye, June 2015. Unless otherwise noted all further quotes come from this research project.
4 Interview with the late Prof. Dr. Naason Munyandamutsa conducted on November 3, 2015, in Kigali, Rwanda.
5 An interview with a GAERG member conducted October 6, 2015, in Kigali, Rwanda.
6 An interview with a *Benishyaka* representative conducted October 13, 2015, in Kigali, Rwanda.

Bibliography

Amnesty International. (2004, April 6). *Rwanda: "Marked for death", rape survivors living with HIV/AIDS in Rwanda.* https://reliefweb.int/sites/reliefweb.int/files/resources/EB00B99701B8EFE185256E6E005CD886-ai-rwa-06apr.pdf

Blumer, H. (1969). *Symbolic interactionism: Perspective and method.* Prentice-Hall.

Denov, M., & Piolanti, A. (2019). Mothers of children born of genocidal rape in Rwanda: Implications for mental health, well-being and psycho-social support interventions. *Health Care for Women International, 40*(7–9), 813–828.

Dunlap, E., Stürzenhofecker, G., Sanabria, H., & Johnson, B. D. (2004). Mothers and daughters: The intergenerational reproduction of violence and drug use in home and street life. *Journal of Ethnicity in Substance Abuse, 3*(2), 1–23. https://doi.org/10.1300/j233v03n02_01

Ellsberg, M., & Heise, L. (2005). Researching violence against women: A practical guide for researchers and activists. *World Health Organization and Program for Appropriate Technology in Health.* https://path.azureedge.net/media/documents/GBV_rvaw_front.pdf

Gishoma, D., Brackelaire, J.-L., Munyandamutsa, N., Mujawayezu, J., Mohand, A. A., & Kayiteshonga, Y. (2014). Supportive-expressive group therapy for people experiencing collective traumatic crisis during the genocide commemoration period in Rwanda: Impact and implications. *Journal of Social and Political Psychology, 2*(1), 469–488. https://doi.org/10.5964/jspp.v2i1.292

Hassan, J. (2003). *A house next door to trauma: Learning from Holocaust survivors how to respond to atrocity.* Jessica Kingsley Publishers.

Hazelwood, R. R., & Burgess, A. W. (1995). *Practical aspects of rape investigation: A multidisciplinary approach* (2nd ed.). Garland Press.

Herman, J. L. (1995). Complex PTSD: A syndrome of survivors of prolonged and repeated trauma. In G. S. Everly, & J. M. Lating (Eds.), *Psychotraumatology: Key papers and core concepts in post-traumatic stress* (pp. 87–100). Plenum Press.

Jewkes, R., Sen, P., & Garcia-Moreno, C. (2002). Sexual violence. In E. G. Krug, J. A. Mercy, L. L. Dahlberg, & A. B. Zwi (Eds.), *The world report on violence and health* (pp. 147–182). World Health Organization.

Kantengwa, O. (2014). How motherhood triumphs over trauma among mothers with children from genocidal rape in Rwanda. *Journal of Social and Political Psychology, 2*(1), 417–434. https://doi.org/10.5964/jspp.v2i1.334

McGarty, C. (2014). Twenty years after genocide: The role of psychology in the reconciliation and reconstruction process in Rwanda. *Journal of Social and Political Psychology, 2*(1), 377–386. https://doi.org/10.5964/jspp.v2i1.449

Pennebaker, J. W., Zech, E., & Rimé, B. (2001). Disclosing and sharing emotion: Psychological, social, and health consequences. In M. S. Stroebe, R. O. Hansson, W. Stroebe, & H. Schut (Eds.). *Handbook of bereavement research: Consequences, coping, and care* (pp. 517–543). American Psychological Association. https://doi.org/10.1037/10436-022

Reid-Cunningham, A. R. (2008). Rape as a weapon of genocide. *Genocide Studies and Prevention, 3*(3), 279–296. https://doi.org/10.1353/gsp.2011.0043

Republic of Rwanda. Ministry for Local Government, Department for Information and Social Affairs. (2002). *The counting of genocide victims: Final report.* https://genodynamics.weebly.com/uploads/1/8/3/5/18359923/minaloc_translated_document.doc

UN General Assembly, *Prevention and punishment of the crime of genocide*, 9 December 1948, A/RES/260, available at: https://www.refworld.org/docid/3b00f0873.html [accessed 16 January 2022]

Woolner, L., Denov, M., & Kahn, S. (2019). "I asked myself if I would ever love my baby": Mothering children born of genocidal rape in Rwanda. *Violence Against Women, 25*(6), 703–720.

Zraly, M., Rubin, S. E., & Mukamana, D. (2013). Motherhood and resilience among Rwandan genocide-rape survivors. *Ethos: Journal of the Society for Psychological Anthropology, 41*(4), 411–439. https://doi.org/10.1111/etho.12031

Part III

Justice and Memory through Artistic Expression

9 An Open Grave

The Kigali Memorial and the Aesthetics of Memorialization

Tawia B. Ansah

Introduction

In 1995, I visited Rwanda as part of a United Nations human rights mission.[1] Like many of the members of Fest'Africa, referenced in Anna-Marie de Beer's chapter in this volume, *Remembering Rwanda Through Transnational, Multivocal Narrative*, I too experienced the aftermath of genocide in Rwanda with both a Western and an African sensibility, having grown up in Ghana, Britain, and the United States. I visited several places where Tutsis had been massacred, a small number of the literally hundreds of sites that had been identified.[2] Some of these sites of massacre were already being preserved as memorials to the dead. Churches, ravines, outdoor latrines, and abandoned school buildings were filled with the remains of the dead where they had fallen. In 1995, a year after the genocide, these sites were unmediated, that is to say, they told the story of what had happened without filters, overscripts, or prompts. There was nothing formal or aestheticized about them; they were not monuments or "public art" (Young, 1994).

What struck me then was how, both in African and in Western culture, each site represented a dual desecration. On the one hand, they were evidence of a massacre, showing without ambiguity the truth of what had happened. This evidentiary purpose of the sites seemed almost to require the exposure of dead bodies. In this sense, they were crime scenes, and the desecration of the dead was instrumental. On the other hand, there was a conflicting value: the unburied represented a radical rupture from the traditional observance and maintenance, through burial rites, of the border between the living and the dead. In that sense, there was nothing instrumental or purposive to militate against the desecration.

As I stood on a knoll by the church at Ntarama, I thought of how that border between the living and the dead, one that would have been represented by the appropriate traditional burial rites, had been swept away. I imagined, as I walked through the site, that I had sullied the hallowed ground, that the unburied would be angry, that their spirits roamed the earth, like Polyneices after Creon's prohibition against his burial (Sophocles, 458 BCE, 1954, p. 195),

DOI: 10.4324/9781003228592-12

and like the ghosts in Veronique Tadjo's (2000) novel, *The Shadow of Imana* looking for someone to bury them in order to sacralize their abandoned bodies (p. 41, see also Tadjo, 2002).

Those walks took place almost three decades ago. Within that time, Rwanda has created formal monuments to the fallen victims of the genocide. I have not gone back to Rwanda to see them, but I have visited them virtually, online. I see the difference between the unfiltered sites I had visited and the more managed and aestheticized memorializations that have been created since.

In this chapter, I take a virtual walk-through Kigali Genocide Memorial Centre – the flagship memorial to the 1994 genocide of the Tutsis (Yusin, 2016) – in order to consider how much of the tragic past it has captured. What does the memorial say about Rwanda and her people today, and how does it reference, or not, the sites of massacre strewn about the country, the other memorial sites?

Much has been written over the years about the government's efforts to manage and maintain those sites since those early days, to create memorials to the fallen (Bickford & Sodaro, 2010; Bolin, 2019). I was interested in how that work was undertaken and how the "static product" (Young, 1994, p. 5) of today captured the history, the violence, and the trauma of the past, how it represented in monumental form the collective effort toward transitional justice, and the creation of a post-genocide Rwandan identity. I was interested in what happened, or what happens, to memory in the process, when memorialization and unburial collide. What, I wondered, does the latter expose regarding the efforts pursuant to the former?

In his extensive study of monuments, defined as "a subset of memorials,"[3] James E. Young (1994) notes the following:

> In this age of mass memory production and consumption, in fact, there seems to be an inverse proportion between the memorialization of the past and its contemplation and study. For once we assign monumental form to memory, we have to some degree divested ourselves of the obligation to remember. In shouldering the memory-work, monuments may relieve viewers of their memory burden.
>
> (p. 5).

Young (1994) goes on to note, however, that,

> If part of the state's aim…is to create a sense of shared values and ideals, then it will also be the state's aim to create the sense of common memory, as foundation for a unified polis. Public memorials, national days of commemoration, and shared calendars thus all work to create common loci around which national identity is forged.
>
> (p. 6).

Focusing on monuments to past events rather than other forms of memorial, Young (1994) cautions that "neither memory nor intention is ever monolithic: each depends on the vast array of forces – material, aesthetic, spatial, ideological – converging in one memorial site" (p. xii). His aim, in *The Texture of Memory: Holocaust Memorials and Meaning*, is to "highlight the process of public art over its often static result, the ever-changing life of the monument over its seemingly frozen face in the landscape." Memory sites are "fundamentally interactive [and] dialogical" spaces (Young, 1994, pp. x, xii).

In my virtual walk through the Kigali Memorial, I wanted to know whether Young was right, and whether the monument (museum-memorial) did in fact carry the burden of memory-work for, rather than with, the observer. I found that I was drawn to those artifacts both inside and outside of the museum-memorial that underlined the coherence as well as the ruptures of the museum-memorial's formal elements. As such, I found it helped to think about the formal elements toward an interpretation of the memorial and its meanings through the aid of related disciplines such as film, literature, and art.

Thus, my walk through the site attempts two things. First, to recognize, appreciate, and underline the extent to which memory sites may indeed bear the work of memorializing massive events such as genocide, how they remember with as much detail and as much authenticity as possible. This is particularly true of monumental memorials organized by the state, with a particular objective in view. The memorial's plotline, with a beginning, a middle, and an end (stages on the walk) creates a narrative and suggests a cabined response to the past. As I left the virtual site, I could see in the distance images of the city's new skyscrapers, a gleaming landscape symbolizing Rwanda's bright, ecstatic future (Yusin, 2016). I left with a feeling of the coherence of the monument's narrative project.

Second, however, I wish to consider the risks inherent to the monumental form of memorializing an event. Much like spectacular prosecutions of genocide and human rights perpetrators, memorializations such as the one in Kigali function as a bulwark against denial. Monuments too, like trials, are "constructed to serve pedagogic and commemorative ends" (Douglas, 2001, p. 182). Monuments, like trials, attempt to calibrate an official and univocal version of the events. But as Lawrence Douglas (2001) has noted, the legal narratives projected through the performance of trials contain moments of disjuncture that go against the narrative grain. These moments make us question what we observe and experience of the trial (p. 171).[4]

The Kigali monument presents the bones of the dead and the partially exposed coffins in the grounds outside the museum. The unburied or partially buried, their hovering presence between the worlds of the living and the dead, are colonized by the monument and their stories collapsed into the larger, memorial framework. Their sacrifice is for this greater, instrumental good: the evidence that genocide took place here, that masses were killed in the name of *ethnie*. Straddling the border, the unburied and partially buried represent the moments of disjuncture within the narrative coherence of the monument.

As both a cultural artifact and a political statement, I observe the memorial through the artifacts of other memorial forms: literary, filmic, and artistic. I am interested in the ways monuments, while dialogic and fluid, also critique their own univocality, by which I mean the monument's intention to create a specific narrative or national identity.

I explore the meaning, as a moment of disjuncture, of the "open grave" motif on the museum grounds. I focus on this motif, rather than the bones on the shelves within the museum, because the experience of looking down into the graves and of walking on them, albeit virtually, reminded me of my actual walk through the raw sites of massacre a year after the genocide. I observed that the artifact of the open grave on the grounds of the museum is integral to the whole exhibit – as it references aspects internal to the museum displays, such as the bones on the shelves, as well as the rural sites of massacre around the country. And yet, the open grave in the garden seemed peripheral also to the narrative of the monument, as it sits outside the museum memorial proper and monument's coherent construction of the history and the events of 1994.

Part 1 of this chapter describes Kigali Genocide Memorial, particularly the open gravesite on its grounds. Using both Western and African literary and cultural examples, I reflect upon the open grave trope as a window onto the work that memorials do in relation to the events memorialized. Part 2 considers the open grave concept in relation to memorial art, or art that tells the story of an event. I use the work of French classical painter Nicolas Poussin as an example and draw upon his work for the language and methods of an aesthetic analysis.

I conclude that in the monumental form of memorial, intended to create an official narrative and interpretation of the events, the disjunctive moments are also moments of erasure, of forgetting, or of suppression. Those moments or currents may elucidate the memorial, may shift the burden of memory onto the observer. This shift occurs when we consider the formal elements of the structure, and pay attention to the dislocated, abstracted elements – here, the open grave motif – outside the narrative project itself.

In short, if monumental memorial is an instance of transitional justice, it is also a highly politicized locus of nation-building and national identity. It tells the story of how the genocide should be remembered to create a coherent, managed, and consistent post-genocide identity. In Rwanda, the attempt to build an identity predicated on the story of the genocide, told from the "official" point of view, has also been an exercise in eliding and suppressing inconvenient, even brutal, aspects of the history and politics of Rwanda in the shadow of genocide (Ansah, 2006; Reyntjens, 2013, p. 129).[5] This chapter uses an aesthetic lens, meaning that it employs aesthetic references and theory, to review the formal elements of the memorial itself, in order to critique the memorializing effort of Rwanda's primary national memorial site in Kigali. I attempt to uncover what is symbolically buried within the memorial's "open grave."

Memorial Museum

Toward the end of Sophocles' play *Antigone*, Tiresias the seer warns King Creon that the "unburial" of Polyneices will have dire consequences:

> Know well, the sun will not have rolled its course
> many more days, before you come to give
> corpse for these corpses, child of your own loins.
> For you've confused the upper and lower worlds.
> You sent a life to settle in a tomb;
> you keep up here that which belongs below
> the corpse unburied, robbed of its release.
> Not you, nor any god that rules on high
> can claim him now.
> You rob the nether gods of what is theirs
> (Sophocles, 458 BCE, 1954, p. 195).

In 1995, a year after the genocide, the massacre sites in Rwanda were raw. There was no denying that this massive human rights atrocity, recognized internationally by states and non-state parties as a legal genocide, had subverted the ordinary course of the universe: life, death, burial, and the communal rituals of mourning.

Often considered the "crime of crimes" (Schabas, 2009), genocide is characterized by the widespread and systematic massacre of innocents simply because of who they are as a people based on race, ethnicity, nationality, or religion. Twenty-eight years after the genocide in Rwanda, as part of the effort to contend with its past and transition into its future, the question remained: how those raw memorial sites would be managed and presented, how an abnormal phenomenon may have become "normalized" through the edifice of monuments and other forms of memorial.

In 2004, the government opened the most formal and perhaps most managed of its memorials to the genocide at the Kigali Genocide Memorial Centre (Aegis Trust – Rwanda, 2004). In the museum, there were the exhibits: powerful reconstructions of the events, with voices and script, photographs and film clips. There were the stories of the victims and the survivors rendering for the observer, for a brief time, an immediate experience. There were bones on a shelf. Outside the museum there are gardens, waterfalls, a monument to the fallen United Nations Belgian soldiers, a wall of names, and walkways. This seemed to be designed as a "negative space" for contemplation and reflection.

At the outer border of the grounds were fourteen mass graves, marked by simple concrete slabs, that contained the remains of 250,000 victims who died in the Kigali prefecture. One of the tombs had a latticed window jutting out of its surface. Looking into the window, an observer would see rows of coffins, each covered with purple and grey cloth emblazoned with a white cross (Kigali Genocide Memorial Center, n.d., images).

Whilst the gravesites in the countryside may have been less elaborate (less "monumental") in terms of the collection of items on display compared to those within the "museum" proper, the motif of an open grave was often present. At Ntarama, for instance, the bones of the dead were laid out in several places, including shelves and tables in a basement room one entered via a short staircase from the church floor.[6] Through the motif, then, we are invited to see not just evidence of the dead, but their actual remains. In Kigali, the visual representation of the dead is mediated: first, by the architectural and artistic exhibits within the museum and grounds of the memorial; and second, by what is visible in the open grave itself.

The Kigali Memorial's open grave display, with the enclosure and in/visibility of the bodies within the tomb, seems to go a step further in rendering the motif more abstract: through a glass window we see into a mass grave, but we see no remains as such. The question then becomes how this abstract open grave implicates the massive and explicit projection of the museum exhibits within: the voices on the tapes, the clothes, pictures, piles of machetes, and the piles of femurs and other bones. Despite its marginal and off-center location, it is somehow integral to unfolding or, indeed, decomposing the ways the museum memorial, as monumental art, tells its story.

Considered aesthetically, the *location* of the open grave in Kigali may be as significant as the fact of its being a part of the memorial to genocide. This leads to a reflection on the role of the unburied, the open gravesite, in literary and artistic representations of death in the context of a massive atrocity. In other words, the open grave in Kigali, through its external locus and abstraction, references not only other gravesites of the Rwanda genocide (in the countryside), but also the *trope* of the unburied and exposed body and its role in genocide memorial as such, taking the Rwandan genocide as an example.

To consider the trope of unburial in memorial monuments and art, I turn again to the idea of the open grave represented in the Sophocles play referenced above. At the heart of *Antigone* is an unburied body that we never see on the stage. It is the fact of unburial that propels the plot and undergirds the play's critique of the law. Its off-stage visualization is mediated by what the various parties say about it. The first introduction to Polyneices's unburied corpse is from Antigone herself, who reports on the king's edict that, unlike the body of Polyneices' brother Eteocles, who also fell in the siege against Thebes, "none may bury him and none bewail,/but leave him unwept, untombed, a rich sweet sight/for the hungry birds' beholding" (Sophocles, 458 BCE, 1954, p. 160). This is because the king has decreed Polyneices a traitor and, as such, a person who has defiled himself. In this sense, his non-burial is legally sanctioned. Antigone declares that "I never shall be found to be his traitor," indicating to her sister Ismene that she will bury her brother and break the law. This first conversation between the sisters propels the plot (Sophocles, 458 BCE, 1954, p. 160).

The next time we encounter the body (off-stage) is in the description from the guard who, fearing liability, stutters out the "terrible tidings" that, "Someone left the corpse just now,/burial all accomplished, thirsty dust/strewn on the flesh, the ritual complete" (Sophocles, 458 BCE, 1954, p. 167). After dreadful threats from King Creon, the guards unbury the body by sweeping the dust away. They resume the watch. Antigone returns to rebury the body and pour libations, whereupon she is captured and brought before the king (Sophocles, 458 BCE, 1954, pp. 172–173). Ultimately, the king reverses the edict. We learn, at the end, that Polyneices is given proper burial rites: "The dogs had torn [his body] all apart" but, with the gods' permission, "we gave the final purifying bath,/then burned the poor remains on new-cut boughs,/and heaped a high mound of his native earth" (Sophocles, 458 BCE, 1954, p. 199). The burial rites come too late, of course, to have prevented the suicides of Princess Antigone, Prince Haemon, and the queen.

The unburied body exerts enormous discursive power within the play and, by extension, within the Western literary imagination. A passage from Chinua Achebe's seminal novel, *Things Fall Apart*, suggests something similar within the African literary tradition. As with Polyneices, the main character, Okonkwo, falls afoul of the ancient laws of the land. Okonkwo's unburied body, by customary decree, is deemed to be self-defiled, in this case because he committed suicide. Okonkwo's village is in transition. He kills himself rather than face the new colonial justice for having beheaded an official messenger of the foreign, self-appointed District Commissioner. But that act of violence, an instinctive act of rebellion, was itself in defense of the precolonial norms that were being destroyed under the new colonial order. As one of the community leaders noted at the town meeting that precipitated the killing of the official messenger,

> All our gods are weeping. Idemili is weeping, Ogwugwu is weeping, Agbala is weeping, and all the others. Our dead fathers are weeping because of the shameful sacrilege they are suffering and the abomination we have all seen with our eyes.
>
> (Achebe, 1958, 1994, p. 203).

We learn of the protagonist's unburied body when the District Commissioner comes to arrest Okonkwo and finds instead a group of his friends, bereft at his loss. "We can take you where he is, and perhaps your men will help us," one of them says (Achebe, 1958, 1994, p. 207). The men lead the Commissioner outside the compound and into the bush, where they find Okonkwo's body dangling from a tree. It follows:

> "Perhaps your men can help us bring him down and bury him," says Obierika. "We have sent for strangers from another village to do it for us, but they may be a long time coming."
>
> The District Commissioner changed instantaneously. The resolute administrator in him gave way to the student of primitive customs. "Why can't you take him down yourselves?" he asked.
>
> "It is against our custom," said one of the men. "It is an offense against the Earth, and a man who commits it will not be buried by his clansmen. His body is evil, and only strangers may touch it. That is why we ask your people to bring him down, because you are strangers."
>
> "Will you bury him like any other man?" asked the Commissioner.
>
> "We cannot bury him. Only strangers can. We shall pay your men to do it. When he has been buried we will then do our duty by him. We shall make sacrifices to cleanse the desecrated land."
>
> (Achebe, 1958, 1994, p. 207).

The novel ends with the Commissioner thinking about the book he will write upon his return to London, a book of laws based on his observations during the time that "he had toiled to bring civilization to different parts of Africa" (Achebe, 1958, 1994, p. 209).

In the result, the novel's movement completes a spatial and symbolic movement "off-stage": from the villages, where the action of the novel has taken place, to the bush where a dangling body that we do not see embodies the rupture within the African fabric created by the presence of the colonial masters. The rupture is so severe that they, the Africans, cannot even attend to their own sacred burial rites. The desecration of that porous border between the living and the dead is exposed in this unburied body, this open grave.

In both of the above literary uses of the open grave/unburied body motif, the subject lies elsewhere, but highlights the decomposition of the action – customs, norms, and culture – on-stage. Returning to Kigali, one may translate this template to the "normative" memorial site as being "on-stage," and consider the effects of the partially buried but undisclosed/abstracted body in the open grave as being "off-stage." What does the off-stage open grave motif on the grounds of the memorial signify in the on-stage story?

Kigali Genocide Memorial was created and largely funded by the British anti-genocide nonprofit Aegis Trust, and received its template from the Yad Vashem Holocaust Memorial Project (Bolin, 2019, p. 345). Given this legacy, the memorial memorializes genocide with a script, so to speak, that is Holocaust inspired. As such, it raises the question: to what extent do we "see" Kigali through a lens that references the Holocaust as *the* genocide of the last century?

A commemoration inspired by other commemorative models is suggestive. Part of the Holocaust-infused memorialization of the genocide in Rwanda may simply be to tell a story of atrocity in Africa that is similar in kind to the events that occurred during the European wars. But using the Holocaust as the lens through which to see the genocide also lends a certain kind of universality, authority, and stamp to the Rwandan story's reconstruction. This point is partly made by Young (1994) in his aforementioned assessment of the burden-shifting risk pursuant to monumental memorials of mass atrocity as such; that the monument will carry, in a sense inscribe, our response to the horror (p. 6). If that inscription is overlaid by the reference to another, epochal event, we carry the burden of memory work here, in Rwanda, even less and render the memorial ever more univocal. My argument is that, notwithstanding this projection of the monument, the off-stage locus of memorial has the capacity to literally and figuratively dislocate and shift the univocal gaze.

The question becomes: what do we really "see" within the open tomb? What does the representation of an open tomb that does not disclose the unburied body – that renders the sacral body's exposure off-stage, so to speak – signify? This question was posed dramatically within the opening scenes of the Alain Resnais (1959) movie *Hiroshima Mon Amour.* An exchange takes place between the two protagonists that registers the difficulty of dialogue, of words, in the wake of human devastation. The protagonists are simply identified as "He" and "She": a Japanese businessman and the Frenchwoman with whom he has a brief, intimate affair, the latter in Hiroshima to make a film "about peace." Their affair is illicit, since both are married. In the opening scene, we see two naked bodies intertwined in an embrace. They are covered in a kind of glistening dust. The voiceover in French of both parties, as called for by Marguerite Duras's (1961/1994) script, is "flat and calm, as if reciting" (p. 2). Indeed, that is how their voices sound in the film:

HE: You saw nothing in Hiroshima. Nothing.
SHE: I saw *everything. Everything.*
HE: No. You saw nothing in Hiroshima.
SHE: The hospital, for instance, I saw it. I'm sure I did. There is a hospital in Hiroshima. How could I [not?] help seeing it?
HE: You did not see the hospital in Hiroshima. You saw nothing in Hiroshima.
SHE: Four times at the museum....
HE: What museum?
SHE: Four times at the museum in Hiroshima.
Four times at the museum in Hiroshima. I saw the people walking around.
The people walk around, lost in thought, among the photographs, the reconstructions, for want of something else, among the photographs, the photographs, the reconstructions, for want of something else, the explanations, for want of something else.

Four times at the museum in Hiroshima.

…

HE: You saw nothing in Hiroshima. Nothing.
SHE: The reconstructions have been made as authentically as possible.
The films have been made as authentically as possible.
The illusion, it's quite simple, the illusion is so perfect that the tourists cry.
One can always scoff, but what else can a tourist do, really, but cry?
I've always wept over the fate of Hiroshima. Always.
(Duras, 1961/1994, p. 15).

What comes across in the incantation from *Hiroshima* is the extent to which memorial, whether as museum or art/film, stages a stylized struggle between competing narratives and perspectives. In Kigali Genocide Memorial, the gray slabs beneath which lie the coffins delimit the view of the dead as such, lying in their graves. At this level, there is an *a priori* expectation of delimitation, of opacity: we are not supposed to see the dead. On the contrary, the point of a grave is that the dead be rendered invisible to us, clothed in reverent, ritual detachment. The window disrupts the line and returns the dead to the living, in the abstract (since we do not see the bodies).

The window also invites a series of unfolding delimitations. First, the window is divided into six panes, which visually disrupt the view within. At any given angle, we see a line, a border, with the visual field broken up and somewhat narrowed by the window frames. As a result, like the view of the museum in *Hiroshima*, the visual field is refracted, "for want of something else." Second, as noted, the coffins are covered with purple or grey cloth, emblazoned with large white crosses. This itself is a further delimitation of the perspective. We do not see the coffins themselves (Genocide Archive of Rwanda, n.d.).

Third, as noted, this is a window through which we look into an open grave and see nothing, not even, strictly speaking, an open grave. Visually, of course, that seems to be the point, as if we are invited to "see" by a process of occlusion and reflection. No bodies, such as the rooms full of skulls and femurs; no death-in-action, or death as it happened, as in the photographs and reconstructions of the "Genocide" section of the museum. At a certain angle, we see our own reflection in the glass of the latticed window. Thus, not even the "official" narrative of genocide ideology is projected here.

Finally, the open grave negates, in a sense, the ritual finality of a death, since the dead *as* enclosed are exposed to our gaze, robbed of a certain restful detachment from the world of the living. The decomposing body is symbolically, but not literally, relocated to a space within the visual field, juxtaposed against our own reflection. The relocation of the body is mediated, managed, sanitized, and aestheticized. Within the context of a museum and its artifacts that have attempted to recreate the horror of genocide as vividly as possible, the unburied or partially buried body represented by open grave motif unpacks and critiques that recreation or "composition." It represents, so to speak a decompositive element.

The open grave, in short, highlights the managed and aestheticized structure of the Kigali memorial and its reconstruction of the events of 1994. As eloquently expressed in *Hiroshima*, what we "see" in the open grave is juxtaposed against what and how we "see" within the museum. The former is symbolic of the latter: we gaze at our reflection superimposed upon a series of covered coffins, and we reflect upon how the museum, "made as authentically as possible" as a memorial to the past events, has shifted the work of memory from the observer to itself. "You saw nothing at Hiroshima. Nothing" (Duras, 1961/1994, p. 15).

Recently, there was some controversy over a new memorial to the Holocaust in the form of a book, described by journalist Jodi Rudoren (2014) as a "coffee-table monument of memory." In this book of 1,250 pages by Phil Chernovsky, the single word "Jew" occurs six million times. In Rudoren's *New York Times* book review, an interview with the book's author describes the visual effects as follows:

> When you look at this at a distance, you can't tell whether it's upside down or right side up, you can't tell what's here; it looks like a pattern...That's how the Nazis viewed their victims: These are not individuals, these are not people, these are just a mass we have to exterminate.
>
> (Chernovsky, 2014, as cited in Rudoren, 2014).

Chernovsky is then quoted as describing how, upon closer inspection, a more individuating perspective emerges:

> Now get closer, put on your reading glasses, and pick up a 'Jew'... That Jew could be you. Next to him is your brother. Oh, look, your uncles and aunts and cousins and your whole extended family. A row, a line, those are your classmates.
>
> (Chernovsky, 2014, as cited in Rudoren, 2014).

Rudoren (2014) notes that there have been other such experiments on expressing "the anonymity of victims and the scale of the destruction," such as in the collection of "six million paper clips" by eighth graders in a small Tennessee town, or the "seemingly endless piles of shoes and eyeglasses on exhibit at former death camps in Eastern Europe" She notes a comparison between the book's project and the:

> multimillion-dollar effort over many years by Yad Vashem, the Holocaust memorial and museum here [in Israel], that has so far documented the identities of 4.3 million Jewish victims. These fill the monumental "Book of Names," 6 ½ feet tall and 46 feet in circumference, which was unveiled last summer at Auschwitz-Birkenau.
>
> (Rudoren, 2014).

In the Memorial, behind the slabs stands a wall that represents an analogous project to that of the *Book of Names*. The wall resembles a smaller version of the Vietnam Memorial in Washington, D.C., here inscribed with the names of the victims of the genocide in Rwanda (Genocide Archive of Rwanda, n.d.). On a large black rock mounted nearby is a text that seems to sit between the Chernofsky book with its intimation of the "anonymity and scale of the destruction" (Rudoren, 2014), and the Yad Vashem project with its intent to specify the individual murders. The text on this rock, like the open grave memorial, reiterates something like a "necessary" negation at the heart of memory work:

> If you must remember,
> Remember this…
> The Nazis did not kill
> Six million Jews…
> Nor did the *Interahamwe* kill
> A million Tutsis,
> They killed one and then another,
> Then another…
> Genocide is not a single act of
> Murder,
> It is millions of acts of murder.
> (Genocide Archive of Rwanda, n.d.)

Through its various artifacts Kigali Genocide Memorial reaches for a kind of universal language of memorializing massive events, in part by linking Rwanda to other genocidal events. Principal among these references is the Holocaust. As the above inscription suggests, the link assumes a certain kind of stylized representation of the Holocaust that is then modeled by Kigali. The link underlines the project of memorial monuments as both universal and univocal.

But precisely by being both universal and univocal, monuments constrain what it is possible to see and, in effect, to know. The Kigali memorial to the genocide of 1994 projects a specific composition, or theory, of genocide as related to the Holocaust and, through that representation, to other genocides of the 20th century. In this section, I have suggested that the open grave, in its ostensibly affirmative and transparent form (mass graves revealed beneath the glass window), nonetheless complexly critiques that univocal narrative. We see "nothing" through the open window; we experience an opening onto death and decay, but we do not see death and decay. We see a crucifix replicated, prolific and emphatic, beneath the stone. The window is a gap in the stone, a sheen of glass that is broken up into smaller panes, further disfiguring the view within.

It is in this sense of interruption, of the gap, that the open grave both complements and fragments the narrative of genocide projected by the museum memorial. It does so by disclosing the stylization of memory work undertaken by memorial. It shapes the museum experience by exposing the extent to which *as* an aesthetic experience it is also, always, a national, political, and cultural enterprise. The open grave confronts us with the incompleteness of the monument to memory. We see our own faces reflected in the glinting glass.

In sum, if, as the films and novels discussed here suggest, the view into the grave denies or complicates the univocality of the memorial space by registering alternative modalities of memory or alternative sites for memory-work, then it also symbolically calls into question what we "see" within the "authentic" museum exhibit itself. The unburied body in canonical literary works such as Sophocles' and Achebe's signified and propelled a counter-monumental narrative. Here also, we look through the window of the gravesite and reflect upon the tension between re-presenting the dead in that negative and opaque space *off-stage* and the elaborate, "authentic" staging of death on-stage.

Art and the Burden of Memory

> "The law of art is the opposite of the rule of law."
>
> (Douzinas & Nead, 1999).

In this part, I wish to explore further this idea that the decompositive elements of memorialization are key to understanding the way monuments work to remember and to forget, to bear the burden of memory work and, off-stage, the ways this project and projection of memorializations are potentially decomposed within the artistic gaze.

As noted, a monument, as a work of art, is composed of elements that can be analyzed – decomposed, so to speak – to show how the work projects a certain representation. This chapter has approached the analysis of the memorial as a visual display with intimations of performance – on-stage, off-stage, etc. – and here I extend the reference to the visual arts in a more classical form. I use the work of Nicolas Poussin as a painterly representation of the underlying theme here: the critical and centrifugal force of an exposed, unburied body, as depicted in his *Landscape with the Ashes of Phocion* (1648). This painting, like Resnais's *Hiroshima* and Achebe's *Things Fall Apart*, is suggestive regarding the relationship between aesthetics and politics, and thus may elucidate the tension between composition and decomposition within memorialization.

As with the play *Antigone*, the trope of an open grave is central to the composition of Poussin's *Landscape with Ashes*. Like the open mass grave artifact in Kigali, the painting depicts a kind of interruption, but here it is foregrounded within the representational frame.

The observer's visual line is drawn upward from the scene of a woman in a blue robe crouched over in the left of the foreground. Beside her is a dark-skinned woman. The latter's body is twisted to reveal the back of her head to the viewer. We follow this woman's gaze. Unfurled before her are manicured gardens and playgrounds, and beyond this scene is a gleaming white Grecian temple. Behind the temple, a massive rock formation towers beneath a blue sky with billowing white clouds.

At first, the picture seems serene; the figures at play before the temple are small, some in repose and others in motion. The eye falls again to the two women at the front. The one standing is alert, guarding her mistress as the latter gathers something on the ground with her bare hands. As one looks down, the eye is again drawn upward, the perspectives counterposed. The scene loses its initial serenity and becomes dramatic. The line that draws the eye upward and outward powerfully connects foreground and background scenes. Because the lines are primarily vertical, the elements that are arranged horizontally, so to speak, lend themselves at a symbolic level to what may be analogized, as per the previous discussion, to an off-stage/on-stage relation. Here is a description, provided by the museum where the painting is housed:

> The solemn grandeur of the subject is conveyed by the rigid structure, geometrical organization and perfect calm of the landscape and townscape. The classical, even heroic setting for the event is dominated by the central temple and hill and by the dark massed trees on either side.
> (Wall text, Walker Art Gallery, *Landscape with the Ashes of Phocion*, 1648).

The story behind the painting is one of treachery and betrayal. Phocion is one of the subjects of Plutach's *Lives* (Plutarch, c.200 AD, 1919). The museum exhibit includes this description of the scene:

> Phocion was a great Athenian general and statesman of the 4th century BC. He was executed for treason on a false charge contrived by his political enemies. His body was ignominiously ordered out of Athens to Megara where it was burnt. In this painting his grieving wife is shown collecting his ashes
> (Wall text, Walker Art Gallery, *Landscape with the Ashes of Phocion*, 1648).

Plutarch records the following on the death of Phocion and the conduct of his widow. Phocion's death, he writes,

> ...coincided with the traditional Athenian parade of Zeus. It was decreed that the corpse could not be buried in Attica; neither could anyone cremate it. A hired man brought it across the Megarian frontier. There the body was burned. Phocion's wife set up an empty tomb, brought Phocion's bones and heart home by night, and buried them there. Soon afterward, the Athenians had a change of heart;

> they were properly reburied, at public charge, and a bronze statue was erected [to Phocion]...
>
> (Plutarch, c.200 AD, 1919, p. 231).

The painting explores similar themes to those within the previous discussion on the unburied body: as in both Sophocles and Achebe, the body becomes the site of sacrilege, and legally sanctioned burial rites are denied it. Likewise, its exposure is central to the narrative that issues from its off-site locus. Here, however, the ashes are foregrounded within the artistic composition. Analyzing the painting's composition does explicitly what is implicit within the aforementioned literary works, and may provide a more direct analogy to the interplay between the open grave and the museum within the memorial.

The painting is cerebral, as Poussin's contemporaries, such as Gian Lorenzo Bernini noted, (Keazor, 2007, p. 16) and is composed of "vertical and horizontal elements that meet at right angles to each other" (Keazor, 2007, pp. vii–viii). Henry Keazor (2007), in his massive study of Poussin's work, also notes the following:

> Stylistically speaking the road winding between rough terrains, littered with clumps of trees and shrubs, establishes the pre-eminence of line: these landscapes are first and foremost *drawn*. Like Domenichino, Poussin is seeking to convey the continuity of planes, from front to back, and the relations between them by means of strongly linear motifs, such as roads, undulations, or waterways.
>
> (pp. 69–70).

Two features of the painting stand out: first, the crouched figure of the widow as she gathers the ashes, guarded by the "contorted posture" (Rose, 1996, p. 25) of the servant. The widow's headdress and sleeve, bright white in contrast to the dark surroundings, is shaped as an arrow pointing toward the servant and suggests the appearance of denuded bone. Second, the servant's gaze encompasses the entire landscape. This construction directs the vectors to the servant as the lens, so to speak, through which to apprehend the composition. The visual line points up to the servant's waist at a forty-five degree angle, then up along her torso to the spiraling motion of her shoulders and hands, stretched out in a tense gesture of balance. The half-turned head, her compendious gaze in relation to the breathtaking scene, complements the tension in her arms and shoulders. Likewise, her body interpolates the foregrounded tragedy and the placidly majestic city from which the two women are abandoned. The composition is enclosed and enshrouded by the darkly shaded trees.

This painting by Poussin was the first to be examined by Sister Wendy Beckett in her 1992 BBC series, *Odyssey*. Sister Beckett posits a theory of what the picture means: "the gesture of the wife bending down to scoop up the ashes as an act of perfect love" (Rose, 1996, p. 25), an act opposed to the "inherent" injustice of the law represented by the indifferent city on the hill. In her own study of the same painting, Gillian Rose (1996), in *Mourning Becomes the Law: Philosophy and Representation,* disagrees with Sister Beckett's apolitical interpretation. She suggests that Phocion's fate was "the result of tyranny temporarily usurping good rule in the city" (p. 26). For Rose (1996), unlike Beckett, the widow's gesture is political, a "protest against arbitrary power" (p. 26), whence the painting represents a political act. Indeed, the widow's gesture directly references Antigone's handful of dust with which to cover the corpse of her brother (Sophocles, 458 BCE, 1954, p. 167).

Although opposed to each other, both Beckett's and Rose's interpretations involve a view of the widow's act as an interruption: on the one hand, the perdurable tragedy of redeeming love as always and already beyond the law, and on the other, the justice of the city orders (democracy) temporarily usurped by tyranny. Thus, both Beckett and Rose include in their divergent interpretations a common theme: that the scene within the foreground is "other" to the scene beyond it.

Additionally, what is foregrounded in the scene *composes* the visual landscape, along the vectors described above, even as it breaks up. The scene thus represents an interruption, a breakdown or a *de*composition of the orders. Although the widow is the starting point, her sleeve points to the servant's contorted body as the line along which to apprehend the scene. In this sense, it is the tense body of the servant, rather than the ashes, that is central to the frame of the composition. At the same time, at an immediate, visual level her body symbolizes the dyadic, deconstructive nature of the composition as a whole. The brown slave juxtaposed against the white buildings; the agitated female bodies projected against the stolid, phallic, rocks and buildings; the sense of inner turmoil within the furtive gaze, in relation to an outer calm; a tempestuous past in relation to an indifferent, celebratory, and playful present; death and dejection foregrounded in a backdrop of majestic wealth.

The composition thus appears to be a story of belonging and exile, of competing narratives within the project of the city itself. The women are foregrounded and other, but this is an otherness extruding from the city walls precisely because it is formative, febrile, and mythopoeic. Finally, the women are situated within a "gap," bordered and framed by a low, truncated wall, between Attica and Megara and, in a sense, inside and outside of both. The scene gives perfect visual access to foreground and background even as it cuts the one from the other: on-stage, serenity and power; off-stage, tension, and risk.

The ashes are elemental to the composition as its subject, yet they occupy an imaginative space that is outside and other to the symbolic orders represented by the scene behind them. They sit outside the vectors of power that issue from the servant's body. In this complex way, the painting shows the critical interpellation of off-stage and on-stage action in a way that differs from the previous discussion of the open grave motif. The foreground decomposes the narrative structuration of a city (of law, per Beckett and Rose) as impervious, eternal, impassive. The dark body in torsion is complemented by the heavy foliage and billowing clouds above. The city is encompassed by a roiling, passionate drama at both the heart and the periphery of the classical composition. The painting suggests the effort, precisely a political struggle, to contain the ferment within the formal structures, made to appear more enduring, enlightened, and desirable in their grandeur. In short, the tense body of the servant bears witness to an inner and outer conflict (Keazor, 2007, p. 21).

How does the painting by Poussin elucidate the themes in the Kigali Genocide Memorial? The moment of reflection beside the grave with the latticed windows recalls some of the themes at play in the painting. The open grave functions within the larger frame of the museum much like the ashes within the painting. We see it off-site or off-center, but its elemental power is apprehended mainly through a more central, on-stage figuration: the servant's tense body in one case, the museum's attempt at immediacy in relation to the experience of genocide in the other. Both are vectors within the creation of an authoritative narrative. Both sit outside the wall of the city/museum and in the realm of secrecy, reflection, and furtiveness. They sit within a semi-darkness, an intimate sacrality of purpose.

By analogy to the painting, the open grave is part of the official narrative of the genocide, part of the complete, univocal enunciation and mediation of victims' voices. As such, the museum and the memorial represent the discursive containment of a deeper silence: the unsaid, perhaps unspeakably complex, history behind the genocide; the complexity of *anti*-monumental memorial.

In the memorial museum, there are parallel stories arranged *seriatim* within the memorial site. Thus, within the museum section, we begin at the threshold "Wasted Lives" exhibition that attempts to universalize the genocide in Rwanda by relating it primarily to the Holocaust but also to other genocides: Cambodia, Gujarat, Armenia, Darfur, and many others. We then move to the second part, "Genocide," divided into "Before," "During," and "After" (Genocide Archive of Rwanda, n.d.). Outside the museum, we then pay homage to the dead within the gardens, waterfalls, inscribed walls, and the burial grounds. The story is one of genocide past and remembrance, in order to incorporate a lesson in "redemption," and a warning (Bolin, 2019). Rwanda's fast-paced development from the most dangerous African nation to one of the internally safest on the continent highlights this layered narrative structure that cabins the past (McConnell, 2011; Kigali, 2010). In this way, the story told by the memorial is horizontal.

But the open grave motif posits an alternative or a counter-memorial, similar to the one explicated in Poussin's *Ashes*. The servant in that painting does not cabin the tension between the city and the widow but mediates it. She provides a window into the dyadic worlds of order and exile between which her body is interposed and balanced. Both worlds then become possible to imagine and become visible through her labor. The servant's body twists away from her mistress, away from the observer, facing the city. The gesture is precarious and protective, the repository of the widow's loss and the risk of exposure. In the corner of this richly vectored multivalence centered on her body we see, like an open wound, the desecrated and redeemed remains of the dead (Plutarch, c.200 AD, 1919, p. 233).

Conclusion

The analysis of the open grave motif in the Poussin paintings extends the idea of the unburied body off-stage and explicates that "other scene" within the foreground. In the Kigali Genocide Memorial, that "other scene" is indexed by the open grave off-stage, within the memorial grounds. A common theme in both the story of genocide as told by the museum and within the new criminal code is that these events were discrete and contained, with a beginning, a middle, and an end: the end of *ethnie*, the burial of the past.[7] The other scene, the off-stage unburied body, troubles that template.

Today, the Rwandan economy is thriving, and the people live in relative peace. The memorial in Kigali tells a univocal story of the events of 1994 as properly confined to a violent and receding past. This narrative strategy would seem to make perfect sense as you walk through the clean streets of Kigali surrounded not by death and mayhem but by tall, gleaming skyscrapers, the modern artifacts of wealth and prosperity. This is a far cry from standing on the knoll in Ntamira, the smell of death hanging in the air. Yet you wonder, as you walk, whether a national memorial to the genocide might have told a different story, one that did not relegate the messiness of *ethnie* to the past (Prunier, 1995), to a forbidden place within the current imaginary.

Such a memorialization might have the potential to give new meaning to the term "genocide" itself: addenda about the complicity of elites, for instance, within the construction of *ethnie*; about the consequences of *ethnie* suppressed, once more, to the subconscious of the national psyche, subject to political reactivation. Such an idea of genocide is more troublesome, more "vertical" or vertiginous. Instead, we are invited to think horizontally, to see genocide as (truly) genocide if it is "like" the Holocaust. Along those horizontal lines, the open grave is out there, distant from the exhibit, a space for reflection beyond and at a critical distance from the museum itself.

The open grave signifies for both the Western and the African visitor the importance, through burial rites (or their absence), of observing the borderline between the living and the dead. The open grave is a metaphor for the work of memory at the margins. It recalls and references the memorial sites out there in the countryside, dotting the landscape like scars, where the ghosts that roam the earth seeking burial, trailing with them the sense of loss and grief, escape even the grandest efforts at monumental, coherent memorialization. As Richard Brody (2012) notes, as we walk through the museum and the gardens in Kigali, that memorials must be countervailing, because, "memory isn't passive; it's an act of resistance – the edge that cuts a path into the future."

The window above the tomb is a reminder that the view from within the Memorial is always and already decomposed, that we need to find those spaces of dislocation to enable us to look back at formal composition with, so to speak, a recompositive gaze, to see what memorial has undone in relation to memory. The open grave invites us not to forget, then, what lies beneath the luminous, perdurable city projected from memorial's enclosed and monumental finality.

When seen as artistic expression, these moments of dislocation within monumental memorials break with finality and become the locus of a participatory form of memorializing (Shefik, 2018). This form of art, as Sherin Shefik reminds us, is where countervailing memory is projected as a "web of connections" (Garnsey, 2016, as cited in Shefik, 2018, p. 315) between at least two competing forces: the urgency to "remember" in a certain way (by placing a violent past firmly within the past), and the imperatives of justice that require a more complex form of memory and memorializing. Kigali Genocide Memorial, as monumental art, suggests the former, a passive form of remembering the genocide in 1994. I have argued in this chapter that the open grave motif, as a critique of the memorial's objective, opens toward the latter: the irreducibility of memorialization within a univocal state narrative, shifting the burden of memory back to us.

Notes

1 United Nations Assistance Mission to Rwanda (UNAMIR), established by UN Security Council Resolution 872 on October 5, 1993.

2 On-site visits in Rwanda, September-October 1995.

3 Rwanda has a legal definition of memorial. See Wolfe (2020): "Law *N°56/2008 of 10/09/2008 Governing Memorial Sites and Cemeteries of Victims of the Genocide Against the Tutsi in Rwanda*. This law...[d]efines a genocide memorial site as 'a place where victims of genocide were buried and which has a special history in the planning and execution of Genocide,' Article 2" (p. 6).

4 Douglas (2001) makes a point about the tendency to simplify the historical record and thereby monumentalize the victims: "In any trial, the prosecution will attempt to define as sharply as possible the radically distinct normative universes inhabited by victims and perpetrators" (p. 171). But through Primo Levi he warns that this bears a cost: "Levi has observed that simplification is 'useful as long as it is recognized as such and not confused for reality,'" (p. 182). One "moment" of disjuncture within the prosecution's narrative comes about when the testimony of a survivor suddenly links to the accused (Eichmann) through the motif of the open mass grave: "Here, then, a story whose details suggest the figurative prose of a biblical allegory forges a remarkable link between the accused and a survivor" (p. 182).

5 Reyntjens (2013) argued that in the aftermath of the genocide, "The RPF has employed various means – rigged elections, elimination of opposition parties and civil society, legislation outlawing dissenting opinions, and terror – to consolidate power and perpetuate its position as the nation's ruling party" (p. 129). Much of this is predicated on what Reyntjens calls the cynical use of a "genocide credit" by the ruling party.

6 On-site visits, September-October 1995.

7 The temporal jurisdiction of the International Tribunal for Rwanda is from January 1 to December 31, 1994. See the ICTR Statute, at http://www.unictr.org/ (accessed June 17, 2020).

Bibliography

Achebe, C. (1994, 1958). *Things fall apart*. Penguin Books.

Aegis Trust – Rwanda. (2004, April 7). *10 years on: Shaping the memory of Rwanda's genocide* [Press Release]. https://repositories.lib.utexas.edu/bitstream/handle/2152/4391/3490.pdf?sequence=1&isAllowed=y

Ansah, T. (2006). Sovereignty, identity, and the 'Apparatus of Death'. *New England Law Review*, *40*, 529–540.

Bickford, L., & Sodaro, A. (2010). Remembering yesterday to protect tomorrow: The internationalization of a new commemorative paradigm. In Y. Gutman, A.D. Brown, and A. Sodaro (Eds.), *Memory and the future* (pp. 68–86). Palgrave Macmillan. https://doi.org/10.1057/9780230292338_5

Bolin, A. (2019). Dignity in death and life: Negotiating *Agaciro* for the nation in preservation practice at Nyamata genocide memorial, Rwanda. *Anthropological Quarterly*, *92*(2), 345–374. https://doi.org/10.1353/anq.2019.0018

Brody, R. (2012, July 30). In memoriam: Chris Marker. *The New Yorker*. https://www.newyorker.com/culture/richard-brody/in-memoriam-chris-marker

De Beer, A. Remembering Genocide Through Transnational, Multivocal Narrative [chapter 11 in this book]

Douglas, L. (2001). *The memory of judgment: Making law and history in the trials of the Holocaust*. Yale University Press.

Douzinas, C., & Nead, L. (Eds.). (1999). *Law and the image: The authority of art and the aesthetics of law*. University of Chicago Press.

Duras, M. (1994). *Hiroshima Mon amour*. (Seaver, R. Trans.). Grove Press. (Original work published 1961.)

Genocide Archive of Rwanda. (n.d.). *Kigali genocide memorial*. Retrieved July 26, 2019, from http://www.genocidearchiverwanda.org.rw/index.php/Kigali_Genocide_Memorial

Keazor, H. (2007). *Poussin*. Taschen Books.

Kigali Genocide Memorial Center. (n.d.), images. Retrieved August 20, 2021, from https://www.google.com/search?q=images+of+kigali+memorial+centre&client=safari&rls=en&tbm=isch&source=iu&ictx=1&fir=RdAL7ALyyoaHSM%252CxnyqRfsLgrEUgM%252C_&vet=1&usg=AI4_-kRGdvV6nqZufZvoI7VORJIJttd-bw&sa=X&ved=2ahUKEwiD5vOs7L_yAhUNHc0KHbGLB6AQ9QF6BAgVEAE#imgrc=RdAL7ALyyoaHSM&imgdii=BKL3PIQeIxpVmM.

Kigali Genocide Memorial Centre. (n.d.). Retrieved July 27, 2019, from http://www.kigalimemorialcentre.org

Kigali, J. L. (2010, August 9). Philip Gourevitch on Rwanda: Returning to Rwanda. *The Economist*. http://www.economist.com/blogs/baobab/2010/08/philip_gourevitch_rwanda

McConnell, T. (2011, January/February). One man's Rwanda: Philip Gourevitch softens some hard truth. *Columbia Journalism Review*. https://archives.cjr.org/feature/one_mans_rwanda.php

Plutarch. (1919). *Plutarch lives: Sertorius and Eumenes; Phocion and Cato the younger*: (Vol. VIII). (B. Perrin, Trans.). Harvard University Press. (Originally published *circa* 200 AD.)

Poussin, N. (1648). Landscape with the ashes of Phocion [Painting]. Walker Art Gallery, Liverpool, UK. https://www.liverpoolmuseums.org.uk/artifact/landscape-gathering-of-ashes-of-phocion

Prunier, G. (1995). *The Rwanda crisis: History of a genocide*. Columbia University Press.

Resnais, A. Director (1959). *Hiroshima Mon amour*. Argos Films.

Reyntjens, F. (2013). *Political governance in post-genocide Rwanda*. Cambridge University Press. https://doi.org/10.1017/CBO9781107338647

Rose, G. (1996). *Mourning becomes the law: Philosophy and representation*. Cambridge University Press

Rudoren, J. (2014, January 25). Holocaust told in one word, 6 million times. *The New York Times*. https://www.nytimes.com/2014/01/26/world/middleeast/holocaust-told-in-one-word-6-million-times.html?searchResultPosition=1

Schabas, W. A. (2009). *Genocide in international law: The crime of crimes*. Cambridge University Press. https://doi.org/10.1017/CBO9780511575556

Shefik, S. (2018). Reimagining transitional justice through participatory art. *International Journal of Transitional Justice*, *12*(2), 314–333. https://doi.org/10.1093/ijtj/ijy011

Sophocles. (1954). *Antigone* (D. Greene & R. Lattimore, Trans.). Washington Square Press.

Tadjo, V. (2000). *L'ombre d'imana: Voyages jusqu'au bout du Rwanda*. Actes sud.

Tadjo, V. (2002). *The shadow of imana: Travels in the heart of Rwanda* (V. Wakerley, Trans.). Heinemann.

Wolfe, S. (2020). Memorialization in Rwanda: The legal, social, and digital construction of the memorial narrative. In E. M. Zucker & D.J. Simon (Eds.), *Mass violence and memory in the digital age: Memorialization unmoored* (pp. 19–44). Palgrave-Macmillan. https://doi.org/10.1007/978-3-030-39395-3_2

Young, J. E. (1994). *The texture of memory: Holocaust memorials and meaning*. Yale University Press.

Yusin, J. (2016). The itinerary of commemoration in the Kigali Memorial Centre: On trauma, time and difference. *Culture, Theory and Critique*, *57*(3), 338–356.

10 Remembering Rwanda through Transnational, Multivocal Narrative

Anna-Marie de Beer

Introduction

"Genocide staggers the imagination," write Kevin O'Neill and Alexander Hinton (2009, p. 1) in the introduction to their edited text on genocide, memory, truth, and representation. It is the sheer scale of genocide that indeed has this impact on our imagination; the numbers, the inconceivable images, the questions it poses about mankind and evil (O'Neill & Hinton, 2009, p. 1). In this chapter, I argue that collective cultural trauma, such as the genocide of the Tutsi in Rwanda, requires multivocal and even transnational representation of its manifold memories.[1] This may hold true for any form of commemoration of mass violence, but my focus is on textual/literary representations of this event.

The Rwandan genocide narrative seems to have evolved through a series of stages; scholars from the West were quick to write about the genocide, and after a period of time, African intellectuals added their voices to these efforts. Rwandans themselves started testifying to their experiences, often at first with co-authors who were more experienced in writing, and eventually writing their own stories. On this continuum, there has been a range of genres and positionings, from journalistic texts to testimonies, in addition to fictional narratives and even graphic novels.[2] These narratives counteract a potentially monolithic story of the past, which could perpetuate the binaries and categorization that have been so detrimental to Rwanda, by providing a plurality of perspectives.

This chapter on the memory of the genocide engages with the following questions:

> How are the devastating events remembered on the individual and collective levels, and how do these memories intersect and diverge as governments in post-genocidal states attempt to produce a monolithic "truth" about the past? How are representations of a violent past structured by one's positioning as a survivor, perpetrator, witness, government official, scholar, activist, legal professional, journalist, or ethnographer?
>
> (O'Neill & Hinton, 2009, p. 4).

DOI: 10.4324/9781003228592-13

The "positioning" of particular interest to me is one that Geoffrey Hartman (1998) calls the "intellectual witness," a term which refers to those who attempt to represent an event that they did not experience firsthand, but nevertheless feel compelled to write about. Hartman posits that due to its collective impact and the extent of the trauma, the representation of genocide necessitates an interaction between "artistic intellect" and "communal memory" and the art form that I focus on is literary representation of the genocide.

Similarly, Ervin Staub (2006) states that in a "community-oriented" society such as Rwanda, where the genocide was a form of group violence, healing efforts require a collective response that extends beyond the individual (pp. 872, 874). Although Staub focuses on interventions conducive to psychological recovery and reconciliation after mass trauma, the importance of offering a collective response also holds true for representations of the memory of genocide. If healing efforts are to include all role-players in the society, including groups that may have been marginalized by the current system, then commemorative artistic representation would do well to create a space for a multiplicity of genocide narratives, and modes of memory.

I have argued elsewhere that interdependent, shared forms of storytelling provide "an alternative voice to individualist-orientated Western discourses" and resonate with the indigenous African communitarian notion of *Ubuntu* and its focus on solidarity, inclusivity, and social harmony (De Beer, 2020, p. 18). When I speak then of a collective voice or response, I am not referring to the type of collective memory that Erin Jessee (2017) has described as a "dominant, national, official, or public memory" (p. 145) and that endangers the voice of the individual and foregrounds certain ways of remembering. I speak of the opposite, a space in which a range of voices and memories can be articulated and included.

Post-genocide transitional justice, specifically in the form of historical and symbolic redress, relies heavily on narratives, both official and unofficial, that add to the constantly evolving and plural body of collective knowledge about the genocide (Wolfe, 2014). It is commonly accepted that "truth telling" plays a key role in the process of transitional justice and for enabling reconciliation to take place. Establishing the truth is of utmost importance to the victims (Staub, 2006, pp. 880–881).

However, due to the personal and subjective nature of memories, memory and truth are often uneasy bedfellows. In addition, there are different "dimensions of truth" such as "forensic or factual truth; personal or narrative truth; social or dialogue truth; and healing or restorative truth," that dictate the varied needs of different groups during the transitional justice process (Lambourne, 2009, p. 39).[3] Furthermore, when stories about the genocide are told and retold as representing the truth of the genocide, it is important to contextualize them, especially those "iconic stories" which transmit specific messages that can be interpreted in different ways (Jessee, 2017, p. 150). Researchers therefore agree that the "truth" of genocide is complex and must be jointly negotiated (Dauge-Roth, 2010, p. 172; Staub, 2006, p. 880).

My interest lies in the role that art/fiction can play in the development of such a shared, plural, story that these scholars advocate. I would suggest that artistic, imaginative representation creates a space for complex and even "contesting representations" of the genocide that can include the "fragmented and clashing memories" of the different role-players (O'Neill & Hinton, 2009, p. 5). Such representations add to our collective understanding by revealing the complexity of the roots of violence and its consequences and providing a more "differentiated" image of the various role-players and their lived experience of the genocide (Staub, 2006, p. 877).

This type of artistic representation would include perspectives expressed by the eloquent voices of seasoned writers who employ their art in configuring the stories from the genocide. It would also make a space however for those voices that unsettle because they tell their stories in partial or angry ways, or the voices of those who do not have the benefit of intellectual distance from the event. Kenneth Harrow (2005) implies that even the reader's voice should be included in this multiplicity of voices, stating that the story that needs to be told is one "from which the reader cannot escape responsibility" (p. 40).

In this chapter, I do not consider art as a tool which attempts to provide a comprehensive "truth" about historical events. Rather, I see it as a means to provoke dialogue and reflection, to open spaces for disruption and contradiction, to include that which perturbs and disturbs us, and to implicate the reader. Admittedly, some representations are created in order to serve political purposes and can be used in the furthering of atrocities. Just like memories, voices can be flawed or prejudiced; nevertheless, that should not prevent us from creating spaces for an array of voices to be heard. My approach for illustrating this point is to explore the literary project, known as the Fest'Africa project or *Rwanda: écrire par devoir de mémoire* (Rwanda: writing as a duty to memory). I look at its contribution to the creation of a shared representation of the genocide, due to its polyphonic, transnational nature.

The Project *Rwanda: Écrire Par Devoir De Mémoire*

This collective, commemorative, project was undertaken by a group of Francophone African intellectuals from seven different African countries four years after the genocide. Their goal, as African writers and artists, was to unite in order to demonstrate solidarity with their Rwandan brothers and sisters and break the near-silence that had been maintained on this subject by African intellectuals up to that point.[4]

The majority of the project participants were neither Rwandan nor were they eyewitnesses to the genocide. They did not claim to have written the "truth" of the genocide; in fact, many acknowledge that their renditions contain fictional and imaginative elements interwoven with stories told to them by survivors. In terms of representation, however, they have added a valuable dimension, precisely because of the variety of stances, genres, and perspectives that they offer and the unique composition of the group: transnational, yet African.[5]

In preparation for writing on the genocide, the participants of the project traveled to Rwanda for a three-month stay, visiting genocide sites, prisons, and orphanages, and met with survivors, perpetrators, returnees from exile, foreigners, and other inhabitants of post-genocide Rwanda. There were subsequent journeys by some of the authors as not all of them could participate in the original journey and others felt the need to go back again. The project comprised various stages including these follow-up visits, festivals, and book readings as well as some artistic outputs. The texts that were eventually published between 2000 and 2002 as a concrete output of this initiative included travel accounts, novels, and a poetry anthology, by seven of the authors from Djibouti, Chad, Guinea, Senegal, Côte d'Ivoire, and Burkina Faso.[6] Two further texts included in the project were by Rwandans: one essay by a Tutsi who was in exile during the genocide, and one testimony by a genocide survivor.

Véronique Tadjo's (2000)[7] travel account represents a range of perspectives, inviting us to listen to the voices of victims, perpetrators, bystanders, and even the dead. Her initiation into the history of the genocide is presented as a personal journey, both literal and metaphorical, which transforms the author and allows her to reflect on the meaning of evil. The reader is invited to participate in this journey of listening and discovery.

Abdourahman Waberi (2000)[8] similarly writes a travel account, describing fragments of his physical and interior voyage in order to represent the collective experience of the Rwandans. His metanarrative demonstrates an awareness of his exterior position and the incapacity of language to transmit the horror of genocide.

Boubacar Boris Diop (2000)[9] constructs his novel around Cornelius, a protagonist who has not personally experienced the genocide. He develops poignant interactions between this exile returning to post-genocide Rwanda and the inhabitants he encounters there. It is at the genocide sites, and especially at Murambi, that his quest will lead him to new perspectives, and to entering into dialogue with these different voices.

Monique Ilboudo (2000)[10] writes from the perspective of a single survivor, Murekatete. Unlike the other writers, Ilboudo does not evoke the difficulty of writing about the genocide. Contrary to what happens in Diop's novel, a pilgrimage to the genocide sites undertaken by Murekatete and her husband does not offer new or therapeutic perspectives. In fact, this journey of horror destabilizes and finally destroys the marriage and lives of this couple. They do not work through the experience, and Ilboudo's text acts out the repeated and continued trauma of genocide.

Tierno Monénembo (2000)[11] offers us the genocide from the point of view of Faustin, a young boy who represses the memory of his parents' death and wanders around looking for them. Orphaned, disoriented, severely traumatized by the genocide, and stripped of innocence, he plunges himself into the circle of violence by killing his best friend, whom he catches having sex with his little sister. In the end, he is condemned to death for this act by a society that we feel has caused his demise in the first place. The genocide is only directly referenced in rare instances in this novel, but Faustin's emotional detachment and final derailment is shown to be a direct consequence of it.

Koulsy Lamko's (2002)[12] allegorical account of the genocide interweaves three narratives. The first narrative belongs to a raped and murdered Tutsi queen, whose spirit is metamorphosed into a butterfly. The second is that of a young Tutsi exile, the queen's niece, who has never lived in her own country but visits it after the genocide. The third account deals with an exiled Tutsi soldier who wanders from country to country.

Nocky Djedanoum (2000) works through the medium of poetry, a form of expression which through its slow and meticulous processes captures the profound impact of genocide. Like Ilboudo and Diop, he underlines the importance of physical sites of significance to the genocide. His focus, however, is not on the mass killing sites, but on Nyamirambo, a neighborhood in Kigali that gives the volume its title and where a part of the Muslim community refused to participate in the genocide. His writing expresses his solidarity with the Rwandans and, in spite of the difficult subject matter, presents us with a lyrical homage to life, culminating in his final poem entitled: *Manifesto for Life*.[13]

Vénuste Kayimahe (2002) is a survivor, the only participant in the project who personally experienced the genocide. He takes great issue with the betrayal of Rwanda by the French government, and this becomes the main and recurring theme of his account. Although he subsequently published further work, at the time of writing this first text, he was not a professional writer like the others. Furthermore, his intention was not, in the first place, literary or fictional. He is an eyewitness who testifies angrily to his personal experiences and those of his loved ones.

The second text from the project by a Rwandan writer is the essay by Jean-Marie Rurangwa (2000), exiled from his country at a young age to neighboring Burundi. His text, which can be translated as, *The genocide of the Tutsis explained to a foreigner,* attempts to do just that, analyze the origins and consequences of the genocide to those who were not there. One of the main themes in the text is the impact of being in a perpetual state of exile.

A Transnational, Transcultural Memory Project

Although a plethora of genocide narratives have been written in the wake of the Fest'Africa project, it still remains the most prominent example of artistic solidarity and collective representation of the genocide of the Tutsi by a transnational group of writers. The project has been analyzed through other lenses, but I look at it here as an initiative that offers a plurality of perspectives and as a form of "traveling" or transcultural memory. It also serves as an example of an initiative that heeds the growing call among scholars to decolonize trauma theory.

The Fest'Africa project embodies transcultural memory as a form of what Astrid Erll (2011) calls "travelling memory," engaging with "the incessant wandering of carriers, media, contents, forms, and practices of memory, their continual 'travels' and ongoing transformations through time and space, across social, linguistic and political borders" (p. 11). The project members engaged with the memory and testimonies of Rwandans they had listened to, whilst carrying their own burdens of traumatic memories from their home countries. Their own life stories tell us that the majority of them experienced some form of exile, civil war, or dictatorship. They have lived in various countries on the continent, have written about traumatic issues related to postcolonial Africa, and are concerned with the transmission and preservation of memory and culture.[14]

Exploring the roots of the seven non-Rwandan authors is a way of thinking about their role in making the memory of the genocide "travel." Not only because they physically crossed borders to go to Rwanda, and were themselves transformed by what they saw there, but also because they brought with them their own perspectives which were both individual and collective, non-Rwandan yet African. They were in the unique position of not being victims of the genocide and yet they shared a common painful history; that of European colonization (Hitchcott, 2009, p. 152). Due to their dual position of being outsider/intellectual witnesses, yet African they were able to enter into a "dialogic productivity of remembrance" through listening to the Rwandan testimonies and configuring them into literary texts whilst carrying with them the consciousness of the other historical traumas that the continent had been subjected to: colonialism, slavery, exploitation, and exile (Rothberg, 2009, p. 654). This process set in motion a type of "cross-communal" remembering in the African context which could ultimately lead to solidarity and "transcultural empathy," not only for the writers but for those reading their texts (Craps & Rothberg, 2011, p. 518).

Furthermore, as widely recognized, published authors they contributed in carrying the memory of the genocide outside the borders of Rwanda. They transposed the stories into artistic genres such as poetry, prose, and symbolic accounts which would transmit the story of the genocide on a different emotional level and to a different type of public than those who read mostly journalistic and historical accounts.

Almost twenty-eight years after this commemorative project was initiated, memory studies scholars are increasingly exploring the relevance of transnational and transcultural memory. The transnational turn that is not only gaining relevance in memory studies but also in fields like literary studies and migration studies is a multifaceted concept which encompasses the notion of "'transit,' emphasising movement in space across national borders, but it also stands for 'translations,' the cultural work of reconfiguring established national themes, references, representations, images and concepts" (Assmann, 2014, pp. 546–547). To my mind, this project constitutes an example of the type of memory initiative that contains such reconfigurations, translations, and "cross-border multidirectional links – in the form of analogies, allegories, transnational agents, and transferable symbols" (Rothberg, 2014, p. 655).

One of the main themes of the project is for example places of memory like the genocide sites and the effect they have and the role they play, not only for survivors, but for foreign visitors trying to grasp the enormity of the genocide. Historical sites of memory and their attachment to lived experiences as well as the visceral effect they may have on visitors or survivors is a concept that has universal value and travels across cultural and national borders.

The project creates an intertextual and multicultural network of symbols, themes, and analogies that becomes evident when reading the different texts. The motif of traveling, for example, is used throughout as an analogy for discovering the horror of genocide. It is equated to a type of unsettling, destabilizing journey into the heart of the darkness of genocide. It also embodies the process of learning how to listen appropriately to the genocide story and demonstrating solidarity as an outsider witness.

Another such example is the narrative of Mukandori, a victim referenced in almost all the texts, and whose story has traveled far beyond the borders of Rwanda. This Tutsi woman whose remains are buried at Nyamata memorial, and who was tied up, raped, and impaled has become a cross-cultural symbol of the sexual violence and inhumane acts of genocide.

The tale that Véronique Tadjo includes in her travel diary about the deceased who angrily roam the streets of Kigali is a type of allegory for the consequences of the genocide on the invisible, spiritual world, a world that is integral to the traditional African belief system about death. This tale has the power to resonate across borders and throughout the continent because of its engagement with the connection between the visible and the invisible world.

Rothberg (2014) argues that such memory initiatives that move beyond state borders have the potential to open up a space for different types of voices because they can "unsettle scalar hierarchies and challenge the hegemony of state-sponsored remembering and forgetting" (p. 655).

The project embodies "multidirectional memory" through its "acts of connection" (Rothberg, 2009, p. 654). These writers embarked on a memory process that clearly involved "ongoing negotiation, cross-referencing, and borrowing," including from their own native contexts and other historical events such as the Holocaust (Rothberg, 2009, p. 3). This type of multidirectional remembering uses a memory from one context as a "prism" for another. The process creates links between different historical traumas, and looking at one historical trauma through the lens of another helps us to gain a better understanding of the event (Assmann, 2014, p. 550).

When engaging with the colonial roots of the genocide, Abdourahman Waberi draws from the global awareness of the Holocaust by quoting Primo Levi in an attempt to explain the genocide in Rwanda. Véronique Tadjo, in turn, uses the identity politics and plight of the refugees in her native Côte d'Ivoire as a "prism" for talking about Rwanda. She also establishes striking parallels between post-genocide Rwanda and post-apartheid South Africa, linking two key historical traumas on the continent.

Nocky Djedanoum (2000) poetically evokes histories of collective suffering and shared victimhood on the African continent, notably the slave trade in Senegal, stating that they will "bow down before the memories [of their] slave grand-parents" from Gorée Island (p. 35).[15]

As is clear from the various examples, the contribution of this project in terms of multivocality, transnationality, and multidirectionality becomes especially apparent when it is read as a collective narrative and not as nine separate works.

Recontextualizing Trauma Theory

Another valuable contribution of the project is its engagement with a non-Eurocentric context of trauma, mourning, and storytelling. The project echoes concerns raised by researchers who attempt to recontextualize trauma theory. As developed in Western contexts, trauma theory does not necessarily consider the "sustained and long processes of the trauma of colonialism" and colonial violence in non-Western contexts. Nor does it consider that such traumatic experiences in these settings are often collective rather than individual (Visser, 2015, p. 252). Processing trauma in such contexts entails the "construction and interrogation of the history of colonialism and decolonization" through telling its stories. This is why literature can potentially provide "narrative shape and meaning" to experiences that have had adverse effects on the collective identity of previously colonized societies (Visser, 2015, p. 258). Engaging with the trauma of the Rwandan genocide includes telling the story of how colonization in Rwanda contributed to the origins of the genocide. It implies focusing on the collective nature of the trauma that the community has been subjected to and interrogating the ways in which colonization shaped the collective identities of the Rwandan people. As discussed below in the section on the polarization of identities, the project authors wrote extensively about the harmful influence of colonialism on identity formation in Rwanda.

Another area of expansion of classic trauma theory that is relevant to the Rwandan context regards being open to "non-Western belief systems and their rituals and ceremonies in the engagement with trauma" (Visser, 2015, p. 250). The authors embed references in their texts to the traditional Rwandan processes of mourning, appropriate burial rituals and beliefs regarding the afterlife and the deceased. This belief system is in fact the inspiration for Tadjo's chapter on the way in which the spirits haunt the living because they have not been buried accorded to the customs. It also provides the narrative framework of Lamko's novel, in which the spirit of the deceased protagonist roams the hills of Rwanda in the form of a Butterfly, searching for someone who will bury her body and perform the necessary burial rites before she can depart to the afterlife.

The authors also demonstrate their interest in "recuperation, and psychic resilience," other key concerns that are central to decolonizing trauma theory (Visser, 2015, p. 254). Several authors, namely Monénembo, Ilboudo, and Tadjo, depict the victims' struggle in the aftermath of the genocide, in particular orphans and those who have experienced rape and the loss of close family members.

Another theme that is often present in postcolonial literature and pertinent to the context of Rwanda is the "complexity of the entanglement of complicity, agency, and guilt," and in particular complicity with oppressive regimes (Visser, 2015, p. 258). This issue is addressed through the project, but especially by Diop and Waberi through their focus on the power of propaganda and a culture of submission to authority, as well as the role played by Western countries and previous colonial powers such as Belgium and France.

Finally, trauma scholars encourage an awareness of the importance of "oral modes of narrative and their ritual function in indigenous communities," and this is a stylistic element that is integral, for example, to the work of Tadjo who interweaves oral tales into her realistic travel diary (Visser, 2015, p. 259).[16] Another significant instance is the use of traditional Rwandan proverbs by most of the project authors, especially when interpreted within the paradigm of proverbs as an expression of shared cultural and communal wisdom.

Fearing the Other: The Polarization of Identities

Due to the different styles and genres of the authors and the range of backgrounds they come from, the project provides an array of perspectives on the genocide. The purpose of this section is to illustrate this diversity through specific examples from the texts. I do this by looking at how they engage with a factor commonly seen as one of the root causes of the genocide and the mass participation in it. Staub (2019) has listed the following factors that typically lead to mass violence:

> difficult social conditions (economic decline, political disorganization and chaos, great social changes, ongoing conflict between groups), and cultural characteristics—a history of devaluation of the victims, past group trauma that makes the world look dangerous, and a hierarchical and authoritarian culture
>
> (p. 60).

I discuss how the project deals with one of these, namely the devaluation of the victims through a process of polarization and racialization of identities in Rwanda.[17] As the authors from the commemorative project travel through Rwanda and research its history, they reflect on the opposition between Hutu and Tutsi identities, an instance of what Véronique Tadjo (2002) calls the "physical fear of the Other" (p. 10). They engage with this polarization in their texts by problematizing or subverting it, blurring the clear distinction between the prevailing and commonly opposed binaries of Hutu/native/perpetrator versus Tutsi/foreigner/victim.

One of the literary strategies they employ is to assign hybrid or complex identities to their protagonists, calling into question the assumption about ethnic groups being monolithic. This strategy aligns itself with Staub's (2006) suggestion that moderate Hutus who opposed the genocide should be acknowledged and that the perpetrator group should not be rejected as a whole, but instead that there is a need to create a differentiated view of them (p. 877).

Tadjo's (2002) attempt to implicate the reader becomes evident through the way in which she asks us to reflect on our own fear of the Other, and search our hearts about the (in)humaneness of our own reactions to those who are different from us.[18] She suggests that this form of polarization and of fearing the Other which leads to violence, is not intuitive but learned: "*Creating* foreigners. *Inventing* the idea of rejection. How is ethnic identity *learned*?" (p. 37, my emphasis).

By drawing direct parallels to her native Côte d'Ivoire, and to South Africa, Tadjo (2002) points out that fear of the Other and concomitant interethnic hatred is a universal phenomenon, and not something for which we can condemn only the Rwandans. Instead, she notes, the genocide was an event that "concerned us all. It was not just one nation lost in the dark heart of Africa that was affected" (p. 3).

Tadjo also questions preconceived notions about stereotypical ethnic identities by depicting a gallery of diverse and complex characters. Her travel diary is peopled with inhabitants of Rwanda who represent victim, perpetrator, bystander, exile, and foreigner. Some of them are victim in one situation and perpetrator in another. These characters are presented in nuanced ways, and sometimes she seemed to deliberately refrain from assigning them ethnic identities, simply presenting us with the suffering and consequences of genocide in the lives of human beings, without labeling or categorizing them.[19]

Tadjo illustrates how Rwandans came to internalize the ethnic categorizations imposed on them by colonial powers, especially with regards to physical appearances (Semujanga, 2008).[20]At the same time, she warns us not to trust appearances: "A woman of slender build moves along the road. She is tall, she must be a Tutsi. [...] You cannot safely rely on physical appearance alone. Not all the Tutsis are tall. Not all the Hutus are stocky in build" (Tadjo, 2002, p. 17). These descriptions which are linked to collective identities are not to be trusted, and yet they were widely used during the genocide and reinforced by anti-Tutsi propaganda:

> On the radio we heard that the grave wasn't yet full, that we had to help to fill it. They told us: 'If you're not sure if it is a Tutsi, all you have to do

> is to look at him, his size, his face, you just have to look at his delicate little nose and break it […]'
>
> (Tadjo, 2002, pp. 104–105).

Another textual strategy used to question the validity of ethnic identities in Rwanda is underlining the fluidity and confusion associated with them. Both Tadjo and Monique Ilboudo describe experiences of characters mistakenly identified and treated as Tutsis (De Beer, 2020). These incidents illustrate the arbitrary way in which these categories were sometimes assumed and assigned – a dangerous practice in circumstances where one's identity could mean one's death.

The female Hutu protagonist in Ilboudo's (2000) novel is attacked and left for dead simply because she is fleeing and therefore assumed to be Tutsi: "I was a fugitive, and therefore guilty. I was condemned without any form of trial, and didn't even have the time to present them with my identity card" (p. 45). Tadjo (2002), in turn, describes the plight of a young girl from Zaire who is raped by the *Interahamwe* and her baby killed because she looks like a Tutsi and is caught hiding from the militia. By including these incidents, the authors suggest that in addition to the Tutsis at whom the genocide was aimed, there were other victims, who also have painful stories to tell.

Another approach used by the authors to question the polarization of ethnic identities is to include protagonists born from interethnic marriages. Their situation reflects the reality of many Rwandans who were born from such marriages. In certain cultures, such alliances are of little concern and carry no dangerous consequences. However, if one interprets the choice of a Hutu person to marry a Tutsi within the context of the highly influential *Ten Commandments of the Bahutu,*[21] the dire consequences of this choice become clear.

The Commandments were a political manifesto, and not a religious document, and yet, the tone of the document is dogmatic and the rules are based on stereotypical assumptions. The agenda is clear: Hutus should not make alliances of any kind with Tutsis, the population is divided into clear categories of "us" and "them," and boundaries are drawn between these two groups which may not be crossed without fatal consequences. Those who do not obey are considered traitors. The first of these Commandments (1990) reads as follows:

> Every Hutu must know that the Tutsi woman, wherever she may be, is working for the Tutsi ethnic cause. In consequence, any Hutu is a traitor who:
>
> - Acquires a Tutsi wife;
> - Acquires a Tutsi concubine;
> - Acquires a Tutsi secretary or protégée.

For those who lived by the Hutu Commandments, a mixed marriage was a taboo act and the project authors acknowledge the authoritarian influence of this document in Rwandan society. They demonstrate how disobeying these rules would somehow be punished in the same way as when individuals break the Biblical Ten Commandments. In other words, betraying the *Ten Commandments of the Bahutu* would attract divine retribution.

Tadjo demonstrates the importance and key influence of this document by quoting it in its entirety while suggesting that in spite of this, not all Hutus followed its prescripts.

Waberi's interpretation of the Ten Commandments clearly illustrates the societal change described by Josias Semujanga (2008) who notes how the former value system in Rwanda, which advocated reciprocity, was progressively replaced by new narratives and codes of behavior in the run-up to the genocide (p. 102). Waberi (2016) announces the values of the Commandments in the normative tone of an Old Testament prophet teaching the Biblical Ten Commandments, and even urges the listeners to verify for themselves in their "Bible[s]," foregrounding the perceived "divine authority" of this prescriptive document:

> Marriage outside of one's ethnic group must be prohibited. This makes perfect sense and is in accordance with the Scriptures and in keeping with the guidelines promulgated by our social revolution. Likewise civil servants [...] may not be distracted by their devilish women [...] I can see from your reaction that you think I am exaggerating – go ahead and seek advice from our friends the White Fathers, dive back into your Bible [...]
>
> (p. 17).

He thus demonstrates the stature and influence of this political document; it is elevated to the status of Holy Scriptures and has become a sacred document (De Beer, 2020, p. 126).

Monique Ilboudo (2000) takes her references to the Ten Commandments a step further by depicting the consequences of defying their rules. The father of Murekatete, the protagonist, is a brilliant young Hutu with a promising career who does not allow society to dictate his personal choices, and marries the woman whom he loves, who happens to be a Tutsi. However, he is killed in a mysterious way, and the novel implies that his death is caused by his nonconformist stance and choices. His daughter Murekatete will make a similar choice. Though the patrilineal system observed in Rwandan society allows her to claim a Hutu identity, she chooses to marry a Tutsi. This choice will lead to the loss of her Tutsi husband and eventually her children during the genocide. Once again, the implication is clear: if one chooses to disregard the Ten Commandments of the Hutu, "divine" punishment will follow.

This attitude is embodied in Alfred Ndimbati, Murekatete's neighbor, whom Ilboudo (2000) describes as a purist who detests "ethnic mixing more than anything," and in whose eyes the offspring of such a marriage is a "hutsi," an unnatural, inferior mixture, the "worst of species" (p. 36).[22] Examples of such "hutsi" abound in the texts from the project; they are often the protagonists whose stories complicate the formal rhetoric of ethnic binaries. In many instances, the Hutu characters demonstrate their choice of ignoring the Commandment prescriptions by first marrying a Tutsi, and second choosing to die with the Tutsi partner during the genocide rather than abandon them.

In other cases, the Hutu characters betray their Tutsi partners and even orchestrate their deaths. Diop's (2006) protagonist discovers that his Hutu father was responsible for the murder of his Tutsi mother and "hutsi" siblings during the massacre at Murambi. His childhood friend, Jessica, warns him that in his quest to learn more about the genocide he still has much suffering ahead and a "long path to take in [his] heart and in [his] mind" (p. 79).

Indeed, Cornelius's journey of discovery involves the painful realization that although he was not present during the genocide, it is an essential part of his life history. His initial intention is to write an absurd drama about the genocide, but once he discovers that he is the "son of a monster," he knows that henceforth "the only story he had to tell [is]his own: the story of his family" (Diop, 2006, p. 78). This comment is a subtle reference to the plight of the participants of the project, intellectual witnesses who, confronted with the consequences of fearing the Other, come to realize that Rwanda's story is in many ways also their own. Diop (2006) describes the profound unease of many inhabitants in post-genocide Rwanda as follows: "He had suddenly discovered that he had become the perfect Rwandan: both guilty and innocent" (p. 78).

The project illustrates how colonization profoundly shaped the collective identities of the Rwandan people in unimaginably harmful ways and laid the ground for the genocide decades later (Visser, 2015, p. 258). The previous examples demonstrate how the authors use their art to discredit the validity of stereotypes regarding ethnicity and alterity in order to invite the post-genocide society and the reader to go beyond simplified categories of Tutsi and Hutu, victim and perpetrator, us and them, and above all to acknowledge the universality of mankind's capacity for evil.

The authors find ways to include the voices of non-traditional victims in the narrative, thus counteracting the exclusion and alienation of those often marginalized in post-genocide Rwanda. In the face of ethnic categories, which are imposed ideologically to serve political purposes, they introduce us to the universality of the Rwandans we meet on the pages of their texts. The diversity of the characters reminds us not to fall prey to stereotypes of the country and its people. The authors lead us to question our own fear of the Other by portraying their characters in ways that free them of their constructed otherness.

The authors show how categorization through physical appearances has been internalized by the Rwandans, simultaneously questioning this notion and demonstrating the fluid nature of these categories as well as the arbitrary ways in which they were often constructed.

They present us with the suffering of traditional and non-traditional victims, perpetrators and bystanders. By placing their choice of characters from mixed ethnicities against the backdrop of the authoritarian framework of the *Ten Commandments of the Bahutu*, these authors remind us of the imposed nature of ethnic taboos, and illustrate their painful consequences and impact on the lives of individuals. Their texts demonstrate how the fear of the Other in its many forms contributed to genocidal acts, but at the same time, the authors deconstruct the notion of otherness.

Conclusion

The aim of this chapter was to ascertain how the literary project *Rwanda: écrire par devoir de mémoire* contributes toward a plural representation of the story of the Rwandan genocide. The narrative of the project texts leads to a more differentiated understanding of key concerns on the genocide and away from simplistic narratives that, as Jessee (2017) warns, may "serve to deepen, rather than diminish, lingering divisions" (p. 156). In this chapter I have shown how one such area of concern – the imposed polarization of collective identities – is addressed by the literature. This discussion demonstrates that literary authors, through their art, not only dramatize these issues through a variety of characters and settings, but also open them up for dialogue. Furthermore, their intercultural, transnational approach allows for the transmission of empathy and solidarity across borders and cultures; it is a type of "cross-communal remembrance" that can lead to a greater understanding of the injustices that others have suffered and generate "alliances between various marginalized groups" (Craps & Rothberg, 2011, p. 518). The project further remains a landmark example of postcolonial trauma literature and its engagement with trauma in non-Eurocentric contexts.

Its narratives and counternarratives add to a more nuanced perspective on the genocide's origins and consequences, one of Staub's cited requirements for post-genocide community reconciliation. Such an endeavor leads us to appreciate the value of providing space to the many diverging voices on the genocide, and counteracts the perpetuation of a monolithic truth in imaginative ways.

In reading these texts, one could focus on their deficiencies and silences, which, as I have pointed out, do exist. The scope of Rurangwa's text, for example, is rather limited because he identifies so strongly with the victim group. Kayimahe's is decidedly less literary, and his testimony is disturbingly angry and accusatory. Djedanoum's poetry is profound and deeply moving, but at times he emphasizes the notion of solidarity with the Rwandan people to a point that makes the reader uncomfortable. Waberi's text is extremely fragmented and therefore difficult to read. Diop, Ilboudo,

Tadjo, Monénembo, and Lamko have fictionalized the stories of people who lived through a genocide that they themselves never experience. However, one can also simply read them as nine voices among many, each prompting us in its own unique way to ask our own questions and add our own voices to the dialogic encounters that promote empathy, solidarity and cross-cultural understanding.

Notes

1 This concept is illustrated in more depth in my analysis of the nine texts of the literary project *Rwanda: écrire par devoir de mémoire* (De Beer, 2020).

2 For more on this continuum of genres, read Kerstens (2006).

3 Lambourne refers to Stephan Parmentier's (2003) model of transitional justice which takes note of these different types of truth (pp. 203–224).

4 For more details about the project, its aims, and contributions, consult Hitchcott (2009). There were other artistic endeavors associated with the project but I am focusing on the literary output here.

5 For more on the unique composition of the group, consult Hitchcott (2009).

6 The following texts were published through the project:
Murambi: le livre des ossements (2000), a novel by B. Boris Diop from Senegal;
L'aîné des orphelins (2000), a novel by the Guinean writer Tierno Monénembo;
Murekatete (2000), a novel by Monique Ilboudo from Burkina-Faso;
La phalène des collines (2002), a symbolic account by Koulsy Lamko from Chad;
L'ombre d'Imana: voyages jusqu'au bout du Rwanda (2000), a travel account by Véronique Tadjo from Côte-d'Ivoire;
Moisson de crânes : textes pour le Rwanda (2000), a travel account by Abdourahman Waberi from Djibouti;
Nyamirambo ! (2000), a poetry anthology written by Nocky Djedanoum from Chad;
Le génocide des Tutsi expliqué à un étranger (2000), an essay by the exiled Rwandan Jean-Marie Vianney Rurangwa; and
France-Rwanda : Les coulisses du génocide, témoignage d'un rescapé (2002), a testimony by the Tutsi survivor Vénuste Kayimahe. Where possible, citations of these authors are taken from published English translations of their texts. In such cases, I do not provide the original French citations. In cases where I did not have access to English translations, I use my own translations and provide the original French.

7 All Tadjo citations are taken from Véronique Wakerley's translation of the original text: Tadjo (2000).

8 All citations from Waberi's text are taken from Dominic Thomas's 2016 translation of the original text published in 2000.
Kindle page numbers are provided.

9 Translated by Fiona McLaughlin (Diop, 2006).

10 All citations from Ilboudo's text are my translations from the original French.

11 Translated by Monique Fleury Nagem (2004).

12 All citations from Lamko's text are my translations from the original French.

13 "*Manifeste pour la vie.*"

14 Véronique Tadjo is an acclaimed writer, academic, and artist, born of an Ivoirian father and a French Mother. She was born in Paris, grew up in Côte d'Ivoire, and has lived in many different countries on the continent and elsewhere. She has published novels and poetry and facilitated numerous workshops in

writing and illustrating children's books. Her work focuses on preserving memory and advancing African cultural heritage, with a particular interest in oral traditions and the reinterpreting of traditional myths and legends.

Abdourahman Waberi is a novelist, poet, essayist, and journalist who was born in Djibouti and grew up in Northeast Africa before moving to France. Like Tadjo, he opposes amnesia and silencing and he has expressed a sense of literary commitment toward his home country. His work deals with themes of nomadism, exile, war, and the traumas of colonization and independence in Africa.

Boris Diop is an established and celebrated Senegalese novelist, journalist, essayist, and screenwriter whose work often combines political analyses, fiction, and history. He writes mainly in French but has also published in Wolof.

Monique Ilboudo is an essayist, author, and human rights activist from Burkina Faso who focuses on women's issues. She writes about the plight of women, conflicting relationships between Africans and Europeans and the African society and its taboos and prejudices.

Guinean author and biochemist, Tierno Monénembo, has lived in Algeria, Morocco, and France and has written on the relationship between identity, exile, and memory after having fled the dictatorship of his country. His work combines political and literary engagement and he is known as a writer who subverts and rewrites dominant discourse through the use of polyphony and counternarratives (Migraine-George, 2013).

Poet, playwright, novelist, author, scriptwriter, lecturer, and actor Koulsy Lamko was born in Chad. Exiled because of the civil war, he has lived in Burkina Faso, Togo, Côte d'Ivoire, Rwanda, and Mexico. He has won numerous prizes for his dramas, and founded and directed the Center for the Arts and the Theater in the National University of Rwanda, where he has also taught performing arts and creative writing.

Nocky Djedanoum, initiator of this commemorative writing project, is an exiled journalist and author from Chad who founded the French-based literary and artistic festival, Fest'Africa, aimed at reuniting and celebrating artists and writers from the African diaspora.

Vénuste Kayimahé was born in Rwanda and worked as audiovisual technician at the Franco-Rwandan Center of Cultural Exchange in Kigali at the time of the genocide. He has lived in exile in Kenya, Germany, and Mexico before returning to his native country. His written testimonial has been made into a documentary, and in 2014, he published his first novel which also takes place in Rwanda at the time of the genocide.

Poet, essayist, and playwright Jean-Marie Rurangwa was born in Rwanda but spent many years in exile at a refugee camp in Burundi. The main theme of his work is the ordeal of exile, and he writes about political abuses, the effects of colonization, the ill-treatment of refugees, and the hope for unity and reconciliation in his country. He subsequently fled from Burundi to Italy and has since lived in Brussels and returned to Rwanda. He currently resides in Canada.

15 All citations from Djedanoum's text are my translations from the original French.

16 In my analysis, (De Beer, 2020), I explore more in-depth how the project engages with many of these elements; the integration of oral modes of storytelling, traditional views on death, mourning and burial customs, resilience, for example among genocide rape victims, as well as the notion of guilt, agency, and complicity.

17 Read Mamdani (2002) and Sow (2009) for more information on the historical process of polarization of these identities and its harmful consequences.

18 See De Beer (2016, pp. 47–49) for a more detailed discussion on Tadjo's attempt to implicate the reader and her inclusion of silenced and marginalized voices in her account.

19 A more detailed discussion of Tadjo's nuanced representation of these various inhabitants can be found in De Beer (2016, pp. 47–48). Consult also Semujanga (2008, p. 177).

20 See also De Beer (2020, p. 80).

21 The *Ten Commandments of the Bahutu* was a document published in December 1990 in the Hutu Power, anti-Tutsi Kinyarwanda newspaper, *Kangura*, and is a much-cited example of anti-Tutsi propaganda. It labels Tutsis as the enemy, prescribes discriminatory behavior toward Tutsi women, forbids business partnerships or dealings with Tutsis, suggests reserving strategic positions and educational opportunities for Hutus, and promotes Hutu ideology. A copy of this document as published by *Kangura* is available at https://genocidearchiverwanda.org.rw/index.php/Kangura_No_6. The translated version of the Ten Commandements of the Bahutu can be found at: https://www.un.org/en/preventgenocide/rwanda/assets/pdf/exhibits/Panel-Set2.pdf

22 Original text : *'détestait plus que tout le mélange ethnique. À ses yeux, les hutsi, cet alliage contre-nature, était la pire des espèces.'*

Bibliography

Assmann, A. (2014). Transnational memories. *European Review*, *22*(4), 547–556. https://doi.org/10.1017/S1062798714000337

Craps, S., & Rothberg, M. (2011). Introduction: Transcultural negotiations of Holocaust memory. *Criticism: A Quarterly for Literature and the Arts*, *53*(4), 517–521.

Dauge-Roth, A. (2010). *Writing and filming the genocide of the Tutsis in Rwanda: Dismembering and remembering traumatic history*. Lexington Books.

De Beer, A.-M. (2016). Véronique Tadjo and the masks and shadows of Rwanda. In S. Davies Cordova, & D. Wa Kabwe-Segatti (Eds.), *Écrire, traduire, peindre - Véronique Tadjo - writing, translating, painting* (pp. 43–63). Présence Africaine.

De Beer, A.-M. (2020). *Sharing the burden of stories from the Tutsi genocide: Rwanda: Écrire par devoir de mémoire*. Palgrave Macmillan.

Diop, B. B. (2000). *Murambi: Le livre des ossements: Roman*. Stock.

Diop, B. B. (2006). *Murambi: The book of bones* (F. Mc Laughlin, Trans.). Indiana University Press.

Djedanoum, N. (1999). Le Rwanda, terre de recueillement de mémoire. Retrieved from http://nocky.fr/ecrits-inedits/ (site discontinued; printed version retained by author).

Djedanoum, N. (2000). *Nyamirambo!: Recueil de poésies*. Le Figuier, Fest'Africa.

Erll, A. (2011). Travelling memory. *Parallax*, *17*(4), 4–18. https://doi.org/10.1080/13534645.2011.605570

Harrow, K. W. (2005). "Ancient tribal warfare": Foundational fantasies of ethnicity and history. *Research in African Literatures*, *36*(2), 34–45. https://doi.org/10.1353/ral.2005.0118

Hartman, G. (1998). Shoah and intellectual witness. *Partisan Review*, *65*(1), 37–48.

Hitchcott, N. (2009). A global African commemoration – Rwanda: Écrire par devoir de mémoire. *Forum for Modern Language Studies*, *45*(2), 151–161. https://doi.org/10.1093/fmls/cqp003

Ilboudo, M. (2000). *Murekatete: Roman*. Le Figuier, Fest'Africa.

Jessee, E. (2017). The danger of a single story: Iconic stories in the aftermath of the 1994 Rwandan genocide. *Memory Studies*, *10*(2), 144–163. https://doi.org/10.1177/1750698016673236

Kayimahe, V. (2002). *France-Rwanda: Les coulisses du génocide: Témoignage d'un rescapé*. Dagorno.

Kerstens, P. (2006). Voice and Give Voice': Dialectics between fiction and history in narratives on the Rwandan genocide. *International Journal of Francophone Studies*, *9*(1), 93–110. https://doi.org/10.1386/ijfs.9.1.93/1

Lambourne, W. (2009). Transitional justice and peacebuilding after mass violence. *International Journal of Transitional Justice*, *3*(1), 28–48. https://doi.org/10.1093/ijtj/ijn037

Lamko, K. (2002). *La phalène des collines*. Serpent à Plumes.

Mamdani, M. (2002). *When victims become killers: Colonialism, nativism and the genocide in Rwanda*. Princeton University Press.

Migraine-George, T. (2013). *From francophonie to world literature in French: Ethics, poetics, and politics*. University of Nebraska Press.

Monénembo, T. (2000). *L'aîné des orphelins*. Seuil.

Monénembo, T. (2004). *The oldest orphan* (M. F. Nagem, Trans.). University of Nebraska Press.

O'Neill, K. L., & Hinton, A. L. (2009). *Genocide: Truth, memory, and representation*. Duke University Press.

Parmentier, S. (2003). Global justice in the aftermath of mass violence. The role of the international criminal court in dealing with political crimes. *Annales Internationales De Criminologie - International Annals of Criminology - Anales Internacionales De Criminología*, *41*(1), 203–224.

Rothberg, M. (2009). *Multidirectional memory: Remembering the Holocaust in the age of decolonization*. Stanford University Press.

Rothberg, M. (2014). Locating transnational memory. *European Review*, *22*(4), 652–656. https://doi.org/10.1093/ijtj/ijn037

Rurangwa, J.-M. V. (2000). *Le génocide des Tutsi expliqué à un étranger: Essai*. Le figuier.

Semujanga, J. (2008). *Le génocide, sujet de fiction? Analyse des récits du massacre des Tutsi dans la littérature Africaine*. Nota bene.

Sow, S. (2009). *Esthétique de l'horreur: Le génocide Rwandais dans la littérature Africaine*. (Doctoral dissertation). https://hdl.handle.net/1911/61863

Staub, E. (2006). Reconciliation after genocide, mass killing, or intractable conflict: Understanding the roots of violence, psychological recovery, and steps toward a general theory. *Political Psychology*, *27*(6), 867–894. https://doi.org/10.1111/j.1467-9221.2006.00541.x

Staub, E. (2019). Promoting healing and reconciliation in Rwanda, and generating active bystandership by police to stop unnecessary harm by fellow officers. *Perspectives on Psychological Science*, *14*(1), 60–64. https://doi.org/10.1177/1745691618809384

Tadjo, V. (2000). *L'ombre d'Imana: Voyages jusqu'au bout du Rwanda*. Actes Sud.

Tadjo, V. (2002). *The shadow of Imana: Travels in the heart of Rwanda* (V. Wakerley, Trans.). Heinemann.

Ten commandments of the Bahutu Kangura (1990, December). *Kangura*, 6.

Visser, I. (2015). Decolonizing trauma theory: Retrospect and prospects. *Humanities, 4*(2), 250–265. https://doi.org/10.3390/h4020250

Waberi, A. A. (2000). *Moisson de crânes: Textes pour le Rwanda*. Serpent à Plumes.

Waberi, A. A. (2016). *Harvest of skulls*. (D. Thomas, Trans.). Indiana University Press https://www.amazon.com/dp/B01N4OMMHO/ref=dp-kindle-redirect?_encoding=UTF8&btkr=1#detailBullets_feature_div

Wolfe, S. (2014). The politics of reparations and apologies: Historical and symbolic justice within the Rwandan context. In S. E. Bird & F. M. Ottanelli (Eds.), *The performance of memory as transitional justice* (pp. 43–58). Intersentia. https://doi.org/10.1017/9781839700651.004

11 Fictions of Justice in Post-Genocide Films

Conflict Resolution and the Search for Reconciliation

George S. MacLeod

Introduction

In the opening scene of American director Lee Isaac Chung's (2007) fictional feature film *Munyurangabo,* the eponymous protagonist (called simply "Ngabo") contemplates a machete left unattended in a market in Rwanda's capital city of Kigali. Many viewers will recognize the machete as an iconographic object, representing both the brutality of the 1994 genocide against the Tutsi in Rwanda, as well as the mass participation of the rural citizenry. Ngabo steals the machete and, in the following scene, contemplates its bloody blade. The blood suddenly disappears to signal that Ngabo is in fact imagining an act of future violence, the murder of the man who killed his father. The visual of the machete stained with imaginary blood captures the violent nature of revenge fantasies, as well as a climate of fear in post-genocide Rwanda, and testifies to the film's power to produce meaning through visual symbols that appropriate the quintessential imagery associated with genocidal violence.

Deploying the machete as a symbol of revenge is one way that Chung uses the medium of film to problematize questions of memory and reconciliation surrounding the 1994 genocide against the Tutsi. While *Munyurangabo* shows the dangers that vigilante justice may pose to reconciliation, Haitian director Raoul Peck's (2005) fictional feature film *Sometimes in April* shows that official mechanisms of justice can be equally flawed. In considering the International Criminal Tribunal for Rwanda (ICTR), Peck's film depicts a legal response to genocide which struggles with a burden of proof that is too high, coddles its high-profile detainees, and leaves survivors angry and embittered.

As Rwanda enters the first decade since the genocide in which neither institution is in operation, the legacy of the ICTR and *gacaca* courts are hotly contested subjects of debate amongst scholars and Rwandans.[1] *Munyurangabo* and *Sometimes in April* are notable as two of the only globally circulating films about the 1994 Tutsi genocide set primarily in the genocide's aftermath, rather than during the genocide itself. While there has been considerable scholarly attention to representations of the 1994 Tutsi

DOI: 10.4324/9781003228592-14

genocide in fictional films (Cieplak, 2010, 2018; Dauge-Roth, 2010, 2017; Edwards, 2018; Hitchcott, 2020), significantly less attention has been paid to what fictional representations of post-genocide legal institutions (both local and international) can teach us about the complex intersections between personal memory, the desire for justice, and the advantages and shortcomings of institutions such as the ICTR and the *gacaca* courts. Conversely, scholarship on transitional justice in Rwanda from the domains of political science, anthropology, and international law has paid scant attention to how the institutions they study are incorporated into fictional filmic narratives such as *Munyurangabo* and *Sometimes in April* (for a notable recent exception see Katila, 2021). Analyzing these two post-genocide films as not just "fictions of genocide" but as "fictions of justice" can provide valuable insight into the ICTR and the *gacaca* courts' contemporary legacies.

Two Unique Films Showing the 1994 Tutsi Genocide

In the last few decades, both Rwandan and non-Rwandan filmmakers have directed and produced a number of films on the 1994 genocide against the Tutsi. Notable examples include *100 Days* (2001),[2] *Hotel Rwanda* (2004), *Beyond the Gates* (2005), *A Sunday in Kigali* (2006), *Shake Hands with the Devil* (2007), *Kinyarwanda* (2011), *Grey Matter* (2011),[3] *Birds are Singing in Kigali* (2017), and *94 Terror* (2018). As Alexandre Dauge-Roth (2010) emphasizes, the significance of these films is, to a large extent, their ability to shape narratives of the genocide for Western viewers: "Because these movies are aimed at Western viewers…they put forth a version of history that both conditions what is judged to be worthy of memory and determines the lenses that give the genocide of the Tutsi the possibility of readability" (pp. 170–171). While much has been written on this filmic corpus' depiction, for Western viewers, of historical narratives and individual memory, this chapter takes a new perspective through a focus on the representation of collective transitional justice mechanisms such as the *gacaca* courts and the ICTR.

While *Sometimes in April* includes substantial flashbacks to 1994, it differs from other high-profile films on the genocide by centering its narrative not on the violence itself, but on Rwanda's uneasy transition to peace ten years after the genocide. The films differ vastly in their scope. Produced by HBO, *Sometimes in April* aspires to offer a comprehensive view of the genocide, its aftermath and the relevant geopolitical actors who failed to prevent it. *Munyurangabo* was shot on a shoestring budget using local, nonprofessional actors and has the raw feel of an independent film. It privileges individual stories over broader discussions of Rwandan history and the culpability of the international community. Yet, on a fundamental level, both films are preoccupied with the same questions of vengeance, reconciliation, and individual responsibility, and how these notions are influenced by existing governmental and juridical structures. In close analyses of the films' narratives, I will show how they criticize and legitimize specific practices of justice in post-genocide Rwanda, while also being attentive to how privileging sentimentality (for the sake of narrative closure) undermines these critiques.

I focus on three institutions which are largely responsible for shaping the public discourse surrounding accountability and reconciliation in post-genocide Rwanda. First, there is the ICTR established by the United Nations (UN) in November 1994 and headquartered in Arusha, Tanzania until its official closure in December 2015. Second, I consider the *gacaca* court system, a form of community justice created by the Rwandan government that existed from 2001 until 2012.[4] Finally, there is the Rwandan state itself, whose official discourse has banished the mention of ethnicity and urges national unity and reconciliation amongst Rwandans, with the stated aim of permitting Rwandans to move on and preventing the reoccurrence of genocide. While the objective of the Rwandan state's rhetoric is laudable, it is crucial to note it also serves to mask the anger and psychological scars which make such reconciliation difficult, if not impossible, for many survivors, some of whom are forced to live in close proximity to those involved in the killings.

All three of these institutions (the ICTR, the *gacaca* courts, and the Rwandan state) perpetuate a similar self-justificatory narrative: that accused perpetrators will be tried through a fair and objective trial; and that the guilty will be punished, allowing survivors to move on and the country to be reconciled. Such a narrative, I argue, is inherently fictional, eliding the complex range of dynamics within post-genocide Rwanda, as well as the inherent flaws of the justice system itself. For many survivors, even if they acknowledge the importance of judicial mechanisms, it is hard not to be disturbed by their shortcomings. As Tutsi survivor Esther Mujawayo writes: "I'm telling you, for me, justice is impossible. I don't believe it: the witnesses don't speak, the victims are suspected, and the guilty, protected. While waiting, those that survived pass away. Justice won't bring them back…" [author's translation] (Mujawayo & Belhaddad, 2011, p. 243). To say, like Mujawayo that "justice is impossible" is another way of emphasizing that the narratives used by the courts and the Rwandan government can be considered "fictions of justice." It's important to note, however, that to call them "fictions of justice" is not to dispute the importance of well-functioning transitional justice mechanisms. Rather, what interests me is the way in which the narratives that judicial mechanisms use to describe their work are incorporated within the fictional narratives of the films themselves. Do the films accept these narratives as they are, or do they view them as "fictions of justice," self-justificatory rhetoric that risks presenting an idealized vision of what the judicial process can accomplish?

Compassion and Revenge in *Munyurangabo*

Set in the years following the 1994 genocide, *Munyurangabo* features two teenage boys – Ngabo, a Tutsi, and his friend Sangwa, a Hutu – as they set out to exact revenge for Ngabo's parents who were killed in the genocide.

On their way to Ngabo's village, they stop at Sangwa's hometown for the latter's first visit in three years. Initially scolded and shunned by his father for abandoning the family, Sangwa soon regains their esteem through his natural charm and hard work. Meanwhile, Ngabo, a genocide orphan, finds himself ostracized by his hosts when they learn he is Tutsi. He watches, with a mix of bitterness and longing, the pleasant domestic life that Sangwa enjoys. When Sangwa declares that he no longer wishes to accompany Ngabo on his quest for revenge, Ngabo reveals their plan to Sangwa's father, who beats his son and throws him out of the house. Ngabo tells the sobbing Sangwa that they are no longer friends and continues alone to his old village to kill his father's murderer. Upon arrival in the village, he stops for lunch where a young man, noticing Ngabo's machete, volunteers to recite for him a poem he has written for National Liberation Day entitled *Liberation is a Journey*. The six-minute poem preaches the virtue of reconciliation and national unity, heaps praise on the Rwandan Patriotic Front (RPF), and urges young Rwandans to work hard for the good of the nation. He finishes, and the film cuts to Ngabo holding his machete, standing in front of a squat, mud-brick dwelling. He enters and finds his father's murderer shivering beneath a small blanket. The man says he has AIDS and asks for a drink of water. In the film's final scene, Ngabo fills up a jerry-can of water for his father's murderer.

While the film's ending suggests the efficacy of the government's rhetoric on reconciliation, the beginning of *Munyurangabo* shows quite the opposite: the prevalence of anti-Tutsi sentiment that mirrors pre-genocide political discourse, and an unwillingness on the part of both Ngabo and Sangwa's Hutu family to reconcile (Hilker, 2009). These simmering ethnic tensions are revealed gradually as Chung makes no explicit references to the genocide until 26 minutes into the film. Even when Ngabo reminds Sangwa, in the film's twentieth minute, that the purpose of their journey is to "kill a man," it is not explicitly stated that it is a revenge killing against a genocide perpetrator. In choosing initially not to mention the genocide, Chung allows the viewer to reflect on the subtle ways in which the genocide makes its presence felt within Rwandan society and within the film. The gradual revelation of ethnic tensions lurking below the surface mirrors, to an extent, the situation in current Rwanda. According to Eugenia Zorbas (2009), ordinary Rwandans in the mid-2000s (when *Munyurangabo* was filmed) were initially reluctant to admit the continued presence of ethnic-based thinking, since the government had banned mentions of ethnicity, but would eventually admit that such divisions and modes of thought still exist. Indeed, current scholarship shows how these hidden divisions have persisted into Rwanda's much more recent past (Blackie & Hitchcott, 2018; Caparos et al., 2020; Russell, 2019). While his initial portrayal of ethnic discord appears subversive, Chung will eventually undermine this through his legitimation of official Rwandan government discourse at the film's end.

The eruption of ethnic tensions occurs a third of the way into the film, when Sangwa's father spouts virulent anti-Tutsi statements to his son.

The father views Sangwa's friendship with Ngabo as a troubling indifference to the insidious character of Tutsis. That this initial conversation happens inside and at night adds to its illicit quality. The father says:

> That boy you are with, don't you know he's a Tutsi? Don't you know Tutsis are nasty? They have put our people in submission now. Now I'm suffering because of them. They tried to put me in prison even though I'm old. And yet you walk with them? Hutus and Tutsis are enemies. Don't you know?

The father turns Ngabo into the village scapegoat, blaming him unjustly for a litany of problems, including the illness of their neighbor's son. Without using the word Tutsi, the father excoriates Ngabo in language that recalls pre-genocide anti-Tutsi rhetoric (Rothbart & Bartlett, 2008):

> Ever since you came, there's only trouble, trouble everywhere. Even my kids are sick. Because of you, everything is going badly. Sangwa, you brought this to our home. Look what you brought to our home. Why else is this happening? You have no shame?

Even though he never refers to Ngabo's ethnicity to the boy's face, the father's treatment of his son's friend suggests that discrimination persists even as its purveyors learn to be judicious in how and when they verbalize their feelings. As Susan Thomson (2018) writes concerning the Rwandan government's re-education programs for perpetrators: "[I]nstead of promoting a sense of national unity and reconciliation, it teaches these men, the majority of whom are ethnic Hutu, to remain silent and not question the RPF's vision for creating peace and security for all Rwandans" (p. 332). In a sad irony, it is Ngabo, the orphan and survivor, who is met with suspicion and hostility, seen both as a reminder of the genocide and as a potential threat to the family's security. As Alexandre Dauge-Roth (2010) writes, survivors are often seen "as a parasitic presence…a disturbance that prevents others from fully embracing the present by obliterating the traumatic legacy of genocide" (pp. 8–9). The dynamics of hostility and exclusion, which predated the genocide, thus continue in the film's present, along with an essentializing vision that sees all Tutsis as an indiscriminate threat to stability and security, one of the main rationales the Hutu-powered government had given for the genocide (Kimonyo, 2016).

Ngabo in turn responds to this rejection by blaming all Hutus for the deaths of his parents, saying that "my life would have been better without them," a totalizing rhetoric that suggests his own need to find a scapegoat for the loss of his family. "You don't know that life is hard," he exclaims to Sangwa:

> You have a family, a mother, and a father. You know why my life is like this? Why my life is hard? It's because of your relatives. Because Hutus killed my family…What's more, I bet your father was involved in the killings.

It is Ngabo's blanket condemnation of Sangwa's relatives that suggests his own internalization of a racialized discourse that now threatens to poison his relationship with his friend, and impedes the process of reconciliation that the government espouses. It is unclear if his accusations against Sangwa's father are based on any evidence or are simply motivated by anger at his friend who no longer wants to go along with his revenge scheme. "The way he looks at me when he enters the home shows me that he was among them," he says.

While neither the ICTR nor the *gacaca* courts have been mentioned at this point in the film, the climate of paranoia can be seen in part as stemming from the overwhelming demands on Rwanda's post-genocide judiciary system. With so many perpetrators and no way to give them a thorough trial, establishing the innocence or guilt of a potential killer such as Sangwa's father is not an easy process, and doubt about who participated in the genocide persists. In turn, because the father knows he could be denounced, justly or unjustly, or become the victim of a vigilante revenge killing, he is deeply suspicious of Tutsis. Furthermore, it is the knowledge that his father's killer has not been adequately punished that pushes Ngabo to undertake a quixotic quest to enact justice himself, a vengeance he is ill-prepared to carry out. What is crucial to note is how the film foregrounds the effects of this failure of justice mechanisms on individuals and their families, noting how these unresolved questions of culpability interfere with individuals' natural desires for psychological stability. In this climate of suspicion and fear, where the government's pleas to reconcile are ignored and vigilante justice is deemed necessary, Ngabo appears condemned to a life of exclusion outside of any family structure.

The film uses prison imagery to suggest the sad irony that it is the survivors who are condemned to a psychological prison as a result of their irreparable losses. Around the midpoint of the film, Ngabo speaks with Sangwa's friend Gwiza, revealing for the first time the pain of losing his father. After this, he returns to Sangwa's home where the family is gathered in the central courtyard sharing banana beer and laughing. Ngabo walks silently past them into an adjacent room, but continues to watch the family through a window that has three black vertical bars. The scene is shot primarily from Ngabo's point of view, suggesting a prisoner looking through the bars of his cell. He watches as Sangwa's father promises to build Sangwa a house and the mother encourages him to be a good son and listen to his parents. The injustice of Ngabo's figurative imprisonment underscores the limits of the official juridical responses to the genocide against the Tutsi. Perpetrators walk free while survivors such as Ngabo are excluded because of the prejudice of non-survivors who see them as a threat. More broadly, it suggests the fiction of any justice or reparation system that cannot liberate or compensate those whose wounds are not physically verifiable. No reparation can restore Ngabo's lost parents, which is precisely what he seems to yearn for as he watches his friend and this tableau of domestic bliss from his figurative prison cell.

Appropriating Propaganda for the Sake of Narrative Closure

While the first two-thirds of *Munyurangabo* offer an unsparing and nuanced look at the possible difficulties faced by orphans such as Ngabo, the film's conclusion takes a sentimental turn that undermines some of its previous critiques. *Hotel Rwanda*, the most commercially successful film regarding the genocide, has been frequently criticized for its own feel-good ending in which the protagonist, Paul Rusesabagina, is reunited with his family after saving hundreds of Tutsis from being massacred. As Lena Khor (2012) notes, *Hotel Rwanda* uses "the deployment of sentimental rhetoric to artificially resolve sociopolitical problems" (p. 219). Despite its initial unflinching portrayal of Ngabo's survivor experience – moments of fellowship and joy punctuated by intense feelings of isolation – *Munyurangabo* opts for a similarly sentimental ending. This ending also legitimizes government rhetoric that works to marginalize survivors, even as it claims to speak for them and work for their interests.

This abrupt change in tone occurs in the final 20 minutes of the film, after Ngabo has abandoned Sangwa to exact revenge on his own. After silently surveying the ruins of his family's house, he stops to eat lunch at a small restaurant, where he engages with the young man who has composed the National Liberation Day poem. In this moment, the film shifts from a more thoughtful portrayal of the challenges survivors, particularly orphans, face in social integration, to an almost prescriptive suggestion that survivors have a particular (if not sole) responsibility for the country's stability post-genocide. The manner in which the six-minute poem is filmed is especially revelatory. During the entire sequence, in which the poet declaims on the importance of a unified Rwanda, and the need for forgiveness and moving on, Ngabo's face is not once shown. This choice on Chung's part, presumably to foreground the importance and centrality of the speech to the film's aims, has the troubling effect of marginalizing and excluding Ngabo's reactions to this exhortation to forgive and move on, while also not giving him space to respond.

The poem, the anonymous poet informs Ngabo, is called *Liberation is a Journey*. He begins by addressing all Rwandans inside and outside of Rwanda, reminding them that they all speak the same language and descend from a common culture. The poem emphasizes the role of children in the genocide, presumably causing Ngabo to reflect on whether he, as a child, is a part of a similar process of violence:

> Let's remember how liberation came, unleashing heavy burdens in my youth. When I was young and just a child, I played in mud and heard of hate. Rwanda readied children for war, children chosen and armed against enemies. I heard that Tutsis were roaches and should be stomped; with tails like snakes they should be killed. We were given bows and spears and foreign countries gave us guns.

He describes how he saw Muslims and Christians working together "joined by machetes and their will to kill." He recites that "Rwanda's youth led the battle, don't you see that this is injustice?" As Jastine Barrett (2019) shows, young people did play a significant role in the genocide, participating in the killing, rape, looting, and denunciation of those in hiding. However, this moment in the film suggests a false comparison between Ngabo and the young *génocidaires*, an accusatory stance that does not take into account the substantial differences between his desire for revenge and youths incited to violence during the genocide.[5] The poem also echoes the "good old days" rhetoric of the government, suggesting that Rwanda was a peaceful, harmonious paradise before it was contaminated by genocide. This oversimplification of the political repression and social dynamics of pre-genocide Rwanda is often used by the RPF to explain why national unity should come naturally to Hutus and Tutsis (Buckley-Zistel, 2009).

The political character of the speech is made explicit with the poet's unqualified praise for the RPF, the subject of inquiries related to human rights abuses and ongoing violence in the Democratic Republic of Congo (Goehrung, 2017; Straus & Waldorf, 2011). The poem highlights this:

> And the RPF army I was taught to hate, decided it was time to defend Rwanda...I will thank them [the RPF] wherever I am. Their heroics will be known worldwide. From Darfur in Sudan to the Comoro Islands, they will be admired. And I'll see them the way the Pope sees his church.

The poet asks the RPF to "free us from poverty and illiteracy since liberation is a journey." The poem uncritically lauds the RPF as the "defenders" of Rwanda who stepped in to stop the fighting and restore the country to its harmonious pre-genocide state, saying "no" to the continued violence and bloodshed and engaging in a fight for "truth." While the RPF's role in stopping the genocide is undeniable and their governance of Rwanda in its aftermath has seen many positive developments, such uncritical praise of the RPF amounts to propaganda, especially since there is nothing in the film that offers an alternative perspective on the RPF. At this point, the film's narrative and the RPF's narrative and ideology merge, with the film legitimizing the Rwandan state's rhetoric without contextualizing it.

There are moments in which the poet's word choice betrays the poem's ideological framing. For instance, he says that it gives a "bad image for Rwanda" when children who cannot afford soap are picking tea and coffee for export to foreign markets. This formulation suggests more concern for the image of Rwanda projected for the West than the plight of the Rwandans he describes. The relevance of the speech for Ngabo is most evident when it turns toward the issue of revenge killings and transitional justice. "Will it [Rwanda] remain a cemetery without peace?" the poet asks. "Don't you see that this is injustice?" In the context of the speech, however, the duty not to enact revenge is linked with the idea of the "image" of Rwanda. Even if one wholeheartedly endorses such exhortations to peace, the question is framed as what is good for the Rwandan nation, in essence suggesting that those who seek revenge are bad Rwandan citizens.

In another telling passage, the poet offers unequivocal praise for the *gacaca* court system:

> What happens in the village genocide courts? Let justice liberate. Let truth replace lies in Rwanda. Sitting together in the grass without division or hate. Without lying to each other. As we live in peace and the guilty seek forgiveness...As we battle against hate, I wish you all the best.

The line "battle against hate" recalls the rhetoric against divisionism and hate speech that the RPF government often uses to suppress free speech (Rose, 2015) as well as unjustly imprison political opponents (Jansen, 2014). More fundamentally, the use of the *gacaca* courts as a symbol of reconciliation and national unity leaves no room within the film for a more in-depth questioning of its mechanisms and consequences. While numerous scholars have emphasized the positive aspects of the *gacaca* courts (Gasanabo, 2019; Ugorji, 2019), the trials have also resulted in revenge killings, the traumatization of witnesses, and the release of killers into the very communities they had victimized (Brounéus, 2008; Rettig, 2008; for an alternative perspective see Caparos et al., 2020). Chung's stance is blanket praise of the *gacaca* courts, foreclosing a more nuanced representation of post-genocide Rwanda. The harmonious vision that the poet gives of Rwandans sitting unified side-by-side is itself a fiction, a self-serving piece of RPF rhetoric that in the context of the plot is used to shame Ngabo into acknowledging that his plans for revenge run counter to the RPF's notions of national unity. The hate the poet describes can also refer to that which the victims harbor toward the killers, a hate, which, Ngabo is lectured, stands in the way of a peaceful, undivided Rwanda (Russell, 2019; Waldorf, 2009). While one does not question the poet's ultimate goal of peace, his unequivocal moralizing toward those who harbor hate for the killers glosses over the complex and varied origins of these natural feelings of hate and vengeance. As the survivor Esther Mujawayo writes in her memoir, *SurVivantes* (Mujawayo & Belhaddad, 2011), it is possible for survivors to feel hate for the killers while making a conscious decision not to act upon their feelings.[6]

When Ngabo finds his father's killer dying of AIDS, shivering under a thin blanket and begging for water, his decision to help the man rather than carry out his revenge scheme can be read as a laudable act of compassion. The suggestion that he would be moved by the man's suffering and find himself incapable of killing another human being is highly plausible, and suggests a willingness on Ngabo's part to envision a path to rebuilding his life not based on a continuation of violence. What is critical to note here is not the ethics of Ngabo's choice, but rather the way in which the film frames his choice through its juxtaposition with the National Liberation Day poem. Ngabo's decision is thus seen as influenced by, or at the very least in accordance with, RPF reconciliation ideology, a move that takes attention away from his own agency, and implicitly endorses the RPF's problematic rhetoric. I am by no means suggesting that Ngabo has a right to kill, but rather that the film shows a character who models the behavior mandated by the Rwandan state, at the expense of a more complex exploration of the motivations and consequences of Ngabo's conciliatory gesture.

In the film's final scene, as Ngabo draws water from a well, Sangwa appears beside him. The implication is that to restore this lost interethnic friendship, Ngabo must first show compassion for the man that killed his family. Joyful music plays over the closing credits, suggesting that Ngabo's choice will restore some measure of collective joy. What is missing in these final moments is some interrogation of the complexity of Ngabo's decision to help the man who killed his family. What concrete steps, in addition to putting aside his revenge fantasies, does Ngabo need to rebuild his life? The film (and the RPF rhetoric that it echoes) implies that personal forgiveness is sufficient, a vast oversimplification of the daily struggles that survivors such as Ngabo have faced. What is contradictory in *Munyurangabo*'s representation of the survivor experience is the way in which the film offers such a nuanced portrayal of present-day Rwanda, and the haunting and destructive presence of the genocide and hate rhetoric, only to present a facile conclusion for the sake of narrative resolution. The sentimental ending works to prevent reflection on some of the more nuanced aspects of the survivor experience and makes the film uncomfortably close to a propaganda piece, a sharp departure from its initial even-handed portrayal of the genocide's aftermath. In short, Chung ultimately appropriates the utopian vision of the Rwandan state in a way that marginalizes the very survivors whose story the film claims to tell.

The Limits of Justice in *Sometimes in April*

Sometimes in April is routinely praised as the "productive counter-example" (Khor, 2012, p. 219) to the oft-criticized *Hotel Rwanda* (Dauge-Roth, 2010; Edmondson, 2007; Hitchcott, 2020). As Elizabeth Goldberg (2007) writes *à propos* of Peck's film:

> The tremendous potential of film to dramatize for mass audiences the stakes of the unfolding, immeasurably consequential narrative of human rights and their violations is finally being unleashed with the kind of experiments in points of view and temporality that put to the test the old truism that every story is a hero story
>
> (p. 56).

Derrick Alan Everett (2009) sees *Sometimes in April* as a validation of the ICTR and the *gacaca* system, claiming that the film "shows a functioning international legal justice system in which accused *génocidaires* suffer from the ramifications of their actions" (p. 127). In this section, I eschew the Manichean comparisons with *Hotel Rwanda* that the film often inspires. Instead, I explore how *Sometimes in April* critiques both the international justice system and the concept of justice as a whole. Through these critiques, *Sometimes in April* exposes the "fictions of justice" of the ICTR, especially from the perspective of survivors and their families who have lost everything, even as it suggests the vital necessity of these flawed mechanisms.

Peck's film tells the story of Augustin, a Hutu and former Rwandan army officer, whose Tutsi wife and children were killed during the genocide. Augustin did not participate in the killings, but his brother Honoré hosted a show at the state radio channel *Radio Télévision Libre des Mille Collines* (RTLM), spewing hate speech as the massacres were underway. The film alternates between scenes of the 1994 genocide and of Rwanda in 2004, where Augustin has become a teacher and his brother is imprisoned at Arusha awaiting trial for his work at RTLM. Augustin receives a letter from Honoré begging him to come see him at Arusha, and the film's present-day narrative is structured around Augustin's journey and his reluctance and fear to confront his brother. After initially refusing, he finally meets with his brother who tells him that he was unable to keep Augustin's children from being murdered at a roadblock. Honoré tells Augustin that Augustin's wife stole a grenade to blow herself up along with a group of *génocidaires* to save Tutsis sheltering in a church. There is no tearful reconciliation between the brothers at the meeting's end. They sit in silence for several moments and the film cuts to Augustin leaving his hotel in Tanzania, returning home to his pregnant fiancée.

The film's scenes of the genocide itself are unsparing and graphic. We see a room full of schoolchildren, including Augustin's daughter, shot at point-blank range. The camera slowly pans across a room of gravely injured refugees lying in a church. In the days following the genocide, Augustin walks in shock past grotesque, decaying corpses. The fear, grief, and anguish of those attempting to survive the three-month genocide are poignantly represented. The film also shows the discussions of high-ranking American diplomatic officials as they make the decision not to intervene, arguing that they have no strategic interest in Rwanda and that it is not their responsibility. These bystanders, the film implies, bear some responsibility for the genocide, and yet can never be held accountable since there is no judicial mechanism to punish those who did not directly participate. Their impunity is one example of how the film shows the fictional qualities of the justice narrative, and how this is a source of angst and constant frustration for genocide survivors.

Sometimes in April foregrounds this question of bystanders and responsibilities by displaying a Martin Luther King Jr. quote at the beginning of the film: "In the end, we will remember not the words of our enemies but the silence of our friends." This idea of passive participation in the genocide, which the justice process does not or cannot always prosecute, runs throughout the film. Furthermore, the question of what precisely constitutes participation in genocide is problematized through the figure of Augustin's brother Honoré, a radio host who promoted divisive genocidal rhetoric but did not himself participate in the killings. Honoré personifies this liminal figure who may or may not be brought to justice, slipping through the cracks of the criminal justice system. *Sometimes in April* critiques the ICTR but also acknowledges its potential to create spaces for dialogue that can reveal previously unacknowledged aspects of the genocide. Indeed, while the film shows witness testimony and legal arguments from within the space of the courtroom, it also privileges the liminal spaces outside the courtroom itself – the cellblocks, and even the hotel rooms where visitors and witnesses at Arusha are staying – as crucial spaces for fostering dialogue about the genocide and the way in which it affects survivors in present-day Rwanda. Throughout the film, these spaces on the periphery of the ICTR system are foregrounded as places where transformative acts of remembrance occur in ways that have personal significance for the actors and victims of the genocide.

The film opens with a brief chronology of the historical events that led to the genocide before cutting to footage of former President Bill Clinton, one of the most publicly repentant of the genocide's Western bystanders, delivering a speech post-genocide where he emphasizes the importance of "never again." We zoom out to a classroom of teenage Rwandan students watching the film in 2004, ten years after the genocide occurred. As the audience at the press conference applauds Clinton's speech, the students sit in skeptical silence. They ask their teacher, Augustin, if the genocide could have been stopped, introducing the question of prevention and the ethical conundrum of the responsibility of bystanders.

As mournful string music plays, the camera slowly pans to the outside of the school showing a yellow banner which reads *Journée nationale du souvenir* [National Day of Memory], soaked by a driving rain. But precisely what is being remembered, and by whom? The film asks us to look beyond the official channels of memory, interrogating the difference between the RPF's official memory and the individual memory of survivors, killers, and bystanders.

The first indication of how the international criminal justice system will structure the movie occurs when Augustin returns home from school to find a letter from his brother, Honoré, who is imprisoned in Arusha. In a belated acknowledgement of his own agency, Honoré writes in his letter that, "I finally realized that I was an actor in this tragedy." Honoré says that he wants to tell Augustin the truth about what happened to Augustin's wife and children, and requests that Augustin visit him at the ICTR prison in Arusha. Augustin is ambivalent about going to see his brother, understandably because of the painful memories it evokes. The brother's imprisonment functions symbolically to show the estrangement between the two and the way the genocide obliterates or disrupts family structures. Like *Munyurangabo*, *Sometimes in April* links the functioning of the justice system to family relationships, showing how the two are intertwined.

At the insistence of his fiancée, Augustin agrees to undertake the journey. He sits watching his brother's trial, hidden behind two-way glass. In front of several stern judges wearing black robes and white wigs, Honoré describes a gradual realization that what he did was wrong: "I now recognize that the radio program I did for RTLM was criminal and that many people were killed for it." He claims that during his stay in prison: "I became aware that I was guilty," but that he had not confessed because of pressure from his fellow detainees. Augustin watches skeptically. It is unclear whether Honoré is genuinely repentant or is simply confessing in the hopes of a reduced sentence. The focus, however, is less on the judicial process itself than on Augustin's reaction, and his confrontation with his brother. The tribunal provides Honoré space in which to express himself, and it is clear that his potential crocodile tears are as much about effecting a sort of family reconciliation as about confessing his actual guilt. A flashback showing an insouciant Honoré at the radio station during the genocide casts further doubt on the veracity of his claims, as well as on the ability of the justice system to bring about true repentance.

On a narrative level, the importance of this courtroom scene within the film is not related to whether or not Honoré is guilty (the audience has already seen flashback scenes where he is spewing hate speech on the radio during the genocide). Instead, the courtroom is also a space where individuals like Augustin must confront the emotional impact of uncovering the genocide's past. The viewer is asked to focus not just on the past event that the testimony describes, but on the psychological impact of the testimony being made public in the present moment. The film suggests that unearthing the past is necessarily a fraught endeavor for those who must listen and be reminded of these traumatic events, even if it is done as part of a necessary process of transitional justice.

Like *Munyurangabo*, *Sometimes in April* uses the visual image of the prison cell to show some contradictions of the justice system, although, unlike Chung's film, it remains more consistent in its critiques. While visiting his brother in Arusha, Augustin walks by the prisoners in their clean, ordered cells. He observes the prisoners praying or speaking calmly around a table. This order and tranquility contrasts with the chaotic, violent, overcrowded spaces of the genocide: Augustin's ransacked house in which the floor is covered with his wrecked possessions, the church packed with wounded Tutsis where his wife finds refuge, the swamps strewn with dead corpses. In abrupt cuts from these scenes to the tidy prison cells, the film visually suggests how the justice system attempts to impose order on the messy reality and memory of genocide and prompts the viewer to reflect on what is hidden by this containment. What justice is this, the viewer may wonder along with Augustin, which permits these perpetrators to live in such comfort?

After passing these scenes of calm, Augustin is greeted by the symmetrical sight of two identical, empty chairs, at opposite sides of a small table. The ordered symmetry of the room and the furniture contrast with the complex amalgam of emotions visible on his face. Unable to confront his brother, Augustin leaves abruptly. One is left with the ironic sense that it is those within the prison, seen praying and calmly chatting, who have a better mastery of their emotions than those without.

Peck again creates a contrast between the cellblock and Augustin's hotel room in Arusha, a dark, claustrophobic space that symbolizes how Augustin remains trapped by his traumatic past. As in *Munyurangabo*, the visual containment of the character suggests the irony of an unjust psychological imprisonment, asking the viewer to consider the full meaning of the terms "justice" and "prison." Alone with his grief and confusion, Augustin hears sobs from an adjacent room. We learn that the person crying is a rape survivor who has come to Tanzania of her own volition to testify before the tribunal as a surprise witness. Later in the film, a grief-stricken Augustin is crawling around like a caged animal on the floor of his hotel room. He knocks on the wall to signal the attention of the woman that he heard crying. Communicating through the wall like prisoners, Augustin and the surprise witness experience a fleeting moment of connection, but still remain separated by a traumatic past which, ironically, they share.

The fictional quality of the justice narrative plays out within the courtroom as well, in the arguments that the defense uses to exonerate Honoré. His lawyer attempts to deny the link between speech and violence, suggesting that without empirical, visual proof, one cannot be convicted:

> It is true that my client admits his *moral* guilt. But where is freedom of the press? Or freedom of expression? My client was an intellectual, a man of letters. Did anyone actually see my client butchering people?… Is he a murderer because he stood on a political principle? Where is the blood on my client's hands?[7]

This burden of empirical proof that the lawyer demands also underscores the importance of film, a visual medium, in creating new images that, albeit fictional, can contribute to the historical discussion surrounding the genocide. The lawyer's focus on the lack of empirical evidence also shows the way in which the constraints of the juridical sphere can limit discussions of guilt and responsibility, potentially liberating those with figurative blood on their hands.

An almost parallel scene occurs later in the film, when the woman that Augustin encounters through his hotel room wall describes her experience as one of a group of women who were raped during the genocide.[8] Employing a respectful but skeptical tone, the defense lawyer questions her, asking where the defendant was at the time of the rapes, and verifying, as the witness has implied, that the defendant was not involved. "I felt that he could have protected us but he did nothing," she replies. The lawyer continues, "Did the defendant ever participate in the rapes?" "I never saw him rape anybody," she says, "but he didn't protect us… He was the coach, encouraging his players." Though the outcome of this particular trial is not specified, the implication is that legal technicalities may prevent the man from being convicted. The film shows the psychological toll of the rape survivor's exposure to a humiliating cross-examination, but also suggests some possible benefits to her participation in the tribunal even if she does not achieve a conviction. She has been given an official forum to express herself and to encounter Augustin, who provides her with some much-needed sympathy and compassion. When the judge asks why she decided to come to Arusha and testify voluntarily, she replies that it was important to show how the accused had betrayed the women that he could have protected from being raped. "When a person leads assassins, he is also an assassin." While the Arusha tribunal has prosecuted some of those who urged the killings, the scene underscores how the judicial system may never engage in nuanced discussions of guilt, thus denying justice and closure to surviving family members such as Augustin.

The most explicit critique of the Arusha tribunal comes near the film's end, when Augustin calls his fiancée, Martine, to explain his frustrations. Describing what he has seen over the past few days, he exclaims: "This thing doesn't make sense. They're all here. Everyone who planned genocide is here. I saw Bagosora,[9] here. They get AZT medicine while rape survivors are dying of AIDS, it's like a fucking health club!"[10] Trying to reassure her fiancé, Martine replies,

> "Well I guess the killers are the stars of the show."
>
> "Is this what this is? A show? A big show?"
>
> "We need the tribunals. I know they have their shortcomings, but it's a way to get through it, a way to move on."
>
> "It's a way for everybody to wash their hands, so nobody has to feel bad, so we can pretend there was justice."

Augustin states explicitly what the film itself has been suggesting visually since the beginning: that the international justice system creates its own fiction of order, completion, and justice that serves to absolve the international community of further responsibility. Having ignored the genocide as it occurred, they create transitional justice mechanisms to punish the guilty, creating the false illusion that the genocide can ever be truly "in the past" for those who continue to live with its effects (Akhavan, 2001; Gasanabo, 2019; Palmer, 2015; Schulz, 2015). In addition, the "stars" of the genocide (as August calls the *génocidaires*) are given a privileged status that perversely mirrors that which they held when the genocide took place. Martine's defense of the tribunals, even as she acknowledges their shortcomings, is also consistent with the film. Indeed, the film's ending suggests that without

Arusha, Augustin would not be able to explore his past in a way that would allow him to understand his anger and grief. In a broader sense, it is not the tribunals that Augustin is critiquing. It is the shortcomings of all judicial systems, which often serve other motives than their stated aims and can never truly restore what the defendants are charged with having destroyed. The film wishes to highlight the emotional toll this "fiction of justice" places on the victims of genocide, even as these institutions of justice are crucial to Rwandans' ability to rebuild post-genocide.

Sometimes in April differs notably from *Munyurangabo* in its continual questioning of the efficacy of the justice system and its claims to provide closure and definitive answers to its participants. The film focuses on Augustin's quest for answers about the genocide and the necessary, if often infuriating and unsatisfactory, role of the ICTR in his journey of discovery. A more nuanced understanding of how these systems function, the film suggests, depends on considering the spaces around and outside of the official narrative. It is within these liminal spaces, created by the justice system but not strictly a part of it, that conversations and encounters necessary for gaining understanding can occur.

A Positive Depiction of Grassroots Justice

The positive depiction of the *gacaca* courts in *Sometimes in April* provides a notable contrast with the film's frequent criticisms of the ICTR. The few scenes in the film showing the *gacaca* courts suggest its superiority over the ICTR, which is portrayed as removed from everyday Rwanda and overly preoccupied with legal technicalities.[11] The first scene of a *gacaca* hearing begins from a distance, showing groups of Rwandans sitting outside on the grass, a marked contrast to the closed, aseptic confines of Arusha. There is an implication of grassroots participation, and transparency. That the proceedings take place entirely in Kinyarwanda, as opposed to English, implies a more authentic access to the truth. Considering the shortcomings of the *gacaca* courts mentioned previously – the retraumatization of witnesses, revenge killings by the families of perpetrators – this overwhelmingly positive representation of the *gacaca* courts, as opposed to the ICTR, is puzzling. It is one area where *Sometimes in April* offers a positive portrayal of a particular justice system for narrative reasons at the expense of a more even-handed representation of post-genocide transitional justice. As Bert Ingelaere (2016) writes, "…the enthusiasm for grassroots transitional justice processes runs well ahead of evidence that they are effective. Because these processes operate outside the mainstream, knowledge gaps and blind spots exist" (p. 3, see also Doughty, 2016).

Within the fictional universe of *Sometimes in April*, the *gacaca* court becomes a space where survivors can show agency, and also serves to critique the ICTR's preoccupation with legalese and technicalities. The judge overseeing the *gacaca* proceedings states: "If anyone can testify, please stand up." After a moment of silence an unidentified woman rises:

> I know this man. He came through my yard pushing two of the victims. A woman named Madeleine Mukasano and a man named Dieudonné. When he arrived at my neighbor's house, that man over there hit Dieudonné with a machete and then cut Madeleine's feet off. I saw it with my own eyes. I speak the truth.

By linking the *gacaca* courts with speaking the "truth" the film seeks to highlight inefficiencies within the ICTR proceedings, implying that the *gacaca* comes closer to offering real justice. In providing a forum for ordinary Rwandans, the film suggests that they contribute to a process of reconciliation and allow true justice to occur, far from star prosecutors speaking legalese and using spurious logic to defend murderers.

The film's final scene takes place at the *gacaca* trial of a group of men accused of participating in the massacre of 120 schoolgirls. Augustin's fiancée Martine was one of the only survivors. The judge asks if anyone recognizes the accused killers and Martine walks calmly into frame, stating: "I was there, I'm a survivor." Ending the film at the *gacaca* court continues its depiction of these spaces as a place for ordinary Rwandans to express themselves, speaking the truth about their traumatic experiences. As in *Munyurangabo*, the *gacaca* courts serve a narrative function, creating a sense of resolution that does not allow for a more complex reflection on the complexity of these local tribunals, a reflection that must acknowledge the retraumatization of witnesses and the reduced sentences for killers who confessed (see Kochanski, 2020; Thomson & Nagy, 2011). Again, the point is not to suggest that such a depiction of *gacaca* is wholly without merit, but rather to show how in using *gacaca* to critique the ICTR and to give the film closure, Peck leaves no room for these criticisms in *Sometimes in April*. As in Munyurangabo, the filmmaker appropriates the *gacaca*'s self-justificatory narrative to legitimize the film's ending, creating closure by suggesting that *gacaca* offers a level of justice that the ICTR cannot provide.

Conclusion

Overall, the depiction of the *gacaca* courts and the ICTR within *Munyurangabo* and *Sometimes in April* raises important questions of the lessons fictional film can teach us about the processes of memory and justice in post-conflict spaces. Both films rely on Rwandan government narratives of reconciliation and justice to provide narrative closure in a manner that legitimizes and favorably depicts a system that is inseparable from Rwandan state ideology. This appropriation of a particular justice narrative should caution us to be attentive to how fictional films position themselves, and are positioned, in relationship to the judicial processes that they depict. In the case of the two films in this study, by legitimizing the *gacaca* court as a site of authentic transitional justice, the films work in concert with the Rwandan government, advancing the rhetoric of *gacaca* as a form of comprehensive, totalizing justice that will allow Rwanda to reconcile and heal. While this is a laudable goal, it is important to view an uncritical presentation of the *gacaca* courts as an ideologically inflected choice that risks turning certain characters into symbols at the expense of their individuality and interiority. Thus, while narrative fiction can help us understand the broader implications of transitional justice systems on both the individual and collective level, the need for narrative closure can act as an impediment to a more balanced representation of these systems and their ability to facilitate justice and reconciliation.

Notes

1 For further discussion and debate on the ICTR and *gacaca*, see Chapters 5 and 6 in this volume; Gasanabo (2019); Longman (2017); Palmer (2015); and Thomson (2018).

2 *100 Days* was produced by the prolific Rwandan filmmaker Eric Kabera, who is also the founder of the Rwanda Cinema Center, which has trained Rwandan filmmakers and organized the Rwanda Film Festival known as "Hillywood." Kabera's filmography also includes the 2004 documentary *Keepers of Memory* (director and producer) and the 2008 documentary *Iseta: Behind the Roadblock* (co-producer).

3 Along with Eric Kabera's *100 Days,* director Kivu Ruhorahoza's *Grey Matter* is one of the few globally circulating fictional feature films about the genocide from a Rwandan filmmaker. The film earned Ruhorahoza the 2011 Tribeca Film Festival's Jury Special Mention for Best Emerging Filmmaker.

4 Though the ICTR officially closed in December 2015, certain cases related to the 1994 genocide continue to be adjudicated through the United Nations International Residual Mechanism for Criminal Tribunals.

5 This problematic equivalency between *génocidaires* and survivors forms the basis of some survivor memoirs. See for instance Immaculée Illibagaiza's (2006) memoir *Left to Tell.*

6 She writes *à propos* of genocide: "…I don't wish for this [genocide] to happen to my worst enemy. I would not wish this tragedy on anybody in the world [translation mine]" (p. 257).

7 In December 2003, the ICTR did convict two Rwandans, Ferdinand Nahimana and Jean-Bosco Baraygwiza, for propagating hate speech at RTLM (see MacKinnon, 2009). Although Peck had not completed filming at the time of the *Nahimana* decision, he does not address the case in the film, misleadingly suggesting that those who worked at RLTM were unlikely to be prosecuted. However, as Diane Orentlicher (2005) points out, controversy remains over the legal precedents used to justify this decision and the ICTR's authority to prosecute for hate speech. Thus, while glossing over a significant decision of the ICTR, *Sometimes in April* nonetheless highlights the legal grey area concerning the propagation of hate-rhetoric, and the way the juridical burden of proof can allow those whose moral culpability is unquestionable to remain unpunished. For a more recent discussion, see Badar and Florijančič, (2020).

8 Some have questioned the efficacy of the ICTR in bringing justice to the rape victims and survivors of the 1994 genocide (see Nowrojee, 2005).

9 A colonel in the Rwandan military and one of the masterminds of the 1994 genocide, Théoneste Bagosora received a sentence of life imprisonment from the ICTR that was reduced to thirty-five years upon appeal (ICTR-98-41-T).

10 The ease with which detainees at Arusha received antiretroviral drugs compared to rape survivors in Rwanda is seen by many as an emblem of the tribunal's failure to provide true justice. While a 2004 policy attempted to make antiretroviral drugs available to women who testified at Arusha, those who did not testify were not eligible for this particular program (see de Brouwer & Chu, 2009).

11 For more on the implications of the ICTR's location outside of Rwanda, see Schulz (2015).

Bibliography

Akhavan, P. (2001). Beyond impunity: Can international criminal justice prevent future atrocities? *American Journal of International Law, 95*(1), 7–31. https://doi.org/10.2307/2642034

Badar, M., & Florijančič, P. (2020). Assessing incitement to hatred as a crime against humanity of persecution. *The International Journal of Human Rights, 24*(5), 656–687. https://doi.org/10.1080/13642987.2019.1671356

Barrett, J. C. (2019). *Child perpetrators on trial: Insights from post-genocide Rwanda.* Cambridge University Press.

Blackie, L. E., & Hitchcott, N. (2018). 'I am Rwandan': Unity and reconciliation in post-genocide Rwanda. *Genocide Studies and Prevention: An International Journal, 12*(1), 24–37. https://doi.org/10.5038/1911-9933.12.1.1480

Brounéus, K. (2008). Truth-telling as talking cure? Insecurity and retraumatization in the Rwandan gacaca courts. *Security Dialogue, 39*(1), 55–76. https://doi.org/10.1177/0967010607086823

Brown, A. (Director) (2011). Kinyarwanda [Film]. AFFRM.

Buckley-Zistel, S. (2009). Nation, narration, unification? The politics of history teaching after the Rwandan genocide. *Journal of Genocide Research, 11*(1), 31–53. https://doi.org/10.1080/14623520802703608

Caparos, S., Rutembesa, E., Habimana, E., & Blanchette, I. (2020). The psychological correlates of transitional justice in Rwanda: A long-term assessment. *Psychological Trauma: Theory, Research, Practice, and Policy, 12*(7), 774–784. https://doi.org/10.1037/tra0000583

Caton-Jones, M. (Director) (2005). Beyond the Gates [Film]. IFC Films.

Chung, L. I. (Director) (2007). Munyurangabo [Film]. Almond Tree Films.

Cieplak, P. (2018). History, trauma and remembering in Kivu Ruhorahoza's *Grey Matter* (2011). *Journal of African Cultural Studies, 30*(2), 163–177. https://doi.org/10.1080/13696815.2016.1244476

Cieplak, P. A. (2010). Alternative African cinemas: A case study of Rwanda. *Journal of African Media Studies, 2*(1), 73–90. https://doi.org/10.1386/jams.2.1.73/1

Dauge-Roth, A. (2010). *Writing and filming the genocide of the Tutsis in Rwanda: Dismembering and remembering traumatic history.* Lexington Books.

Dauge-Roth, A. (2017). Comment faire entrer cela dans le cadre ? Répondre cinématographiquement au et du génocide contre les Tutsis du Rwanda : 1994–2014. In V. Brinker, C. Coquio, A. Dauge-Roth, É. Hoppenot, N. Réra, & F. Robinet (Eds.), *Rwanda, 1994–2014. Histoire, mémoires et récits* (pp. 255–278). Les Presses du Réel.

De Brouwer, A.-M., & Chu, S. K. H. (Eds.). (2009). *The men who killed me: Rwandan Survivors of sexual violence*. Douglas & McIntyre.

Doughty, K. C. (2016). *Remediation in Rwanda*. University of Pennsylvania Press. https://doi.org/10.9783/9780812292398

Edmondson, L. (2007). Of sugarcoating and hope. *The Drama Review*, *51*(2), 7–10. https://doi.org/10.1162/dram.2007.51.2.7

Edwards, M. (2018). *The Rwandan genocide on film: Critical essays and interviews*. McFarland & Company, Inc.

Everett, D. A. (2009). Public narratives and reparations in Rwanda: On the potential of film as promoter of international human rights and reconciliation. *Northwestern Journal of International Human Rights*, *7*, 103–131.

Favreau, R. (Director) (2006). A Sunday in Kigali [Film]. Equinoxe Films.

Gasanabo, J.-D. (2019). Peace in Rwanda: Balancing the ICTR and "Gacaca" in postgenocide peacebuilding. In A. Kulnazarova, & V. Popovski (Eds.), *The Palgrave handbook of global approaches to peace* (pp. 173–191). Springer.

George, T. (Director) (2004). Hotel Rwanda [Film]. MGM Distribution Co.

Goehrung, R. (2017). At issue: Ethnicity, violence, and the narrative of genocide: The dangers of a third-term in Rwanda. *African Studies Quarterly*, *17*(1), 79–100.

Goldberg, E. S. (2007). *Beyond terror: Gender, narrative, human rights*. Rutgers University Press.

Hilker, L. M. (2009). Everyday ethnicities: Identity and reconciliation among Rwandan youth. *Journal of Genocide Research*, *11*(1), 81–100. https://doi.org/10.1080/14623520802703640

Hitchcott, N. (2020). Seeing the genocide against the Tutsi through someone else's eyes: Prosthetic memory and *Hotel Rwanda*. *Memory Studies*, *14(5)*, 935–948. https://doi.org/10.1177/1750698020959811

Hughes, N. (Director) (2001). 100 days [Film]. Vivid Features.

Ingelaere, B. (2016). *Inside Rwanda's gacaca courts: Seeking justice after genocide*. The University of Wisconsin Press.

Jansen, Y.-O. (2014). Denying genocide or denying free speech? A case study of the application of Rwanda's genocide denial laws. *Northwestern Journal of International Human Rights*, *12(2)*, 191–213.

Katila, A. (2021). Unearthing ambiguities: Post-genocide justice in Raoul Peck's *sometimes in April* and the ICTR case Nahimana et al. *International Journal of Transitional Justice*, *15(2)*, 332–350. https://doi.org/10.1093/ijtj/ijab008

Khor, L. (2012). The politics of sentimentality and postsentimentality. *Peace Review*, *24*(2), 219–226. https://doi.org/10.1080/10402659.2012.696018

Kimonyo, J.-P. (2016). *Rwanda's popular genocide: A perfect storm*. Lynne Rienner Publishers.

Kochanski, A. (2020). The "local turn" in transitional justice: Curb the enthusiasm. *International Studies Review*, *22*(1), 26–50. https://doi.org/10.1093/isr/viy081

Kos-Krauze, J., & Krauze, K. (Directors) (2017). Birds are singing in Kigali [Film]. Kino Ŀwiat.

Longman, T. P. (2017). *Memory and justice in post-genocide Rwanda*. Cambridge University Press.

MacKinnon, C. A. (2009). Prosecutor v. Nahimana, Barayagwiza, & Ngeze. Case no. ICTR 99-52-a. *The American Journal of International Law*, *103*(1), 97–103. https://doi.org/10.2307/20456724

Mujawayo, E., & Belhaddad, S. (2011). *Survivantes : Rwanda - Histoire d'un génocide*. MetisPresses.

Mulindwa, R. (Director) (2018). 94 Terror [Film]. LIMIT Production.

Nowrojee, B. (2005). *"Your justice is too slow": Will the ICTR fail Rwanda's rape victims?* United Nations Research Institute for Social Development.

Orentlicher, D. F. (2005). Criminalizing hate speech: A comment on the ICTR's judgment in the prosecutor v. Nahimana, et al. *Human Rights Brief*, *13*(1), 1–5.

Palmer, N. (2015). *Courts in conflict: Interpreting the layers of justice in post-genocide Rwanda*. Oxford University Press.

Peck, R. (Director) (2005). Sometimes in April [Film]. HBO Films.

Rettig, M. (2008). Gacaca: Truth, justice, and reconciliation in postconflict Rwanda? *African Studies Review*, *51*(3), 25–50. https://doi.org/10.1353/arw.0.0091

Rose, H. (2015). Speak no evil, hear no evil, do no evil: How rationales for the criminalization of hate speech apply in transitional contexts. *Willamette Journal of International Law and Dispute Resolution*, *22*(2), 313–342.

Rothbart, D., & Bartlett, T. (2008). Rwandan Radio broadcasts and Hutu/Tutsi positioning. In F. M. Moghaddam, R. Harre, & N. Lee (Eds.), *Global conflict resolution through positioning analysis* (pp. 227–246). Springer. https://doi.org/10.1007/978-0-387-72112-5_13

Ruhorahoza, K. (Director) (2011). Grey Matter [Film]. Scarab Studio Films.

Russell, S. G. (2019). *Becoming Rwandan: Education, reconciliation, and the making of a post-genocide citizen*. Rutgers University Press.

Schulz, P. (2015). Justice seen is justice done?' – Assessing the impact of outreach activities by the International Criminal Tribunal for Rwanda (ICTR). *Croatian International Relations Review*, *21*(74), 63–93. https://doi.org/10.1515/cirr-2015-0017

Spottiswoode, R. (Director) (2007). Shake Hands with the Devil [Film]. Seville Pictures.

Straus, S., & Waldorf, L. (2011). *Remaking Rwanda: State building and human rights after mass violence*. The University of Wisconsin Press.

The Prosecutor v. Bagosora, Kabiligi, Ntabakuze, Nsengiyumva (Judgement and Sentence) ICTR-98-41-T (18 December 2008)

Thomson, S. (2018). *Rwanda: From genocide to precarious peace*. Yale University Press.

Thomson, S., & Nagy, R. (2011). "Law, power and justice: What legalism fails to address in the functioning of Rwanda's gacaca courts. *International Journal of Transitional Justice*, *5*(1), 11–30. https://doi.org/10.1093/ijtj/ijq024.

Ugorji, B. (2019). Indigenous dispute resolution and national reconciliation: Learning from the gacaca courts in Rwanda. *Journal of Living Together*, *6*(1), 153–161.

Waldorf, L. (2009). Revisiting *Hotel Rwanda*: Genocide ideology, reconciliation, and rescuers. *Journal of Genocide Research*, *11*(1), 101–125. https://doi.org/10.1080/14623520802703673

Zorbas, E. (2009). What does reconciliation after genocide mean? Public transcripts and hidden transcripts in post-genocide Rwanda. *Journal of Genocide Research*, *11*(1), 127–147. https://doi.org/10.1080/14623520802703707

12 Memory and Photographs of Unrepresentable Trauma in Rwandan Transitional Justice

Sonya de Laat

Introduction

Beginning on April 7, 1994, and continuing for 100 days, 800,000 to over one million Tutsis were murdered along with moderate Hutus who opposed the extremist government. The genocide of the Tutsi has been characterized as the most swift and – for lack of a better term – most efficient genocide of the 20th century (Des Forges, 1999; Kuperman, 2001; Lemarchand, 2004). Nearly three decades have passed since the horrifying event, yet this does not lessen the importance of continued reflection, dialogue, and action in response to this genocide and its aftermath. By the time of its tenth commemoration, the number of photographs taken of the aftermath of the genocide overtook those which were taken during the actual period of mass slaughter. In subsequent years, many more photographic projects have been undertaken. These have included works by photojournalists and visual artists representing the violence of genocide, the number and diversity of victims, and individual and collective experiences regarding the immediate and long-term consequences of the genocide.[1]

The medium of photography, like other visual arts, has been called into the service of working through difficult histories. Art has been recognized and often used for its potential to assist societies, communities, and individuals work through difficult issues (Bisschoff & Van Der Peer, 2013). Many works of art were (and continue to be) created in the aftermath of the Holocaust of the Second World War, so it is not surprising that the same would follow after the Rwandan genocide. Photography is the one art form that has been, if not most widely used, then at least most widely circulated because of its place in the mass press. This chapter is a reflection of a photographic project I undertook in response to Moller and Ubaldo's (2013) question: "What forms of photography might enrich the lives of ordinary people in Rwanda?" (p. 131). The reflection is interleaved with critiques of and by visual scholars and artists on the promise and limits of the medium's ability to represent seemingly unrepresentable experiences of suffering and trauma. The *Memory* –>

DOI: 10.4324/9781003228592-15

Witness (read: memory to witness) project contains photographs taken of Rwandan landscapes that may appear benign or beautiful, but that contain "metaphysical scars," which are affective wounds felt at a deeper level than those left on the skin or other surfaces (Burnet, 2012, p. 89). In many ways, these metaphysical scars can be more debilitating or difficult to adapt to than physical injuries because their force can surface in unexpected ways. As such, viewing the photographs can draw attention toward and can reinforce trauma experienced by survivors. They can also act as points of contact and entry for sharing a collective memory that is far from homogenous, and far from local. As scholarship on the 1994 genocide expands to reflect on potential harms caused when individuals or the state downplay or ignore experiences of those who have survived the trauma of genocide, it is important to recognize that suffering remains often just beneath the surface of seeming resolution and rebuilt lives (Grzyb, 2019; Jessee, 2017; Longman, 2017).

No one can know the suffering experienced by another. But for many survivors, having their experiences acknowledged – even if not fully understood – is crucially important. Acknowledging the personal and collective experiences of genocide and the ways in which trauma insidiously affects peoples' quotidian existence is, in itself, a form of historical and symbolic justice. These forms of justice are "essential to creating a successful transitional justice framework" as they can support other forms of redress including formal criminal, reparatory, and legislative actions, and informal ones such as psychological counseling and peace-building initiatives (Wolfe, 2014). Using the ambiguity of photography to its advantage, *Memory –> Witness* is about recognizing the everydayness of trauma, and the historical legacy of genocide left in its wake as a vital step in continuing to right wrongs. What follows is a look at the hopes and the limitations of photography for trauma survivors and for distant witnesses during the long period of transition after genocide.

The chapter begins with a chronology of photography during and after the genocide, paying particular attention to its role in representing suffering and supporting attempts at social reparations. I then describe the aesthetic experience that catalyzed the *Memory –> Witness* project, which is then presented with details of its content and intent. The project's title emerged from a conversation with a survivor who encouraged distant (spatial and temporal) spectators to listen to and share memories of the genocide. While I hesitated to do so, recognizing the potential for perpetuating colonial hierarchies or continuing to speak for others, taking on the role of distant witness – it was explained – meant a distribution of the burden carried by victims/survivors. Intuitively, witnessing leads to creating memories, but in this case, memories that survivors shared through this exhibition invite distant spectators to become witnesses in order to continue the work of justice and peace.

Aesthetics in the Aftermath of Genocide

Despite "the impression that this event was 'over-covered' by the media, there is a paucity of photographs from the genocide" (Roskis, 2007, p. 238). Some of this can be attributed to the technology available at the time of the mass killings. Smartphones did not exist, digital photography was in its infancy, and there were few – nearly inaccessible – outlets for the average person to share images or video clips of what they were witnessing. The professional war photographer or foreign correspondent was not as popular or as competitive a profession as it is today. Any sustained attention on this small African country also competed with more popular news items of the time such as the OJ Simpson murder trial and musician Kurt Cobain's suicide. The majority of foreign photojournalists active on the continent in early April 1994 were in South Africa covering the violence and excitement surrounding the first democratic election in that country since the fall of Apartheid. By all estimates, there were only five to six photographers in Rwanda on April 7, all of whom evacuated with other foreigners during the first few days of the genocide (Roskis, 2007, p. 239).

Moller and Ubaldo (2013) suggest that the relative abundance of post-genocide photography might be a result of Western guilt: that the late attention through art is a way of making up for not intervening while the genocide raged (p. 131). It also is possible that photography is being used to correct misrepresentations circulated by the press and by social and political leaders at the time. Dominant discourses in the press in 1994 cited the genocide as intertribal warfare (Doyle, 2007; Grzyb, 2009; Melvern, 2000). Reports characterized it as spontaneous, chaotic, and the settling of ancient scores; it was always described as horrifying and bloody.[2] In their attempt to leave no trace of their victims or of their heinous crimes, *génocidaires* managed to keep nearly all killings off camera, rendering the events and their effects more difficult to trace (Hughes, 2007; Roskis, 2007). The few photos that came out of Rwanda during the genocide were images of foreigners being evacuated, disfigured human remains, refugees in neighboring countries, and Rwandan Patriotic Front (RPF) forces advancing on the capital.[3] The shocking images and the stock-in-trade captions found in mainstream international press hardly invited deeper engagement or empathic connections between spectators and subjects.

Many different styles of photography, from documentary to conceptual, have been and continue to be used to draw spectators into events and experiences. Pictures of the supremely shocking to the sublimely beautiful are deployed every day in the name of rousing solidarity and of learning more about the human condition. For the *Memory –> Witness* exhibition, I could have displayed photographs of artifacts from the memorial sites. I could have shown photographs of piles of clothing, of bones, of row upon row of bleached skulls. I *have* shown such images before, for various purposes: to describe the materiality of memorial sites or to talk in more historical terms about the genocide. I have heard reactions from audience members that these images are horrific, disturbing, and shocking. Some photographers use shock as the aesthetic of choice. Internationally acclaimed conflict photographer James Nachtwey (2000) has famously been quoted as saying that his photographs are meant to ruin the viewer's day.[4] Alternatively, I could have attempted to make the pictures more artful. For Sebastiao Salgado, another internationally acclaimed photographer, "beauty" is his photographic calling card. His sweeping vistas and mastery of black and white tonal ranges render his images utterly awe-inspiring (Slagado, 1994).[5] As Roland Barthes (1957) posited, shocking images risk shutting people down (p. 117). So too can the strikingly beautiful. Shock and beauty are very nearly the same: indeed, Nachtwey's images have been equally praised for their formalist style and beauty and vilified for their ability to shock (Linfield, 2010, p. 236). Thus, images of the grotesque and the gorgeous can send us into the realm of the sublime where there is little room for political engagement (Sontag, 2003, p. 81). However, shocking and breathtakingly appealing pictures can also be a "call to action" or an invitation to engage (Moller, 2013, p. 86). This equivocation of the image depends on how photographs are mobilized and the context in which they are applied. Enticing spectators to become familiar with genocide survivors and support actions for peace and justice through photography is what I attempted with my project, but – as other artists have learned – is not without its challenges.

The Chilean visual artist Alfredo Jaar has experimented with photography that can provoke and stir spectators while avoiding the risks inherent with appalling or awe-inspiring aesthetics. Through twenty-one different installations, Jaar's *Rwanda Project, 1994-2000* was at its core a sincere attempt at a deep understanding of the phenomenon of genocide. Despite it being a sustained reflection, Jaar conceived each piece as a response to the one before; yet each was also a self-declared failure (PBS, 2007). Wanting to avoid exploiting or re-traumatizing victims, Jaar was troubled and challenged by "skepticism of the representability of genocide" (Moller & Ubaldo, 2013, p. 86). Jaar's installations used photographs in a variety of ways to try to bring himself and the viewer closer to the experience of genocide through different points of entry. In two separate pieces, close-up images of the eyes of a survivor, Gutete Emerita, were displayed as a large-scale print and reproduced as a massive mound of slides to signify personal and collective experiences of genocide respectively. In his "Real Pictures" installation, Jaar, wanting to avoid encouraging voyeurism, presented a series of black boxes said to contain hundreds of pictures. With the images' descriptions in white text on the outside, spectators' attention was meant to be drawn to key elements and messages of the photographs, thus diminishing the possibility of them simply satisfying a morbid curiosity. Jaar's work sought to generate empathy, solidarity, and intellectual involvement of the spectators as a response to the "barbaric indifference" of foreign actors at the time. Yet Jaar also recognized that each installation could only do so much (PBS, 2007). Despite the variety and volume of his works, there was no guarantee of spectators becoming engaged. Regardless, Jaar persisted. Although criticism has been leveled at the *Rwanda Project*, the ingenuity of the work and its sensitivity to the victims, particularly to the preservation of memory and to the interpretation or translation of experiences, offered much for me to consider when preparing my own exhibit (Mirzoeff, 2005).

Specifically, I see a parallel between Jaar's use of photography in his exhibits and political theorist Mark Reinhardt's reflections on the limits of photography. Reinhardt turns to Stanley Cavell's philosophy of acknowledgement to locate a principled approach to the medium. Reinhardt (2007) concludes that "photographs fail morally and politically when what they invite from a responsive viewer is something less than acknowledgement; this ethical and political failure is tied to the pictures' aesthetic strategies and effects" (p. 31). Acknowledgement, in this vein, is:

> ...precisely what it is that we must offer when confronted with human suffering. It is the difficult, often painful, and thus often avoided act of responding appropriately to the pain of others...To avoid acknowledgement is, fundamentally, to refuse to grapple with one's relation to another.
>
> (Reinhardt, 2007, p. 31).

Acknowledgement requires a willingness to go beyond simply knowing, in the abstract, that suffering exists in our world. It means trying – in spite of inevitable futility – to deeply comprehend the source and content of that suffering. This concept of acknowledgement provides a powerful lens with which to interpret projects offering possibilities for historic and symbolic justice: without an earnest attempt at connecting and understanding, other forms of redress are less likely to develop, or be less comprehensive.

Other photographers, exploring issues and experiences of the genocide through the more familiar forms of portraiture and documentary photography, also exhibit this acknowledgement. Focusing on topics such as children born of rape, orphans, child-headed households, the aftereffects of surviving sexual and other violence, justice and reconciliation, and the intimacy of the killings and subsequent peace processes, these projects have aimed to create deep recognition of these post-genocide phenomena.[6] Appearing in newspapers, magazines, public galleries and stand-alone publications, such projects contribute to larger discourses on rape as a genocide crime, the mutability of victim and perpetrator categories, and the possibilities or processes of restitution. Though not the products of so sustained an engagement as Jaar's, they do invite further consideration of the historical and political causes and the social impacts of genocide. However, as laudable and necessary as such projects are in raising awareness and spreading knowledge of the atrocities and aftereffects of genocide, they have circulated almost exclusively within Western contexts, where the visual culture around images of suffering conventionalizes the recognition of sufferers as objects of pity. This is ultimately a failure of acknowledgement, in Cavell's sense; as objects they are only understood in one dimension (i.e., pitiable), which is not fully human. One possible way to overcome this is to reorient the concept of audience, broadening it to be inclusive of those represented in the pictures, rather than only conceiving of audiences a being distant (predominantly western/northern) spectator. In this way, projects would necessarily take on different shapes since people represented – and often objectified – in the images become part of a critical audience challenging the ways they are portrayed. The result may be collaboration and co-creation, or even self-directed works.

The legal and political scholar Jens Meierhenrich created a project with broader publics in mind: including Rwandans, and people engaging with the genocide for the first time. The project focused on what he calls – borrowing from Pierre Nora – *lieux de memoire*: "Genocide memorials, informal and otherwise, that have emerged – and some that have vanished" (2010). These "sites of memory" include places of refuge, killing, or other violence. Several of the informal sites pictured that Meierhenrich includes are ones that disrupt official narratives or challenge decisions on whose memories are worth preserving. The project is about acknowledging that "disagreement exists concerning the *purpose* of remembering the dead of the genocide as well as over appropriate *ways* of doing so" (2010). There is no doubt of the project's value in terms of memory preservation, regardless of the fact that the project could never be complete: sites were already dismantled, ploughed under, or washed away before Meierhenrich began to make his photographs. Meierhenrich's work contributes tremendously to historic and symbolic justice by acknowledging the past. My project is about the ways in which similar *lieux* affect the present through the ghostly presence of traumatic experiences. In terms of its relation to trauma, visual art is said to:

> ...[illuminate] traumatic experience through the sideways glance, allowing the viewer to apprehend what can only be shown indirectly, allusively and in sometimes surprising ways. Perhaps even more so than literature, film, or theatre visual art affects viewers in ways that are non-narrative and non-cognitive, in affective and emotional ways that are unsuspected, sometimes uncomfortable, raising contradictory or unresolved feelings
>
> (Apel, 2002, p. 3).

In a complementary way, Susan Sontag (2003) said that it is not photographs that help us understand, it is narratives (p. 91). Pictures may provide a wealth of information, but little in the way of meaning without the help of the ideologically influenced hand of a creator, a distributor, or even a spectator. When meaning is not provided or is insufficient, photographs can then "haunt" (Sontag, 2003, p. 91). They may actively unsettle us, niggling away in our mind, fomenting, distilling, or they may gather dust in our internal archive. They may drive us to learn more, inviting us to engage below the surface level of the image. They may also remain dormant or come to the fore when roused from slumber. In a way, photography operates similarly to trauma. Unlike other experiences, traumatic ones are those that have lingering or uncanny affects: "The event is not assimilated or experienced fully at the time, but only belatedly, in its repeated possession of the one who experiences it" (Caruth, 1995, p. 4). Trauma survivors may only come to terms with or come to a full understanding of their experience after repeatedly encountering recollections of the experience after the fact. Similarly, a photograph may help those who have not experienced a violent event come to understand its potential lingering effects for victims by being revisited by (i.e., not being able to forget) a picture relating to such traumatic experiences and subsequently plundering its depths.

On their surface, photographs appear deceptively simple. We believe that the meaning is uncomplicated, that they transparently transmit the world. To a point, they are doing this; it is what makes photography different than most other visual arts. Photographs are of a reality to the extent that "they bore witness to the real" (Sontag, 2003, p. 26). But they are always fragmentary and abstract. They never are, and never can be, the whole story. This is because photographs connect multiple stories, with multiple vantage points converging on one picture. Indeed, as visual theorist Ariella Azoulay (2012) describes photography, the camera is manufacturing an image of encounters and a "complex field of relations" of actors and actions contributing to the photographic situation (pp. 92, 113). It is up to the spectator to unfold those interconnected stories, to actively engage with how they relate to each other. This process is more likely to be initiated when patterned encounters with pictures (e.g., routines of reading the news) get disrupted.

Indeed, contemporary trauma scholarship has been linked to photography. Ulrich Baer (2002), who explored trauma's psychological dimensions through images of former Second World War death camps, and 18th-century medical pictures, claims that photography "provide[s] special access to experiences that have remained unremembered yet cannot be forgotten" (p. 7). Troubled memories, ghostly hauntings, and spectral apparitions are phenomena associated with both photography and trauma. Baer locates the connection between photography and trauma through the nonliteral aspects of the medium that reference or gesture to experience in an almost mimetic way to experiences of trauma. For instance, overgrown and "inhospitable" landscapes of former Nazi death camps, scenes of apparently "nothing," provide spectators with a sense of "premonition of uncanny aura – that something has disappeared," something associated with horrific crimes against humanity (Baer, 2002, p. 77). Yet, the limits of photography, no matter its application, are such that spectators will never attain full comprehension. Hence the specter: photography allows for proximity, and can bring meaning, but not more. Despite the limitations, there remains value in attempts by photographers to explore, probe, or represent trauma with an aim to induce in spectators moral repulsion or related sentiments. Sliwinski (2013) persuasively argues, in a similar vein as Cavell's concept of acknowledgement, "the painful labor of attending to others' suffering, might be the very beginning of responsibility [to care, to intervene] itself" (p. 159).

More recently, Margaret Iversen has situated the trace of trauma through more literal and indexical aspects of the medium (2017, p. 16). For the contemporary spectator encountering a seemingly unending stream of images of traumatic or trauma-inducing scenes, Iversen provides welcome guidance on how to engage with critical awareness to representations of more horror than seems possible. She writes, "photography has the potential to restore the link, severed by the shock effects of modern life, between voluntary and involuntary memory, between the individual and the collective" through the association of symbolic elements that may recur in images – the semiotic elements of pictures – to aid in accessing meaning (2017, p. 108). It is not so much photographs themselves that provide access to individual experiences of the traumatized. Rather, the ties and links between images across time and space can connect us as we continue to strive, in Cavell's and Sliwinski' senses, for acknowledgement and responsibility.

It should come as no surprise that genocide survivors use similar words as photographers and art critics when referring to the trauma they experienced. Ghosts, hauntings, and specters inhabit the narratives and lingering effects – or more precisely, the ongoing lived realities – of trauma. With the growing nuance in genocide scholarship, and the broad applicability of photography in representing, expressing, or accessing individual and collective impacts of one-sided acts of extermination, there is opportunity to link genocide to its wider social, political, and global connections via photography. Indeed, the medium can reach beyond superficial assessment of genocide, accommodating broader experiences and definitions of its survivors, such as victims, perpetrators, rescuers, or bystanders (Jessee, 2019, p. 176). Photography can shed light on instances that were not acknowledged as significant, but that remain unsettled. In this way, pictures can provide insights into the operation of trauma, while at the same time help people work through trauma. My photographic project, always approached as one for a broadly conceived transcultural and transgenerational audience, is about drawing attention to lingering aspects of places of troubled and traumatic memory in contemporary Rwandan landscapes to explore the roots and bitter fruits of the genocide. The images enable exploring beneath the surface of the landscapes to gain proximity to the traces of trauma that everyone victimized by genocidal forces may be living with. However influential the work and approaches taken by the visual artists and theorists discussed here have been to the overall development of *Memory -> Witness*, it was only possible for me to engage with them after having been inspired to create the project through a particular aesthetic encounter in Rwanda.

An Aesthetic Encounter with Tall Trees and Long Stories

The *Memory –> Witness* project developed gradually; it was not preconceived prior to the making of its photographs. It emerged from a culmination of contingencies that brought into focus my personal aesthetic encounter with the physical and imagined country of Rwanda and its numerous genocide memorial sites. There are eight national memorial sites in Rwanda, with the largest concentration in the southern part of the country. Most of the national memorials are located at massacre sites; many are churches where local Tutsi and moderate Hutu sought refuge (Des Forges, 1999; Wolfe, 2020). Although each site is unique, containing evidence and ghosts of different circumstances, experiences, and horrors, they also show patterns of violence, suffering, and death.

In 2013, I had the opportunity to visit Rwanda, its national memorial sites and museums, and its numerous local memorial sites.[7] While traveling from one site to the next, there were repeated artifacts: personal effects, clothing, bones, weapons used to torture and kill, mass graves, and the faded dried flowers from the previous year's commemoration ceremony. Even the guides' stories echoed each other: the downing of the President's plane, outbreaks of violence, fleeing to traditional places of safety, violations of refuge sites, horrifying massacres and violent deaths with the types of weapons on display, tallying the dead, and the small numbers of survivors. Though each location had its own specifics, there was still a chilling pattern revealing the calculated and prepared nature of the genocide. Ironically, the repeated stories of the guide's narrations seem scripted and monotonous. That is banality of genocide: Murder becomes "routine," particularly to the killers. In the case of Rwanda, it was normalized (and euphemized) to the point that it was called *work* (Des Forges, 1999; Lemarchand, 2004).

After visiting memorial sites in cities, towns, villages, and roadsides, my senses began to shut down. The relentless assault of hate, discrimination, greed, ignorance, violence, and pain emitting from each site was overwhelming. I noticed an instinctive defense mechanism forming; I was beginning to use my camera as a shield to hide behind. The repetition of elements at the sites further hardened this shield. With each exposure, another protective coating was applied. The result was a thick layering of a sense of anticipation bordering the mundane. Then we visited Bisesero.

Located in the hills of Rwanda's Western Province, Bisesero is different than all the other sites. It is unique because it is the site of the largest resistance against *génocidaires* (Matthews, 1997). It is further distinguished from other sites because the memorial is not built on the actual site of resistance. Most memorials sit on grounds where massacres took place, in effect hallowing that ground. This memorial is instead built on what had been, until its construction, a bare hill (Meierhenrich, 2011).[8] No church, no school, and no shed had previously existed on this site. It overlooks the actual hill where the resisters held their ground, but not in any explicitly symbolic or instrumental ways. It is "over there with the trees" our guide said, pointing in the direction of other hills. On the one hand, the distance of this memorial from the actual place of resistance and battle adds to the reverence for that hill through a sort of sacred untouchability. On the other hand, it can result in feeling that the memorial is inauthentic. When so many other memorials are places of blood and violence, this space lacks that physical proximity that could otherwise lend it force. These aspects formed part of my initial ambivalence to the site.

The memorial, whose construction began in 2004, is an architectural wonder. A winding pathway snaking up the hillside connects nine buildings that symbolically represent the sectors where resistance fighters came from. My first impression of the memorial was that its style was excessive, an impression likely influenced by the contras between the site and the surrounding geographic context. To get to the memorial site required over thirty kilometers of travel on steep and deeply rutted dirt roads leading from the lakeside town of Kibuye. The winding road passed through numerous mud-home villages and countless family farm plots. The modern and solid cement and plaster construction of the memorial site presented a dramatic difference. Additionally, compared to the other sites we had visited where the buildings were overwhelmed with piles of clothes, personal effects, neat stacks of bones, and row upon row of skulls, Bisesero was bare. The symbolism of strength, unity in resistance, and eventual defeat is powerfully inscribed in the architecture. At the time of this visit, however, the physical state the memorial left me feeling, it was both lacking and overdone. Under construction for 10 years, the memorial's buildings were numerous but cavernous; all were still almost entirely empty, save one.

Before heading up the hillside, we were led to a corrugated metal shed near the base of the memorial. Unlike the nine concrete buildings constituting the formal structure of the memorial, this shed appeared rudimentary, provisional, and huge. Contained within it were the remains of 15,000 bodies (African Rights, 1997). The bones had been moved to the shed several years ago when it was discovered that one of the mass graves at the top of the hill had sustained weather and root damage and was leaking (Grzyb, 2019, pp. 185–98). Eventually they would be reburied by the time of my subsequent visit. This shed was not part of the official tour; it was also not part of the official memorial exhibit. I was left wondering what the site would be like once complete. My sense was that this site would be tremendously affective. On a return visit in February 2015, I was able to see the repaired mass grave and the addition of a roofed structure over the grave area. The official buildings now housed, in room after room, the skulls and long bones that had been temporarily stored in the shed. The memorial, though still incomplete, certainly reinforced the routinization of killing so chillingly characteristic of genocide. In 2013, however, my impressions led me to different sensations.

Our guide, who survived the genocide in a different part of the country, led us through the empty buildings, up the snaking walkway, and past symbolic features such as the paths' construction material transitioning from concrete, to stone, to dirt. She took us past a mass grave in which the leader of the resistance was given a place of honor amidst the others who fought and died with him. We also walked by the damaged and open mass grave from which the bones in the shed had been removed. Eventually she led us to a forest. To me, and several of the others I was traveling with, this site was incongruous, so different from the rest of the Rwandan landscape we had been traveling through in the previous days. It was so unexpectedly familiar, so much like the landscapes of my country, Canada. It was like the campsites in so many of my fondest memories. The tall trees, the powerful scent of pine, the thick bed of pine needles cushioning my feet, it was so much like home. I let myself be enraptured by the beauty. It was a welcome shady respite from the heat of the day, a calm place so contrary to the intense driving of the past few days, not to mention the punishing, dusty drive up through the hills to get to this spot. It seemed to be such a comforting place; so apparently distant from the extremes of emotions we experienced in our visits to memorial sites and from our talks with survivors.

As I let myself be transported by the sublime beauty to distant memories created in a far-off place, I heard the guide explain that survivors come to this site each year to commemorate the 50,000 loved ones lost. Under the protection of trees donated by the former Belgian colonial government, survivors camp for the duration of time that the resisters held their ground. For nearly one hundred nights, survivors from the surrounding communities come here – not to the actual hill of resistance, which would be more in keeping with other overnight vigil practices held at other massacre sites – but to these pines (Meierhenrich, 2011). I was shocked and jarred back into the moment, reminded that beauty could be deceptive. That beauty is able to lull us into a sense of comfort, a superficial, anemic encounter with our world. The beauty of this spot overwhelmed me. I forgot that it could conceal so much more depth.

Unlike the other memorial sites, where I was affected by the physical proximity to the 20-year-old artifacts, it was the temporal and physical proximity to the survivors' ritual expression of grief and commemoration in that expanse of trees that affected me most powerfully at Bisesero. That this bucolic spot was one of mourning, grief, and bittersweet celebration of lives lost in the most horrific of ways. That the surrounding hills rolling in bright green tea bushes, banana groves, and maize, could and did in fact represent trauma, violence, and suffering to survivors. In fact, any one, or all, of the "thousand hills" of Rwanda contained traces of the genocide, particularly for survivors. This sense was substantiated by a survivor I spoke with upon my return to Canada – his response to my comment on the apparent beauty of Rwanda was that to him each hill represented loss, suffering, and sadness.

Though the physical scars on the landscape and buildings have largely been cleared away, or incorporated into official memorial sites, it is in these otherwise unidentified vistas that the story of the genocide continues in subtle and insidious ways. The landscapes may have changed – new trees planted, old buildings torn down – but the hills still hold memory for the survivors. "Everyday" locations and beautiful panoramas hold "metaphysical scars" that continue to reverberate the trauma of the genocide decades later (Burnet, 2012, p. 89). Such scars are not ones seen on peoples' bodies, or the ones still visible on buildings (such as those on the Rwandan Parliament building). They are scars that exist at a deeper – even unconscious – level. Survivors I met in Rwanda and in Canada talked extensively about their physical and the emotional trauma, the fading, and the manifest scars of loved ones lost, found, buried, and reburied. These narratives were never easy to listen to, as they must not have been easy to retell. But in sharing these stories, the community of witnesses expands in space and in time. It becomes the responsibility of all those witnesses – direct victim, eyewitness, secondary and distant witnesses – to continue sharing.

The newfound sense of responsibility I gained via my encounter at Biserero is what I wanted to inspire in visitors to my photographic exhibition. My goal was to encourage spectators to accept my visual invitation to gain a deeper knowledge of the causes and outcomes of genocide; in effect, to acknowledge rather than simply recognize its occurrence. In this sense, the photographs could be a response to the question: "What forms of photography might enrich the lives of ordinary people in Rwanda?" (Moller & Ubaldo, 2013, p. 131). By engaging spectators who have varying degrees of separation to the genocide and to Rwanda, these photographs could – in a small, incremental way – offer opportunities for symbolic redress by drawing attention to the lingering power of trauma and to the multidimensionality of survivors.

The *Memory —> Witness* Photographs

The *Memory —> Witness* exhibit was on display in the central branch of the Hamilton Public Library in Ontario, Canada, from April 1, 2014, to May 16, 2014.[9] The exhibit was also on display, by invitation, at the twentieth commemoration ceremony held in Hamilton, Ontario, by the local Rwandan community. The majority of the *Memory –> Witness* exhibit consists of brightly hued landscape photographs. The prints are large; one of the four panoramas extends beyond ten feet in length. The scale renders it difficult for viewers to take in all at once. They have to scan the scene as they would an actual panorama. The bright hues and rich saturation, though exaggerating natural colors, compensates for the fact that these are photographs, abstract prints, and not real places. While the pictures are mainly of verdant scenery, they are not typical landscape photographs.[10] Digitally "stitched" together from a series of exposures made at random times of the day, (Figure 12.1) or from somewhat blurred images made from a moving car, these are quotidian landscapes: everyday scenes of hills, trees, and earth. The scenery, the dimensions, and the saturation are meant to draw the viewers in, to hold their attention.

Figure 12.1 Digitally “stitched” photograph from the *memory → witness* exhibition entitled “I feel at home here” by the author.

Through the prints' titles, spectators are drawn deeper into the photographs. The titles are quotes from survivors I talked with, or whose words were immortalized in Jean Hatzfeld's *Life Laid Bare* (2007). They address the speakers' acts of survival, their continuing fears, and the trauma they continue to endure. The photographs are meant to encourage spectator engagement. Their words label the prints, rather than more typical geographic or temporal markers, as a means of hooking viewers' attention in the same way that the guide's story of the overnight vigil at Bisesero caught me. The combination of serene scenes juxtaposed with the words of survivors, along with the careful curation of the images constitutes a deliberately executed exhibition.

Displaying the photographs in public spaces was also deliberate. The intent was for people who might not normally go to galleries to stumble upon the images. In democratic spaces, those who have not had much experience with the power of art will have an opportunity to be drawn in. Those who have had little or no exposure to the worst genocide in a generation can be persuaded to learn more. When displayed in the library, a list of books for further reading was included. This deliberate structuring of the exhibit was suggested by the exhibit's title: *Memory -> Witness*. One would be correct to wonder if the title should be reversed: that witnessing leads to memories. However, memories, once shared, can draw people previously unconnected, unaware, or even unconcerned with the events into the narrative.

When photography is considered as a medium that deals in events, as opposed to simply being a tool that records them, pictures become points of entry into phenomena that otherwise seem fixed in time or separated by great distances. Azoulay's (2012) conception of the "situation of photography" refers to the way in which photography is implicated in the ongoing development of events, even possibly initiating them simply with the presence of a camera, the discussion of a photograph, or the hypothetical existence of either (p. 15). For Azoulay, photographs are records of encounters rather than of occurrences. As such, the pictures I took in Rwanda immediately articulated to the broader photographic situation of the Rwandan genocide. The images contributed to extending this event by creating a different continuum (or entry point) through which survivors and newcomers could converge and connect. With this conception of photography in mind, I exhibited the prints with the conscious intent of them creating a civil space in which different burdens of responsibility would present themselves. Exhibiting the images as part of an ongoing – rather than past – event linked through trauma, through survivors, through distant witnesses, offered opportunities to create links across great temporal and geographic divides. As a result, there is the potential to reach the kind of acknowledgement that could benefit ordinary Rwandans, one that includes accepting the (often painful) relation to someone's suffering.

The largest photo in the exhibit is entitled "*Mille collines, mille coliques*: every hill represents painful memories." The image is of rolling hills of tea

Figure 12.2 Photograph entitled, "I will always tremble whenever I hear voices raised among the leaves of the Banana groves", for the *Memory → Witness* exhibit by the author.

at the Gisovu tea plantation between the lakeside town of Kibuye and the hilltop at Bisesero genocide memorial. Tremendous pain and sadness are in those hills, yet they look soft, inviting, and full of vitality. The photograph reveals its depth to spectators as they engage with the text, the image, and the narrative interwoven between the two. It is this sort of action the juxtaposition of the otherwise benign pictures and the contrasting text is meant to encourage throughout the exhibit. Other landscapes include pictures from Lake Kivu, banana groves, and the pine trees at Bisesero entitled "Understand this: the genocide will not fade from our minds. Time will hold on to the memories, it will never spare more than a tiny place for the solace of the soul," "I will always tremble whenever I hear voices raised among the leaves of the banana groves," (Figure 12.2) and "I feel at home here," respectively (Hatzfeld, 2007).

The pictured scenes may appear benign or bucolic, but for some survivors at certain times of the year (or perhaps for others at all times), these pictured scenes refer to tremendous hate, greed, and violence. Given the way in which trauma is understood to operate, these differing affective encounters with landscapes and memory may vary depending on the person, the time of year, or any number of reasons. The horrors hidden in these landscapes exemplify the "metaphysical scars" that are connected to the physical world – having been born of it – but that are only visible to the mind's eye as it connects to affect and memory (Burnet, 2012, p. 89). Yet, some of those same landscapes also evoke love, comfort, and homecoming. This is how guides and other survivors talk about the act of staying with human remains while camping in the Bisesero hills or staying overnight at other memorial sites and mass graves. Many people have not been able to locate their family members' remains; as a result, forests, hillsides, riverbanks, and other formal or informal landmarks across the country become *familial* places. This is a kind of beauty in itself.

The landscape photographs are bookended by the only two photographs that include people. Opening the exhibit is a close-up portrait of a gently

Figure 12.3 Final photograph in the *Memory → Witness* exhibition entitled, "Redemption," by the author.

smiling woman. The concluding photograph is of a hand holding a smartphone displaying a photograph of a modern Rwandan home. More so than the others in the exhibit, these two photographs point to the *ongoing* nature of the post-genocide narrative. Bookending the exhibit with these two images suggests the nonlinear nature of this narrative. The genocide is not experienced as something that has come and gone; rather, it underlines and overarches individual and interconnected lives.

The final photograph of the exhibit is entitled *Redemption* (Figure 12.3). In fact, it is a photograph of a photograph. It depicts the house built by Léon, a survivor who was a teenager at the time of the genocide. A sign of achievement, the house might suggest that he has "moved on" from the past. But the past is with Léon every day: he works as a guide at national genocide memorial sites. He is also an academic who has studied the political climate leading to the outbreak of genocide. He is also a father, a husband, and – by traditional Rwandan cultural standards – has achieved the status of a responsible male in the building of his own home (Sommers, 2012). This is not a house built to erase the past, but rather to honor it. His family home was lost in the genocide, along with almost all of his family members. The values instilled in him by his parents before they were murdered inspired Léon to make his life as good as could be, to honor them, and allow their memories to live on through him and his family. *Redemption* indeed.

Conclusion: Intentions in Tension

Despite my good intentions, I realize that these photographs are forevermore ambiguous. In the exhibit alone, they are rhetorical, polemical, mnemonic, symbolic, and stylistic. This is both deliberate and unintentional.

I cannot separate the political from the aesthetic, just like I cannot determine each spectator's interpretation or response. Although photography is limited in its ability to convey experience and affect, and spectators may not be willing or able to follow through with the opportunities photography offers, these challenges do not constitute grounds for the medium's dismissal. Even with limitations, "[photographic] representations are nevertheless necessary because they acknowledge the survivors' need for recognition" (Moller & Ubaldo, 2013, p. 140). As such, it is in the act of paying attention to and respecting the suffering of others, despite never being able to fully understand it, that historic and symbolic justice fundamentally emerges (Sliwinski, 2013). This is tellingly evidenced by comments from visitors to the *Memory –> Witness* exhibit:

> Blood and gore are not always necessary to tell of horror. The picture of the pines with some stumps here and there are just as potent;
>
> Thank you for telling our pain and our resurrection;
>
> *Merci infiniment de nous rappeler notre vécu à travers ces photos* [Thank you immensely for reminding us of our experiences through these photos];
>
> *Ces images qui montrent une autre face de ce beau pays connu pour son malheur. Bravo!* [These images show another side of this beautiful country known for its misfortunes. Congratulations!]

As an additional act of symbolic justice, the memories of those who would otherwise be forgotten also exist in the *Memory –> Witness* images. In an attempt to obliterate all traces of the identity, individuality, and humanity of their victims, *génocidaires* also destroyed official portraits, snapshots, and family photo albums during the genocide, as a form of symbolic violence against the Tutsi (Hatzfeld, 2007). Many of the identity cards that essentially became death sentences to the Tutsis who carried them were defaced and tossed in the shrubs and hills. Family albums and snapshots were equally mistreated or incinerated, leaving their ashes to be carried by the wind. In a sense, for some, the landscapes thus contain traces, refer to the spectral evidence of those who were killed. Along with symbolic justice, photography can assist with the labor on the long road of transitional justice. The ambiguity of the photographs opens space to delve beneath the surface of the experience and lives of those who were the primary target of the genocide. Responsive to recent scholarship bridging gaps between victims and perpetrators, bystanders and rescuers, photography enables exploration of the suffering of all and the common origins of the traumas they have endured (Jessee, 2017, p. 260).

Within the study of transitional justice, photography opens up possibilities to access difficult knowledge and work through troubling experiences. Ultimately, the intention is to remind those who come into contact with these (or any other media for that matter) that to look at someone, or to look at a photo, is *not* enough to understand them. Engaging with this genocide at this time is about acknowledging that, though a story may no longer be in the headlines, it is not over, it has not been resolved. Each photographic project, this one included, offers opportunities to identify and work through aspects of the long process of transitional justice. Through photography, the stories continue. Trauma borne by survivors is something that they will live with for the rest of their lives. For succeeding generations, it will be experienced as historical trauma, trauma that the medium of photography can draw attention to and help explore. The burden of the trauma can be lessened by being shared. Exploring the multiple narratives converging on the photographic plane is one way to distribute the weight of that burden.

Notes

1 For example, see: Abdelaziz (2007); Cowart (2011); Heine, (2019); Hugo (2014); Jaar (1998); Lyons & Straus (2006); Nachtwey (2011); Peress (1995; 2019); Salgado (1994); and Togovnik (2009).

2 For instance, see *New York Times*, 14 April 1994, A12; *New York Times*, 9 April 1994, A6; and Grzyb, 2009.

3 For instance, see the following articles from *New York Times*: April 12, 1994, A6; April 15, 1994, A3; May 14, 1994, A3; April 10, 1994, A1; May 1, 1994, A16; May 17, 1994, A8; May 24, 1994, A3.

4 "I don't want to let people off the hook. I don't want to make these pictures easy to look at. I want to ruin people's day if I have to. I want to stop them in their tracks and make them think of people beyond themselves." (Nachtwey, 2000).

5 Salgado has been criticized for aestheticizing suffering, yet there is nothing romantic in the claim he made at his presentation, "Genesis, Royal Ontario Museum Exhibit Launch" on May 2, 2013, of feeling "dead inside" after this photographic experience. He was unable to produce a photographic project for nearly a decade afterward.

6 See note 1.

7 The trip was an experiential learning component of a graduate course on media and the 1994 Rwandan genocide taught by Dr. Amanda Grzyb, in the Faculty of Information and Media Studies at Western University, Canada.

8 The Bisesero memorial site also overlooks a village inhabited predominantly by survivors. Nearly 50,000 resisters lost their lives, only about one thousand survived. Retrieved June 15, 2020 from: https://genocidearchiverwanda.org.rw

9 The photographs can be viewed at: Series Statements on www.sonyadelaat.weebly.com (Accessed September 23, 2019).

10 The conventional practice of formal landscape photographers is to foster or fortify appreciation of the natural environment or invoke a sense of serenity. Photographers use natural (time of day), mechanical (filters, digital post-production), and other techniques to enhance or highlight certain features in the landscapes. Encouraging specific appreciation of those elements rather than of the landscape's symbolic or metaphysical qualities.

Bibliography

Abdelaziz, M. (2007). *Portraits of genocide*. Retrieved September 23, 2019, from http://www.un.org/en/preventgenocide/rwanda/exhibits/portraits.shtml

African Rights (1997). *Resisting genocide: Bisesero, April–June 1994*. African Rights.

Agamben, G. (1998). *Homo sacer: Sovereign power and bare life*. Stanford University Press.

Apel, D. (2002). *Memory effects: The Holocaust and the art of secondary witnessing*. Rutgers University Press.

Azoulay, A. (2012). *Civil imagination: A political ontology of photography*. Verso.

Baer, U. (2002). *Spectral evidence: The photography of trauma*. MIT Press. https://doi.org/10.7551/mitpress/6398.001.0001

Barthes, R. (1957). *Mythologies* (R. Howard & A. Lavers, Trans.). Hill and Wang.

Bisschoff, L., & Peer, S. V. (Eds.) (2013). *Art and trauma in Africa: Representations of reconciliation in music, visual arts, literature and film*. I. B. Tauris.

Burnet, J. E. (2012). *Genocide lives in us: Women, memory, and silence in Rwanda*. The University of Wisconsin Press.

Caruth, C. (Ed.) (1995). Introduction. In C. Caruth (Ed.), *Trauma: Explorations in memory* (pp. 3–12). John Hopkins University Press.

Cowart, J., (2011), My take: If Rwandans can forgive killings, we can forgive the waitress. CNN Belief Blog. Retrieved January 9, 2022 from: https://religion.blogs.cnn.com/2011/11/07/my-take-if-rwandans-can-forgive-killings-we-can-forgive-the-waitress/

Des Forges, A. L. (1999). *Leave none to tell the story: Genocide in Rwanda*. Human Rights Watch.

Doyle, M. (2007). Reporting the genocide. In A. Thompson (Ed.), *The media and the Rwanda genocide* (pp. 145–159). IDRC Books/Les Éditions du CRDI.

Grzyb, A. F. (2009). Media coverage, activism, and creating public will for intervention in Rwanda and Darfur. In A. Grzyb (Ed.), *The world and Darfur: International response to crimes against humanity in Western Sudan* (pp. 61–94). McGill-Queen's University Press.

Grzyb, A. F. (2019). Unsettled memory: Genocide memorial sites in Rwanda. *The Brown Journal of World Affairs, 25(2)*, 185–198. Retrieved January 9, 2022 from: https://bjwa.brown.edu/25-2/grzyb-unsettled-memory-genocide-memorial-sites-in-rwanda/

Hatzfeld, J. (2007). *Life laid bare: The survivors in Rwanda speak* (L. Coverdale, Trans.). Other Press.

Heine, O. (2019). *Rwandan Daughters*. [Photographs]. In K. Monks, Rwandan rape survivors and their children, 25 years later. *CNN*. Retrieved September 23, 2021 from: https://www.cnn.com/interactive/2019/04/africa/rwandan-daughters-cnnphotos/

Hughes, N. (2007). Exhibit 467: Genocide through a camera lens. In A. Thompson (Ed.), *The media and the Rwanda genocide* (pp. 231–234). IDRC Books/Les Éditions du CRDI.

Hugo, P. (2014, April 6). *Portraits of reconciliation*. [Photographs] In S. Dominus, Portraits of reconciliation. *The New York Times Magazine*. https://www.nytimes.com/interactive/2014/04/06/magazine/06-pieter-hugo-rwanda-portraits.html

Iversen, M. (2017). *Photography, trace and trauma*. University of Chicago Press.

Jaar, A. (1998). *Let there be light: the Rwanda project 1994-1998*. Barcelona: ACTAR.

Jessee, E. (2017). *Negotiating genocide in Rwanda: The politics of history*. Palgrave MacMillan; Springer.

Jessee, E. (2019). Oral History and the Rwandan genocide. *The Brown Journal of World Affairs, 25(2)*, 169–184.

Kuperman, A. J. (2001). *The limits of humanitarian intervention: Genocide in Rwanda*. Brookings Institution Press.

Lemarchand, R. (2004). The Burundi genocide. In S. Totten, & W. S. Parsons (Eds.), *Century of genocide: Critical essays and eyewitness accounts* (pp. 321–387). Routledge.

Linfield, S. (2010). *The cruel radiance: Photography and political violence*. University of Chicago Press.

Longman, T. (2017). *Memory and justice in post-genocide Rwanda*. Cambridge University Press. https://doi.org/10.1017/9781139086257

Matthews, J. (1997). Resisting genocide: Bisesero, April–June 1994. [Photographs]. In African Rights. *Resisting genocide: Bisesero, April–June 1994*. African Rights.

Meierhenrich, J. (2010). *Through a glass darkly: Genocide memorials in Rwanda 1994-present*. Retrieved September 23, 2019, from http://maps.cga.harvard.edu/rwanda/home.html

Meierhenrich, J. (2011). Topographies of remembering and forgetting: The transformation of lieux de memoire in Rwanda. In S. Straus, & L. Waldorf (Eds.), *Remaking Rwanda: State building and human rights after mass violence* (pp. 283–296). The University of Wisconsin Press.

Melvern, L. (2000). *A people betrayed: The role of the West in Rwanda's genocide*. Zed Books.

Mirzoeff, N. (2005). Invisible again: Rwanda and representation after genocide. *African Arts, 38(3),* 36–96. https://doi.org/10.1162/afar.2005.38.3.36

Moller, F. (2013). *Visual peace: Images, spectatorship and the politics of violence*. Palgrave Macmillan.

Moller, F., & Ubaldo, R. (2013) Imaging life after death: Photography and the 1994 genocide in Rwanda. In L. Bisschoff, and S. V. de. Peer (Eds). *Art and trauma in Africa: Representations of reconciliation in music, visual arts, literature and film* (pp.131–151). I. B. Tauris. https://doi.org/10.5040/9780755604302.ch-006

Nachtwey, J. (2000, September 15). *James Nachtwey photographs*. Nieman Reports. Retrieved January 9, 2022, from https://niemanreports.org/articles/james-nachtwey-photographs/

Nachtwey, J. (2011, April 6). When the world turned its back: James Nachtwey's reflections on the Rwandan genocide. *Time Lightbox*. https://time.com/3449593/when-the-world-turned-its-back-james-nachtweys-reflections-on-the-rwandan-genocide/

PBS. (2007). *Protest: Featuring artists Nancy Spero, An-My Le, Alfredo Jaar, and Jenny Holzer*. ART:21, S4 Ep2 | 53m 28s | Aired: 11/3/2007. Retrieved January 9, 2022, from: https://www.pbs.org/search/?q=Alfredo+jaar.

Peress, G. (1995). *The silence*. Scalo.

Peress, G. (2019, April 10). *The silence*. [Photographs]. In P. Gourevitch. The silence: 25 years since the Rwandan genocide. *Magnum Photos*. Retrieved January 9, 2022, from: https://www.magnumphotos.com/newsroom/conflict/gilles-peress-silence-25-years-since-rwandan-genocide/

Lyons, R., & Straus, S. (2006). *Intimate enemy: Images and voices of the Rwandan genocide*. Zone Books.

Reinhardt, M. (2007). Picturing violence: Aesthetic and the anxiety of critique. In M. Reinhardt, H. Edwards, & E. Duganne (Eds.), *Beautiful suffering: Photography and the traffic in pain* (pp. 13–36). University of Chicago Press.

Roskis, E. (2007). A genocide without images: White film noirs. In A. Thompson (Ed.), *The media and the Rwanda genocide* (pp. 238–241). IDRC Books/Les Éditions du CRDI.

Salgado, S. (1994, June 5). *A killer in the next tent: The surreal horror of the Rwandan refugees.* [Photographs]. In R. Rosenblatt. A Killer in the Eye. *The New York Times Magazine.* (Section 6) Retrieved January 9, 2022, from: https://www.nytimes.com/1994/06/05/magazine/a-killer-in-the-eye.html?searchResultPosition=386

Salgado, S. (2013). *Genesis.* Exhibited at Royal Ontario Museum February 1, 2012-September 2, 2013.

Sliwinski, S. (2013). A painful labor: Photography and responsibility. In M. B. D. Pia, & J. Elkins (Eds.), *Representations of pain in art and visual culture* (pp. 150–162). Routledge.

Sommers, M. (2012). *Stuck: Rwandan Youth and the struggle for adulthood.* University of Georgia Press.

Sontag, S. (2003). *Regarding the pain of others.* Picador.

Togovnik, J. (2009). *Intended consequences; Rwandan Children born of rape.* Aperture.

Wolfe, S. (2014). *The politics of reparations and apologies.* Springer.

Wolfe, S. (2020). Memorialization in Rwanda: The legal, social, and digital constructions of the memorial narrative. In E.M. Zucker & D. Simon (Eds.), *Mass violence and memory in the digital age: Memorialization unmoored* (pp. 19–44). Palgrave Macmillian. https://doi.org/10.1007/978-3-030-39395-3_2

13 Rwandan Youth Speak! Memory and Justice through Poetry

Ashlee Cawley and Stephanie Wolfe

Poetry by Jessica Gatoni, Bliss Light Nshokeyinka, Claudine Karangwa Ingabire, Fred Mfuranzima, Guy Cadeau, and Innocent Byiringiro

Introduction

The task of compiling a poetry collection comprised of the works of others is fraught with difficulty – selecting and arranging poems to form a collective narrative while still honoring the original artistic voice of each poem presents a challenge. For this project, Rwandan poets were asked to submit poetry regarding genocide, justice, peacebuilding, transformation, memory, or similar topics.

To honor the original style and intent of the poets – no usage edits were made – leaving the poems largely untouched.[1] Of the submissions, patterns emerged in the eye of the editor, and they were arranged accordingly. Furthermore, the collection shares the artistic voices of Rwandan youth grappling with the legacy of their country in the shadow of genocide: survivors, second-generation survivors, diaspora, and those residing in Rwanda: accounts of sorrow, confusion, memory, and renewal. In this chapter, poets display grief, explore the genocide's legacy, and demonstrate abiding expressions of hope. To provide further context, the chapter concludes with an interview with second-generation survivor of the genocide, Jessica Gatoni, whose poetry is featured in this collection.

GRIEF

Part 1: Nothing But "The Void"
Jessica Gatoni

Snatched away
By the genocide
Swept away
By rivers
Blown away
In the wind
Rotten completely

DOI: 10.4324/9781003228592-16

In the burning sun
Leaving me with
Nothing But 'Void'

I picked up the ashes
Of our memories
And clung onto them
Hoping to eternalize them
I held onto them
In my grey matter
But to my dismay
What resurfaced
Doesn't have
Your smell
Your shape
Your face
Your smile
Your looks
Your life
Nothing but 'Void'

Just a dull color
Like the long dark days
Consuming me alive
Inch by inch
Just a grey mark
Glooming my future
Slowly but surely
Nothing else
But 'Void'

As I dig deep to remember
What used to be our home
Yes, dearest beloved
Our comfort zone
Is no more
No wall to hit
To ease my frustrations
No more stone to turn
To find your remains
No more mass grave
To search for your whereabouts
Nothing But 'Void'

I am terrified
What if …
Due to this void

I am unable to remember
Your smile
Your voice
Your walk
Your looks
Your jokes
What if …
Due to loss of sanity
My memory fades away
And I am left with
Nothing but 'Void'?

I am numb
I am dumb
Should I catch
A glimpse of you
In the blowing wind
Or in the blinding dust
Give me a sign
Give me a clue
To fill this void
You left behind
Before I lose
All my senses

A Bloody Night
Bliss Light Nshokeyinka

What a bloody night
A hell of life
Opportunity of knife
When the people alive cried
Dead ones I don't know
But milk was made red

No one could read
Or get a piece of bread
Because all were ready
To produce death in them
And I couldn't realize

That one could make a release
A rainy and heavy night
All days without light
As they lost their sight
Even those ones bright

Embraced such sorrows
Under death shadows

What kind of thinkers
Behaving like magicians
Whose mind was dark
Full of a deadly mark
Aiming at destroying
Our country developing!

People were crawling
Others praying
Priests preaching
Interahamwe butchering
Dogs barking
Our sounds were lamenting

I recall that dark day
And another red night
A one's breathing
Of a bundle of fearing
Children crying
Calling perpetrators fathers

Girls getting pierced
And raped forcibly
Beating all unceasingly
Friends turning into enemies
Entering prisons with no case
Oh! What a beloved country!

Bushes became our homes
Sharing them with dogs
Coming to hunt us
Sent by our hunters
While lungs got slight
To make us tight

Agony and hatred
Captured many innocent
Since they were made spies
Without a sender
So as to butcher them
After their dehumanization

Strength stops
My pen gets tired
Remembering my parents

As I stood at current
A branchless tree
O God, get my heart!

Voices That Call Memories
Fred Mfuranzima

For you are memories
Crying into my pen
Breathing into my poem
I shadow box myself to sleep with

My pen ink cries your dreams
Remembrance of your screams
Gets me accommodations at inn
Of rain forests then I moan my poem but not loud

And cry for you silently till daybreak wakes my pain
In the morning sun set reads to my hurts at night
Place I am always at when it rains
I cry, no matter if it's in the dark or in the light

For you are a memoir, my dreams are not jumping on
But off jump a thousand hobbling pains
These wounds doctors cannot hear with words
And don't have words for, am so glad that I arrested it in my songs and poems

A young girl sings across mount Kigali
All day it rains, she gets her liberated anger under house
Arrest them in her songs and poems
And throw them in flood chorus to Nyabarongo River

I believe myself into a singer bound in willingness
To trade pain for metaphors
And lines and rhymes
That owes their styles to your tale

I still hit my road sick in pain or full of joy, but always in smile
It is your world; you cry something and look up fine
It is your world, you cry something and heard voices fine
When your voices go back to memory, never again.

La Trompete Trompeuse
Bliss Light Nshokeyinka

Le jour revient encore
Couvrant une forte colère

Entrant dans mon pauvre Coeur
Aménant une forte menace
La trompête trompeuse
J'étais dans une brousse verte

La croyant un bon refuge
Qui par hasard me décevait
M'amenant un bruit dérangeant
Qui par mes Oreilles
Ouvra un mauvais appel
Elle prend un bon son

Comme celui d'une belle chanson
Mais elle était comme celui du serpent
Dans le jardin d'Eden
Qui lui trompa malignement
Disant que Dieu est mauvais vraiment
Elle était en soit soulageante

Avec une voix mélodieuse
Alors qu'elle était une malaise
M'appelant de sortir vite
Et pourtant elle voulait m'inviter
A la mort si vite

Sortant avec espoir
Pensant que c'était mon devoir
Avec souci de recevoir
Un reservoir du salut
Mais on voulait me salir
Oh trompête trompeuse!

Etant avec ma mère
Nous y sortions en fierté
Avec un Coeur apaisé
Curieux de revoir le soleil
Mais une effrayante rencontre
Quelle trompête trompeuse

On la tua sur place
Sans prendre même une pause
On la viola sauvagement
Et si cela regagne mon moi
Je me met à mort
En souvenir de son amour

Je n'ai aucune cicatrice
Cicatrice corporelle
mais mon Coeur est très lourd

Qui me fait devenir sourd
Et quand je pense à la vie
Je n'ai rien à dire

Mère de ma chair
Souvenir de mon Coeur
Poursuite de mes rêves
Toutes mes nuits t'appellent
De venir me voir
Mais toujours c'est au revoir

J'en suis toujours triste
Quand je vois toute piste
Qui dirige où tu fus tuée
Des larmes couvrent mes joues
Et mon stylo me dit non
Stop! Laisse ça.

LEGACY

Part 2: Streams of Living Water
Jessica Gatoni

Psalms 1:3 Reads: "And he shall be like a tree planted by the rivers of water, that bringeth forth his fruit in his season; his leaf also shall not wither; and whatsoever he doeth shall prosper."

When I feel the most at peace
There are streams of water cascading over pillars of stones
Ever flowing.
The whooshing sounds are often accompanied with the melodies of a pan flute,
In my mind…
The wind is softly blowing -
I hum a tune.
I am reminded of hard things that are cleansed

Scripture is also healing,
It tells me:
You are a tree,
With rivulets of water nourishing you,
With roots planted in eternity,
With leaves that will never wither,
Bearing fruit in your season,
In your time.
You are prosperity,
In your living testimony,

And in your memories.
This is the story of a survivor.

As I travelled through my country
For the first time,
To the Land of a Thousand Hills,
Where it is said that God Himself Sleeps;
A mythos short of unreal because that is where I believe I first felt God.
I dreamt about my long-lost great grandparents,
I imagined my ancestors telling me:
There are things that outlive us,
Things of which you have no control over,
Things that permeate the sands of time.
Your spirit fills the gap between these lines,
If but only for a moment

My mother would watch as I built sandcastles as a child.
The grains of sand would adhere to the water like a bridge to a foundation.
I would mold each wall and build a house I thought would last forever.
Until the winds changed, the tide swept in and washed over my forever.
I learned quickly that homes cannot be built with strong gusts of winds.
Though these walls crumbled, dissipated by the shore,
My mother never spoke of changing weathers.
Instead, she simply held my hands and swayed my arms back and forth like a pendulum,
Stomped her feet to the ground, beat by beat and told me we were made to dance.

My father would tell me stories in my native tongue as if they were my own,
Though I spoke my language in fragments,
I saw glimpses of the past in his eyes.
They were subtle and meek but told tales so deep that they reached the most ancient of times,
Of minstrels and poets lulling the crowds,
Sculptors and painters that materialized our beautiful Mother into simple mounds.
Thousand hills…still… climate,
Revealed the secret that *Imana yirirwa ahandi igataha i Rwanda*
God Spends his days everywhere else but falls asleep in Rwanda
Voices echoing…. *Humura Rwanda nziza*
breathe beautiful Rwanda

Though some oral traditions may be lost with time,
Dance is also a form of communication.
Intore is the dance that bridges the gap.

It tells tales of the tribe passed on from generation to generation.
Dancers whose stealth, mirth, matched their serene resound
Their movements are repeated mnemonically,
Keeping memory of ancient ancestors,
Kings, queens, warriors, heroes.
We remember their fight,
We remember their songs.
Draped up in a silky fabric bells ringing on our feet,
Our *mishananas* adorn our bodies,
We are the embodiment of history!
This is my own story as a First-Generation immigrant from Rwanda

Someone Please Explain
Cadeau Guy

Born from a dark room where there is no explanation of what you see
Born from a family with a complicated story
Where you don't know why your uncles were murdered
Where you don't understand why people who have the same language, same color, and same culture could…

Once I asked my mother
why did they kill them because they were Tutsi? How did they become Tutsi?
Mum said, because back in time a Tutsi had to have more than ten cows…
Why would someone be killed because of cows that died a hundred years ago?
My mum looked at me, she told me, "I don't know"
Then who should I ask?
But they were our neighbors…
My mum tells me yes…
Then had you done something to them long ago?
She told me again, "I don't know"

Can someone please explain why someone was killed because he was born in a family that he didn't choose?
Can someone tell me why a mother would kill her own baby because she had him with a Tutsi man?
Can someone tell me why…

After all the questions we had after genocide, we have understood nothing
From nothing, we can't understand how classmates could hate you enough to kill you while you were friends
Even old people and wise people can't give me a satisfying answer

Do I have to live with all that confusion?
Or should I believe that humanity didn't exist at that time

Because the only reason you can give me to understand why you would kill is that you were out of your mind.

When Rape Is A Tool Of War
Jessica Gatoni

Women are the spoils of war.
Their bodies pillaged,
Wealth plundered
With lips of red like velvet,
Skin of silk,
Black diamonds in their eyes.
Rubies in their cheeks
Their shapes targeted,
They are mounds of rolling hills
Figures of 8,
Hourglasses,
Counting down to the second,
Every facet of their image will be made enemy.

When Rape is a tool of war
They say you are no longer a body
You are the fragment of parts
Fitting construct of a world that wills you to look like glass only to shatter.
You are the breaking of ribs,
The undoing of creation,
The penetrating wounds calling for destruction
Stripping you bare,
Tearing through skin
Spilling crimson hued violence.
The wolves will tell you that flesh was never yours,
They howl at the moon, yet it towers over them.
Which is to say,
If the only victor of war is death,
You are always bellied antithesis,
Cradling new life
Like a battle cry
In the oceans within you,
Wells deeper than anatomy,
Nestling the young ones left behind under your breast.
You are the wave
Carrying the tides of the forgotten.

You raised new generations
With wombs and care

You nurtured the corporeal
Built spirit from the ashes
Made lush grass from tumbleweeds
Honoring you will not take words
As you have remained stoic in your miracles.
You are chronicled in the masses,
Women, like you, who bear the weight of humanity
In tips, grasping to the ends.

The Legacy To Reckon With
Claudine Karangwa Ingabire

Once upon a time, Rwanda was a beautiful place of peace and harmony, of love no agony. But, I was told that my home was once in vain, that my people were divided, killed, and died in pain.

Then, I remember when I was too young eager to know my Dad told me, that when I will grow I will understand though.

My mind filled with so many whys?

Cause I have heard stories of brothers and sisters who were thrown in lakes and rivers, families who were completely wiped out, uncles and aunties who lost their identities and roots.

And today, as we gather together to remember them, we remember them, for we can preserve their memories to bleed solutions from their tragedies.

And we remember them, for we can mourn their absence, to live as if it was their existence. We remember them, for we can break the chains of discrimination to harvest fruits of education. And we remember them, for we can build the Rwanda we want always moving on the front.

Rubyiruko rwiza
Mizero y'ejo hazaza,
Mashami yashibutse ku babyeyi batwibarutse,
Nimucyo twibuke imiryango yacu yazimye,
Shenge ntibakazime twararokotse,
Dusenyere umugozi Umwe
Twimika ubumwe.

And never forget that we are always told that we are tomorrow, we are a new chapter of change we want to create. And we are a generation lighting candles of hope and dignity, of values and prosperity.

Losing them after all these years, may it instill in us resilience to collect people's broken pieces.

Erega turi u Rwanda, nous sommes le Rwanda
Uri u Rwanda, tu ès le Rwanda
Nanjye ndi u Rwanda, et moi aussi je suis le Rwanda.

> *À nos chèrs parents, amis, frères et soeurs qui ont été tué pendant le genocide perpetré contre les Tutsi en 1994.*
> *Le malheur qu'on a vecu de leur avoir perdus ne doit pas nous faire oublier le bonheur de leur avoir connus.*

Even though our families' chains are broken, and nothing seems to be the same, there is hope that our children and children of our children will link them again. So that in the future we can live in a world free of genocide.

And the struggle continues.

HOPE

Kwibuka 22: Remember, Unite, Renew
Part 1 Commemorate
Jessica Gatoni

To **remember**,
We walk tombs, catacombs of memories painful to process.
It is hard to digest,
How the land of milk and honey, green lush pastures, mounding hills, streams of rivers;
Became drenched in red;
Sticky from remnant splatters of decay,
Shards of metal trapped in skulls,
Sharp reminders of history,
In Memorandum…
Rwanda, we struggle to find the words, to **remember**:

Gisozi, in the heart of your city,
Tales of how evil is sown, grown, and harvested.
We saw a timeline from a structured majesty, to an invaded territory, to a shattered country.
Images played in our minds like a cacophonous melody,
A dissonant beating of drums…
We bore witness to the aftermath of hatred spewed by tongues,
Gums carrying bodies, balled up fists like bombs.
Encased in glass were fragmented human bones and skulls,
Testimonies and photographs bringing them to life but…
There were too many voices forever silenced.
I wondered, if this world would ever understand the ubiquity of death,

In Bugesera,
Ntarama and Nyamata;
Hallowed were the grounds upon which we walked,
For they were dichotomous to the foundation they were built on.

Where there was no sanctuary, no mercy or humanity in rewritten commandments
Founded in destruction and where the Tutsi sought refuge in vain.
Slain in churches, laid on sacrament tables;
Their leftover belongings were collected, cleaned, and placed meticulously by an altar;
There are still bodies being uncovered to this day.

Murambi, in the city of Butare,
Once a school now a memorial of mummified bodies exhumed and the magnitude of loss is felt in your senses.
The dizzying smells of lime, preserved bodies are etched in memories;
A mother shields her baby
Her last message of humanity to the world.

In a country no bigger than the size of Belgium
Or the state of Maryland
There are 265 memorials and 113 designated cemeteries

This is the legacy of genocide.
The stories here were apparent, inescapable, the failures were evident, but this was not THE END.
Rwanda, you have survived by living by knowing life with the anguish of reliving, but you remember.
Kwibuka means to remember.
Yet, your thousand hills are silent, serene, peaceful, an example of how Mother Nature quells the lawlessness of man.
Rwanda, you have refused to be overcome and found that in solidarity you can reclaim dignity in your beautiful land.

Part 2 Lessons Learned

We were made to dance
When we swing our arms back and forth like a pendulum
Stomp our feet beat by beat by beat
We are bridging the gap between past, present and future
Our solutions are rooted in tradition
Flesh storing memories of ancestors, warriors, protectors, kings, queen
Singers, and poets lulling the crowds
Today, we remember their songs, and fight

To **unite** we become the clay
Molded before the form is born,
We are the cement, that is laid before the concrete has had days to set;
A foundation rebuilding, paving new roads along the way
Because we do not choose who we are, where we come from; where we have been, but we decide where will go

So look nowhere in particular,
But see everything,
Hear what your soul has to show you,
And love enough to decode the sorrow.
Love enough to forgive…
Sorrow is a loan,
Without it would we have ever grown?
Sorrow is a loan,
Without it would we have ever known?
The price of death, the value of life, the importance of reconciliation
As a new day dawns over us, we can begin **anew**
It is possible, we have lived, survived, and achieved it.

A Brave Face
Innocent Byiringiro

What if I had a choice, what if I had this art!
To listen to that voice, deep inside my heart
That tells me to embrace, all the pain of the past
And then decide my fate, which lays in my hands?

One thousand hills, two thousands secrets
O Rwanda you've seen, the one worst disgrace
Now it's time you may chill, and just take a deep breath
So the world may see, the other side of your brave face

You've seen the worst of all and then from then
You rose up above, away from hell
Technology in Kigali - a sign of hope
Corrupt leaders have gone - you make us proud

Let's not forget our past, from where else can we learn?
Bloodshed of our innocent friends, beg us a hand for this land
All their pain was not in vain
We've got to make Rwanda great again

Unemployment can go, we've got Made In Rwanda
Agaciro Development Fund leaves us with no wonder
To whether we can build this nation, *nta nkunga dukesh' amahanga*
Please come and see the rest #visitrwanda
I know you will make it, stretch those wings and flip that fear
The whole world is watching, as you brainstorm the next idea
You will be the hub for Africa, your cities will be cleaner
You've got your people to prove it, you may already be a winner

Far ahead is where we aim, and our eyes we fix
From our sweats is where we gain, and list our needs

This land will be marked forever
And its heroes will always deliver

The World I Dream Of
Claudine Karangwa Ingabire

What If God would create flowers of one colour? What If God would create one race? The world would not be colourful.

For clouds in the sky have different shades, that's how people were born with different races. We all know that Black is beautiful, so White is also wonderful.

Just like how rainbows are born among lights and rains, to soothe viewers' eyes and remove all pains, that's how people should look at each other through the twinkle of their eyes, which sparkle for only love.

Because people just flock like bright sun rays, that's how they should light flames of warmth. Avoiding any room that may lead to any form of discrimination, but unity that may lead to work together in cooperation.

The world I dream of is…

Where I treat you with humanity not discerning who you are. Either Christian or Muslim with different faith to never fall apart, and I accept our differences, or at least to help you ease your sorrows and scars.

And I embrace our diversity for I know that conflicts never lead to victory, but only welcome grudges and hate.

I don't judge you, shame and call you names, just to understand that we were born with different heights, whether you are short or tall because we deserve the same human rights.

The World I dream of is…

Where I see you as a neighbour whom we share the same fence, not the one we argue until violence but as a human who welcomes God's providence.

I respect your values and norms, to let you enjoy the bliss of your rejoices.
I don't care if you are a singer and I am an actor we can join our talents.
And I don't care if you are white and I am black we can join our abilities.
I don't care if you are from Asia and I am from Africa we respect our different cultures.
For we can exchange our different views and ideas with flexibility so that nobody may suffer.

For we may value our uniqueness and choices day-to-day.
For we know that peace only begins first with yourself and through little things we do every day.

Let us all blend our races and ethnic voice as an opportunity to avoid any prejudice to progress with peace: Let it be known, all around the world from heaven to earth.

Too Young
Jessica Gatoni

They said, they said we were young,

Too young,

to say the word "genocide".

As I stood on a platform, sometimes too small
to see past a podium,

I would gaze upon a crowd of survivors,
brothers, sisters, friends, and strangers alike and
recite poems entitled,

"I survivor of genocide," or "My dream in the
aftermath of a genocide"

But I was too young

My body was too fragile to understand the
trauma of a survivor

My lips were too innocent to utter words my
mind could not fathom, words like:

Murders by machete, pools of bloodshed used
to cleanse an entire ethnic group; vermin they
were called, infestations of *inyenzi*
(cockroaches) to be crushed by the sole of a
shoe.

Soulless people who feared no God
meticulously orchestrated the destruction of a
people, theirs.

Led by a hatred sowed by the seeds of a
curiously divisive African history; one whose
lines of separation were only truly drawn by the
ink of their oppressors, and the sword of their
brethren.

Our Elders; keepers of our legacy, guardians of
our secrets

Young men; heirs and holders of our heritage, future bearers of new lives

Young girls; daughters, mothers, infants none were too young to be savagely violated, torn apart and stripped, brutalized and silenced.

Their voices are ours...

At that age I would simply read aloud a poem and recite word for word, all the mannerism and movements memorized, the inflections and intonations perfected, the tone of the piece was properly set.

The nature of mass murders and the psychology of a genocide perpetrator, the science of death completely eluded me.

The traumatization of the survivor, the mending of their hearts, and the task of rebuilding our country fazed me.

However one glimmer of lucidity managed to penetrate my infant mind and seep in an adage, far uncommon to the people of Rwanda and that is: The life we live should never be taken for granted.

Rwanda has come from so far, and the pride of this country is apparent not only in its endeavors to rebuild the corners of its borders, but also in reaching out and serving as global leaders in their own right.

Our journey is one to be captured and eternalized; it deserves accolades and glory, risen from the ground up and mounted on a pedestal for all to see, it should be reveled in its sheer beauty.

This tiny spec of land one of the smallest in the African continent, is home to some of the brightest visionaries, innovators, entrepreneurs & brilliant minds.

They have rebuilt our motherland and propelled us forward to a vision of self-reliance and sustainability.

It is now the task of the youth to ensure that this vision is upheld.

> *Agaciro kacu*, our dignity, is a creed that has
> been carried on from generation to generation.
> Let it be the flame that ignites us and burns
> brightly within our hearts.
>
> We, the youth of Rwanda are empowered by
> the strength and sacrifice of our people.
>
> I do decree that we will be united in this mission
> to bring continued growth and prosperity to our
> BEAUTIFUL country.
>
> Let us never forget the atrocities of genocide,
> let us honor the lives of those who perished
> unscrupulously before us and let us, bring new
> hope…

Epilogue – Interview with a Poet, Jessica Gatoni

Jessica Gatoni, a second-generation survivor of the genocide, still remembers the clickety-clack of the typewriter as her mother wrote poems and poetry during her childhood. Having lived as refugees in Kenya during the genocide, Jessica, her mother, and sister immigrated to Canada following the genocide in 1994.

> I was about four years old and I didn't know what had happened, but I clearly remember my mother trying to express to us what had gone on. Now I know that she'd gone back and seen what had happened in Rwanda and was deeply affected by it. My dad and brother were separated from us, and they were trying to find a way for us to be reunited. The only thing that she could do at that time was to write a lot. I remember seeing her write and being very emotional. I remember trying to understand why she was being like that.

Jessica's mother, a poet and playwright, used art to come to terms with the genocide. Jessica, as well as other children of the Montreal Rwandan community, participated in her mother's performance art.

> We would gather together as a community, and as kids, we would perform skits. We started to conceptualize that something terrible happened and started to understand that it was a reality for survivors of the genocide. So, as we got older, and heard more testimonies of loss and violence, the things that we performed became more vivid, more painful, and real.

As Jessica aged, she took after her mother and pursued poetry writing, also taking part in spoken word performance poetry. She wrote her first poem about the genocide in response to a journalist's disapproval of her involvement in her community's performance art,

> There was a certain point when a journalist at one of the events wrote an article that said these are not words that children should be saying – that we were too young to talk about genocide – and should not be a part of these things. My mom had to reply to that and say this is something that we have to learn about, and that we, as Rwandans, grow up learning about the genocide that occurred in our country. These are unfathomable tragedies that people – men, women, and children – went through and it is something that cannot be taken away. You can't really dull that and minimize the effect and the depth of the genocide, and it's still something that current and future generations to come will have to work through and unpack.

Following those comments, Jessica wrote a poem expressing her frustration with the sentiment that she was too young to discuss the genocide it was, after all, an intrinsic part of her history and her identity. Though Jessica is a poet of many subjects, this poem remains her favorite.

> At the time, I was asked to write a poem about the genocide for the twenty-first genocide commemoration at the United Nations. I was thinking back to my memories reciting poetry written by my mother when I was a child...So, with that poem, I was going through a period of life where I felt like I really couldn't understand what had happened in my country, but I could still connect with it and empathize. The purpose of writing and telling that story was to highlight that it is a shared part of the history of Rwanda. In the poem, I also commend the work that has been done to make the country as peaceful as it is today. Rwanda's recovery is an important part of its legacy and one that is awe-inspiring. I can only write poetry from a personal perspective, as a person who grew up in the Diaspora and who went back to Rwanda somewhat later in life. However, I cannot and would not change the fact that I'm Rwandan and I hope to continue using art to tell my country's story.

Looking forward, Jessica plans to continue writing poetry and contributing artistically.

> I know Rwandans all over the world have a distinct artistic voice that needs to be heard. There is no one else but the Rwandan people who can tell this story in their own way, and having ownership over that narrative, is of utmost importance to me. Our voices and experiences need to be heard. I want to continue writing poetry and sharing stories with this in mind.

In doing so, Jessica joins a generation of young Rwandan artists, both those within the diaspora and living within Rwanda, composing art and the spoken word to share the memory of the genocide and its aftermath in a way only they can tell.

Thinking back on her childhood in the shadow of genocide, Jessica recalls a conversation:

> Recently I was talking to one of my childhood friends (Rwandan), and she could remember so much of what we did and performed, even quoting things. It helped me realize how meaningful it was to have those experiences as a young child and be able to talk about such a traumatic event. Even when I think about my career goals, it's within the frame of mind that I'm Rwandan, because I hopefully will do something that contributes to my country – that's how I would like to frame my decisions. And I really do have so much hope for my country. I've seen so much progress. It's something that really invigorates you and makes you want to be a part of that.

Perhaps then, it is appropriate to consider Jessica's favorite artistic piece.

> I really identify a lot with the play that my mom wrote called *Reclaiming Our Voices*.[2] I still reread it. It was a full cathartic release of a time in her life where she just shared everything – talked about everything, and it was so hopeful because it's a love story. It's a story about people from both sides falling in love and trying to mend the wounds of their country.

In using poetry to grapple with the legacy of the genocide in their country, the artistic voices of Rwandan youth explore the complexities of memory, grief, and hope in a manner that academic prose cannot. As a collection, the poems featured in this chapter convey the power of the individual experience within the context of unimaginable collective loss. As the next generation of Rwandan youth enters adulthood and public life, they will assume their roles as leaders of Rwanda, authoring the story of their country in a way only they can.

Notes

1 Poems were solicited across social media networks and among social circles. Most poets had a point-of-contact through the nonprofit Never Again Rwanda. It was not specified that poetry needed to be composed in English; however, as the language of solicitation was in English, this likely had an influence on submission content. As such, most of the poetry submitted is in English, but one is in French and some contain phrases in French and Kinyarwanda.

2 Reclaiming Our Voices by Jeanne d'Arc Byaje

Part IV
Conclusions

14 Conclusion

Tawia B. Ansah

The Latin word *penumbra* expresses the outer fringes of an experience, the moment in time, space, and memory that resides within the shadow of the event. In the aftermath of the 1994 genocide in Rwanda, this is where we are. Justice within the shadow seeks to capture the outlines, to articulate and give voice to the violence and the loss, the sense of human fracture, and the transition to humanity and renewed belonging.

This volume clarifies the need to understand the efficacy of memory and memorializing in the context of a multifaceted and horrific event such as the one-hundred-day genocide of the Tutsis in Rwanda. The volume shows how, even several decades later, genocide is still apprehended piecemeal, through a meld of perspectives, and through an interdisciplinary lens. The contributions range from individual stories and experiences of Rwandan survivors, witnesses, and poets, to analyses of the legal mechanisms and their interplay within the local efforts to memorialize and commemorate the genocide. Uniquely, within the literature on the genocide, all the authors of the volume are either Rwandans or foreigners who visited Rwanda in the aftermath of the genocide. Each of us, whether insiders or outsiders, felt profoundly the effects of the experience. Each of us grappled with its meaning for law, literature, art, and memorials. Each chapter, in diverse ways, contended with the meaning and content of identity in the wake of an event predicated on ethnic divisions. The memory of that violence must somehow function as the handmaid of a new Rwanda, and a new global pluralism.

In Rwanda, justice and memorialization mean many things: accountability, preservation, and critique of *lieux de mémoire*, reparations and institutional reforms, protection of the most vulnerable in society after the genocide, and/or political reconciliation. In Rwanda, memory is both a legalistic and an imaginative project, a fundamentally participatory undertaking. As such, in its representations and analyses of monuments, museums, photography, and artistic expression such as poetry and stories, the volume engages the burden and the work of memory across a spectrum of disciplines.

DOI: 10.4324/9781003228592-18

Although the story of Rwanda's genocide has been told many times in the last 28 years, this volume attempts something new in its de-siloed approach to memory and justice. In the sections on legal process, we see the overlap between institution-building and the emphasis on the rule of law in a nation where both have been destroyed. We see the challenge of preserving memory as a function of the legal process. The testimonies of child survivors overlap both the legal processes described, and the need to preserve and archive their unique perspective of the genocide and the legacy of trauma. The chapters speak to the recovery from trauma as part of the transition from the shadow of genocide toward a sustainable future.

In the section on artistic expression in the aftermath of genocide, artists and writers analyze justice and memory work from multiple methods. The chapters here examine memorial commemoration and its cultural and political effects, the creation of collective memory through fiction and poetry, and the emotional evocations of photography. Underlying the whole is a sense that justice in transition is intimately linked with the imaginative enterprise, which is itself in crisis. The Rwandan genocide, the event itself, beggared the imagination. The planning and execution, the scale and speed, and indeed the intimacy of the destruction of human lives in one hundred days: this inhumanity was unprecedented. Art and literature reach into the experience of genocide and its aftermath, offering the possibility of catharsis, elucidating memory, and hinting at rehabilitation.

The volume presents an interplay between the empirical, scholarly works and these works of the imagination, suggesting that the work of memory, fused as it is with the pursuit of justice under genocide's shadow, is intrinsically interdisciplinary. Twenty-eight years later, the work of memory matters more than ever. Today's global political discourses on nationalism, with their dependence on racial and ethnic divisions, are strikingly similar to the discursive prelude to the 1994 genocide in Rwanda. As it makes its contribution to the project of justice in Rwanda, this volume highlights the importance of working within a pluralistic register to understand and to counteract the ideology of genocide. The volume is an affirmation of humanity's promise beyond this shadow.

"Cut down in their prime"

Photograph by Sonya de Laat

Index

Note: Page references in *italics* denote figures and with "n" endnotes.

academic discourse: on Rwanda 47–49; on Rwandan genocide 47–49
Achebe, Chinua 173, 179, 181
Aegis Trust 174
aesthetics: in aftermath of genocide 230–235; and long stories 236–239; and tall trees 236–239
Africa: Canadian media descriptions of violence in 54; Western nations on 56; white expertise on 48; *see also* Rwanda
Aiding Violence (Uvin) 63
AIDS *see* HIV/AIDS
Akayesu, Jean Paul 93
Amin, Idi 135
Antigone (Sophocles) 171, 172, 179
Apartheid 230
Appui aux victimes de violence sexuelles project: beyond expectations of 152; data collection methods 153–154; economic consequences 155–156; psychological consequences 154–155; qualitative data analysis 154; safe space, creation of 152; safe space, importance of 156–160; selection criteria 153; social consequences 155–156
art, and burden of memory 179–184
"artistic intellect" 189
Arusha Accords 26, 141
Association des Etudiants et Éleves Rescapés du Genocide (AERG) 37–38, 162
Association Rwandaise 83
Aukerman, Miriam 111
Azoulay, Ariella 234, 241

Baer, Ulrich 234
Bagambiki, Emmanuel 4
Bagosora, Theoneste 62
Baraygwiza, Jean-Bosco 224n7
Barrett, Jastine 214
Barthes, Roland 231
Beardsley, Brent 56
Beckett, Sister Wendy 181–183
Benishyaka 162, 163n6
Bernini, Gian Lorenzo 181
Berry, M. 146
Beyond the Gates 208
Biblical Ten Commandments 199
Birds are Singing in Kigali 208
Bisesero: memorial site 236–238, 241–242, 245n8; Tutsi resistance in 31
Bizimungu, Pasteur 37
Black, D. 58–59
A Bloody Night (Nshokeyinka) 251–253
Book of Names 178
Boutros-Ghali, Boutros 94
A Brave Face (Byiringiro) 262–263
Brody, Richard 185
Brown, Kris 125
Browning, Christopher 122
Burgess, A. W. 161
Burundian Hutu refugees 61
Byiringiro, Innocent 262–263

Cain, Kenneth 51
Canada: and Rwandan genocide 53, 63; Rwandan genocide perpetrators living in 57
Canadian humanitarians 58–60; contrasting articles on Rwandan genocide survivors 58–59; showcasing masculine transcendence 58

Canadian media coverage: Canadian government response to genocide 54–56; coverage of Canadian humanitarians 58–60; coverage of genocide trials 57–58; media as injustice 60; media frameworks and perspectives 53–54; of Rwandan genocide 53–60
"Can There Be a Political Science of the Holocaust?" 121
Caplan, Gerry 62
Cappeliez, M. 53–54
Cassese, Antonio 113
Catholic Church 138
Cavell, Stanley 232–233, 235
Chakravarty, Anu 116
Chari, T. 53
Chernovsky, Phil 177–178
Chiasson, P. 57
"Child soldiers: Romeo Dallaire's wrenching return to Africa's 'gang warfare'" (Thompson) 58
child survivors' testimonies: collecting 69; digitizing 71–72; from Gitarama prefecture 76; overview 67–68; psychological trauma 76–80; Rwandan genocide 67–86
Chung, Lee Isaac 207
civil society: and human rights 104; and Rwanda post-genocide reconstruction 9–10, 105
civil society organizations (CSOs) 93; local 101; role in Rwanda reconstruction process 100–102
Civil War 26, 132
Clinton, Bill 218
Cobain, Kurt 230
colonialism: role in Rwandan genocide 72; and Rwanda 6, 55
Commission Nationale Lutte Contre le Genocide (CNLG) 84
"communal memory" 189
communal symbolic reparations 120
compassion: and films 50, 52; in *Munyurangabo* 209–212
corruption: anti-Rwandan 135; religious 139; and trials 99
Crimes Against Humanity and War Crimes Act 57

Dallaire, Roméo 25, 32, 49, 51–52, 139
Dauge-Roth, Alexandre 50, 208, 211
de Greiff, Pablo 106, 106n4, 118, 120
Des Forges, Alison 137, 140
Diop, Boubacar Boris 191–192, 196, 200, 201, 203n14
discourse: academic 47–49; popular culture 49–53
discrimination 211; and Belgians 72; ethnic 22; systemic racial 44
dissent: by community 81–82; by friends and relatives 82; by neighbors and good samaritans 82; by school administrators 81
divisionism 22
Djedanoum, Nocky 192, 195, 201, 203n14, 203n15
"double genocide" 132–146
Douglas, Lawrence 169, 185n4
Drumbl, Mark 112
Duras, Marguerite 175

Eight-Point Programme 135–136, 141
Ellsberg, M. 154
Emerita, Gutete 231
Erll, Astrid 193
ethnic discrimination 22
ethnicity 209–210; leadership positions based on 72; paternal 25; and Rwandan Patriotic Front (RPF) 135–137; stereotypes regarding 200
Everett, D. A. 217

Fair, J. E. 54
Faridah, Nyampinga 34
Fest'Africa project *see Rwanda: écrire par devoir de mémoire*
fictions of justice in post-genocide films 207–224
films: fictions of justice in post-genocide 207–224; post-genocide (*see* post-genocide films); showing Tutsi genocide (1994) 208–209
Florea, S. 101
Fonds d'Assistance aux Rescapés du Génocide (FARG) 83
Forces Armées Rwandaises (FAR) 137

gacaca courts/justice system 9, 12, 15n16, 38–39, 41, 41n4, 46, 93, 110, 144, 207–209, 212, 215, 222–224; *vs.* conventional justice mechanisms 96; criticism of 98–99; establishment of 96; and local justice 115–116; preparations for 97; role of 96–98; support of 98–99

Gatoni, Jessica 249–251, 255–257, 258–259, 260–262, 264–268
génocidaires 9, 35–36, 45–46, 54, 68, 214, 217, 221, 224n5, 230, 236, 244
genocidal rape: challenges faced by victims of 150; defined 150; female survivors of genocidal rape 150–154, 160; importance of safe space 156–160; physical and emotional intrusion of 155; psychological and social effects of 157
genocide: aesthetics in aftermath of 230–235; as "crime of crimes" 171; "double genocide" 132–146; legal mechanisms addressing 8–9; "machete" 112; memorials (*see* memorial(s)); role of radio in 27; *see also* Rwandan genocide
genocide against Tutsi people 11, 13, 102, 110, 113, 207, 208; and *gacaca* courts 99; and human capital 101; and justice 93; and NAR 101; safe space for women raped during 150–163; through children memories 21–41, 67; and transitional justice 92; *see also* genocide; Rwandan genocide
The genocide of the Tutsis explained to a foreigner (Rurangwa) 192
Genocide Survivors Support Network (GSSN) 40–41
Gersony, Robert 140
Gersony Mission 140
Gewirtzman, David 39–40
Gigliotti, S. 51
Gitarama prefecture 68, 69–71, *70*; experiences of children in 76, 85; intervention/support provided to children from 83–84
Goldberg, E. S. 216
A Good Man in Hell 50–51
grassroots justice 222–223
Great Lakes refugee crisis 37
Greenberg, Mark 71
Grey Matter 208, 224n3
Groupe des Anciens Etudiants Rescapés du Génocide 39
Group of Former Genocide Survivor Students (GAERG) 162
group sharing 157–158
Grzyb, Amanda 245n7
guhahamuka 75
Guy, Cadeau 257–258
Habyarimana, Juvenal 21, 25, 31–32, 132, 135, 138
Hamber, Brandon 111, 118, 120, 122
Harrow, Kenneth 190
Hartley, Aidan 51
Hartman, Geoffrey 189
Hassan, J. 161
Hatzfield, Jean 61, 241
Hazelwood, R. R. 161
Healing of Life Wounds program 59
Hearty, K. 119
Heise, L. 154
Herman, J. L. 161
Hinton, Alexander 188
Hiroshima Mon Amour 175–177, 179
historical justice 45, 46, 64
HIV/AIDS 156, 160, 210, 215, 221
Holocaust 140, 178, 183, 184, 194–195, 228
Hope for Rwanda's Children 59
Hôpitaux Universitaires de Genève (HUG) 150, 151
Hotel Rwanda (film) 49, 52, 208, 213, 216, 217
Hotel Rwanda ou Le Genocide Des Tutsis vu par Hollywood (Ndahiro and Rutazibwa) 52
Hron, Madeline 47, 61
Humain Avant Tout 63
humanitarians *see* Canadian humanitarians
human rights: abuses and criminal prosecutions 91–92; and civil society 104; memoirs 51; and NAR 102, 104; nongovernmental reports 57; violations 111, 113, 115–117, 123
Human Rights Watch 67, 98
100 Days 208, 224n2, 224n3
Hutu people 6–7; and Belgian colonial rule 72; disenfranchisement 6; extremist faction 24–31; extremists killing of Tutsis 72; government and RPF 7; and radio spreading hate 27; resistance by 80–81; *see also* Rwandan genocide

Ibreck, Rachel 118
IBUKA 68, 69, 71–72, 73
identities, polarization of 196–201
Ilboudo, Monique 191–192, 196, 198, 199, 201, 203n14
Imanishimwe, Samuel 4
individual narratives 121–122

Ingabire, Claudine Karangwa 259–260, 263–264
Ingabire, Victoire 143
ingando (solidarity camps) 69, 136; and ethnic transcendence 136; political teachings of 141
Ingelaere, Bert 98, 116, 222
Inside Rwanda's Gacaca Courts: Seeking Justice After Genocide (Ingelaere) 98, 115
"intellectual witness" 189
Interahamwe 7, 30–31, 32, 35–36, 42n9, 68, 80, 81, 138, 141, 198
International Association of Genocide Scholars 47
International Criminal Tribunal for Rwanda (ICTR) 4, 8–9, 46, 62, 92, 143, 207–208, 209, 224n4, 224n7, 225n9; contributions to reconciliation 112–114; establishment of 93, 110, 112; Kamatali on 94; and local justice 115–116; objective of 93
International Tribunal for Rwanda 186n7
inzibutso 123
IRIN (Integrated Regional Information Networks) 98
Iseta: Behind the Roadblock 224n2
Iversen, Margaret 235

Jaar, Alfredo 231
"Jean Apologize for Canada's role in Rwanda" 56
Jessee, Erin 189, 201
John Paul II, Pope 139
justice: grassroots 222–223; historical 45, 46, 64; limits, *in Sometimes in April* 216–222; local 115–116; nonjuridical 117–124; overview 91–93; and peace 92; within Rwanda 91–106; symbolic 45–46, 64; through poetry 249–268; transitional (*see* transitional justice)

Kabalisa, Leo 58–59
Kabera, Eric 224n2, 224n3
Kabgayi Catholic Church Center 139
Kabgayi Catholic Mission 71
Kagame, Paul 37
Kamatali, Jean-Marie 94
Kangura magazine 73, 204n21
Kayibanda, Grégoire 71, 135, 138
Kayimahé, Vénuste 192, 202n6, 203n14
Kayiranga, Théobald 22, 30–31, 35–36
Keazor, Henry 181
Keepers of Memory 224n2
Khor, L. 213
Kielburger, Craig 59–60
Kielburger, Marc 59–60
Kigali Genocide Memorial 143; art and burden of memory 179–184; Memorial Museum 171–179; overview 167–171
King, Charles 121–122
King, Martin Luther, Jr. 217
King, Regine 58–59
Kinyamateka 71
Kinyarwanda 208
knowledge production: about Rwandan genocide 47, 63; colonial tradition of 46; and racialized power relations 48–49, 62; refugees as objects of 54; white Western domination in academic 49
Kothari, U. 48
Krog, Antjie 13
Kwibuka 22: Remember, Unite, Renew (Gatoni) 260–262
Kwibuka commemoration ceremonies 121, 123

Lambourne, W. 202n3
Lamko, Koulsy 192, 196, 202, 203n14
Landscape with the Ashes of Phocion 179
La Trompete Trompeuse (Nshokeyinka) 253–255
Law and Reality: Progress in Judicial Reform in Rwanda 98
Leave None to Tell the Tale (Des Forges) 140
Lederach, J. P. 116
The Legacy To Reckon With (Ingabire) 259–260
Levi, Primo 195
Liberation is a Journey 210, 213
liberation of Rwanda 31–36, 136–137, 142
Life and Death in Nyamata: Memoir of a Young Boy in Rwanda's Darkest Church (Ndizeye) 38
Life Laid Bare (Hatzfeld) 241
Ligue Rwandaise pour la promotion et le defense des droits de l'Homme 101
Lives (Plutarch) 180
local justice: and *gacaca* courts/justice system 115–116; and ICTR 115–116
Longman, T. P. 143–144, 146

MacCharles, T. 56
"machete" genocide 112
Malkki, Liisa 61
Mamdani, Mahmood 126, 203n17
Manifesto for Life (Djedanoum) 192
Mann, L. 146
material reparations 117–118
Médecins du Monde 151
Meierhenrich, Jens 233
Melvern, Linda 11, 143
memorial(s): importance of 122; Kigali Genocide Memorial (Gisozi) 123; spaces in Rwanda 122–124; as symbolic reparations 121
memorialization efforts 92
memory/ies 3, 125; of genocide in Rwanda 10–12; public 121–122; through poetry 249–268; of unrepresentable trauma in transitional justice 228–245
Memory - Witness exhibit/photographs 239–243
Mfuranzima, Fred 253
Minh-ha, Trinh T. 61
Mironko, Charles 94
miti yikinyarwanda 75
Moller, F. 228, 230
Monénembo, Tierno 191, 196, 202, 203n14
Mourning Becomes the Law: Philosophy and Representation (Rose) 182
Mouvement Révolutionaire National pour le Développement (MRND) 42n9
Mugesera, Leon 9, 57
Mugonero Church massacre 27
Mujawayo, Esther 209, 215
Mukandayisenga, M. R. 67
Mukeshimana, Eugenie 24
"multidirectional memory" 194
Muna, Bernard 94
Mungwarere, Jacques 57–58
Munyagishari, Bernard 9
Munyandamutsa, Nasson 74, 152
Munyurangabo 207, 208; compassion in 209–212; revenge in 209–212
Murekatete, Jacqueline 21–22, 26, 29–30, 34; Genocide Survivors Foundation 40; immigration to United States 39–40
Museveni, Yoweri 7
Mutua, M 56, 57, 60

Nachtwey, James 231
Nahimana, Ferdinand 224n7
narratives: appropriating propaganda for sake of 213–216; individual 121–122; state 121–122; therapy 84
Nassilah, Nyinawumwami 34
National Commission for the Fight Against Genocide 84, 103, 121
national courts 95–96
National Unity and Reconciliation Commission 95, 103
Ndahiro, A. 52
Ndizeye, Omar 27–29, 34; and AERG 37–38; life after genocide 37
Never Again Rwanda (NAR) 10, 38, 93, 151, 268n1; human rights program 102, 104; overview 101; Peacebuilding Institute 102–104; peacebuilding program 102–104; in societal healing and reconciliation 104–105
New York Times 53, 177
Ngirumpatse, Pauline 63
94 Terror 208
Nishimwe, Consolee 23–24, 27, 32–35, 40
nonjuridical justice 117–124
non-material reparations 117–118
Nothing But "The Void" (Gatoni) 249–251
Nshimye, Jason 24, 31, 34
Nshokeyinka, Bliss Light 251–255
Ntakirutimana, Elizaphan 27
Ntaryamira, Cyprien 25

Obote, Milton 135
October war 7
Odyssey 181
OJ Simpson murder trial 230
Olick, J. K. 118–119
O'Neill, Kevin 188
Operation Turquoise 31–32, 35
Organic Law N° 40/200 of 26/01/2001, Setting Up "Gacaca Jurisdictions" and Organizing Prosecutions for Offences Constituting the Crime of Genocide or Crimes Against Humanity Committed Between October 1, 1990 and December 31, 1994 114
the Other 196–201

Palmary, I. 120
Palmer, Nicola 99, 114
Parks, L. 54
Parmentier, Stephan 202n3
Paul, Jean 39

peace: defined 92; and justice 92
Peacebuilding Institute 102–104
Peck, Raoul 207, 216
Peskin, V. 144
photographs: *Memory - Witness* 239–243; of unrepresentable trauma in transitional justice 228–245
Plutarch 180
poetry: justice through 249–268; memory through 249–268
polarization of identities 196–201
popular culture discourse, and Rwanda 49–53
post-genocide films: compassion in *Munyurangabo* 209–212; fictions of justice in 207–224; limits of justice in *Sometimes in April* 216–222; positive depiction of grassroots justice 222–223; propaganda for narrative closure 213–216; revenge in *Munyurangabo* 209–212; showing 1994 Tutsi genocide 208–209
Poussin, Nicolas 170, 179, 181, 183, 184
professional counseling 157–158
Prosecutor v. Bagosora 25
The Prosecutor v. Elizaphan Ntakirutimana & Gerard Ntakirutimana 27
psychological trauma: of children from genocide 76–80; and traditional Rwandan culture 75
public memory 121–122

racialized power relations 48–49
racism: anti-Rwandan 135; and Rwandan survivors 63
Radio Muhabura 73
Radio RTLM 73
Radio Rwanda 26
Radio Télévision Libre des Mille Collines (RTLMC/RTLM) 26–27, 217, 219, 224n7
rape *see* genocidal rape
Razack, Sherene 48, 49, 50–51, 59, 63
reconciliation: defined 95; ICTR's contributions to 112–114; NAR in 104–105; in Rwanda 93–99
Reinhardt, Mark 232
Remembering Rwanda 15 47
reparations 91; legal programs 119; material 117–118; non-material 117–118; symbolic 117–124
resistance: bribing to survive 82–83; by churches and religious people 80; by community 81–82; by friends and relatives 82; by neighbors and good samaritans 82; by persecuted Hutu and Tutsi people 80–81; during Rwandan genocide 80–83; by school administrators 81
Resnais, Alain 175, 179
revenge: killings 132–146; in *Munyurangabo* 209–212
Rever, J. 134, 144
Reyntjens, F. 143, 144, 146, 186n5
rights of persons with disabilities 106n3
Robbins, J. 118–119
Roht-Arriaza, N. 118
Rose, Gillian 182–183
Rothberg, M. 194
Rudoren, Jodi 177
Ruhorahoza, Kivu 224n3
Rurangwa, Jean-Marie 192, 203n14
Rusesabagina, P. 52–53
Rutazibwa, N. 52
Rwafa, U. 50
Rwanda: academic discourse on 49; and colonialism 6; French intervention in 31–32; genocide 24–31, 44; genocide education in 60; hate media 73; justice in 46; justice within 91–106; liberation 31–36; popular culture discourse on 49–53; post-genocide 37–41; post-genocide reconstruction 9–10; pre-genocide 22–24; quota system 22; targeted murders in 7–8; transformation within 91–106
Rwanda Cinema Center 224n2
Rwanda Defence Force (RDF) 134, 144
Rwanda: écrire par devoir de mémoire 190–192, 202n1; fearing the Other 196–201; polarization of identities 196–201; transnational, transcultural memory project 192–195; trauma theory 195–196
Rwandan Civil War 134–135, 140, 143, 146n11
Rwandan genocide 24–31, 63, 67, 172, 188, 195, 228, 241, 272; absence of Rwandans as experts on 47–48; academic discourse on 47–48; Canadian media coverage of 53–60; causes of 72–73; and children 75; child survivors' testimonies 67–86; digitization of documents on 71–72; discourse and Western knowledge producers 44, 47; popular culture

discourse on 50; representation of 44; resistance during 80–83; survivors 84; and trauma 74–75; understanding killings 140; Western-produced film representations of 50; *see also* genocide; genocide against Tutsi people
Rwandan Patriotic Army (RPA) 132; killings 137–140
Rwandan Patriotic Front (RPF) 7–8, 26, 35–36, 37, 132, 135, 146n4, 210, 230; composed of Tutsi in exile 73; Eight-Point Programme 135–136, 141; and ethnicity 135–137
Rwandan speechlessness 61–64
Rwanda Project, 1994-2000 231–232
Rwanda's Untold Story 15n21, 132
Rwandese Alliance for National Unity Congress 135

safe space: creation 152; importance 156–160; for women raped during genocide 150–163
Salgado, Sebastiao 231, 245n5
savages-victims-saviors paradigm 56, 60
Second World War 228, 234
Semujanga, Josias 199
The Shadow of Imana (Tadjo) 168
Shake Hands with the Devil (Dallaire) 25
Shake Hands with the Devil (film) 48, 49, 50, 52, 208
Sharangabo, Ntare 45, 48, 62
Sharangabo, Patrick 58–59
Shefik, Sherin 185
Shoah Foundation 85n1
Shooting Dogs 51–52
Sibomana, Father Andre 13
Simusiga 68
"situation of photography" 241
Sliwinski, S. 235
Small, A. 47
societal healing, and NAR 104–105
Someone Please Explain (Guy) 257–258
Sometimes in April 207, 208, 224n7; limits of justice in 216–222; as validation of *gacaca* system 217, 222; as validation of ICTR 217–218
Sontag, Susan 233
Sophocles 171, 179, 181
Sow, S. 203n17
state: narratives 121–122; and Rwanda post-genocide reconstruction 9–10
Staub, Ervin 189, 196–197, 201
Stealing the Pain of Others 50
Streams of Living Water (Gatoni) 255–257
Sundaram, A. 134
A Sunday by the Pool in Kigali 51
A Sunday in Kigali 208
symbolic justice 45–46, 64
symbolic reparations 117–124; communal 120; genocide memorials as 121

Tadjo, Véronique 168, 191, 194, 195, 196–198, 202–203n14, 202n7
Taylor, L. K. 116
Ten Commandments of the Bahutu 198–199, 201, 204n21
Tested to the Limit: A Genocide Survivor's Story of Pain, Resilience, and Hope (Consolee) 40
The Texture of Memory: Holocaust Memorials and Meaning 169
Things Fall Apart (Achebe) 173, 179
Thompson, Allan 58
Thomson, Susan 143, 144, 146, 211
Too Young (Gatoni) 264–266
Toronto Star 53, 54, 55, 57
traditional Rwandan culture 75
transformation: economic progress of Rwanda 100; within Rwanda 100
transitional justice 10–12, 14n3, 228–245; defined 3–4, 92, 111; memory of unrepresentable trauma in 228–245; overview 110–111; photographs of unrepresentable trauma in 228–245; and political reconciliation 5; role of 92; Rwandan context 111–117
trauma: defined 74; psychological and traditional Rwandan culture 75; psychological of children, from genocide 76–80; and Rwandan genocide 74–75; theory, recontextualizing 195–196
"travelling memory" 193
truth commissions 91
Tutsi people 6–7; and Belgian colonial rule 72; children's testimonies on atrocities faced by 68; genocide against 13, 21–41, 63; quota system 22; as refugees 28–29; resistance 31; resistance by 80–81
Twa people 6, 14n6, 25, 72

Ubaldo, R. 228, 230
Ugandan Bush War 7
Umurungi, Jeanne 63
United Nations (UN) 10, 21, 140, 209; Committee Against Torture 57; human rights mission 167
United Nations Assistance Mission to Rwanda (UNAMIR) 139, 141, 185n1
United Nations High Commission for Refugees (UNHCR) 138; Gersony Mission 140
United Nations International Residual Mechanism for Criminal Tribunals 224n4
United Nations Security Council (UNSC) 8, 46, 112; Resolution 929 31; Resolution 955 93, 126n3
University of South Florida (USF) Holocaust and Genocide Studies Center (HGSC) 71
unrepresentable trauma: memory and photographs of 228–245; in transitional justice 228–245
USC Shoah Foundation Visual History Archive 67
Uvin, Peter 63, 94
Uwilingiyimana, Agathe 25–26
Uwinkindi, Jean 9

Vambe, M. 47, 48–49, 62
Voices That Call Memories (Mfuranzima) 253

Waberi, Abdourahman 191, 195, 196, 199, 201, 202n8
Waldorf, Lars 116
"Wasted Lives" exhibition 183
Western and Local Approaches to Justice in Rwanda (Uvin and Charles) 94
Western filmmaking: narrative choice of 51; portrayal of Westerners 51–52; representation of Rwandan genocide 50; *see also* films
When Rape Is A Tool Of War (Gatoni) 258–259
white experts: on Rwandan genocide 61–62; use of creative license in genocide stories 62
white moral authority 62
white supremacy 63
"Why did Ottawa ignore warnings of Rwandan genocide?" (Black) 55
Wilson, R. A. 118
Wolfe, Stephanie 5, 8, 11, 45, 121
World Bank 72
The World I Dream Of (Ingabire) 263–264

Yad Vashem Holocaust Memorial Project 174, 178
Young, James E. 168–169, 175
Youth Association for Human Rights Promotion and Development 101

Zegeye, A. 47, 48–49, 62
Zorbas, Eugenia 210
Zraly, M. 161

Printed and bound by CPI Group (UK) Ltd, Croydon, CR0 4YY

07/10/2024

01041767-0008